MW00531805

# WILLS & INVENTORIES
# OF
# LINCOLN COUNTY TENNESSEE
# 1810 – 1921

By

Helen C. & Timothy R. Marsh
Shelbyville, Tennessee

COPYRIGHT © 1989
    By Southern Historical Press, Inc.


All rights reserved.  No part of this publication may be reproduced, stored in a
retrieval system or transmitted in any form or by any means without the prior
written permission of the author.

**SOUTHERN HISTORICAL PRESS, INC.**
c/o The Rev. Silas Emmett Lucas, Jr.
P.O. Box 738
Easley, South Carolina 29641-0738

ISBN 0-89308-654-1

## PREFACE

Lincoln County, Tennessee was created by an Act of the Legislature passed the 14th day of November 1809 at Knoxville, Tennessee. The said Act to be in force from the first day of January 1810. The parent county was Bedford. There were few settlers in the county before 1806.

The Abstracts of Wills in this book were copied from the Court Records, located in the Lincoln County Court Clerk's Office in Fayetteville, Tennessee and the State Library and Archives in Nashville, Tennessee.

While no records have been destroyed by court house fires, it should be pointed out that a considerable number of records were lost or destroyed during the Federal occupation of the town of Fayetteville during the Civil War. This included some of the early Inventory and Administration of Estates Records.

An earlier Will Book was published by us in 1977. It was a limited quanity edition and soon sold out. Due to continued request for the book we decided to reprint this new edition with extended dates to December 1921.

May this brief glimpse through the doors of the past of the lives of the people spread upon the pages of this book help perpetuate their memory while being useful to this and future generations.

The authors,
Helen Crawford Marsh
Timothy Richard Marsh

# WILL & INVENTORY

## INDEX

## WILL BOOK AND INVENTORIES - 1810

Page 1   **WILLIAM ROSEBROUGH,** of Montgomery County, Kentucky.   Wife,
Margaret.   Seven children: Dorcas, Orpha, Milly, Rhoda, Samuel,
William, and Alexander John.   A step-daughter Rebeckah Sloan.   Owned 300 acres
in Tennessee.   Executrix: Wife Margaret Rosebrough.   Signed March 20, 1809.
Witnesses: James Harris and Samuel A. Harris.   Proven February 25, 1811.
Recorded November 10, 1812.   There is an inventory list.

Page 8   **DAVID McCRACKING.** Wife Elizabeth.   Children: James, David, Joseph,
Ann Mary Burch, Elizabeth Pirce, Mary Varnal, Margret Spraley, Sarah
Brown, E--er Jones, Cintha Birck, and youngest daughter Malinda.   Executors: Wife
Elizabeth McCracking, George Pirce and Thomas Jones.   Signed January 20, 1812.
Witnesses: Susannah Norwood and William Norwood. Proven August 24, 1812.

Page 10   **PARRISH SIMS,** of Georgia and West of the Indian Territory.   Wife
Grizel Sims.   Mentions children but not named.   Executors: Wife Grizel
Sims, William Sims and Benjamin Murrell.   Signed November 26, 1807.   Witnesses:
James Sims, James Witty, George Whitenton and Jamima Sims.   Proven May 25,
1812.

Page 12   **SARAH BIGGERS,** of Williamson County.   Son Joseph.   Daughters,
Agnes Dryden, Eleanor.   Mentions other daughters but not named.
Executors: Kimbrough Ogilvie and James Reid.   Signed January 7, 1811.   Witnesses:
Robert Biggers and James Julion.   Proven February 26, 1812.   Inventory list.

Page 16   Inventory and Sale of **ALEXANDER GRAY'S** Estate.   Recorded
November 14, 1812.

Page 18   Inventory and Sale of property of **SARAH BIGGERS, DECEASED.**
Recorded May 29, 1812.

Page 19   Amount of Estate of **ELEANOR BIGGERS.**   Her guardian, Robert
Elliott.   Recorded August 29, 1812.

Page 20   Sale of Estate of **BENJAMIN LUMBY,** deceased.   Recorded August 27,
1812.

Page 22   **WILLIAM BLAND,** deceased.   Sale and list.   Recorded May 26, 1812.

Page 23   Inventory of property of **ROBERT SIMSON,** deceased.   Recorded
November 26, 1812.

Page 24   **ABRYHAM ADAMS.** Wife Agness.   Daughter Sarah Adams.   Nephew
Abryham Adams.   Has land in South Carolina, Chester District on
Rocky Creek.   Executors: Wife Agness Adams and Richard Wyatt and Samuel
Little.   Signed April 4, 1812.   Witnesses: John Murphy, Archibald Boyd and Samuel
Boyd.   Proven August 24, 1812.

Page 26   Inventory of the Estate of **JOHN DANIEL,** deceased.   Recorded
February 9, 1813.

Page 27   Inventory of Sale of personal property of **WILLIAM FRAME,** deceased.
Recorded February 9, 1813.

Page 27   Inventory of Sale of **JACOB INGLE,** deceased.   Recorded March 5,
1813.

Page 31   Inventory of Estate of **LEVIN READY,** deceased.   Approved May 22,
1813.

1

Page 31　**THOMAS YOUNG,** deceased.　Wife Mary Young.　Nine children: William, Elizabeth Beard, Mary Beard, Jemima, Sally, Majary, Nancy, Daniel and Franky N. Young. Executor: Son William Young. Signed February 18, 1813. Witnesses: Woodson Haley and Ely Sanders. Recorded November 2, 1813.

Page 33　**ANDREW BUCHANAN.** Wife Gennet. Son Leander. Daughters Sinthy, Levicy, Gincy, Betsey and Peggy Buchanan. Executors: Brother Samuel Buchanan and John B. Buchanan.　Signed April 10, 1813.　Witnesses: John A. McKinney, John Davis and Samuel Buchanan. Recorded November 6, 1813.

Page 35　Provisions for Widow Elizabeth Reedy.　Recorded November 17, 1813. Sale of Estate of **LEVIN REEDY**, deceased.

Page 37　**ALIJAH HOMES (HOLMS),** deceased.　Left items to Mrs. Porter. Recorded November 23, 1813.

Page 38　October 25, 1813, **ALIJAH HOLMS**, deceased.　Items listed for eight days attendance when sick, etc. Recorded November 23, 1813.

Page 38　Inventory of **JOHN HARRIS,** deceased. Recorded November 23, 1813.

Page 39　**ALEXANDER MOORE.**　Friend Andrew Smith and friend Patrick O'Callaghan.　Had land in Allegheny County, Robertson Township, Pennsylvania.　Executor: Patrick O'Callaghan. Signed March 22, 1813. Witnesses: John V. McKenney and James Bright. Proven November 23, 1813.

Page 40　Inventory of Estate of **ROBERT PATTON,** deceased.　Recorded November 2, 1813.

Page 41　**WILLIAM CROSS.** Wife Delila Cross. Four children: Nancy Powhatten, James and Etheldridge.　Owned land in Davidson County.　Executor: Wife Delila Cross.　Signed January 25, 1814. Witnesses: Moses Driver and John Mailer. Proven February 7, 1814.

Page 42　Sale of Estate of **ROBERT PATTON,** deceased.　Recorded March 15, 1814.

Page 45　Inventory of **DAVID PHILLIPS,** deceased. Recorded March 15, 1814.

Page 45　Inventory of **ABSOLEM WHITSETT,** deceased. Estate. Recorded March 15, 1813.

Page 46　Inventory of Estate of **JOSHUA SIMPSON,** deceased.　Recorded March 15, 1814.

Page 47　Inventory of Estate of **WILLIAM CROSS,** deceased.　Recorded May 3, 1814.

Page 49　Sale of Estate of **PETER CAIN,** deceased. Recorded April 25, 1814.

Page 49　**LEMUEL P. MONTGOMERY, ESQ.,** deceased. Land in Campbell County near the Town of Jacksborough.　Mentions his brothers and sisters but not by name. Executors: James Trimble, Jenkins Whitside and Thomas M. Corsey. Signed March 4, 1814.　Witnesses: George C. Witt, John Maze and Robert Buchanan. Proven May 2, 1814.

Page 51　Inventory of Estate of **RICHARD BIRD,** deceased.　Recorded July 19, 1814.

Page 51　Inventory of Estate of **SAMUEL WHITE,** deceased.　Recorded August 18, 1814.

2

Page 52    Inventory returned. **JOEL McCREARY,** deceased. Recorded August 18, 1814.

Page 53    Inventory returned. **ELIZABETH PHILLIPS,** deceased. Recorded August 19, 1814.

Page 54    Sale of Property of **ARTHUR PARR,** deceased. Recorded August 19, 1814.

Page 54    Sale of Property of **DAVID SHELTON,** deceased. Recorded August 19, 1814.

Page 56    Estate of **WILLIAM FRAME,** deceased. Recorded August 19, 1814.

Page 56    Sale of Property of **JOSHUA SIMPSON,** deceased. Recorded August 20, 1814.

Page 58    Inventory of **JAMES GRANT,** deceased. Recorded August 20, 1814.

Page 58    Account of **ROBERT PATTON,** deceased. Recorded August 26, 1814.

Page 59    **HENRY PORCH,** deceased. Recorded August 27, 1814.

Page 60    Inventory of Estate of **JOHN COBB,** deceased. Recorded December 22, 1814.

Page 60    Inventory of Estate of **HENRY PORCH,** deceased. Recorded December 22, 1814.

Page 61    Amount of Sale of **ELIZABETH PHILLIPS,** deceased. Recorded December 23, 1814.

Page 62    Amount of Sale of **JOEL McCREARY,** deceased. Recorded December 23, 1814.

Page 65    Agreeable to Letters of Administration to me, August Term 1814, directed to the Estate of **JESSE W. JONES,** deceased, and I can not find no property of the deceased but his bounty and pay as a Regular Soldier and are in the possession of Jesse George which he will not give up without a Law Suit, a true inventory by me, Joseph Kelly, Administrator. Recorded December 26, 1814.

Page 65    Allowed Martha Harris, wife of **JOHN HARRIS,** deceased, provisions out of his estate. November 6, 1814.

Page 66    **GEORGE C. WITT,** deceased. Wife Charlotte. Owned lot and house in Fayetteville. Was partner with Dickson Garner with 14 different tracts of land. Brother Thomas Witt. Executors: Francis Porterfield and James Bright. Signed March 20, 1815. Witnesses: Francis Porterfield and Vance Greer. Recorded May 23, 1815.

Page 67    **ROBERT C. KENNEDY,** deceased. Wife Esther. Children: William Edmiston, Hetty Montgomery, Polly McNairy, Marion Lewis and Sally Buchanan, all still Kennedys. Also, Peggy, wife of George W. Martin, Martha Campbell wife of John P. Campbell, Elizabeth Edmiston wife of Vance Greer. Had land on Norris Creek. Executors: William Edmiston, John P. McConnell and William Edmiston Kennedy and wife Esther Kennedy. Signed February 18, 1815. Witnesses: Thomas L. Trotter and Robert L. Dean. Proven May 1, 1815.

Page 71    Inventory of Estate of **DAVID McCANTS,** deceased. Recorded May 25, 1815.

Page 73    Sale of Property of **CHARLES BURKS,** deceased.   Recorded May 25,
           1815.

Page 76    Sale of Property of **GEORGE WOLF,** deceased.   Recorded May 25,
           1815.

Page 77    Inventory of Estate of **WILLIAM CROSS,** deceased.   Recorded May 25,
           1815.

Page 79    **WRIGHT WILLIAMS,** deceased.   Wife Anna Williams.   Mentioned
           children but not by name.   Executors: Joel Pinson, Sampson Williams
and Robert Riley.   Signed November 22, 1814.   Witnesses: Henry Kelso and Brice
M. Garner.   Recorded August 18, 1815.

Page 80    **MOSES DRIVER,** deceased.   Wife Sally Driver.   Mentions his children
           but not by name.   A brother Abner Driver.   Executors: Wife Sally
Driver and Duke W. Sumner.   Signed June 9, 1815.   Witnesses: David P. Monroe and
William Monroe.   Recorded August 18, 1815.

Page 82    A verbal statement made of the disposition of personal property of
           **ANDREW STEWART,** late a Sergeant in Captain John Doak's Company
of Tennessee Volunteers of Mounted Gunmen, who was suddenly taken sick while in
New Orleans, performing a tour of duty as a soldier and died between the 6th and
10th of February 1815, as pronounced as his Last Will and Testament.   "It is my
wish that my brother Joseph Stewart of Knox County of East Tennessee, shall after
his death compile and collect all his personal estate... Cousin Darkus Shaw a silk
dress.   Witnesses: Samuel S. Doak and Christopher E. Lord.   Proven August 7, 1815.

Page 83    **JACOB DANCE,** deceased, of Giles County.     Wife Sarah Dance.
           Children: William, Jacob, John, James, Nancy wife of George Lensly.
Executors: Wife Sarah Dance and son William Dance.   Signed August 25, 1814.
Witnesses: A.Y. Issacs and Thomas Johnson.   Proven August 7, 1815.

Page 85    **HENRY FEATHERSTON,** deceased.     Wife Nancy.     Sons, William
           Grandison Featherston and Edward Harding Featherston.   Mentions his
daughters but not by name.   Executors: Wife Nancy Featherston and brother
Edward Featherston.   Signed November 4, 1814.   Witnesses Alexander Morton and
James Buchanan.   Proven August 7, 1815.

Page 87    **FREDERICK OLIVER,** deceased.   Mentions wife and children but not by
           name.   Signed January 25, 1815.   Witnesses: Thomas Sumners and John
Durley.   Executors: Wife Rosanna and her uncle Enoch Davis.   Proven August 7,
1815.

Page 88    Memo of Sale of **ZAPH MOSLEY,** deceased, by Lucrecy Mosley.

Page 89    **WILLIAM YOUNG,** deceased.   Sold 1 horse for $11.00 and 1 tin trunk
           for $2.00.   Seaborn Brown, Administrator.   June 14, 1815.

Page 89    Inventory of Estate of **AARON BRADLEY,** deceased.   August 4, 1815.

Page 89    Inventory of Estate of **SAMUEL CHAPPALAIN,** deceased.   August 20,
           1815.

Page 89    Inventory of Estate of **THOMAS McBRIDE,** deceased.   May 20, 1815.

Page 90    Inventory of Estate of **JOHN MITCHELL,** deceased.   Recorded August
           25, 1815.

Page 90    Inventory of Estate of **A. STEWART,** deceased.   Recorded August 25,
           1815.

Page 117    List of Sale of **THOMAS SMITH,** deceased.    Recorded December 23, 1815.

Page 118    Inventory of **SAMUEL HODGE,** deceased.    Wife Patsey Hodge. Recorded December 23, 1815.

Page 119    Inventory of **JOHN MILLIKEN,** deceased.    Recorded January 2, 1816.

Page 120    Inventory of **AARON BRADLEY,** deceased.    Recorded January 2, 1816.

Page 121    Inventory of **ANN BLACKWOOD,** deceased.    Recorded January 22, 1816.

Page 121    Inventory of **JOHN COROTHERS,** deceased.    Recorded January 22, 1816.

Page 121    Inventory of **SAMUEL FARRIS,** deceased.    Recorded January 22, 1816.

Page 122    Inventory of **DAVID McCANTS,** deceased.    Recorded January 22, 1816.

Page 123    Inventory of **THOMAS PINKERTON,** deceased.    Recorded January 22, 1816.

Page 124    Inventory of **WILLIAM P. HARDIN,** deceased.    Recorded January 22, 1816.

Page 124    Inventory of **WRIGHT WILLIAMS,** deceased.    Recorded January 22, 1816.

Page 124    Inventory of **WILLIAM LONGMIRE,** deceased.    Recorded January 22, 1816.

Page 125    Inventory of **JOHN HART,** deceased.    Recorded January 22, 1816.

Page 126    Inventory of **CHARLEY SMITH,** deceased.    Recorded January 22, 1816.

Page 127    Inventory of **JOHN KARR,** deceased.    Recorded January 22, 1816.

Page 128    Memo of the Will of **DAVID HOWELL,** deceased.    Wife Mary Howell. Signed October 9, 1815.    Witnesses: Stephen Loyd and Elizabeth Loyd. Proven November 19, 1815.

Page 129    **WILLIAM BEAVER, SR.,** deceased.    Wife Elizabeth Beavers.    Children: William, Michael, Polly Hodge and Sarah Hampton.    Executors: Son William Beavers, Jr. and James Broadaway.    Signed November 5, 1815.    Witnesses: Cornelius Darnell and John Broadaway, Jr.    Proven February 7, 1816.

Page 131    Inventory of **JOHN COROTHERS,** deceased.    Recorded March 13, 1816.

Page 131    January 13, 1816.    Sold to the highest bidders all the property of **SAMUEL HODGES,** deceased.    Recorded March 13, 1816 by Patsey Hodges.

Page 132    I, Jonathan Hays, guardian of Jesse Love and Asa Love, heirs of **HENRY LOVE,** deceased, received $64.00 of the sstate of my wards. Recorded March 13, 1816.

Page 132    Sale of Estate of **JOHN HART,** deceased.    Recorded March 13, 1816.

Page 132    Amount of possession of Sarah Waggoner, widow of **GEORGE WAGGONER,** deceased.    Recorded March 13, 1816.

Page 132    Inventory of **JOHN DOWNING,** deceased. Recorded March 13, 1816.

Page 132    Inventory of **GEORGE C. WITT,** deceased. Recorded March 13, 1816.

Page 133    Inventory of **PLEASANT GRIFFIS,** deceased. Recorded March 13, 1816.

Page 134    Inventory of **ANN BLACKWOOD,** deceased. Recorded March 13, 1816.

Page 135    Inventory of **JAMES CRAWSBY,** deceased. Recorded March 13, 1816.

Page 135    Inventory of **JOHN DOAK,** deceased. Recorded March 14, 1816.

Page 137    Inventory of **THOMAS PHELPS,** deceased. Recorded March 14, 1816.

Page 139    Property sold of **WILLIAM RORAx,** deceased. Recorded May 30, 1816.

Page 139    **PLEASANT GRIFFIS,** deceased. Recorded May 30, 1816. Inventory.

Page 141    Inventory of **ELIZABETH BEAVERS,** deceased. Recorded May 30, 1816.

Page 144    Amount of Sale of property of **JOHN HART,** deceased. Recorded May 30, 1816.

Page 144    Inventory of **AMBROSE BARKER,** deceased. Recorded May 30, 1816.

Page 144    Inventory of **DANIEL MORGAN,** deceased. Recorded May 30, 1816.

Page 145    Return of Property of estate of **JOHN DOWNING,** deceased. All sold. Recorded May 30, 1816.

Page 145    **SAMUEL BARNES,** deceased. Wife Polly Barnes. Three sons, Ansylum Barnes, William Barnes and Robert Barnes. Executors: Robert Edmiston and John Rhea. Signed April 5, 1816. Witnesses: Ansylum Barnes and Jeremiah Barnes. Proven May 8, 1816.

Page 147    **THOMAS WILSON,** deceased. Wife Elizabeth Wilson. Children: James, Thomas, Matthew, Washington, Betsy, Robert and John. Grandson Clinton. Brother Robert Wilson. Executors: Brother Robert Wilson and Samuel Little. Signed February 26, 1816. Witnesses: Robert Wilson, Sr. and Samuel Little and Robert Cunningham. Proven May 9, 1816.

Page 149    Inventory of **ANDREW EDMISTON,** deceased. By Robert E. Edmiston, executor. May 6, 1816.

Page 150    **JOHN MORGAN,** deceased. Wife Mary Morgan. Children: Nancy, Martha, Malinda, Susan, Mary, Charles, Hiram and John. Land in Franklin County, Tennessee. Executors: Wife Mary Morgan and son Charles Morgan and James Bright. Signed November 3, 1816. Witnesses: Joseph Morgan and John J. Whitaker. Proven February 8, 1817.

Page 152    Additional Sale of Property of **ALEXANDER McDONALD,** deceased. Sale on March 20 and 21, 1817. And rented three lots in the town of Fayetteville.

Page 153    Inventory of **JACOB WHITEHEAD,** deceased. Sale of personal property.

Page 153    Inventory of **WILLIAM KING,** deceased. May Term 1817.

Page 154    **WILLIAM WOODY,** deceased. Wife Jane Woody. Children: William Blank, Jane, Sarah Hilton, Biddy Huff, Betsey Buchanan, John and

7

Nancy Fulington. Son-in-law James Buchanan. Executors: Wife Jane Woody and son John Woody and son-in-law James Buchanan. Signed July 16, 1814. Witnesses: Henry Featherston and Alexander Morton and W. Williams. Proven May 5, 1817.

Page 156 **HEZEKIAH LEONARD,** deceased. Brother Griffith Leonard. Will was made before George Leonard and Robert Leonard on March 27, 1817, on his last sickness. Proven May 10, 1817.

Page 157 **ANDREW SPRALDING,** deceased. Wife Martha Spralding. Grandson Andrew Biram Spralding and granddaughter Polly Windom. Signed February 11, 1817. Witnesses: William C. Ables and John Austin. Executrix: Martha Spralding. Proven May 9, 1817.

Page 159 Inventory of **RICHARD BYRD,** deceased. Recorded April 29, 1817.

Page 160 Inventory of **WILLIAM ACUFF,** deceased. Recorded March 14, 1817.

Page 161 Inventory of **WILLIAM BREWER,** deceased. Recorded March 3, 1817.

Page 163 **WILLIAM CAMPBELL,** deceased. Wife Lydia Campbell. Children, George, Elizabeth, Mary Bellar, Nancy Linthecum, Sarah and the youngest daughter Lydia Hunt. Sarah married Shaderick Webster. Executors: Son George Campbell and son-in-law Shaderick Webster. Signed November 23, 1816. Witnesses: George Hopkins, Alexander Moore, G. Campbell and William Bellar. Proven May 10, 1817.

Page 165 **JAMES PYBAS,** deceased. Children: Eldest son Henry Pybas, Benjamin and William Shaw and youngest son James. Daughters: Eldest daughter Esther Pybas, 2nd daughter Catharine, 3rd daughter Selah, and youngest Polly. He lived on west side of Swan Creek. Executors: Isaac Conger and Henry Pybas. Signed March 15, 1816. Witnesses: Kenneth McKenzie and William McKenzie. Proven May 10, 1817.

Page 167 **ALEXANDER WHITE,** deceased. Mentions wife and children but not by name. Mentions William White and Robert M. White. Signed July 7, 1813. Executors: William White and Robert M. White. Witnesses: Aaron Boyd and Nathaniel Brown. Proven May 9, 1817.

Page 169 Inventory of **DAVID TURNER,** deceased. John Buchanan, Administrator.

Page 170 Allowance. **ROBERT LEE,** deceased.

Page 170 Allowance. **WILLIAM WHITEHEAD,** deceased. May 8, 1817. By Commissioners: John H. Zivley, Bernard Prott and George Walton.

Page 171 **ALEXANDER McDONALD,** deceased. Inventory.

Page 172 Inventory of **ANDREW EDMISTON,** deceased. June 18, 1816.

Page 172 Inventory of **WILLIAM DAVIDSON,** deceased. Recorded July 16, 1817.

Page 172 Inventory of **JOHN FOWLER,** deceased. Sarah Fowler, Administrator.

Page 174 **WILLIAM PAYNE,** deceased. Wife Charity Payne. Children: Rachel, William B., Charity, Elizabeth, George Washington, Thomas Jefferson, Susanna, Dianna and Patsey Payne. Also, mentions a Martha Payne, relict of Charles Payne, deceased. Executors: Charity Payne and James Grant. Signed April 3, 1817. Witnesses: Thomas L. Trotter and Jesse Haden. Proven May Term 1817.

Page 176 Settlement of **JAMES CAUSBY,** deceased. Hance Causby,

Administrator. May 6, 1817.

Page 176     Settlement of **JESSE DAVIS,** deceased. Sale on April 19, 1817.

Page 177     Settlement of **JOEL McCRARY,** deceased. With Elijah McCrary, Administrator. May 1, 1817.

Page 177     Settlement of **JOHN KARR,** deceased. Ann Karr, Administrator. April 14, 1817.

Page 178     Allowance for widow and children of **JOHN FOWLER,** deceased.

Page 179     Inventory of **ARNOLD BRUCE,** deceased. Joseph Scott, Administrator.

Page 180     Sale of **WILLIAM CAMPBELL,** deceased. Executors: G. Campbell and S. Webster.

Page 181     Inventory of **JACOB WHITEHEAD,** deceased. Tobias Whitehead, Administrator. August 6, 1817.

Page 183     Settlement of **WILLIAM RUSSELL,** deceased. George Cunningham, Administrator.

Page 184     Settlement of **PLEASANT GRIFFIS,** deceased. John Martin and Nathan G. Pinson, Commissioners. May Term 1817. Inventory, etc. August 2, 1817.

Page 187     Sale of Estate of **PETER CORBELL,** deceased. Inventory. May 26, 1817.

Page 189     Sale of Estate of **JAMES PYBAS,** deceased.

Page 190     Inventory of **CARTER ACUFF,** deceased. August Term 1817.

Page 191     May 30, 1817. Court appointed Willaby Pugh and Philip Koonce to settle with Abner Wells, Administrator of **THOMAS PINKERTON,** deceased.

Page 191     Sale of Property of **MATTHEW SAMPLE,** deceased. May 15, 1817.

Page 191     Settlement. Ordered William Edmiston and William Parr to settle with the Estate of **ALEXANDER WHITE,** deceased.

Page 192     Settlement of Peter Tipps and Jacob Silvertooth on estate of **JOHN TIPPS,** deceased.

Page 192     Settlement of **ALEXANDER McDONALD,** deceased. September 26, 1817. By S.D. Hunter and Polly McDonald, Administrators.

Page 193     Inventory of the Property of **JOSEPH DAMRELL,** deceased. By wife Elizabeth Damrell. November 6, 1817.

Page 195     List of Notes, etc., remaining of estate of **WILLIAM E. RUSSELL,** deceased. George Cunningham, Administrator.

Page 195     Estate of **JESSE CLARK,** deceased. November 1, 1817. Sale.

Page 196     Settlement of Estate of **AARON BRADLEY,** deceased. Jane Bradley and William Rowell, Administrators. Schooling of Rachel Bradley. Mentions Jane, Jesse and Hannah.

Page 197     Settlement of Estate of **ROBERT PATTON,** deceased. Jane Patton,

Administrator. October 29, 1817.

Page 199   Inventory of **CHARLES ADAIR,** deceased. By Samuel Wilson, Executor.
February 20, 1817.

Page 201   **CHARLES BURKS,** deceased. Settlement. January 17, 1818.

Page 201   **WILLIAM P. HARDIN,** deceased to **MOSES HARDIN,** deceased,
November 15, 1816.

Page 202   **THOMAS HEDGECOCK,** deceased. Catharine Hedgecock,
Administrator, August 16, 1817.

Page 202   **WILLIAM McMILLEN,** deceased. Wife Martha McMillen. Children:
John Andrew, William, James, Nancy wife of Jacob Wright, Sally wife
of Edmund Chitwood, Joseph, Thomas, Jane wife of Jonathan Gross, Patsy wife of
Gilbert Marshall, and Polly wife of Hugh Pinkston. Signed April 18, 1815.
Witnesses: Nathan G. Pinson, Samuel Nesbet and A. Bostick. Proven November 8,
1817.

Page 205   Notes due on Estate of **JOHN GAGE,** deceased. Jeremiah Lee,
Administrator. Polly Lee formerly Polly Gage. January 19, 1818.

Page 206   Commissioners for the Estate of **WILLIAM ACUFF,** deceased. John
Park, Administrator. January 1, 1818.

Page 207   **ROBERT BUCHANAN,** deceased. Wife Abnida Buchanan. Mentioned
John Nixon's daughter Betsy Nixon. Executors: Abnida Buchanan and
Samuel Buchanan. Signed July 9, 1817. Witnesses: Samuel Buchanan and John
Nixon.

Page 208   **JAMES ELLIS,** deceased. Wife Sarah Ellis. Children: James, Sarah,
William, Jesse, Hulda Ness, Elizabeth Massey, and Polly Curry.
Executors: Sons, William and Jesse Ellis. Signed September 17, 1817. Witnesses:
William Ellis and Jesse Ellis and James Ellis. Recorded November 8, 1817.

Page 210   **JOSEPH LOONY,** deceased. Wife Caty Loony. Mentioned his children
but not by name. Executors: Abner Buckler and Joshua Nichols. Signed
October 18, 1817. Witnesses: Thomas Henly, John Acuff and Sarah Acuff. Proven
November 4, 1817.

Page 212   Sale of Estate of **ALEXANDER McDONALD,** deceased. March 18,
1818.

Page 212   Inventory of **JAMES CUMMINS,** deceased. April 21, 1818.

Page 213   Inventory of **JAMES PYBAS,** deceased.

Page 213   Inventory of Personal Property of **BENJAMIN McFARLIN.**

Page 214   Settlement of Estate of **SAMUEL CHAPPELAIN,** deceased.

Page 215   Settlement of Estate of **DAVID SHELTON,** deceased. John Silvertooth
and John Dawdy, Administrators. April 18, 1818.

Page 216   Inventory of **SAMUEL CAROTHERS,** deceased. February 26, 1818.

Page 218   Inventory of **ARCHIBALD ALLEN,** deceased. Sold December 6 & 7,
1814.

Page 222   **WILLIAM B. GRISSOM,** deceased. Father Oliver and mother Deannah
Grissom. Brothers and sisters: Wiley, Eaton, Henry, Benjamin, Edward,

Polly Clark, Elizabeth L. Commons and the children of Sally Neil. Executors: Brothers Eaton and Benjamin Grissom. Signed January 23, 1819. Witnesses: William Edmiston, Randolph Grissom and John Davis. Proven January 30, 1819.

Page 225   Inventory of Estate of **WILLIAM CONWELL,** deceased. John Ryal and Polly Conwell, Administrators.

Page 228   Sale of Estate of **WILLIAM McDAVID,** deceased. Nancy McDavid and James McDavid, Administrators.

Page 231   Sale of Estate of **JOSEPH LOONY,** deceased. Joab Buckly, Executor.

Page 231   Additional Sale of **ALEXANDER McDONALD,** deceased. September 20, 1818. By S.D. Hunter, Administrator.

Page 232   **JOHN DOAK,** deceased. William Shaw, Administrator. September 22, 1818.

Page 232   **SAMUEL CUTREL,** deceased. Vance Greer, Administrator to amount collected of Hugh M. Blake. June 1817.

Page 233   Notes and Property belonging to Estate of **HUGH TOMLINSON,** deceased.

Page 235   Inventory of **JOEL HALBERT,** deceased.

Page 236   Inventory of **JOSEPH WHITENBERG,** deceased. Samuel Rosebrough and Jacob Whitenberg, Administrators.

Page 238   **CHARLES LUCAS,** deceased. Wife Polly Lucas. Owns land in Kentucky. Executor: John Donelson. Signed April 17, 1817. Witnesses: William Boon, John T. King, and John Barker. Proven October 1818.

Page 240   Inventory of **WILLIAM McDAVID,** deceased.

Page 241   Settlement of Estate of **ALEXANDER McDONALD,** deceased. October 17, 1818.

Page 245   Inventory of **MARTIN FLYNT,** deceased. July 27, 1818. Richard Flynt, Executor.

Page 246   Inventory of **JOHN KELLY, SR.,** deceased. May 7, 1818. Nancy Kelly and Joseph Kelly, Administrators.

Page 249   Sale of Property of **JOEL HALBERT,** deceased. November 12, 1818.

Page 255   Inventory of **JOSEPH WILCHER,** deceased. November 11, 1818. Francis Fincher, Z. Arnold and J. Ellis.

Page 257   Inventory of **WILLIAM CAMPBELL,** deceased. G. Campbell and S. Webster, Executors.

Page 258   Inventory of **WILLIAM GRICHAM,** deceased. January 30, 1819.

Page 259   Estate of **THOMAS PHELPS,** deceased. Sale of Estate to Britain Phelps. January 16, 1819.

Page 260   Inventory of **JOHN HUGHES,** deceased.

Page 261   Inventory of **JOSEPH WHITENBERG,** deceased. List. January 26, 1819. By Samuel Rosebrough.

Page 288    **JOHN C. BEARD,** deceased.  Mother Polly Moore.  Brother Alexander Moore.  Friends, Mrs. Catharine Garner, Brice M. Garner.  Executor: Uncle Ezekiel C. Loyd.  Signed February 19, 1822.  Witnesses: R. Dickson and William Dickson.  Proven July 15, 1822.

Page 290    **JESSE HAYS,** deceased.  Wife Isabella Hays.  Children: Thomas, Henry, Lucretia Killingworth, Betsy Thompson, John, Mary Moore, Isabella wife of William Holloway, and Sarah Bledsoe.  Executors: Sons, Thomas and Henry Hays.  Signed January 28, 1822.  Witnesses: Joseph Greer, James Simmons and John H. Moore.  Proven April 15, 1822.

Page 293    Amount of Sale of Estate of **THOMAS COMMONS,** deceased.

Page 295    Settlement of Estate of **DAVID SHELTON,** deceased.  Administrators John Silvertooth and John Dawdy.  April 18, 1818.  Witnesses: A.W. Walker and James Clark.

Page 296    **JOSEPH McADAMS,** deceased.  Wife Margarett McAdams.  Children: William, Susannah, James, Irwin, John, Joseph, Hugh and Samuel McAdams and Mary McAdams.  Grandsons: Joseph, son of Irwin McAdams and Joseph, son of John McAdams and Daniel Patterson.  Proven July 21, 1823.

Page 298    **MOSES SATTERFIELD,** deceased.  Wife Elizabeth Satterfield.  Six children: Preston, John, Elizabeth, Hannah wife of Samuel Wallace, Mahala and Catharine Satterfield.  Signed May 24, 1823.  Executors: James Childers and Michael Robertson.  Witnesses: John Cock, Jr., John Martin and Mahala Satterfield.  Proven April 21, 1823.

Page 300    **ROBERT ADAMS,** deceased.  Wife Martha Adams.  Children not named.  Executors: James McCartle and Gilbert Kennedy.  Signed December 1, 1819.  Witnesses: Thomas McGaugh and James Kennedy.  Proven January 17, 1820.

Page 302    **WILLIAM HARRIS,** deceased.  Wife Jane Harris.  Mentions his children but not by name.  Executors: Brother Howell Harris and Henry Scales.  Signed March 2, 1817.  Witnesses: James Tool and William Middleton.  Proven July 17, 1820.

Page 303    **MALCOMB PATTERSON,** deceased.  Wife Mary Patterson.  Children: Elizabeth, Margaret, Alexander, Catharine, Nancy, Archibald and Dunken Patterson.  Signed January 16, 1823?.  Witnesses: Robert Fletcher, William Sanders and Alexander Kennedy.  Proven January 26, 1821.

Page 305    **ROBERT NIX,** deceased.  Wife Susannah Nix.  Executors: Wife Susannah Nix and Elijah Brownfield.  Signed May 22, 1822.  Witnesses: Joel Howell, John Moorehead and John Lindsey.  Proven July 15, 1822.

Page 307    **ARTHUR BROOKS,** deceased.  Wife Fanny Brooks.  Children: William A., Josiah, Rebeccah, Louisa and Thomas F. Brooks.  Executors: Gideon Pillow and Oliver Williams.  Signed November 11, 1819.  Witnesses: James Brooks, Elijah Brooks, Henry Talley and Dunkin Bond and Jesse Riggs.  Proven January 21, 1820.

Page 308    **CHRISTOPHER MILLER,** deceased.  Brother Jacob Miller.  Executors: Nicholas Carriger and Daniel Smith.  Signed February 18, 1822.  Witnesses: Jacob Groce and Thomas Marsh.  Proven April 22, 1822.

Page 310    **WILLIAM REED,** deceased.  Wife Elizabeth Reed.  Children: John, Lewis, William, Elizabeth, James, Benjamin, Nathaniel, Lemuel, Absolom, Fanny and Polly Reed.  Executors: Nathaniel Reed and William Ford.  Signed March 15, 1822.  Witnesses: Benjamin Reed and Lemuel Reed.  Proven April 15, 1822.

Page 311 **THOMAS R. EDWARDS,** deceased. Brothers and sisters: Joshua Dodson, Sister Leathy Dodson, Susannah Dodson and James Dodson. Bequeathed to my sister Leathy Dodson one feather bed, to wit, the bed left with my mother when I left Virginia. Has lands in Granville County, North Carolina, to go to his brother James Dodson, claimed by my father Thomas Edwards, deceased. Executors: Martin Dodson, my step father and Stokley Slayden, both of Halifax County, Virginia. Signed April 23, 1820. Witnesses: Samuel Davis, John Roper, M.D., and James Garrett. Proven January 15, 1821.

Page 313 **MARGARET RORAX,** deceased. Nuncupative Will. The deposition of Cynthy Hunter, Mary Brents, and Nancy Rorax, were present when Margaret Rorax, now deceased, witnessed her make her Will during her last sickness. Daughter Tabitha Hindman and her seven children, William, Eli, Bartley, Silas, John, Margaret and David Rorax. Mentions that John Hindman should not share in any part. Executrix: Daughter Tabitha Hindman. Signed by witness on February 20, 1821. Witnesses: Mary Brent, Cyntha Hunter, and Nancy Rorax with Isaac Conger, Justice. Proven April 16, 1821.

Page 315 **THOMAS BLYTHE, SR.,** deceased. Wife Elizabeth Blythe. Sons and daughter: Elizabeth, a single woman at this time, Thomas Blythe, Jr., Champain Blythe are both Executors. Signed by Thomas Blythe, Sr. on March 2, 1823. Witnesses: Jonathan Floyd and Hezekiah Erwin. May 4, 1823.
Codocil: Daughter Rachel Carr and heirs, daughter Tenasha Dawdy, son Hugh Blythe, daughter Mary Sutton and son Absolum Blythe. Signed May 4, 1823. Witnesses: Jonathan Floyd and Hezekiah Erwin. Proven July 24, 1823.

Page 318 **ESTHER KENNEDY,** deceased. Children: William Edmiston, Martha McConnell, Margaret Martin, Elizabeth E. Graves, Hetty McEwen, Mariam L. Sanders and Mary M. Kercheval and her granddaughter Juliett Elizabeth Kercheval. Executors: Son William Edmiston Kennedy. Signed January 10, 1822. Witnesses: William Edmiston and Elizabeth Ann Edmiston. Proven October --, 1823.

Page 320 Inventory of **CHRISTOPHER MILLER,** deceased. Nicholas Carriger, Executor.

Page 321 Amount of Sale of **JOHN HOPPER,** deceased. By Sarah Hopper, Admr.

Page 322 Missing.

Page 323 Missing.

Page 324 Inventory of Estate of **WILLIAM C. RUSSELL,** deceased. 1816. Recorded December 9, 1823. Administrators: George Cunningham and Patsey Russell.

Page 325 Inventory of Estate of **WILLIAM ACUFF,** deceased. Sold by John Park, Administrator, September 3, 1816. Recorded December 10, 1823.

Page 327 List of Property sold of **THOMAS HEDGECOCK,** deceased, by Caty Hedgecock, Admr. Recorded December 10, 1823.

Page 328 August Sessions, 1816. Ordered Benjamin Guess, Joseph Adkins and Martin Jones to sell off one years provisions to the widow of **THOMAS HEDGECOCK,** deceased, July 30, 1816. Witness: John Enochs, J.P.

Page 328 Amount of Sales of **ANDREW ALEXANDER.** Administrators: Elizabeth Alexander and Archibald Alexander. Recorded December 10, 1823.

Page 328 Sale of Estate of **DAVID DALTON,** deceased. December 10, 1823. Samuel Dalton, Admr.

Page 329 Polly Davidson's allowance, one year supply, November 2, 1816.

Recorded December 10, 1823.

Page 329    Amount of Sale of **RUBEN YEAGER,** deceased.    Augustine Yeager, Administrator.

Page 330    Inventory of **ANDREW ALEXANDER,** deceased.    Recorded December 11, 1823.

Page 331    Amount of Sale of Estate of **BOOKER B. EASTER,** deceased.    February 28, 1816.

Page 332    Last return of Estate of **DAVID McCANT,** deceased.    Sarah McCants, Administrator on February 5, 1823.

Page 333    Settlement of Estate of **JAMES GRANT,** deceased.    May 21, 1816.

Page 333    Settlement with the orphans of **HENRY LOVE,** deceased.    Orphans: Jesse and Asa Love, by guardians William Lee and Jonathan Hays.    June 24, 1816.    Witnesses: William Smith and Robert M. White.    Recorded December 12, 1823.

Page 334    Provisions layed out for Nextley Norris for one year including discharge for six months Militia, November 2, 1816.    Commissioners were William Millard, Nicholas Carriger and Lewis Morgan.    Recorded December 12, 1823.

Page 334    Provisions layed out for widow and children of **JACOB INGLE,** deceased.    Commissioners William Dickson, James Holman and Benjamin Boone.    May 2, 1816.

Page 334    Sale of Property of **THOMAS BLYTHE,** deceased, by Thomas Blythe, Jr. as Executor.    Sold on September 20, 1823.    35 acres to himself for $200.00.    Recorded December 12, 1823.

Page 335    Inventory of **DANIEL MORGAN,** deceased.    April 27, 1816.    Recorded December 12, 1823.

Page 335    Inventory of Property of **HEZEKIAH MORRIS,** deceased.    Recorded December 12, 1823.

Page 336    Amount of Sale of Property of **ALEXANDER McDONALD,** deceased.    September 6, 1816.    Provisions layed out for widow of same on August 31, 1816.    Commissioners were John Archer, Ezekiel Norris and James Bryans.    Recorded December 15, 1823.

Page 339    August 30, 1805.    John Love's account against Mary Love.    Recorded December 16, 1823.

Page 340    Estate of **HENRY LOVE,** deceased, to William Lee, Dir., support of Henry Love's two orphans: Jesse and Asey Love.    Recorded December 16, 1823.

Page 340    Additional return of the Estate of **SARAH BIGGERS** by Kimbrough Ogilvie on August 5, 1816.    Recorded December 16, 1823.

Page 340    Sale of Property of the Estate of **ALEXANDER McDONALD,** deceased, March 18, 1818.    Hire of negro Jacob until March 18, 1819.    Recorded December 18, 1823.    Administrators: Sherwood Hunter and Polly McDonald.

Page 341    Estate of **JUSHUA SIMPSON,** deceased.    Commissioners were R. Dickson and Vance Greer.    Recorded December 7, 1823.

Page 341    Inventory of Estate of **WILLIAM SMITH, JR.,** deceased, by William Smith, Sr., Administrator.    Recorded January Term 1821.

15

Page 342   Statement of Account of Lincoln County with Elizabeth Simpson of
           Fayetteville, this February 4, 1817, by boarding five children for 2
years and 9 months. Polly, Peggy, William, Ruth and John Simpson, the children of
**JOSHUA SIMPSON,** deceased. Recorded December 17, 1823.

Page 342   Inventory of Estate of **CHARLES ADAIR,** deceased, taken February 3,
           1817. Recorded December 18, 1823. Samuel Wilson, Executor.

Page 343   Estate of **SARAH BIGGERS,** deceased, by Executors: Kimbrough Ogilvie
           and James Reed.

Page 343   Robert Elliott, guardian for Elinor Biggers, an idiot.   Settled account
           February 4, 1817.   Commissioners were J. Bright and R. Dickson.
Recorded December 20, 1823.

Page 344   Inventory of **JAMES WARD,** deceased, now in the possession of the
           widow of the deceased on July 21, 1823. John Lain, Administrator.

Page 345   Account of hiring of negroes belonging to the Estate of **EDWARD
TEAL,** deceased.   Francis Teal, Administrator, November 13, 1822.   Recorded
December 25, 1823.

Page 345   Ordered by the Court that Nathan G. Pinson, Phillip Koonce and James
           Holman settle with George Campbell and Shadarick Webster, Executors
of the Will of **WILLIAM CAMPBELL,** deceased. Recorded December 25, 1823.

Page 346   Commissioners appointed to settle with Jonathan Floyd, Executor of
           **WILLIAM N. PATTERSON,** deceased.   Estate proven December 28,
1823. Recorded December 25, 1823.

Page 347   Inventory of Estate of **JONATHAN ESTILL,** deceased.   Recorded
           December 26, 1823.

Page 347   Lincoln County Court, July Term, 1819.   Ordered that David Cowan,
           James Corithers and Stephen Hightower, appointed to settle with John
Buchanan, Administrator of **ARCHIBALD BUCHANAN,** deceased, and made return
at next court. Recorded December 26, 1823.

Page 347   Inventory of Estate of **ARCHIBALD MAYFIELD,** deceased, August 22,
           1822. Recorded December 26, 1823.

Page 348   Ordered by the court at January Term 1818, to lay off provisions for
           widow and orphans of **SAMUEL CARITHERS,** deceased.   February 26,
1818.

Page 348   Court ordered settlement with James Downing, administrator of **JOHN
DOWNING,** deceased. Recorded December 27, 1823.

Page 348   Inventory of **JAMES CUMMONS,** deceased.   Taken April 27, 1818, by
           Charles Tuley, Administrator.

Page 349   Ordered   settlement   with   John   Silvertooth   and   John   Dawdy,
           Administrators of **DAVID SHELTON,** deceased. Recorded December 27,
1823.

Page 349   Inventory of **GEORGE HOPPER,** deceased.   Taken December 15, 1822
           by Lewis Hopper and Joseph Broadway, Administrators.   Recorded
December 27, 1823.

Page 350   Memo of Estate of **JAMES PYBAS,** deceased, November 16, 1822.
           Recorded December 29, 1823.

Page 351    Estate of **SAMUEL CHAPLAIN.**

Page 351    Additional inventory of **J.B. CLARK,** deceased.    July 1, 1821.
            Recorded December 29, 1823.

Page 352    Settlement of Estate of **SAMUEL CHAPALAIN,** deceased.   January 23,
            1818. Recorded December 29, 1823.

Page 353    Settlement of Estate of **WILLIAM CAMPBELL,** deceased.

Page 353    Memo on February 20, 1818 of property of **BENJAMIN McFARLING.**
            Recorded December 30, 1823.

Page 354    Amount of Sale of Estate of **WILLIAM CAMPBELL,** deceased.   July 19,
            1819. Recorded December 30, 1823.

Page 354    Inventory of **WILLIAM WALLACE,** deceased.    By  Mary  Wallace.
            Recorded December 30, 1923.

Page 354    Inventory of **ROBERT ABERNATHY,** deceased.

Page 355    List of Sales of Estate of **JOHN S. HUGHES,** deceased.    Sale on
            February 19, 1819.   Judith Hughs and John S. Price, Administrators.
Recorded December 30, 1823.

Page 357    Inventory of **JAMES PYBAS,** deceased. Recorded December 30, 1823.

Page 357    Inventory of **MR. ----- AMONS,** deceased.   Recorded. December 20,
            1823.

Page 358    Sale of **NATHANIEL TATUM,** deceased.   July 5, 1820.   Edward Tatum,
            Executor.  Recorded December 31, 1823.

Page 358    Settlement of Estate of **EPHRAIM LOYD,** deceased.   July 9, 1822.
            Sarah Loyd, Administrator.   Sale held February 2, 1820.   Recorded
December 31, 1823.

Page 359    Provisions layed off for the widow and children of **AARON PARKS,**
            deceased, made on May 25, 1820. Recorded December 31, 1823.

Page 359    List of Property of Estate of **PRESLEY GEORGE,** deceased, made on
            March 16, 1821. Recorded December 31, 1823.

Page 359    Memo on Sale of Estate of **JOHN WARREN,** deceased, made on May
            10, 1821, by Henry and Willis Warren, Administrators.

Page 360    April Term 1820.   Layed off provisions for support of widow and
            children of **DAVID SAWYERS,** deceased.    May 16, 1820 by John
Crawford, William Crawford and James McConnell. Recorded December 31, 1823.

Page 360    Widow Brown to have one year support on February 18, 1822.   John
            Enochs, Jonathan Floyd and Andrew W. Walker.

Page 360    **ARTHUR BROOKS,** deceased.    February 21, 1822 by Elisha Bagley,
            William Crunk and James Brooks. Recorded December 31, 1823.

Page 360    Inventory of Estate of **CHRISTOPHER MILLER,** deceased.   Taken June
            1, 1822. Nicholas Carriger, Executor. Recorded December 31, 1823.

Page 361    List of Property of Estate of **EPHRAIM LOYD,** deceased.    Taken by
            Collin Campbell and James Gibson. Recorded December 31, 1823.

17

Page 361     Provisions for widow of **THOMAS CUMMINS,** deceased.     Mentioned
             having six children.     February 15, 1822.     By George Blakemore and
Benjamin Woodruff and John W. Blake.     Recorded December 31, 1823.

Page 361     Amount of Sale of Personal Estate of **WILLIAM SMITH, JR.,** deceased.
             By William Smith, Sr.     Recorded December 31, 1823.

Page 362     Inventory of all the movable property of the late **WILLIAM HARRIS,**
             deceased.     Taken by Howell Harris, Administrator, on July 12, 1820.
Recorded December 31, 1823.

Page 362     Administrators and guardian of **GEORGE WAGGONER,** deceased.
             Proceed to sell negro man on August 2, 1822 by Jacob and John
Waggoner, Administrators.     Recorded December 31, 1823.

Page 362     Account of money due the heirs of **WILLIAM TATUM,** deceased.     Polly
             Tatum, Betsey Tatum and John Tatum.     Recorded December 31, 1823.

Page 363     **WILLIAM TATUM,** deceased.     Estate examined by Edward Tatum,
             Administrator on July 25, 1820.     Recorded December 31, 1823.

Page 363     Additional Inventory of Estate of **WLEXANDER McDONALD,** deceased.
             Recorded January 1, 1823 (1824).

Page 368     Inventory of **SAMUEL McGLADEY,** deceased.     Patsey McGladey, Admr.
             1829.

Page 369     Inventory of **HENRY BURNS,** deceased, made on July 24, 1820 by
             Elizabeth Burns.     Recorded January 3, 1824.

Page 370     Settlement of Estate of **SAMUEL BARNES,** deceased, made by George
             Cunningham, guardian for heirs of Samuel Barnes, deceased.     January
21, 1823.

Page 370     Sale of Property of **ANDREW (missing),** deceased, made by William
             Smith, Abraham Simmons and David Buchanan, Administrators, on May
3, 1817 or 1819.

Page 371     Sale of Estate of **WILLIAM MONTGOMERY,** deceased, by Easther
             Montgomery, Administrator on ___ 18, 1822.

Page 374     Inventory of **ARCHIBALD MAYFIELD,** deceased, made by Henry Kelso,
             Administrator.     Recorded January 5, 1824.

Page 374     Inventory of **THOMAS CUMMONS,** deceased, made by Easther Cummins
             and Hugh M. Blake, Administrators.     Recorded January 6, 1824.

Page 375     Amount of Sale for **THOMAS JOYCE,** deceased, by Samuel Crawford,
             Administrator with Charlotte Joyce.     January 6, 1824.

Page 377     Inventory of Estate of **THOMAS JOYCE,** deceased.     Recorded January
             6, 1824.

Page 378     Inventory of Estate of **ISAAC OAKS,** deceased, made by Solomon
             Burford, Administrator.     Recorded January 7, 1824.

Page 379     Inventory of Estate of **DAVID SAWYERS,** deceased, made by John C.
             Sawyers, Administrator, on July 12, 1822.     Recorded January 7, 1824.

Page 380     Settlement of Estate of **ELIZABETH SAWYERS,** deceased.     John C.
             Sawyers, Administrator.     Recorded January 9, 1824.

Page 381　**ARTHUR BROOKS,** deceased. Sale on April 13, 1822. James Brooks, Administrator. Recorded January 9, 1824.

Page 383　Inventory of Estate of **JONATHAN LOONEY,** deceased. John Enochs, Administrator. Recorded January 9, 1824.

Page 384　Inventory of **ROBERT NIX,** deceased. July 16, 1822 by Susannah Nix, Administrator. Recorded January 10, 1824.

Page 385　Sale of Estate of **CAPTAIN WILLIAM BROWN,** deceased. Made by Thomas H. Shaw, Administrator. Recorded January 13, 1824.

Page 387　Inventory of Estate of **ELIJAH HARLEY,** deceased.

Page 388　Estate of **JOHN WARREN,** deceased. Made by Henry and Willis Warren, Administrators. Settled on July 15, 1822. Recorded January 13, 1824.

Page 390　Estate of **RICHARD BYRD,** deceased. April 29, 1817 by Joel Pinson, Administrator. Recorded January 20, 1824.

Page 392　Estate of **RICHARD BYRD,** deceased. To Elizabeth Sanders for nursing and boarding Rebecky Byrd, Polly Byrd, Elliford Byrd, infant children of Richard Byrd, deceased, from April 15, 1814 to March 15, 1816. Recorded January 27, 1824.

Page 392　Inventory of **SAMUEL CARITHERS,** deceased, 1818 by James Carithers and Hampton Bostick, Administrators. Recorded January 28, 1824.

Page 394　**EDWARD TEAL,** deceased. Sold by Francis Teal, Administrator, on November 22, 1821. Recorded January 28, 1824.

Page 397　**RACHEL SMITH,** deceased. By Edward Gore, Administrator, on June 20, 1816. Recorded January 28, 1824.

Page 398　**DAVID SAWYERS,** deceased. Inventory made on April 17, 1820 by John C. Sawyers, Administrators. Recorded January 29, 1824.

Page 399　Inventory of **DAVID SAWYERS,** deceased, made June 6, 1820 by J.C. Sawyers, Administrator. Recorded January 30, 1824. Additional sale recorded January 30, 1824.

Page 401　Inventory of **ELIZABETH SAWYERS,** deceased. Sold November 17, 1821.

Page 403　Provisions for Mary Harley, widow of **ELIJAH HARLEY,** deceased. Made on October 13, 1820. Recorded January 30, 1824.

Page 403　Inventory of **JOHN WARREN,** deceased. Taken by Henry and Willis Warren on June 29, 1820.

Page 404　Inventory of **DAVID SAWYERS,** deceased, by John C. Sawyers, Administrator.

Page 405　Inventory of **ARCHIBALD BUCHANAN,** deceased, made on October 15, 1819 by John Buchanan, Administrator.

Page 405　Inventory of **ARCHIBALD BUCHANAN,** deceased.

Page 405　Received February 5, 1816 of John Buchanan of $8.00 against the Estate of **ARCHIBALD BUCHANAN,** deceased.

Page 406     Inventory of **ARCHIBALD BUCHANAN,** deceased.

Page 407     **DR. A. BARKER,** deceased, made June 21, 1816 by A. Barker, Administrator. Recorded January 7, 1824.

Page 411     **JOSEPH PATRICK, WILL.** Wife Elizabeth Patrick. Children: Sophiah, Austin and Patsey Franklin. Signed September 15, 1823. Witnesses: Thomas Spencer and John Wiseman. Proven January 27, 1824.

Page 412     Inventory of **JOSEPH PATRICK,** deceased. Recorded January 26, 1824.

Page 412     **ELI GARRETT, WILL.** Wife Agatha Garrett. Children not named. Executors: Son Greenberry Garrett and wife Agatha Garrett. Signed December 2, 1823. Witnesses: William Griffis and William Bonner. Recorded February 8, 1824.

Page 414     Inventory of Estate of **ELI GARRETT,** deceased. Recorded February 10, 1824.

Page 416     **ARTHUR DUDNEY, WILL.** Wife Mary Dudney. Sons: John a cripple, Abraham and William Dudney. Son-in-laws Reuben Washburn, James Tool and John Lee. Signed December 2, 1823. Witnesses: James Higgins, Edward Summerford and Benjamin Marshall. Proven in April Term 1824.


## LINCOLN COUNTY, TENNESSEE WILL BOOK # 1

Page 1     **WILL OF JAMES BURNES.** Wife Charlotte Burnes. Sons: Samuel, John W., Wilson A., and William. Daughters: Eldest Leady G. Elons, Betsy W., Rhoda H., and Susanna Burnes. Signed September 30, 1827. Witnesses: H.H. Hopkins and Coleman Smith. Executors: H.H. Hopkins and Coleman Smith. Exhibited in court October 17, 1827.

Page 3     **WILL OF MICIJAH STONE.** Wife Sally Stone. Children: William, Joel, Washington, James, Mary, Hopkins, Martha, Jefferson and another child not named at time of making will, his wife being pregnant, Littleberry, Frances, and Eglantine. Executors: John H. Leftwich and Abner Steed. Signed October 2, 1827. Witnesses: Abel Landis and John Landess. Proven October 15, 1827.

Pahe 6     **WILL OF J. DAVID THWING.** Wife Martha Thwing. Adopted sons, David and Bruce Thwing. Step-son-in-law John Wheeler. Signed June 11, 1827. Executors and witnesses: William B. Benge and Champain Smith. Proven July 21, 1827.

Page 8     **WILL OF WILLIAM MOORES.** Children: Daniel R., Henry, Isaac, Arthur, Samuel, William, Joshua, Josiah, Elizabeth, Phebe, and Jane Rachel Moores. Signed June 6, 1826. Executors: Josiah and Daniel R. Moores. Witnesses: William Owen and Joshua Owen. Proven July 16, 1827.

Page 9     **WILL OF DAVID P. MOORE.** Seven children, William Monroe, Louisa V. Nolen, Polly wife of William Armstrong, Sarah wife of Hugh Wardlow, Susan wife of Abner Blair, Martha F. Harris, and Amanda M. Monroe. Signed: ___ day of ___, 1828. Witnesses: Constant Scales, I.G. Wright, Enos Rust and William Johnson. Proven January 26, 1828.

Page 11     **WILL OF LEWIS MORGAN.** Mentions his wife but not by name. Children: Henry, Smith, Polly, Joab, Edward, and Nancy Merrell. Sons-in-law: Robert Clark, Andy Greer, Joseph Colvert, Pleasant Flemmin, Redden Reddick, and Gideon Austin. Grandson, Andrew Flemmin. Signed November 26, 1827. Witnesses: I.J. Leftwich, Amos Harris and John S. Johnson. Executors: Benjamin Reeves and Zachariah Harrison. Proven January 21, 1828.

Page 13 **WILL OF JOHN BLAKE.** Wife Elizabeth Blake who is also the Executrix. Children: Hugh M., John W., William D., Jane, Sally Marr, and Peggy Scales. Signed September 28, 1824. Witnesses: Brice M. Garner, John C. Garner. Recorded June 26, 1828.

Page 15 **WILL OF SAMUEL BUTLER.** Wife Elizabeth Butler. Children: Constant, Thomas, Tressee Camile, Nancy Caroline, William, Samuel H., John, Edmond, Lewis, and Mary Ann Butler. Owned a lot in Hazelgreen (Alabama). Executors: Joseph Dean and John Pinkerton. Signed October 18, 1826. Witnesses: William Cox and Sealia Cox. Recorded June 26, 1828.

Page 16 **WILL OF MALCOM McCOWN.** Wife Mary McCown. Children: John, Emaline, Lewis, Carrol, Moleen, William Farlow and James Fletcher and Lavina Blair McKown (McCown). Executors: William Borrow and George McKown. Signed February 13, 1827. Witnesses: David Jones, John W. Street and Isaac McCown. Recorded June 26, 1828.

Page 18 **WILL OF JAMES RANDALL.** Mother Catharine Randall of Down Patrick Dawnshire, Ireland. He mentioned his business partner James Muse. Executors: Robert Dickson and John P. McConnell. Signed August 26, 1826. Witnesses: John Morgan, W.L. Martin and John Coleman. Recorded June 26, 1828.

Page 18 **WILL OF GEORGE HEATH.** His Executors are his sons, Nathaniel P. and Abner C. Heath. He mentions his wife and other children but not by name. Signed March 19, 1826. Witnesses: James Frame and William Loca. Recorded June 26, 1828.

Page 19 **WILL OF JAMES CHEATHAM.** Wife Rebecca Cheatham. Four children: Elmer, Solomon, Betsy R., and Albert W. Cheatham. Executors: William Shipp and Joel Pinson. Signed December 12, 1826. Witnesses: Obadiah Pinson, Lewis Shipp and John Robison. Recorded June 26, 1828.

Page 21 **WILL OF MARTHA McMILLEN.** Children: William, James, John, Joseph, Thomas, the heirs of son Andrew, Nancy Wright, Sarah Chitwood, Jane Gross, Martha Marshall and Polly Pinkston. Signed February 27, 1826. Witnesses: David Crook and Jacob Wright, Jr.
Codocil: Mentions a granddaughter Martha Wright. Recorded June 26, 1828.

Page 23 **WILL OF AGNES ALDRIDGE.** Children: Martha Harrison, Elizabeth Simmons, Polly Davis, Tabitha Hightower and her daughter Agnes B. Hightower, Sally Hutcheson, Frances McGowan, Richard, William, and James Baugh Aldridge. Executors: Sons William and James Baugh Aldridge. Signed April 22, 1824. Witnesses: Willie S. McLaurine, Elem Stevenson, and Joseph McCracken and Asa T. Stone. Recorded June 27, 1828.

Page 24 **WILL OF THOMAS PULLEY.** Wife Lydia Pulley. Children: Gideon N., Benjamin C., Thomas W., Letha Thompson, Rhoda Noles, David, and Elizabeth Warren. Executors: Gideon and Benjamin C. Pulley. Signed January 3, 1828. Witnesses: Arch Baxter and John Dusenberry. Recorded June 27, 1828.

Page 25 **WILL OF JAMES SIMMONS.** Wife Katharine Simmons. Children: Polly Erwin and her daughter Lucy Erwin, Agnes Burden, Sally Davis, Katharine Barham, Elizabeth Simmons, Thomas and James A. Simmons. Executors: Sons James A. and Thomas Simmons. Signed March 7, 1828. Witnesses: James Cooper, Abner Freeman, Thomas Simmons, and James A. Simmons.
Codicil: Mentions children of Henry Nichols: James, Aney Spradley, Tabithy Armstrong, Polly Nichols, William Nichols, Catharine Nichols, and Mahaly Nichols, and children of daughter Elizabeth: John and Sinai Simmons.

Page 29 **WILL OF THOMAS ROWNTREE.** Wife Sarah Rowntree. Children: James L., William, Mary and Ann Rowntree and Katharine Shaw, Elizabeth Landess and Nancy Smith. Executors: Thomas H. Shaw and W.F. Long.

Signed April 9, 1828. Witnesses: James Curry, Thomas S. Stovall and W.F. Long. Recorded September 15, 1828.

Page 31 **WILL OF JACOB PRUETT.** Wife Nancy Pruett. Mentions his first wife and children but not by name. He mentions his children by Nancy but not by name. He names one son James A. Pruett. Executors: Wife Nancy Pruett and son James A. Pruett. Signed April 4, 1828. Witnesses: Thomas Spencer, John Pruett and Isham Burnett. Recorded September 15, 1828.

Page 33 **WILL OF EZEKIEL NORRIS.** Children: John M., Harvey, Cynthia, Minerva, William and Emily. Executors: Francis Porterfield, Esq. and Thomas Clark, Esq. Signed January 17, 1827. Witnesses: William Neeld and John McMillen. Recorded January 14, 1829.

Page 34 **WILL OF JAMES WALKER.** Wife Nancy Walker. Children: Carter Walker, Andrew Walker, James Walker, Polly Givins, Milly Walker who married Drury M. Connally also her marriage to James Pearson. Grandchildren: Franklin Walker, Alliline and Franklin Butler, John Ford and Presly Kirkpatrick. Executors: Son James Walker and a friend Abner Steed. Signed November 28, 1828. Witnesses: James Scott and William C. Scott. Recorded March 16, 1829.

Page 36 **WILL OF JOEL BRUCE.** Wife Sally Bruce. Children: Arnold, Joel, Warmley, Letty and Sally Bruce. Executor: Stephen Hightower. Signed January 2, 1829. Witnesses: William M. Rose, John Harrison and James McGowan. Recorded March 20, 1829.

Page 37 **WILL OF KINCHIN HOLCOMB.** Wife Nancy Holcomb. Children: Alfred, Hardy H., Robert N., John and Sarah I. Holcomb. Grandson Richard K. Hightower. Signed: November 15, 1828. Executors: Sons Alfred and Robert N. Holcomb. Witnesses: Joseph McCracken and Daniel Lee. Recorded July 14, 1829.

Page 39 **WILL OF JOHN HARRISON.** Children: Thomas and Middleton Harrison. Executor: Ludy Cauthran. Signed April 9, 1829. Witnesses: Robert Brown, Robert R. Allsup and Morgan Halbert. Recorded July 14, 1829.

Page 40 **WILL OF JAMES BROWN.** Wife Mary Brown. Three sons and six daughters: Alexander, James, William, Martha, Harriet, Clarissa, Ann, Polly, Elizabeth, and married daughter Jane Waggoner. Executor: William Husbands. Signed April 10, 1829. Witnesses: John Brown and Levingston J. Brown. Recorded October 17, 1829.

Page 42 **WILL OF WILLIAM BLEDSOE.** Wife Mary Bledsoe. Sons, John and Lewis Bledsoe. Executor: Lewis Bledsoe. Signed October 13, 1825. Witnesses: A. Isaacs and Thomas Bottom. Recorded October 17, 1829.

Page 43 **WILL OF WILLIAM SMITH.** Children: James C., Mary Murphy, Franky Espridge, John T., Jane Day, William S., Elizabeth Parks, Joanna Auston, and Susannah B. Parks. Signed July 9, 1829. Witnesses: John Brown and T. Cooper. Recorded March 5, 1830.

Page 45 **WILL OF JOHN GUYDER.** Wife Nancy Guyder. Mother Nancy Weathers. Elizabeth Sharp. Signed December 13, 1829. Witnesses: J. McKenny and Francis Patton. Recorded March 5, 1830.

Page 46 **WILL OF BENJAMIN MERRILL.** Wife Susan Merrill. Children: Polly Colvert, Margaret Merrill, Nancy, Benjamin, Iselene and John Merrill. Grandson Andrew Merrill. Executor: John Merrill. Signed June 1, 1829. Witnesses: William Jones, Abner Merrill and Garrett Merrill. Recorded March 5, 1830.

Page 47 **WILL OF JORDON REESE.** wife Polly Reese. Sons: Joel, Gordon R.,

William H., and Littleberry Reese. Daughters: Fanny H. Moore, Polly L. Moore, and Finnetta W. Boone. Executors: Wife Polly Reese, son Littleberry Reese and James Fulton. Witnesses: Charles McKinney, James D. Cole and John P. Cole. Signed February 16, 1830. Recorded May 17, 1830.

Page 51    **WILL OF WILLIAM COWLEY.** Wife Gincey Cowley. Sons: Charley, Drury and George Cowley and a daughter Susan Cowley. Executrix: Wife Gincey Cowley. Signed February 9, 1830. Witnesses: Samuel Ramsey and I. Watkins. Recorded May 17, 1830.

Page 51    **WILL OF JOHN FARRAR.** Wife Elizabeth Farrar. Children: Ten eldest, William, Robert, Miles, John, James, Mary, Sarah Ann, Moses, Aaron, and Franklin. Nine youngest: Francis, Lucy, Nathaniel, Joseph, Nancy, Daniel, David, Betsy and Jane Farrar. Executors: Wife Elizabeth Farrar and William Shipp and Joel Pinson. Signed February 19, 1826. Witnesses: David Cowan, Charles Williams and Eli Cole. Recorded October 8, 1830.

Page 53    **WILL OF JOHN TODD.** Wife Margaret Todd. Children: Samuel, Elzira, Eli Milton, Levi and Betsy Todd. A relation, Ebenizer McEwen. Executor: A relation, Robert H. McEwen. Signed September 4, 1822. Witnesses: James Fulton, Hiram S. Morgan and R.H. McEwen. Proven July 19, 1830.

Page 56    **WILL OF SARAH VANCE.** Children: Nancy _____ and her daughters, Lucinda and Sarah, and Polly Vance, William Vance and his son James, John Vance, and James and grandson Wiley H. Lemby. Executor: Son John Vance. Signed August 18, 1829. Witnesses: Nathan Briley and A. Isaacs. Proven July 19, 1830.

Page 57    **WILL OF THOMAS LINTHECUM, SR.** Daughter Elizabeth Norwood and her sons, Thomas and William and daughter Jane Norwood, and son William Linthecum. Signed August 24, 1830. Executors: John Norwood and James McDavid. Witnesses: Gideon Barnet and George Koonce. Proven October Term 1830.

Page 58    **WILL OF ANN H. McCURDY.** Children: Oldest daughter Mary A.H. Davis and her husband William Davis, Elizabeth L. McKinley and her husband Joseph McKinley and child Joseph McKinley, John H. McCurdy's heirs: one named Lovey A. McCurdy, Nathaniel W. McCurdy, Elijah McCurdy, Rebecca H. Williamson, and Sarahtee H.C. Williamson. Executors: William Davis, John L. Jackson, Nathaniel W. McCurdy, and Elijah McCurdy or any of them. Signed December 31, 1830. Witnesses: J. Pinkerton and Joseph Dean. Proven January Term 1831.

Page 60    **WILL OF JOSEPH GREER.** Wife Mary Greer. Son Joseph Greer. Brothers, John and Thomas Greer. Owned land in Roan County, Tennessee, and in Kentucky. Executors: Wife Mary Ann Greer, son, Joseph Greer, brother, Thomas Greer and John H. Moore. Signed February 23, 1831. Witnesses: Elliott Hickman and Greenfield Buchanan.

Page 62    **WILL OF MARY PARR.** Children: Jane Collier and her husband James Collier, Isham Parr and Fanny Read. Executor: Isham Parr. Signed January 7, 1831. Witnesses: James R. Brown and Benjamin Rives.

Page 63    **WILL OF WILLIAM INGLE.** Wife Sarah Ingle. Five children: Leonard W., Polly, Permelia A., Jacob and Benjamin B. Ingle. Executors: Howell Johnston and Samuel Boone. Signed September 28, 1830. Witnesses: Abner Steed, Howell Johnston, Paul Ingle and Orpah Johnston. Proven September 2, 1831.

Page 64    **WILL OF MORGAN DAVIS.** Children: Elizabeth Smith, Sally Clayton, Ann Williams, and Hannah Halbert, Mary Clayton, John Davis, Amos Davis, and Jesse Davis. Executors: Sons Jesse and John Davis. Signed October 15, 1821. Witnesses: Abraham Sumners and Jacob Allbright. Proven April Term 1831.

**Page 65**  **WILL OF JOHN ROPER.**  Wife Bethany Roper.  Six children: Sarah S. wife of Nathan Bagley, Joseph Roper, William Roper, Michael Cook, wife of David Short, and Henry B. Roper and Candice wife of John Short. Executors: Sons Joseph, William and Henry B. Roper.  Signed June 18, 1825. Witnesses: William Crowder and John Cowden.  Recorded September 3, 1831.

**Page 68**  **WILL OF SARAH STEWART.**  Only mentions her youngest daughter Mary M. Stewart.  Executor: John H. Allen.  Signed February 18, 1832. Witnesses: Josiah Roughton and Isaac J. Roughton.  Recorded April 16, 1832.

**Page 69**  **WILL OF PETER VAUGHN.**  Wife Sarah Vaughn.  Children: William, Samuel, Nancy, Polly and Elizabeth Vaughn.  Signed July 25, 1831. Witnesses: Charles McKinney, William Bright and James Wilson.  Proven October 17, 1831.

**Page 70**  **WILL OF SAMUEL JENKINS.**  Wife Ise Jenkins.  Children: George, James, Sally, and Elizabeth (mentions his children by his first wife). Children by his last wife: Betsy, Jincey, Murphy, Susannah, Cipam (?), Mary, Joseph and Aron Jenkins.  Executors: John Smith, Esq. and William Spencer, Esq. Witnesses: Thomas Spencer and James M. Spencer.  Recorded January 16, 1832.

**Page 71**  **WILL OF DREWRY AUSTIN.**  Wife Betsey Austin.  Sons, Harris and William Phillip Austin.  Granddaughter Anne Bolen.  Mentions Thomas Bolen.  Witnesses: Benjamin Rives, Mathew Carter and Henry S. Gill.  Proven in Court October 25, 1831.

**Page 72**  **WILL OF DAVID READS.**  Son John Hamilton Reads.  Daughter Martha Jane reads.  Brother William M. Reads and brother-in-law William Hamilton.  Signed September 5, 1831.  Witnesses: Eli Taylor, Johnathan Anderson and Hugh Taylor. Proven October 17, 1831.

**Page 73**  **WILL OF BARNABAS BOYLES, SR.**  Children: Rachael Paradise, Sally Reasons, Barnabas Boyles, Nancy, Patsey, Jane and Lucinda Boyles. Signed December 24, 1830.  Witnesses: R.H.C. Bagley and C. Boyles.  Proven October 19, 1831.

**Page 75**  **WILL OF ABEDNEGO FOSTER.**  Wife Nancy Foster.  Son Washington Foster.  Signed February 18, 1832.  Witnesses: R.J. Harrison, Hillery M. Stokes and John S. Johnson.  Proven April 16, 1832.

**Page 76**  **WILL OF JOHN SIVILY.**  Wife Leah Sivily.  Children: Daniel, John, Benjamin, George, Martin, Harrison, Jacob, Elizabeth, Rachael, and Leah Sivily.  Signed April 13, 1831.  Witnesses: Daniel Sivily, John Stacy and Jacob Topp.  Recorded June 18, 1832.

**Page 79**  **WILL OF THOMAS LEONARD.**  Wife Hannah Leonard.  Sons, Griffith and Robert Leonard.  Daughter Hannah Moore and her son Thomas D. Moore.  Executor: Son Griffith Leonard.  Signed July 9, 1829.  Witnesses: Lacy Meeks, John Lovett and Parkes Campbell.  Recorded April 16, 1832.

**Page 81**  **WILL OF HENRY KELSO.**  Children: Mary Kelso, Nancy Roabuck, John Kelso, James Kelso, Elizabeth Henson, Jefferson Kelso, Alford Kelso, Jane Cunningham, Mandada Yeates, Amytis Kelso, and Henry Kelso.  Owned land on south side of Elk River and on waters of Lee's Creek.  Executors: John Kelso and Jefferson Kelso, his sons.  Signed January 5, 1832.  Witnesses: Nimrod Bailey and Elisha Tomison.  Proven June 18, 1832.

**Page 83**  **WILL OF JAMES McFERRAN.**  Wife Nancy McFerran.  Children: James and John McFerran, Mary Moore, and Margaret Pinkerton.  Executors: John Clark, Esq. and Brown Parkison.  Signed December 25, 1831.  Witnesses: William P. Pulliam and Thomas McFerran.  Recorded June 18, 1832.

Page 84 **WILL OF JACOB LANDISS.** Wife Marum R. Landiss. Son William Landiss. Daughter Susan M. Landiss. He owned interest in a tanyard in Jackson County, Alabama, also had interest in a tanyard in Hillsbrough, Franklin County, Tennessee. Executors: Thomas H. Shaw and William S. Smith. Signed June 21, 1832. Witnesses: Thomas M. Battle, Felix G. Sanders, William H. Setliff, James G. Reaves, and John Landiss. Proven July 10, 1832.

Page 84 **WILL OF HENRY HUGHEY.** Wife Betsey Hughey (Elizabeth). Signed March 13, 1832. Witnesses: James Askins and James Henderson. Recorded October 2, 1832.

Page 85 **WILL OF COLLIN CAMPBELL.** Wife Mary Ann Campbell. The niece of his wife, Elizabeth Robertson. Other names listed were: William M. Leonard, George S.C. Leonard, sons of George L. Leonard. Executors: George L. Leonard and Joel Yowell. Signed September 19, 1830. Witnesses: John Clark and William Dewoody. Recorded October 2, 1832.

Page 85 **WILL OF JOSHUA WALLS.** Wife Permelia Walls. Children: Lizetta, Leroy, Theophilus, John Henry, and Andrew Jackson Walls (youngest), and Mayor (Major) Walls. He had land on the headwaters of Swan Creek of Elk River. Signed May 15, 1832. Witnesses: L.H. Owen, Wilson P. Dairy and John Watson. Recorded January 11, 1833.

Page 87 **WILL OF CHARLES COLLIER.** Wife Jane Collier. Son John Collier. Executor: Wife Jane Collier. Signed May 25, 1832. Witnesses: Charles E. McCoy and Joseph B. Kennedy. Recorded January 10, 1833.

Page 88 **WILL OF WILLIAM BLAIR.** Wife Margaret Blair. Sons, John, Alexander and William Blair. He mentions his daughters but not by name. He lived on Swan Creek. Executors: Wife Margaret Blair and his son William Blair. Signed June 22, 1832. Witnesses: Richard Wyatt, John Wyatt and Thomas Moore. Recorded February 5, 1833.

Page 89 **WILL OF ROBERT WILSON.** Wife Mary Wilson. Son Charles T. Wilson. Daughter Jane Woodruff. He has debts owning to him in Virginia and Tennessee. Executors: Wife Mary Wilson and son Charles Wilson. Signed April 22, 1826. Witnesses: H.M. Blake, John W. Blake and Charles Thomson. Recorded December 5, 1832.

Page 90 **WILL OF CHARLES TULEY.** Seven children by 1st wife Polly Tuley: James Wilderness Tuley, Martha Cummings Tuley, John Alexander Tuley, William Hutson Tuley, Samuel Preston Tuley, Elizabeth Caroline Tuley, and Malinda Tuley. Owned land on North Elk River, 5 miles below Fayetteville, 175 acres. Present wife Elizabeth Tuley. Executors: John Clark and David Watson. Signed December 4, 1823. Witnesses: William Moore and John Clark.

Page 92 **WILL OF ALLEN J. KENNEDY.** Wife Agnes Kennedy. Five children: Mary, Ann, John G., Robert A., Agnes, and Martha Kennedy. Also a son of his wife Agnes Kennedy by the name of William Kennedy, by a previous marriage. Executors: William Timmons, George W. Jones, James Bright and Samuel W. Carmack. Witnesses: A.A. Kincannon and Davis Eastland. Signed June 27, 1833. Recorded August 15, 1833.
NOTE: His negro man Jeffrey should remain with his wife Agnes until 1843 or at any time she desires to appropriate money to (by hiring Jeffrey out) send him to Liberia, or to any other country he may choose to go, where he can live as a free person, if he desires, by the year of 1843 or 1844 to remain a slave. He is to stay with his wife Agnes Kennedy.

Page 95 **WILL OF JOHN RUTLEDGE.** Wife Catharine Rutledge. Son William Rutledge. Executors: Wife Catharine Rutledge and son William Rutledge. Witnesses: Joseph Whitaker and Isaac Rutledge. Signed April 8, 1833. Recorded December 15, 1833.

Page 95    **WILL OF MARY WILSON.** Son Charles T. Wilson.    Grandchildren:
           Nancy R. Woodruff, William J. Woodruff, and Benjamin R. Woodruff.
Debts due her in Virginia and Tennessee.  Executors: Son Charles T. Wilson and
William D. Blake. Signed April 20, 1830. Witnesses: James Blakemore and John W.
Blake. Recorded December 15, 1833.

Page 96    **WILL OF REUBIN HUNTER.**  Wife Scintha Hunter.   Children: Polly
           McElroy wife of William McElroy, Sherron Hunter, and Sally Davis wife
of Elijah Davis. Executor: Son Sherrod Hunter. Signed August 11, 1832. Witnesses:
James Higgins and William Edmiston. Recorded December 15, 1833.

Page 97    **WILL OF JOEL JOHNSON.**  Wife Margaret M. Johnson (who is his 2nd
           wife).   Son Ambrose Johnson.   He mentions other sons and daughters
but not by name.   Executors: James Hague and James Fulton.   James Franklin is
guardian of any sons under age of 21 years.  Signed December 5, 1832.  Witnesses:
E.M. Ringo and Samuel Todd. Recorded December 14, 1833.

Page 98    **WILL OF DANIEL WAGGONER.**  Wife Eave Waggoner.   Children:
           Susanna, Henry, Alexander who is the youngest, Catharine, Michael,my
eldest daughter Elizabeth Bateman, Daniel, David and Andrew  Waggoner.
Executors: Sons Daniel and David Waggoner.  Signed July 21, 1833.   Witnesses:
Jacob E. Waggoner and John Bateman. Recorded December 14, 1833.

Page 100   **WILL OF ARMSTEAD PAMPLIN.**   Children: Eldest first: William B.,
           Henry H., Elizabeth, Robert, Armstead, Lucinda, Martha, Joseph,
James, and a granddaughter Susan Waggoner.    Mentions Jacob Waggoner.
Executors: William Pamplin and Joseph Pamplin, his sons.  Signed July 13, 1831.
Witnesses: John Baley and Esrom Loyd. Recorded July 2, 1834.

Page 101   **WILL OF WILLIAM JAMES.**  Wife Jane B. James.  Children: Sarah,
           Jane Dekalb, Thomas, Mark, Walter, and Matthias James.  Step-daughter Caroline
Watson.  Executors: Thomas Massey and William M. Ingle.  Signed December 14,
1832. Witnesses: A. Baxter, John Duke and William C. Kennedy.  Recorded July 2,
1834.

Page 102   **WILL OF ZACHARIAH ARNOLD.**  Wife Charlotte Arnold.   Children:
           Nancy Childress, Mary, Patsey, Malinda, Malissa, Moses, Sanders W.,
and John Arnold and his son William Arnold.   Owned land on south side of Elk
River.  Executors: Son Sanders W. Arnold and son-in-law Jarred Simmons.  Signed
October 3, 1834.   Witnesses: William Griffis, J.W. Hamilton and W.C. Jennings.
Recorded December 4, 1834.

Page 103   **WILL OF JEREMIAH BRYAN.**  Wife Roxannah Bryan.   Children:
           Newton Perry Bryan, William Carroll Bryan, James Bryan, Jane wife of
Elijah Bolen, and Kenny Bryan.  Executors: Joel Swanner and Malakiah Reeves.
Another daughter Mary who married William Justice.  Signed September 5, 1834.
Witnesses: Alvin C. Oliver, Samuel R. Reeves, James B. Gill and Nathan G. Pinson.
Recorded December 5, 1834.

Page 105   **WILL OF THOMAS W. HILL.**  Son John William Hill. Executor: Parkes
           Campbell.  Signed July 19, 1834.   Witnesses: Isham R. Howze and
William Campbell. Recorded December 5, 1834.

Page 105   **WILL OF AMOS DAVIS.**  Wife Elizabeth Davis.  Sons and daughters:
           Jame H., Nathan C., Allen J., J.H., Morgan A., Stephen M., John S.
(youngest), Fanny T., and youngest daughters Sarah Ann and Mary Elizabeth Davis.
Executors: Nephew Morgan Clayton and son James H. Davis.  Signed June 13, 1834.
Witnesses: A. Young, Isaac Moore, Joshua Davis and James Pool.     Recorded
December 4, 1834.

Page 108   **WILL OF SOLOMON REESE.**  Wife Mahala Reese.  Three children not
           named, or any more after death of nine months.  He said that he had

seven children by his first wife, but did not name any or his former wife's name. All his land is in Carroll County, Tennessee. Executor: Cullen E. Sugg. Signed October 11, 1834. Witnesses: William Wofford, Wilie Wingo, C.T. Rose and N.G. Pinson. Recorded December 6, 1834.

Page 109 **WILL OF WILLIAM A. DAVIS.** Wife Polly Davis. Children: Newton C., Cadwallader C., Rufus Columbus the youngest, and Adaline, Eliza Ann, Narcissa P., Theodocia B., Margaret Elizabeth Frances, and Arena Josephine Davis. Executors: Pleasant Bearden and Thomas W. Hays. Signed September 17, 1834. Witnesses: Obadiah Pinson and John P. Davis. Recorded December 6, 1834.

Page 112 **WILL OF JOHN MARR.** Wife Sarah Marr. Children: John M.B. and Eliza Marr. He had 260 acres on Cane Creek. Executrix: Wife Sarah Marr. Signed July 27, 1834. Witnesses: William B. Benge, J.J. Todd and William B. Blake. Recorded December 8, 1834.

Page 113 **WILL OF JAMES BLACKBURN.** Wife Ellenor Blackburn. Five children but not named. Executors: David Blackburn and Ellenor Blackburn. Signed October 4, 1834. Witnesses: W.N.R. Gracy and Jefferson Kelso. Recorded December 9, 1834.

Page 114 **WILL OF WILLIAM PATTERSON.** Wife Rachel Patterson. Children: Eldest son John C., Maria Henderson Patterson, Martha Eliza, William B., David S., James H., and Logan M. Patterson. Executors: Wife Rachel Patterson and son John C. Patterson. Signed April 17, 1833. Witnesses: His wife and son John C. Patterson. For the probate of the above, see Minute Docket at January Term 1835, page 196. Recorded February 23, 1835.

Page 115 **WILL OF WALTER B. SHARP.** Brother Benjamin F. Sharp, sister Elizabeth H. and a sister Nancy Sharp. Names his Aunt Nancy Guyder. He also mentions his mother but not by name. Executor: Samuel Todd. Signed October 18, 1834. Witnesses: Samuel Todd, Hugh Thomison and Elijah Davis. For probate of the above, see Minute Docket at January Term 1835, page 213. Recorded February 23, 1835.

Page 117 **WILLIAM HOWARD.** Youngest son Benjamin Howard, age 19, will be 21 on February 22, 1831. Youngest daughter Faner Parker. Oldest son Christopher Howard. Eldest daughter Sarah Boone. Signed April 2, 1827. Witnesses: Obediah Barnet and William A. Tucker. Executors: Christopher Howard and Benjamin Howard. Probate, see Minutes of April Term 1835.

Page 119 **WILL OF LEONARD MILES.** Wife Mary Miles. Children: Polly Carrithers, Elizabeth Atwood, Sally Martin, Nancy Gee, William Miles, Leonard Miles, Patsey Lindsay, a granddaughter Polly Lindsay. Executor: William Atwood. Signed April 1, 1835. Witnesses: William F. Smith and John Loyd. Proven in April Term 1835.

Page 120 **WILL OF CORNELIUS DARNELL.** Children: Calvin R., John B., and Mary Ann Darnell. Executor: John Broadway. Signed June 21, 1835. Witnesses: William Beavers and William Hopper. Probated July Term 1835.

Page 121 **WILL OF NOAH RYALS.** Wife Rebecca Ryals. Seven children: Mahala, Nancy, William, Mary Ann, Martha Jane, and Eliza Ryals. Executrix: Wife Rebecca Ryals. Witnesses: W.B. Benge and Cad J. Claiborne. Signed October 22, 1835. Proven October Term 1835.

Page 122 **WILL OF WILLIAM R. WARREN.** Wife Sarah Warren. Children: Robert, William, James, Peter, Samuel, Mary, Sarah, Elizabeth, Martha, and Nancy Gean Warren. Signed August 28, 1835. Witnesses: John Gilbert and John Cooper. Proven October Term 1835.

Page 123 **WILL OF FREDERICK CONAWAY.** Wife Winney Conaway. Children: John, Wiley W., Dunsey, Matilda, Pernee, Ann, Green B. and Benjamin

B. Conaway. The Family Bible goes to his wife Winney Conaway. Executors: Son Wiley W. Conaway and Solomon P. Simpson. Signed: December 1, 1835. Witnesses: James R. Cooke and Jesse McClure. Proven in January Term 1836.

Page 124 **WILL OF ROBERT MOORE.** Wife Joannah Moore. Children: Washington Franklin Moore, Amanda Moore, and Martha Hepzeba Moore. Executors: Wife Joannah Moore and James Fulton, Esq. Signed October 4, 1832. Witnesses: William A. Reavis, John Enochs and Jacob Silvertooth. Proven at January Term 1836.

Page 125 **WILL OF ELIJAH McCLURE.** Wife Susannah McClure. Mentions sons but only named one son Aaron McClure. Brother Jesse McClure. Signed April 26, 1831. Witnesses: Thomas McClure and Aaron McClure. Proven at January Term 1836.

Page 126 **WILL OF ISAAC RUTLEDGE.** Granddaughter Ann Rebecca Rutledge and a guardian for her. He mentions other heirs but not by names. Executors: Mark Whitaker, Jr. and Abner Stead. Signed October 23, 1835. Witnesses: J.E. Waggoner and Wade A. Morris. Proven January Term 1837.

Page 127 **WILL OF ELIZABETH HUGHEY.** Eldest daughter Polly, eldest son Washington, second son Robert, daughter Jennetta, son Isaac and youngest daughter Peggy. Executor: James Wilson. Signed May 23, 1836. Witnesses: Joseph Henderson, Mathew Wilson and Washington Wilson.

Page 128 **WILL OF JOHN MURDOCK, SR.** Wife Isabella Murdock. Children: John, Nancy, Elizabeth and Rachel Murdock. Mother Molly Murdock. Executor: William B. Benge. Signed August 6, 1836. Witnesses: Samuel Wakefield and Ezekiel Sanders. Proven at October Term 1836.

Page 129 **WILL OF ANTHONY MULLINS.** Wife Sarah Mullins. Children: Eldest Elizabeth Smith, 2nd Mary Lincity, Margaret Price, William, John, Sarah Bylew, Andrew, Nancy Ricks, Walter, Martin, George, Polly, Milly, Patsey, Vincent, Thomas Jefferson, Pleasant, and Eliza Mullins. Executors: Jesse Bonner, Samuel M. Clay and William Stephens. Signed October 5, 1824. Witnesses: John Paul, Thomas Gillespie, John Vickers, Sr. and John Vickers, Jr.

Page 130 **WILL OF ROBERT R. ALLSUP.** He mentions his three youngest sons as: Robert H. Allsup, Brice M.G. Allsup and Thomas H. Allsup. Another son Ephraim S. Allsup. He mentions his eldest sons and daughters but not by name. Executors: Ephraim S. Allsup and David C. Cowan. Signed August 22, 1836. Witnesses: B.M.G. Allsup and Joseph L. Throp.

Page 131 **WILL OF ZEALOS MILSTEAD.** Wife Elizabeth Milstead. Son Aaron and daughter Sally Milstead. Signed September 22, 1836. Witnesses: Ephraim Dickey and Samuel Lauderdale. Proven at November Term 1836.

Page 132 **WILL OF JAMES SCOTT.** Wife Jane Scott. Children: Elizabeth Jobe, Isabella Turley, Mary Fergueson, Rosetta McDonald, Nancy Mitchell, Rachel Scott, John Scott, and William Scott. Executors: William Moore and Charles Bright. Signed March 24, 1836. Witnesses: Carter Walker and David Cooper. Proven at May Term 1836.

Page 133 **WILL OF DAVIS EASTLAND.** Sister Ann L. Eastland. Brother Cyrus Eastland. Father Ezekiel Eastland. Executor: Ezekiel Eastland, his father. Signed March 9, 1838. Witnesses: Charles McKinney and S.W. Carmack. Proven at April Term 1838.

Page 134 **WILL OF ANN MEANS.** Nephew Alfred S. Templeton, nephew Leander Templeton, nephew Howard Templeton, nephew Hugh M. Templeton, niece Minerva W. Templeton, niece Evaline A. Templeton, nephew and niece Archibald and Polly Templeton and their youngest child William W. Templeton. Other names: Elizabeth Craig, John Shields, Margaret Craig, Nancy Curry, and

Robert Shields. Executors: John Wilson and Cyrus Cathey. Signed July 15, 1835. Witnesses: John McDaniel and John J. Crawford. Archibald Templeton shall be guardian of her children. Witness: John J. Crawford.

Page 136 **WILL OF MOSES CHAMBERS.** Wife Jean Chambers. Names Julia Parks. Grandchildren: John Cook, Catharine Chambers, Jobe Parks and Elizabeth Jane Parks. Executors: Daniel Scivally and John Scivally. Signed August 9, 1837. Witnesses: John S. Johns and John T. Brown and Daniel Parks. He mentioned not laying off a dower. He thinks she (wife) is not capable of managing such, as she has been insane for some 12 years or more. September 15, 1837. Proven November Term 1837.

Page 137 **WILL OF ROBERT STEPHENS.** Son Jerman and his daughters, Tennessee and Mary Stephens, a son James Stephens and his son Robert Randolph Stephens, a son Josiah Stephens, 4th son Henry Stephens, daughter Sarah wife of David Franklin and their two children, Sarah Ann and Theophilus Franklin. Executors: Charles Bright and John Moorehead. Signed November 10, 1835. Witnesses: Henry Warren and J.B. Ramsey. Proven June Term 1837.

Page 139 **WILL OF HIRAM CULBERSON.** Wife Nancy Culberson. Children: Parthenia, Abi, James S., William C., Mary Ann, Thomas, Sarah E., and Hiram F.L. Culberson. Executors: Wife Nancy Culberson and sons James S. and William C. Culberson. Signed April 28, 1836. Witnesses: Jesse Halbert and Morgan Halbert. Proven at September Term 1837.

Page 140 **WILL OF MARGARET McCOY.** Children: Spruce H., David Billings, Samuel William and Elizabeth Wilson. A granddaughter Candess Delina McCoy. Executor: John C. Taylor. Signed May 14, 1837. Witnesses: Ira McKinney and John Wood. Proven September Term 1837.

Page 141 **WILL OF WILLIAM HOBBS.** Sons Nathaniel and William Hobbs. Daughters Nancy and Sally Hobbs. Sons Jesse and Alfred. Grandchildren: Caroline George, Lorenzo Dow Porter, and Susannah Alford Hobbs. He mentioned moving from the State of North Carolina. Executor: Son Nathaniel Hobbs. Signed December 7, 1836. Witnesses: Thomas Fortune and David W. George. Proven January Term 1837.

Page 142 **WILL OF JOHN WHITAKER.** Wife Nancy Whitaker. Children: William, J.J., Joseph Whitaker, Nancy Sebastian and her daughter Nancy W. Sebastian, Benjamin Whitaker, Thomas Whitaker, Daniel Whitaker, Martha King, Madison G. Whitaker and Newton Whitaker. Executors: William Moore and sons John J. and Newton Whitaker. Signed January 31, 1837. Witnesses: John Bailey and William Moore. Proven July 1837.

Page 143 **WILL OF JOHN GRAY.** Wife Mary R. Gray. Children: Elizabeth, Mahala and Frances Gray. Executors: Wife Mary R. Gray and James Bright. Signed October 16, 1832. Witnesses: John King and John Copeland. Proven June 1837.

Page 145 **WILL OF AARON McWHORTER.** Wife Rebecca McWhorter. Children: Betsey, Hugh B. and Matilda McWhorter. Executors: William Strong and Cordel Shuffield. Signed April 4, 1837. Witnesses: Joseph Joins and Elizabeth Moore. Proven July Term 1837.

Page 146 **WILL OF ANNA McCONNELL.** Son Robert McConnell and his wife Patsey. Daughter Sarah T. McConnell. Son John Perry McConnell who is to get the family Bible. Executors: Elijah M. Ringo and A. Bradshaw. Signed July 8, 1834. Witnesses: A. Yell and John L. Morgan. Proven June Term 1838.

Page 147 **WILL OF ABNER C. HEATH.** Mentions his wife but not by name. Executors: Samuel Young and John Copeland. Signed June 13, 1838. Witnesses: James Sorrells and James Frame. Proven August 1838.

Page 148  **WILL OF WILLIAM S. HALL.**  Wife Rebecca Hall.  He mentions his children but only named one daughter Lucinda A. Hall.  Executor: William Thomas.  Signed August 2, 1838.  Witnesses: J.L. Stone and John N. Hayes. Proven October Term 1838.

Page 149  **WILL OF SAMUEL BUCHANAN.**  Wife Sally Buchanan.  Sons: James M., Simpson and younger son William Buchanan.  Daughter Mary Tooley and her two children James and Preston Tooley.  Executors: William H. Tuley and James M. Davis.  Signed May 3, 1838.  Witnesses: Thomas Hines, Thomas H. McGaugh, Samuel Buchanan and Thomas Massey.  Proven October Term 1838.

Page 150  **WILL OF JOSEPH LONG.**  Wife Matilda Long.  Four children: Mary Ann, Robert W., William R., and Albert J. Long.  Executors: Brother William F. Long and Rufus K. Flack.  Signed September 5, 1838.  Witnesses: B.H. Berry, D.M. Beatie and John H. Taylor.  Proven October 1838.

Page 151  **WILL OF JOSHUA GIBSON.**  Names: Newton M. Buchanan, Andrew J. Buchanan, William S. Buchanan and John M. Buchanan, all sons of Samuel S. Buchanan.  Also, Samuel S. Buchanan's four daughters: Louisa, Margaret, Julia and Mary Anna Buchanan.  Executors: James Fulton and Samuel S. Buchanan. Signed January 1, 1837.  Witnesses: James Tool, David Buchanan, Jr. and J.S. Edmiston.  Proven at October Term 1838.
NOTE: He bought land of Robert Braden of Cane Creek and land he bought of John H. Gibson on Buchanan Creek.

Page 152  **WILL OF ABRAHAM SUMNERS.**  Wife Nancy Sumners.  Children: Margaret Coble, Thomas P. Sumners, Abraham M. Sumners, William G. Sumners, and Mary Williamson.  A granddaughter Nancy.  Executors: Sons William G., Thomas P., and Abraham M. Sumners.  Proven in November Term 1838.

Page 153  **WILL OF DANIEL HOLMAN.**  Sons: Isaac, James and John Holman. Daughter Sally Haggard.  Son Hardy Holman, deceased, Hardy's daughter Patsey now the wife of James S. Holman, son Willis Holman, daughter Nancy Holman, Polly wife of Mr. Harrison and was formerly the wife of John Hughes, deceased.  Polly's children by Hughes not names but a child by Harrison by the name of Jesse.  Executors: Son Isaac Holman and William F. Long.  Signed October 12, 1829.  Witnesses: J. Long, John Brown, Jacob Hamilton and William Brown.
Codicil: Mentions his daughter Sally Haggard's children: Sally, Johnson, Dorcas and Joel Haggard.  Signed December 1, 1830.  Witnesses: J. Long, D. Bryant and John Brown.  Proven in October Term 1838.

Page 155  **WILL OF ARTHUR ALBERTSON.**  Wife Elizabeth Albertson.  Brother John Albertson of the State of Indiana.  Father Caleb Albertson, deceased.  He had interest in land (640 acres) granted to the University of North Carolina, founded upon a warrant which issued for the Military Service of Caleb Albertson in the Revolutionary War and was escheated by Act of Assembly of said State and is said to be located in the County of Obion in the State of Tennessee. Friend Robert W. Ragsdale.  He had land on Swan Creek.  Executrix: Wife Elizabeth Albertson.  Signed December 6, 1836.  Witnesses: Ira McKinney and Abraham Barnes.  Proven February 1839.

Page 157  **WILL OF JOHN RHEA.**  Wife Sally Rhea.  Children: William B., Mary B., Susan M., and Brice M.G. Rhea, Altamira Isom and her children by James Ison, Sally Ann Broyles and Pleasant V. Rhea.  Grandchildren: Rufus K. Smith and Frances E. Smith.  Children of Altamira and James Ison: Lewis, Grace, Dave, and Chany Isom.  Executor: James Bright.  Signed December 29, 1838. Witnesses: Andrew Buchanan, Hugh Shaw and Charles McKinney.  Proven March Term 1839.

Page 161  **WILL OF JAMES B. ENGLISH.**  Wife Martha English.  Children: Samuel Lewis English, E.E. English, Eleazer E. English, Montgomery English, and S.L. English.  A son-in-law William Gragg.  Executors: Sons Eleazer,

Montgomery and Samuel L. English. Witnesses: Henry Bryson, A. McMillen and Samuel L. English. Proven in June Term 1839.

Page 163 **WILL OF EDWARD HARRIS.** Wife Catharine Harris. Children: Martha Ann, Eliza, Mary Jane, Rebeccah Agnes and Casandra Louisa Harris. Executors: Amzi Bradshaw and Harmon Cummins. Signed August 10, 1836. Witnesses: John S. Morgan and Edmond M. North. Proven at July Term 1839.

Page 165 **WILL OF BRANSON D. CAPLE.** Mentions his wife but not by name. Children: William, Nancy, Willis, Davy, Crag and Malvina Caple. Owned a house and lot in Lewisburg, Tennessee. Executors: Daniel Whitaker and Pleasant Halbert. Signed August 8, 1839. Witnesses: James Fulgum and Eli Evans. Proven in September Term 1839.

Page 166 **WILL OF HEZEKIAH JORDON.** Wife Martha Jordon. Children: Spencer Leatherwood and wife Clary, John H. Norton and wife Polly, Barnet Burton and wife Malinda. Executors: John H. Horton and Spencer Leatherwood. Signed April 11, 1830. Witnesses: David Byers and Edmond D. Parkes. Proven in October Term 1839.

Page 167 **WILL OF ROBERT STEWART.** Wife Mary Stewart. Children: James, Mary, youngest son Bryson, John, and Arthur Stewart. Executrix: (probably his wife Mary Stewart). Signed August 30, 1839. Witnesses: James Stewart and David A. Black. Proven in December Term 1839.

Page 168 **WILL OF HENRY B. SMITH.** Wife Cynthy Ann Caroline Smith. Children are not named. Executor: William Beavers. Signed June 12, 1840. Witnesses: William Harris and Thomas Mathis. Proven in August Term 1840.

Page 168 **WILL OF WILLIAM GUNTER.** Wife Phoeba Gunter. Children: Joshua Gunter, Hiram Gunter, Polly Gunter, Hughes Gunter, James Gunter, William Gunter, George W. Gunter, and Rebecca Gunter. Executors: Joshua Gunter and Malcom F. Hughes. Signed August 12, 1840. Witnesses: Samuel Ramsey and John Ramsey. Proven at September Term 1840.

Page 169 **WILL OF ABRAHAM CUNNINGHAM, SR.** Wife Nancy Cunningham. Children: Samuel, John, Nancy Groce, James, Joel, Wilson, Mary Breaden, George and Abraham Cunningham,Jr. and daughter Jane and her two sons Jeremiah O. Coulter and Hardy H. Coulter. Executors: Son John Cunningham and Abner Steed. Signed September 8, 1840. Witnesses: Travis Ashby and Wilson Groce. Proven at October Term 1840.

Page 171 **WILL OF HENRY MOORE.** Wife Frances H. Moore. Children: Jordon R. Moore, William H. Moore, Mary L. Beanland and other children not named. NOTE: He mentioned both families but did not explain. Executors: Wife Frances H. Moore and son William H. Moore. Signed September 12, 1840. Witnesses: Joel L. Reese, John Bell and James D. Cole. Proven at October Term 1840.

Page 172 **WILL OF HENRY SWINEBROAD.** Wife Elvira Swinebroad. Mentions his children but not by name. Executors: Boon Wilson, David Smith and William B. Wright. Signed September 20, 1840. Witnesses: Ira McKinney, S.D. Milliken and John Kennedy. Proven in November Term 1840.

Page 173 **WILL OF EPHRAIM DICKEY.** Wife Elizabeth Dickey. Daughter Mary Dickey. Signed September 16, 1840. Witnesses: Alexander Edmiston and Samuel Bell. Proven in November term 1840.

Page 174 **WILL OF JAMES M. DEAN.** Wife Ann Dean. Brother Alvin M. Dean. Brother Harvy M. Dean. Father Henry Dean. Executors: Thomas Dean of Bedford County, Tennessee and B.H. Berry of Lincoln County. Signed September 20, 1840. Witnesses: William G. Rountree and James A. Berry. Proven at October Term 1840.

Page 174 **WILL OF MINTY ALEXANDER.** Son James A.J. Alexander, daughter Milly Susannah Alexander. Mentions Temple Taylor. Executor: Temple Taylor. Signed September 3, 1840. Witnesses: T.S. Williams and John Keller. Proven at December Term 1840.

Page 175 **WILL OF FIELDING McDANIEL, SR.** Third son Evan, second daughter Agnes, other children: Elizabeth, John, Ambrose, Fielding, Charles, William and Coleman Fielding, 9 in number. Ambrose the 2nd son is deceased and left two children. John McDaniel was appointed their guardian, they are John and Robert McDaniel. Ambrose's wife is Rosetta. Executors: Son-in-law Thomas Wakefield and 1st son John McDaniel. Signed July 23, 1839. Witnesses: Hugh Shaw and William H. King. Proven in January Term 1841.

Page 176 **WILL OF ALEXANDER ASHBY.** Wife Lavina Ashby. Children: John L., Rachel E., Frances S., Nathan A., Merrion Jane and Nancy A. Ashby, also Mary Ashby. Executors: William Ashby and Chloe Stealman. Proven in January Term 1841.

Page 178 **WILL OF JAMES CAMPBELL.** Wife Margaret Campbell. Daughters: Elizabeth Lucinda, Mary Ann and Lucinda Wheery. Mentions his son-in-law Lewis Womack. Signed November 30, 1840. Witnesses: Paul Ingle, R.B. Ramsey and William Ramsey. Proven March Term 1841.

Page 179 **WILL OF JAMES GRANT.** Children: Nancy Russell and Charlotta Merrill. Mentions a brother of Charlotta named Asa. A grandson James Franklin Merrill. Executors: Benjamin Whitaker and Josiah McCracken. Signed March 19, 1841. Witnesses: James McCracken, R.B. Mattox and Josiah McCracken. Proven in May Term 1841.

Page 180 **WILL OF ELIZABETH ALBERTSON.** Nephew John Crawford, nephew Henry Crawford, who are the sons of Elias Crawford of Randolph County, North Carolina, niece Elizabeth Russell wife of Ransom Russell of Randolph County, North Carolina, niece Sally Arnold widow of Daniel Arnold. A brother Elias Crawford. To the children of my deceased niece Elizabeth Taylor, all of North Carolina. Executor: Abram Barnes. Signed March 20, 1841. Witnesses: Ira McKinney and Joseph Clark. Proven in May Term 1841.

Page 182 **WILL OF PHILIP FOX.** Wife Ailce Fox. Children: Benjamin, John, Enoch, Nancy Ann, Rebecca, Daniel and Morgan Fox. Executors: Wife Ailcy Fox and James W. Holmes, Esq. Signed July 31, 1841. Witnesses: Thomas Flack and Abner Steed. Proven in September Term 1841.

Page 184 **WILL OF STEPHEN COLE.** Wife Elizabeth Cole. Sons: Isaac R. and Felix G. Cole. Executors: John Cole and Zebulon Parr. Witnesses: Jesse M. Rowling and John Maddox. Proven at September Term 1841.

Page 185 **WILL OF SAMUEL DOBBINS.** Wife Susannah Dobbins. Son John, daughter Elizabeth Pinson and a deceased daughter (not named) wife of Samuel Hall and her children, not named. Signed December 28, 1839. Witnesses: Ezekiel Sanders and T.W. Harper. Proven and recorded October 8, 1841.

Page 187 **WILL OF MARTHA THWING.** Mentions Mrs. Mary E. Wheeler wife of David Wheeler. Mentions her grandchildren but not by name. Executor: James Bright. Signed January 13, 1840. Witnesses: John J. Ramsey and Elisha Bagley.
Codicil: Signed May 23, 1840. Proven and recorded October 8, 1841.

Page 189 **WILL OF ARCHIBALD McELROY.** Wife Elizabeth McElroy. Mentions his children but not by name. Executors: Wife Elizabeth McElroy and Amos Hurley, who is also the guardians. Signed December 18, 1839. Witnesses: W. Bonner, John M. McGaugh, May Buchanan and Anthony Delaney. Proven and recorded October 8, 1841.

Page 190 **WILL OF THOMAS CHILDRESS.** Children: Susannah, Nancy, Thomas D., and Hannah, Polly and Nelly Childress. Signed November 17, 1836. Witnesses: William Stephens, James Hays and Eli L. Hodge. Proven and recorded October 8, 1841.

Page 191 **WILL OF WILLIAM BLAIR.** Wife Ann Blair. Mentions his children but not by name. Executors: John Wyatt and Hugh Taylor. Signed September 3, 1841. Witnesses: Jesse Morton and John Blair and Richard Wyatt. Proven at October Term 1841.

Page 191 **WILL OF CHARLES THORP.** Brothers: Joel, William and Hardin Throp. Land on Bradshaw Creek. Signed February 15, 1840. Witnesses: David C. Cown and James Thorp. Proven at March Term 1840.

Page 193 **WILL OF JOSEPH KENNEDY.** Wife Lucinda Kennedy. Mentions his boys and his father but not by name. Signed December 29, 1839. Witnesses: James E. English, John H. Reece and Andrew M. English. Proven and recorded October 26, 1841.

Page 194 **WILL OF JOHN ALLBRIGHT.** Wife Margaret Allbright. Children: John, Jacob, Mary Ann, William, Matthew, Alexander, Barney Monroe, James Isham and Harvey Allbright. Executor: Robert Drennan. Signed 16, 1839. Witnesses: James Roach and Hamilton Cochran. Proven and recorded October 26, 1841.

Page 195 **WILL OF ISAAC GATTIS.** Sons: Newton, James, Thomas, William Wilson, and daughters: Sophia George, Polly wife of Daniel E. Yarbrough, Eliza Allen, Julian Bready, Elizabeth Cashion, Jane Waggoner, Sarah Brown, Nancy Gattis and Martha Brady. Executors: William Gattis and son-in-law Abner Brady. Signed October 18, 1841. Witnesses: Abner Steed, N. Gattis and Charles Gattis. Proven November Term 1841.

Page 197 **WILL OF ROBERT WILSON.** Wife Hannah B. Wilson. Children: Eldest daughter Elizabeth T. Wilson, 2nd daughter Narcissa L. Sawyers, eldest son Union A. Wilson, 2nd son Matthew T. Wilson, youngest son Robert W. Wilson. Executors: Wife Hannah B. Wilson and William Wyatt. Signed September 17, 1839. Witnesses: Adam Nipp and John Wyatt. Proven in December Term 1841.

Page 198 **WILL OF JOHN PRYOR, SR.** Wife Mary Pryor. Children: John, Nathan, William, Ann R., Estill and Mary Estill. Executors: Three sons, William, John and Nathan Pryor. Signed September 24, 1841. Witnesses: Charles McKinney and W. Bonner. Proven in January Term 1842.

Page 199 **WILL OF NANCY CUNNINGHAM.** Raised Rebecca Allen. Daughter Polly and son-in-law John Cunningham, daughter Nancy, son John Groce and wife Cincinnatta Groce, daughter Elizabeth wife of James Howell and her daughter Nancy Howell, and Rebecca wife of Travis Ashby. Executors: John Groce and Travis Ashby. Signed December 12, 1841. Witnesses: Abner Steed and Alexander Bready. Proven January Term 1842.

Page 200 **WILL OF AARON WELLS.** Wife Mary Wells. Daughter Sally Dobbins. Grandchildren: Alex Dow F. Dobbins, Adeline Dobbins, Caledonia Dobbins, and her heir Rachel, Narcissa McKinney, a great granddaughter Josephine Wood. Executors: Grandson-in-laws: Ira McKinney and John Wood. Signed January 24, 1842. Witnesses: David Smith, William B. Wright, Boone Wilson, Amos Hurley and Isaiah Nerren. Proven and recorded April 12, 1842. Land on Swan Creek, Main and West.

Page 203 **WILL OF PHILIP KOONCE.** Daughters: Burdotty, Juily Woods, Sophia Ann and Patsey Pina. Mentions Andrew McCartney and Amos Small. He mentioned his wife and other members of his family but not by name. Executors: His wife and William McGee. Signed March 5, 1833. Witnesses: George W. Dennis and Andrew McCartney. Proven and recorded April 12, 1842.

Page 204 **WILL OF ROBERT HAIRSTON.** Wife Margaret Hairston. Children: Mary Meek, Manly M., and James N. Hairston. Nephew Robert Meek. Land in Lincoln County. Will made in Marshall County, Mississippi. Land in DeSota County, Mississippi. Executor: Manly M. Hairston. Signed August 12, 1841. Witnesses: J.J. Meek, Robert Jackson and I.F. Davis.
Marshall County, Mississippi, proved October 25, 1841. Signed by clerk November 24, 1841.
Marshall County, Mississippi, Jesse Lewellan, Judge. Certified January 18, 1842. Admitted to record by Lincoln County Court February Term 1842.

Page 206 **WILL OF WILLIAM COLLINS.** Wife Catharine Collins. Children: Nancy and her son Robert T. Collins, Wright P. Collins, Samuel D. Collins, Missouri Ann and Alexander F. Collins. Executors: Thomas McAfee and Ira McKinney. Signed July 8, 1842. Witnesses: A.F. Dobbins, Jacob R. Wright and Henry Turney. Proven and recorded August 9, 1842.

Page **WILL OF MARK WHITAKER.** Children: Rebecca Izard, Nancy Hammonds, John Whitaker, Mary Lucas, Sarah Paysinger, Martha Pegram, Benjamin J. Whitaker, Judah Pruitt, Mark Whitaker, Jr., and Perlina Burton. Executors: Sons Mark Whitaker and Benjamin J. Whitaker. Signed October 30, 1941. Witnesses: John J. Whitaker, William Moore and Joseph Whitaker. Proven October 13, 1842.

Page 210 **WILL OF WILEY C. NEWMAN.** Wife Mary M. Newman. Children: Wiley M. Newman, Moses H. Newman and Martin W. Newman. Executor: Son Wiley M. Newman. Signed August 26, 1842. Witnesses: Eli Couch and Obediah Holloway. Proven and recorded October 13, 1842.

Page 211 **WILL OF JOHN GRAGG.** Wife Jane Gragg. Children: Eliza Jane, Elizabeth and John W. Gragg. Executors: Wife Jane Gragg and son John W. Gragg. Signed February 8, 1842. Witnesses: Henry Bryson and Robert McCalla. Proven November Term 1842.

Page 212 **WILL OF JAMES RUSSELL.** Wife not named. Son William Alexander Russell, daughter Christiana Jane Russell. Mentions John Cown and David Whitfield. Signed October 24, 1842. Witnesses: William B. McCollum and John Gray. Proven and recorded December Term 1842.

Page 213 **WILL OF JOSIAH BRANDON.** Wife Rachael Brandon. Sons: Lemuel, Logan D., Thomas and William Brandon. Mentions his indigent daughters but not by name. Grandson Lemuel S. Woodward. Executors: Sons Lemuel and Logan D. Brandon. Signed January 4, 1840. Witnesses: B.B. Brandon and David Scivally and William Frame. Proven and recorded December Term 1842.

Page 214 **WILL OF JOSEPH HESTER.** Wife Mary hester. Son Wilson W. Hester. Request that James Bright, Sr. shall be guardian for his children, which he does not name. Executrix: Wife Mary Hester. Signed October 25, 1842. Witnesses: J. Bright, M.H. Bonner and Jacob Broyles. Proven and recorded December Term 1842.

Page 217 **WILL OF CYRUS CATHY.** Wife Nancy Cathy. Six children: William A., Cyrus S.H., Mary E., Sarah C., George J.F., and John T. Cathy. Executors: Wife Nancy Cathy and brother Alexander Cathy. Signed September 25, 1842. Witnesses: John Wood, Ira McKinney and William F. Zimmerman. Proven February Term 1843.

Page 218 **WILL OF JOHN O. GRIFFIS.** Wife Martha M. Griffis. Executors: Moses H. Barnes and John Cown. Signed December 21, 1842. Witnesses: S. Gullett, William M. Smith and William A. Griffis. Proven February Term 1843.

Page 219 **WILL OF GEORGE MARTIN.** Children: S. George Martin, William J.H.,

Martin, Martha J.A. Timmins, Celia Ann Martin, Robert Martin, Mary V. Houston, Elizabeth M.L. ____. Grandchildren: Ann Eliza, Mary Catharine, Frances Virginia and two infants, twins, all the children of son C.K.V. Martin, deceased. Executors: Sons, S. George Martin and William J.H. Martin. Signed November 11, 1840. Witnesses: George W. Jones and Samuel Bell. Proven March Term 1843.

Page 220   **WILL OF THOMAS ATWOOD.** Wife Nancy Atwood. Son John Atwood. Appointed George Renegar as guardian of son John Atwood. Mentions other children but not by name. Executor: Enos Wilson. Signed May 12, 1843. Witnesses: John J. Whitaker, Enos Wilson and George Renegar.

Page 221   **WILL OF JOHN VICKERS.** Wife Nancy Vickers. Executors: Joab Nipplin and Uty Sherrell. Signed February 28, 1843. Witnesses: Martin Graves and Aron Boyd.

Page 221   **WILL OF JAMES PYBAS.** Wife Sarah J. Pybas. Sons: Kenneth M. and William J. Pybas. Niece Lucinda Pybas. Executors: John Landess and Sarah J. Pybas. Signed August 1, 1840. Witnesses: John Cunningham and Polly Cunningham.

Page 223   **WILL OF PERLINA BURTON.** Children: Susan Catharine, brother Mark Whitaker is to be the guardian of her sons, Francis Marion, Patrick, Henry Mark, and William. Sister Judah Pruitt is to raise her daughter Susan Catharine. Mentions her father's estate but not by name. Executor: A brother Benjamin J. Whitaker. Signed August 8, 1843. Witnesses: John J. Whitaker, Martha Pegram and George Waggoner.

Page 224   **WILL OF ALEXANDER HUGHEY.** Wife Mary Hughey. Children: Elvira J. Hughey, Parthena Hughey, Mary C. Hughey, Martha L. Hughey, and William Henry Hughey. Signed March 11, 1843. Executrix: Wife Mary Hughey. Witnesses: William B. Bright and J.N. Ruth.

Page 225   **WILL OF MATTHEW PRICE.** Wife Elizabeth Price. Four children: Anna Cown, Sarah Rountree, George Price and John Price. Executors: Sons, George and John Price. Signed February 28, 1829. Witnesses: Kindred Pearson, Thomas Blyth and John Newton.

Page 226   **WILL OF JAMES K. NEECE.** His guardian, Jesse Neece. Mother Huldy Neece. Executrix: Mother Huldy Neece. Signed September 9, 1843. Witnesses: W.W. Gill, W.W. Reese, Jesse Nees and Hardy N. Nees.

Page 226   **WILL OF GEORGE CATHEY.** Wife Elizabeth Cathey. Children: Frances S. Cana and Robert A. Cathey. Executors: William F. Zimmerman and wife Elizabeth Cathey. Signed June 26, 1843. Witnesses: John McDaniel and Alexander Cathey. Proven and recorded November Term 1843.

Page 227   **WILL OF JOHN B. LEATHERWOOD.** Wife Sally Leatherwood. Sons, Elisha, Jesse, Spencer and Norris Leatherwood. Executor: Norris Leatherwood. Signed October 28, 1843. Witnesses: Uty Sherrell and Spencer Leatherwood. Proven and recorded November Term 1843.

Page 228   **WILL OF ELIZABETH BLAKE.** Jane Blake, Sarah Penelope Mary, and John W. Blake. Margaret Scales' heirs, Luchy and Eliza. William D. Blake. Executors: John W. Blake and William D. Blake. Signed December 1, 1843. Witnesses: Joseph McMillen and David P. McMillen.

Page 229   **WILL OF REUBEN WASHBURN.** Sons, John and Abram Washburn. Daughters: Mary, Elizabeth and Louisa Jane Washburn. A granddaughter Charlotte Mourning. Executor: John Thompson. Signed February 20, 1840. Witnesses: L.W. Ledbetter and John A. Dollins.

Page 231 **WILL OF JOHN GIBSON.** Wife Margaret Gibson. Children: Albert G. Gibson, Nancy Gibson, Margaret A. Gibson, Lucinda Gibson, Polly Gibson, Jenetta Gibson, Malinda Gibson, Eliza Gibson, Parke Gibson, John H. Gibson and Felix G. Gibson. Son-in-law John W. Smith who married Lucinda, son-in-law Samuel Crawford, son-in-law Archibald M. Harber, and son-in-law Alfred C. Dickey who married Eliza. Executors: Albert G. Gibson and Felix G. Gibson. Signed June 4, 1840. Witnesses: Isaac Southworth, Joseph B. Hill and Nepoleon Ward. Proven and recorded June Term 1844.

Page 235 **WILL OF JOHN COLE.** Wife Nancy Cole. Sons, William and Joseph Cole. Daughters, Emeline and Nancy Cole. Signed June 3, 1844. Witnesses: Josiah Norwood and Pinkney Pilant. Proven and recorded July Term 1844.

Page 236 **WILL OF HENRY PATTERSON.** Wife Elizabeth Patterson. Six children: Lucy R. Bonner, David F. Robertson, Henderson F. Robertson, Ann F. Bonner, Elizabeth C. Robertson and Mary Robertson. A grandson Henry Robertson, a child of my deceased son William H. Robertson. Mentioned James Shares. Executors: Moses H. Bonner and David F. Robertson. Signed July 9, 1844. Witnesses: James Fulton, John Goodrich and Wilson A. Hester. Proven at September Term 1844.

Page 241 **WILL OF JONAS LEATHERWOOD.** Wife Martha Leatherwood. Only daughter Nancy Wilson. Executors: Boon Wilson, Daniel Leatherwood and George Reece. Signed September 20, 1840. Witnesses: Isa M. King and Davis Smith. Proven and recorded September 9, 1844.

Page 242 **WILL OF ROBERT CUNNINGHAM, SR.** Wife Sarah Cunningham. Children: John and Enoch Cunningham, Frances, Rebecca, Lucinda, Robert, Mary and Sarah and Jane (or James) Cunningham. Executors: Son Wilson Cunningham and son-in-law Francis Bearden. Signed April 20, 1844. Witnesses: W.F. Zimmerman and H.R. Hamilton. Proven at August Term and recorded September 4, 1844. All wanted Wilson Cunningham's name added to the above children. Signed: Francis Bearden, Lucinda Bearden, Robert Cunningham, Sarah Cunningham, John W. Cunningham, Enoch Cunningham, James Cunningham, Mary Bearden, John Bearden, G.W. Sawyers and Rebecca Sawyers. Proven August Term and recorded September 14, 1844.

Page 244 **WILL OF DAVID BUCHANAN.** Wife Margaret Buchanan. Four daughters, Martha, Joanah, Mary and Isabellah. Sons, S.S. Buchanan and David Buchanan, Jr. Joanah married Parke Gibson. Executors: Samuel S. Buchanan and David Buchanan, Jr. Signed August 12, 1844. Witnesses: Thomas W. Buchanan and Felix G. Gibson. Proven and recorded September 17, 1844.

Page 246 **WILL OF JOHN McMILLEN.** Children: Elizabeth Parks, Frances Davidson Robertson, Doak, Charlotte Hardin, William Brown, John Constant Thomas and Elzira Ann. Owned Lot # 14 in Fayetteville, also had 291 acres in Lincoln County. Executors: William T. Ross and Woodruff Parkes. Signed August 21, 1844. Witnesses: E.M. Ewing and W.A. Russell.

Page 247 **WILL OF JOHN DAVIS.** Wife Sarah Davis. Children: Martha Jane, Margaret Elizabeth, Sarah Johnson, Campbell N., Madeline McMullen who is deceased, and Leroy. Two grandchildren of a son Ephraim Davis, deceased. Son-in-law Fielding Parks who married Caroline. Executor: Fielding Parks. Signed: August 9, 1844. Witnesses: Hugh Thomison and A.J. Cunningham.

Page 250 **WILL OF WILLIAM ROWELL.** Wife Katharine Rowell. Children: Esther Mary, Jacob William, David James, John Wesley, Merriah Ann, Samuel Milton, Eliza Jane, and Martha Caroline Rowell. Executors: David James Rowell, John Wesley Rowell and Samuel Milton Rowell. Signed September 4, 1844. Witnesses: William Bland and Samuel J. Bland.

Page 251  **WILL OF JOHN MOORE.**  Two children: Eli Moore and May Hinds. Named a William Johnson.  Executors: Son Eli Moore and son-in-law Thomas Hinds, and "Doc" William F. Smith.  Signed October 22, 1844.  Witnesses: William Moore and B.M.G. Rhea.  Recorded November 21, 1844.

Page 252  **WILL OF HENRY LANDESS.**  Wife Gracy Landess.  Children: Hannah Ford, Polly Green, Gracy E. Tally, Ann who married James F. Smith and is now deceased, Susan Eaton who married Alfred Eaton, John, Joseph Thompson and Henry Harman who left the county.  Executor: Son John Landess. Signed October 21, 1844.  Witnesses: William C. Blake and D.R. Smythe.  Recorded November 21, 1844.

Page 254  **WILL OF JOSHUA GUNTER.**  Children: Franklin Gunter, Wesley Gunter, Clayborn Gunter, William Gunter, and Jasper Gunter and son-in-law John Ramsey.  Executor: Alfred Bearden.  Signed December 4, 1844. Witnesses: A.G. Downing and Robert H. Wheeler.

Page 255  **WILL OF GEORGE WAGGONER.**  Wife Mary Waggoner.  Children: Peter, Margaret, Barbary, Elizabeth, Mary, Fetty, George, John Lewis, Jesse and heirs of son Jacob Waggoner.  Executors: Sons, Jesse and Peter Waggoner.  Signed October 13, 1842.  Witnesses: James W. Holman and B.M. Jones. Codicil: He revokes his son Peter Waggoner as executor and desires his son Jesse Waggoner be sole executor.  Signed November 24, 1844.  Proven and recorded April Term 1845.

Page 257  **WILL OF THOMAS MASSEY.**  Former wife Polly, whose father is John Rains from Davidson County.  Children: Welford R., John R., William P., and Christiana H. Massey.  Present wife Priscilla R. Massey.  Children: Thomas J. Massey and Jane Eliza Clark.  Owned land on Cane Creek also on Coldwater Creek.  Executors: Thomas Hinds and Joseph Clark.  Signed January 15, 1844. Witnesses: William L. Pamplin, Thomas Childs and B.W.D. Carty.  Recorded July 10, 1845.

Page 259  **WILL OF THOMAS CHAPMAN.**  Wife Mary Chapman.  Children: Katharine Wakefield, Delila Brown, Harriet Scott, Mary Ann Kymes, and Jesse Chapman.  Son-in-law John Kymes.  Signed July 29, 1844.  Witnesses: Theo. Harris, William Beavers and Howell Harris.  Recorded July 11, 1845.

Page 262  **WILL OF RALPH SMITH.**  Wife Cyrena Smith.  Children: Alfred, Clarissa, Nancy Smith.  Signed April 12, 1845.  Witnesses: Samuel Hawkins and Joseph B. Smith.  Recorded July 11, 1845.

Page 263  **WILL OF JOEL E. BROWN.**  Four daughters: Elizabeth, Sarah, Martha Jane and Minerva Brown.  Executor: Tunstall Gregory.  Signed May 28, 1845.  Witnesses: William B. Woodruff and Fenton Gregory.  Recorded July 11, 1845.

Page 264  **WILL OF JOHN SUMNERS.**  Wife Rebecca Sumners.  Children: Sally Roden, Margaret, Sellers, Joseph, Jane, Polly Shelton, Robert, and Andrew Sumners and Rebecca Williamson.  Grandchildren: Abner Sumners and Eliza Reed a daughter of Jane.  Executor: Son Robert Sumners.  Signed May 18, 1845. Witnesses: Davis Smith and Pleasant Bearden.

Page 266  **WILL OF THOMAS BLAIR.**  Wife Milly Blair.  Children: Louis C., Nancy, Harrison and John W. Blair.  Executors: Harrison and John W. Blair.  Signed June 5, 1845.  Witnesses: John Smith and Allen Pool.  Recorded July 15, 1845.

Page 267  **WILL OF ANTHONY BAITS.**  Wife Catharine Baits.  Children: Alexander, George, Mary Ready, Anthony, Doak, Jasper, Jane and Tempy Baits.  Executors: Son Alexander Baits and Travis Ashby.  Signed July 1, 1845.  Witnesses: M.W. Yant and Peter Ashby.

Page 268 **WILL OF EPHRAIM KING.** Wife Jane King. Martha G. King, Sarah C. King, Elenor M. Sorrels, Ephraim C. King and Washington A. King. Executors: Son James G. King and James B. Hudson. Signed January 10, 1845. Witnesses: John Landess and Joseph Harkins.

Page 269 **WILL OF BENJAMIN KNOWLES.** Wife Ann Knowles. Children: Martha, Elizabeth, eldest son Jesse, eldest daughter Rebecca wife of Joseph Campbell, Nancy wife of William Thompson, Mary wife of _____ Shelton, and Cyntha wife of Matthew W. Carter. Executors: Crawford Carter and son Matthew Knowles. Signed July 23, 1845. Witnesses: James Hague and A.J. Eslick. Proven and recorded September 15, 1845.

Page 271 **WILL OF DANIEL HALBERT.** Wife Mary Halbert. Mentions his heirs but not by name. Executrix: Wife Mary Halbert. Signed May 9, 1844. Witnesses: Davis Smith and Henry Robison. Recorded September 15, 1845.

Page 272 **WILL OF WILLIAM SOLOMON.** Wife Hasly Solomon. Nine children: William Calvin, John Rhea, James Madison, Mary Louisa, Julia Ann, Elizabeth Jane, Augustus Marion, Bennet Franklin, and Joseph Hamilton Solomon. Brother Jordon Solomon. Executors: James Fulton, James Bright and John V. McKinney and Abner Steed. Signed January 16, 1833. Witnesses: Samuel Rosebrough and A.J. Rosebrough. Proven and recorded September 18, 1845.

Page 274 **WILL OF JAMES R. BLAIR.** Wife Savina Blair. Children: Josiah H., Holman, William B., Martha E., John M., Lewis J., Elizabeth A., and Cassena M., and James E. Blair. Executors: James F. McCown, William C. Bland and John Fowler. Signed September 1, 1845. Witnesses: W.B. Solomon and Samuel J. Bland. Recorded October 25, 1845.

Page 276 **WILL OF COL. JAMES DUFF.** Willed all his slaves to the American Colonization Society to be transported to the African Colony of Liberia to be forever freed. Sister Margaret Smith and sister Elizabeth Campbell. Witnesses: Carson Sloan and William Taylor. Recorded January 19, 1845.

Page 277 **WILL OF VINCENT HERRALSON.** Wife Mary G. Herralson. Three children: James H., Ephraim L. and Elizabeth W. Herralson. Executors: Wife Mary G. Herralson and John L. Henderson. Signed December 30, 1845. Witnesses: M.H. Bonner and Lewis Shipp. Proven and recorded February Term 1846.

Page 278 **WILL OF JOHN AUSTIN.** Wife Elizabeth Austin. Daughter wife of Cecil Thornton. He willed to Hardy Birmingham land in Giles County on the waters of Sinking Creek, 47 acres. Son Andrew W. Austin was willed land in Lincoln and Giles County. Executor: Hardy Birmingham. Signed March 28, 1845. Witnesses: Spencer Leatherwood and B.B. Leatherwood. Proven and recorded at February Term 1846.

Page 280 **WILL OF HENRY WARREN.** Eldest son John E. Warren, son William, daughter Elizabeth wife of Joseph Stephens, daughter Mary wife of James P.D. Rosebrough, son Thomas R. Warren, daughter Sarah wife of Beckworth J. Tiller, daughter Nancy wife of Thomas J. Payne, son Henry, son Benjamin, single daughters Emeline and Caroline Warren. Executors: James Bright and two sons Benjamin and Thomas Warren. Signed January 23, 1846. Witnesses: James Hague and Thomas James.
Codicil: February 24, 1846. Signed February 24, 1846. Proven April Term 1846.

Page 288 **WILL OF ALEXANDER FORBES.** Wife Catharine Forbes. Children: Ann Patterson, James Forbes who is deceased and his daughter Lucinda Forbes, Lucy M., Polly Rainey, Schuyler Forbes who is deceased, Alexander and Martha Gilliland. Executor: Samuel Parker. Signed March 30, 1843. Witnesses: Aaron Boyd and Bazel Leatherwood. Recorded April 1846.

Page 289 **WILL OF HANNAH EVANS.** Malinda Evans wife of John Evans. Dillingtine Evans. Executor: Enoch Hamilton. Signed March 28, 1845. Witnesses: John H. Taylor and John Hamilton. Recorded June 1845.

Page 290 **WILL OF BENJAMIN THURSTON.** Mentioned his wife but not by name. Nine children: Elizabeth Thomison, Parthena S. Isham, Mary C. Summerford, Martha D. Roach and Catharine S. Parkes, Aron Parkes, Oney Parkes, William Parkes, and Joel Parkes, all the children of my deceased daughter Polly Parkes, another son of Polly Parkes is Benjamin Thurston Parkes, and he named a friend Samuel E. Gilliland. He willed 1/8 of an acre of land where he now lives for a burial ground for himself and wife, to be reserved from sale forever. Executors: James Bright and Hugh Thomison. Signed July 11, 1843. Witnesses: E.M. Ringo, G.W. Jones and John C. Rogers.
Codicil: Executor: Hugh Thomison. Signed July 19, 1844. June Term 1846.

Page 293 **WILL OF MILTON HODGES.** Appointed his brother Joseph Hodge of the State of Mississippi, County of Leake, as his attorney. Owns land in Louisiana, Parrish of Lebane. Signed August 2, 1845. Witnesses: Thomas Roe, Samuel Boone and Joel Reese. Proven July Term 1845.

Page 294 **WILL OF ROBERT BUCHANAN.** Children: Pryor Buchanan, Milton Buchanan, Elizabeth Woodward, Jane Buchanan and Mary Buchanan. He owned land on Buchanan Creek above the old factory. Executors: Hiram Buchanan and Alfred Smith. Signed March 5, 1839. Witness: Samuel Buchanan. Proven June Term 1845.

Page 295 **WILL OF ANDREW McCARTNEY.** Seven sons and three daughters: Council, Andrew C., William W., Gray A., James, Thomas, and Rufus and Caroline Ann, Mahala and Mary McCartney. Executor: Jacob Stonebraker. Signed August 13, 1845. Witnesses: Charles H. Edmondson and James Locker. Recorded September term 1845.

Page 297 **WILL OF JOHN W. LEONARD.** Wife Betsey Leonard. Executor: John McDaniel. Signed July 14, 1846. Witnesses: Samuel D. Milliken, Anderson Boone and Wade H. McRee. Recorded October Term 1846.

Page 298 **WILL OF WOODY TAYLOR.** Present wife Nancy Taylor. Children: Louisa and Caroline Taylor, John H. Taylor. Other children: William, Elizabeth, Polly, all born to Nancy Taylor. Executors: Son William A. Taylor of Franklin County and Joseph Adkin of Lincoln County. Signed June 13, 1832. Witnesses: John W. Hamilton and A.C. Hamilton. Proven October Term 1845.

Page 301 **WILL OF THOMAS H. JONES.** Mother Leah Jones. Brother Edmond C. Jones and sister Julia F. Jones. Executor: Griffith Cunningham. Signed (no date). Witnesses: M.H. Bonner and Griffith Cunningham. Recorded November 1846.

Page 302 **WILL OF CORNELIUS SULLIVAN.** Wife Mary Sullivan. Mentions his children but not by name. Executor: Constant Smith. Signed October 25, 1846. Witnesses: John Wood, Robert E. Edmondson and Joshua Hughes. Recorded November 18, 1846.

Page 303 **WILL OF JOHN W. SEBASTIAN.** Brother Joseph Sebastian. Nephew William, the son of Joseph Sebastian. Other names: Jacintha Huey, Martha Hornsby, Sarah Hughs, Isaac Grizzard, and Hetty Polk. He had land in Philips County, Arkansas. Executors: John J. Whitaker and Wiley Grizzard. Signed November 18, 1846. Witnesses: J.F. Whitaker and William L. Moore. Proven at December Term 1846.

Page 304 **WILL OF JOHN HENDERSON.** Mentions his wife but not by name. Children: Mary, John L., James and his two sons E.F. and W.A. Henderson. Executor: Son John L. Henderson and he is to be guardian of his son

James W. Henderson's heirs. Signed September 5, 1846. Witnesses: E.M. Shelton and Norris Leatherwood. Proven December Term 1846.

Page 305 **WILL OF JAMES HAGUE.** Wife Ann Hague. Mentions children but only named one son Robert Hague. Executors: Son Robert Hague and E.M. Ringo. Signed January 11, 1847. Witnesses: William L. Hague and Charles Bright. He had partnership with William S. Hague. Proven February Term 1847.

Page 306 **WILL OF WILSON SCOTT.** Wife A--any Scott. Mentions his children but not by name. He owned 47 acres adjoining John Buchanan. Executor: Constant Smith. Signed February 5, 1847. Witnesses: H.H. Reives and John Williams. Proven and recorded March Term 1847.

Page 307 **WILL OF WILLIAM B. SHELTON.** Wife Mary B. Shelton. Brother Dr. E.M. Shelton. Executor: Brother Dr. E.M. Shelton. Witnesses: Joseph F. Brown, James Dunlap and John J. Clark. Proven and recorded March Term 1847.

Page 308 **WILL OF JAMES MILLS, SR.** Wife Elenor Mills. Children: Sarah Cunningham, Eliza H. Ashby, James W., Nancy C., Margaret Adeline, and Elizabeth Mills. Executors: H. Johnson and Samuel Brown, Esq. Signed May 31, 1847. Witnesses: Jesse Stoctill and Abner Steed. Proven June Term 1847.

Page 309 **WILL OF SAMUEL COLEMAN.** Wife Sarah Coleman. Children not named. Witnesses: Wife and Rebecca and son George Coleman. Signed February 22, 1847. Witnesses: Henry Bryan, George Coleman and H.J. Anderson. Proven June Term 1847.

Page 310 **WILL OF MILLY BARKER.** Three sons and two daughters: McKindre Whittenberry, Joseph N. Whittenberry and Norman H. and Margaret E., and Rebecca A. She mentions another son Charles H. Executor: Son Norman H. Whittenberry. Signed April 2, 1847. Witnesses: Samuel Rosebrough and Franklin R. Moore. Proven July Term 1847.

Page 311 **WILL OF J.A. SIMMONS.** Wife Hannah S. Simmons. Son Joseph Simmons. He mentions his five youngest children and his five oldest children but not by name. Executrix: Wife Hannah S. Simmons. Signed in the State of Texas, County of Dallas, July 23, 1846. Witnesses: John G. Gledwell and Daniel Freeman. Proven July Term 1847.

Page 312 **WILL OF JACK H. LEFTWICH.** Wife Jane Leftwich. Children: L.B., Fanny Bryant, Rebecca S. Gill, Polly R. Reese, Catharine G. Stone, Sarah Jane Neese, Nancy Gill, Fennetta Boon Bryant, Martha Ann Leftwich, also mentions a son L.B. Leftwich has undertaken to raise Patrick Purdom, a grandson of William N. Briant (Bryant). Executors: Wife Jane Leftwich and son L.B. Leftwich and Lewis Newsom and Joel Reese. Signed June 5, 1847. Witnesses: Samuel Boon, W.H. Bailey and J.N. Childres and Elizabeth Swan. Proven July Term 1847.

Page 317 **WILL OF A.B. SHULL.** Wife Eunice B. Shull. Mentions children but not by name. Executors: Wife Eunice B. Shull and Daniel B. Shull. Signed May 4, 1847. Witnesses: William Timmons and Joel Commons. Proven August Term 1847.

Page 317 **WILL OF HENRY TAYLOR, SR.** Wife Mary Taylor. Children: Henry Taylor, Jr. the youngest son, Lucinda Kennedy and Sarah English. Leaves to Sarah Buckes Dickens of the A.R.P. Church's # 2 Vol. Brown Dictionary, Bible and Psalms Book. To Hugh Taylor 1st Vol. Browns Dictionary. He mentions younger children but not by name. Signed November 6, 1845. Witnesses: William Kidd and Samuel H. Sloan. Executor: Henry Taylor, Jr. Proven August Term 1847.

Page 319 **WILL OF AMBROSE TIMMONS.** Wife Nancy Timmons. Children: John,

William, Mary Caldwell, Martha Ann Buchanan, Elizabeth, Abigail wife of Isaac Turney, Charles W. and Thomas Timmons. Three grandchildren: Ambrose T., Nancy and Rebecca Ann Turney the children of my daughter Amanda Turney and Jacob B. Turney. He had land about two miles west of Fayetteville on both sides of the road leading to Pulaski. Executor: (blank). Signed January 2, 1845. Witnesses: B.W.D. Carty, W. Bonner, R.E. Neeld and J. Clark, Jr. Codicil: Signed August 22, 1847. Proven September Term 1847.

Page 322 **WILL OF SALLY RHEA.** Children: Sally Ann Broyles wife of Jacob Broyles, Susan M. McLaughlin, Mary (Polly) B. Smith and her children: Frances S.E. and Rufus Smith, Altamira Isom, Brice M.G. Rhea, Pleasant V. Rhea and William B. Rhea and his wife Nancy Rhea. Executor: Son-in-law Jacob Broyles. Signed June 13, 1844. Witnesses: C. Norman and James Fuller. Proven September Term 1847.

Page 326 **WILL OF JOSHUA EWING.** Wife Mary Ewing. Children: Joshua Calvin, Samuel, William Donate, Elenor, Robert John, James Porter, Eliza and Jane Ewing. Signed June 29, 1842. Witnesses: Zebulon Parr and John M. Ewing. Proven September Term 1847.

Page 327 **WILL OF MOSES STONE.** Wife Peggy Stone. Children: John Stone, Peggy Stone, James A. Stone, Parthenia Stone, Calvin Stone, Emily J. Stone, Marinda Stone, Moses F. Stone, and Emily J. Brown a daughter of Matilda Brown, deceased, who was married to Jesse Brown, Isaac Williams who married Rebecca now deceased. Signed June 29, 1840. Witnesses: James Kyzer and James A. Stone. Recorded October 14, 1847.

Page 328 **WILL OF JOHN CRAWFORD.** Wife Elizabeth Crawford. Children: John, Ezekiel, Emily, Martha Lucinda, Nancy, Elizabeth and Margaret Crawford, seven children. Mentions older children in Arkansas: Hays, William D., James, Naomi, Elenor, Rachel, Nancy, Andrew W., Mary Ann, Margaret and Elizabeth. Executors: Alexander McDonald, William F. Kercheval, Esq. and son John Crawford. Signed January 10, 1846. Witnesses: H.C. Marcel and A.S. Boone. Recorded and approved October Term 1847.

Page 331 **WILL OF JOHN ARMSTRONG.** Mentions his wife but not by name. Son Josiah R. Armstrong. Four grandchildren: John Wesley Armstrong, Jasper Newton Armstrong, George Higgins Armstrong and Sarah Jane Armstrong. Signed December 24, 1846. Witnesses: James D. Cole, L.L. Cole and J.L. Cole. Proven and recorded November Term 1847.

Page 332 **WILL OF JESSE NEES.** Wife Sarah Jane Nees. Mentions children but not by name. Executors: Joel Reese and Dempsey Sullivan. Signed October 30, 1847. Witnesses: W.G. Commons and Samuel Barnes.

Page 333 **WILL OF SARAH SHAW.** Children: Peggy Watson and her children, Jesse B., John M., Sallu, Thomas, Hugh C., Robert F., Mary Jane and Margaret E. Watson and husband Samuel Watson, John J. Shaw and his wife Dicy and their daughter hannah Shaw. Owned land on Coldwater Creek. Also named a grandson William M. Shaw. Executor: Son Hugh Shaw. Signed October 20, 1847. Witnesses: W.B. Rhea and Isaac J. Holman. Proven December Term 1847.

Page 336 **WILL OF JAMES MARTIN.** Willed all to Nathan Pryor's wife Elizabeth Pryor and her heirs, etc. Son John H. Martin, daughter Susan Jane Robertson. Land on east side of Dukes Creek. Signed January 3, 1847. Witnesses: Henry Womack and James Cunningham.

Page 337 **WILL OF ALANSON A. SHERRELL.** Mentions his wife but not by name. He also said of his two children but not by name. Executors: His wife, Joseph L. Sherrell and David S. Patterson. Signed March 8, 1848. Witnesses: Joshua D. Brown and John Madden. Proven April Term 1848.

**Page 338** **WILL OF JOHN McKINNEY.** Eldest son Ethetrin McKinney, son Reuben McKinney and Henry McKinney. He mentioned a younger son but not by name. Signed April 21, 1848. Witnesses: J.D. Brown and Joshua G.W. McDaniel. Proven June Term 1848.

**Page 339** **WILL OF WILLIAM BIRMINGHAM.** Children: Berry, Amanda Jane, Curtis, James M., John, Sarah Cox, Caswell and Caleb and William Birmingham. Executors: Curtis and Berry Birmingham. Signed May 22, 1848. Witnesses: A.J. Higgins, Thomas J. Anderson and Ethetrin McKinney. Proven and recorded August Term 1848.

**Page 340** **WILL OF JAMES FROST.** Children: William C. Frost, John B. Frost, Lucinda Stephens, and Barbara wife of B.M. Jones. Granddaughters: Samantha and Sarah Coble. Executor: William Tolly. Signed August 7, 1847. Witnesses: Felix Davis and James R. Wright. Proven and recorded September Term 1848.

**Page 341** **WILL OF WILLIAM WILLIAMS.** Wife Louisa Williams. Children: Margaret Ann, Mary Ann, Barton, Susan Delong, Permelia Johnson, William Edward, Thomas Stephenson, Samuel Jefferson, and John Clark Williams. Executors: William Stephens and Eli L. Hodge. Signed October 2, 1848. Witnesses: A.M. Allred and James S. Smith. Proven and recorded November 22 Term 1848.

**Page 342** **WILL OF WILLIAM GRIFFIS.** Daughter Lucinda B. Booker, son William A. Griffis, and daughter-in-law Martha Griffis. Grandchildren: John W. Windell and Alfred James Henderson Windell. Executor: Thomas R. Griffis. Signed November 11, 1846. Witnesses: G.W. Jones, R.A. McDonald and J.B. Clements. Proven and recorded November Term 1848.

**Page 344** **WILL OF SAMUEL TATE.** Wife Mary J. Tate. 2nd son James L. Tate, 3rd son Andrew B. Tate, youngest son Robert J. Tate. Daughters (5): Lavina G. Tate, Eliza A. Tate, Agness J. Tate, Sarah M. Tate and Mary K.E. Tate. Eldest son William V. Tate. Executors: Son William V. Tate and wife Mary J. Tate. Signed October 12, 1848. Witnesses: J.V. McKinney and John J. Tate.

**Page 346** **WILL OF JOHN STRONG.** Wife Sarah Strong. Seven children: Polly, Catharine, Elizabeth, Darthula, Samuel C., Matilda A., and Daralee J. Strong. Signed December 5, 1845. Witnesses: Lemuel G. Mead and John H. Sullinger. Proven December 4, 1848.

**Page 347** **WILL OF ALEXANDER WILEY.** Wife Margret Wiley. Daughter Jane Wiley, son Lewis B. Wiley to get land in Tishomingo County, Mississippi, known as the Southeast Quarter Section 7 in Township 2, of Range 80 east of the Bases Meridian, according to the plan of the survey of the Chickasaw Cepien. Son Milton H. Wiley and sister Nancy Wiley. Executor: Son Lewis B. Wiley. Signed December 4, 1848. Witnesses: Robert Drennan and James Wiley. Proven and recorded February Term 1849.

**Page 349** **WILL OF JAMES ELLIS.** Wife Dolly Ellis. Daughter-in-law Judy Ellis. Granddaughter Arena Ellis and her sister Narcissa Walker and Polly. Grandson William Ellis. Signed August 16, 1845. Witnesses: Andrew Buchanan and White Buchanan.
Codicil: Signed August 10, 1848. Witness: Andrew Buchanan. recorded February 1849.

**Page 351** **WILL OF THOMAS L.D. PARKES.** Mentions a wife and children but not by name. Signed December 25, 1845. Witnesses: A son William and a daughter Ann Parkes. Signed January 23, 1846. Witnesses: G.W.S. Hart and Motlow.
Addition: Because of a letter written by A.M. Dean, the will is changed to prevent A.M. Dean from having the liberty to handle any more of his earnings and the balance of Ann's equal, if any, be placed in the Shelbyville Bank or some other institution which may be safe.

Codicil: January 8, 1849. Martin L. Parkes is guardian for Ann Dean. Executors: Wife Eliza Parkes and son William A. Parkes. Witnesses: Abram Sitliff and F.S. Mayfield. Proven and recorded February 1848.

Page 353  **WILL OF JOHN SMITH.**  Wife Nancy Smith.  Three youngest sons: Benjamin Childs, Thomas Jefferson and Napoleon Polk Smith.  Daughter Elizabeth Delana. Sons: Joshua, John N., and William Smith. Owns three tracts of land, two tracts in the State of Georgia and one in Tennessee. Executors: Sons John N. and William Smith. Signed January 26, 1847. Witnesses: William M. Parkes and Alexander McCollock.

Page 355  **WILL OF LEWIS BLEDSOE.**  Wife Fanny Bledsoe.  Grandson James Pinkney Bledsoe.  Great granddaughter and child of my granddaughter Mary Ann Burford.  Daughter Drucillah J. Bledsoe and Sarah Ann Bledsoe also a daughter.  Son James H. Bledsoe.  Son Henry M. Bledsoe.  Son Stephen W.J. Bledsoe.  Daughter Mary M. Bledsoe.  Executors: Henry M. Bledsoe, Stephen W.J. Bledsoe and James H. Bledsoe.  Signed May 10, 1848.  Witnesses: Thomas J. Anderson and W.E. Simms. Proven April Term 1849.

Page 358  **WILL OF HENRY SNOW, SR.**  Wife Anna Smow.  Children: Henry, William, Daniel, two youngest daughters, Catharine Braden and Alchy Braden.  Six other oldest daughters: Rebecca, Honea, Nancy, Mary, Elizabeth and Margaret Snow.  Executor: Son Henry Snow.  Signed April 26, 1844.  Witnesses: Johnathan Tripp and J. Waggoner.
Codicil: His six daughters living in North Carolina. July 20, 1847. Witnesses: J.W. Holman, W.B. Flack and James M. Spencer. Proven May 7, 1849.

Page 360  **WILL OF THOMAS GRANT.**  Wife Frances Grant.  Children: Elizabeth, Mary Jane, George Harison Grant, Charlotte Catharine Grant and Virginia Frances Grant.  Executor: C.W. McGuire.  Signed May 19, 1843. Witnesses: Josiah McCracken and Joseph McCoy.

Page 361  **WILL OF MARY JANE BUCHANAN.**  Father Robert Buchanan, deceased.  Brother Milton Buchanan.  Executor: Andrew Buchanan. Signed April 27, 1849. Witnesses: Howell Harris, Jr. and Henry Clift and Albert G. Gibson.  Recorded June 4, 1849.

Page 362  **WILL OF JOHN BEATY.**  Wife Joana Beaty.  Nine children: Eldest William B. Beaty, Martha who intermarried with Thomas McClellan, Robert Beaty, David M. beaty, John Beaty, Sarah Beaty, Andrew J. Beaty, Josiah Beaty and Jane Beaty.  Executors: Son William B. Beaty and son-in-law Thomas McClellan.  Signed August 9, 1840.  Witnesses: Isaac Southworth and G.M.C. Edmondson (Edmiston).
Codicil: Death of his wife Joana and daughter Sarah Beaty.  Signed December 21, 1841. Witnesses: Isaac Southworth and Thomas B. Eastland.

Page 365  **WILL OF JESSE STILES.**  Samuel Stiles.  Executors: W.M. Newman and Samuel Stiles.  Signed September 20, 1849.  Witnesses: W.H. McLaughlin, Daniel McPhail and James P. Landston. Proven in October Term 1849.

Page 366  **WILL OF JOHN V. McKINNEY.**  Wife not named.  Children: Rane, Mary, Martha and John McKinney.  Executor: Son Rane McKinney. Witnesses: Robert R. McKinney and Charles McKinney. He owned a Drug Store.
Codicil: Sale of Drug Store, etc, by private sale. Daughter Tabitha, daughter Eliza McKinney.  Executors: Sons Rane and John McKinney and his relation Robert R. McKinney.  Owns land in Mississippi.  Signed August 1, 1849.  Witnesses: Charles McKinney, Richard White and James Fulton. Recorded October Term 1849.

Page 369  **WILL OF HARVY ALLBRIGHT.** Mother Margaret Allbright.  Executor: Robert Drennan.  Signed October 1, 1849.  Witnesses: James E. English and Simpson Abbott.
Codicil: October 2, 1849. Witnesses: Simpson Abbott and Alexander Allbright.

Page 370 **WILL OF MOSES HARDIN.** Wife Orpha Hardin. Salina J. Carrigan, Wiley K. Hardin, Moses L. Hardin, Jr., Benjamin W.D. Hardin, Alfred W. Hardin's heirs, and Stanford H. Hardin's heirs. Signed May 12, 1849. Witnesses: Woodruff Parks and Thomas M. Wilson.

Page 371 **WILL OF THOMAS DANCE.** Mentions his wife also children who have already gone from home, except daughter Nancy, but not named. Executrix: His wife. Signed April 3, 1833. Witnesses: Stephen M. Dance, Thomas Dance and Louis Garner and Richard E. Bennett. At court held for Halifax County November 25, 1833. Thomas Dance deceased. Proven in Court and another court held for the said county December 23, 1833. Proven and recorded. Another Court held in August 25, 1834, on Sarah Dance. Witness: William Holt, Court Clerk.

Page 372 **WILL OF PHILIP PHAGAN.** Wife Jane Phagan. Children: Martha, John, Sarah, Mary Dale, Margaret, Elizabeth and Philip T. Phagan. Executors: Wife Jane Phagan and son Philip T. Phagan. Signed November 19, 1849. Witnesses: William Stephens, William D. Bright and William Lay.

Page 374 **WILL OF MARTHA C. McCONNELL.** Son Robert K. McConnell and daughter Mary E. McConnell, son-in-law H.C. Holman. Executors: Robert K. McConnell and W.F. Kercheval. Signed October 3, 1849. Witnesses: Joel Commons and S.M. McElroy. Proven December Term 1849.

Page 375 **WILL OF RACHEL GRAY.** Daughter Frances Smith wife of Francis Smith. Mentions other children but not by name. Witnesses: James Fulton and John T. Morgan.

Page 375 **WILL OF FENTON GREGORY.** Father Tunstill Gregory. Never married. Brother and partner Brown Gregory. Other brothers and sisters: Sarah Eslick, Emily Gregory, Mary Parks, Elizabeth McCartney, John F. Gregory, Rutha A. Gregory and Martha T. Gregory. Said Fenton Gregory died on August 14, 1849. This will was made in the presence of Moses H. Bonner and Tunstill Gregory. Made the will out and signed August 23, 1849.

Page 376 **WILL OF KATHARINE CARRIGER.** Children: Elizabeth Martin, Margaret Mardis, Leonard Carriger, Sarah Ingle, Mary Eaton, Cynthia Boone, Thomas J. Carriger and Christian Carriger, also a grandson Ido Carriger. Executor: Samuel Boone. Signed June 26, 1849. Witnesses: W.H. Bailey and Joel Rees.

Page 377 **WILL OF HENRY BECK.** Wife Louisa C. Beck. Brother Adam Beck. Brother Davanet Beck. Mentions Abraham Barnes, and Dr. John Wood. Executor: Abraham Barnes. Signed April 17, 1850. Witnesses: William Wyatt and Joshua Hughes.

Page 378 **WILL OF GEORGE GEE (A FREE MAN OF COLOR).** Two children: Esther and Cynthia who is owned by Dr. William Bonner. Other children: Mary who is the youngest child by his first wife, mentions other children but not by name. Owns a lot in Fayetteville. Executor: John Goodrich. Signed December 5, 1845. Witnesses: Thomas C. Goodrich and D.W. Russell. George Gee has bought his son Wiley from James Fulton, Robert Farquharson, R.A. McDonald at a price of $1200.00. Want his two daughters bought from Dr. William Bonner, Esther and Cynthia. He wanted his children to be freed, or they could go to Liberia to be a free person. Remaining children are owned by Elijah M. Ringo. Signed November 1, 1848. Witnesses: William Bonner and C.P. Beavers.

Page 380 **WILL OF JOHN MOORE, SR.** Wife Martha Moore. Son James Mc. Moore. Executor: Son James Mc. Moore. Signed March 15, 1849. Witnesses: John M. McFerrin and William G. Moore.

Page 382 **WILL OF MARTHA LEATHERMAN.** Son George Reed. Nancy Ann Wilson wife of Andrew Wilson. Mary Kenedy wife of John Kenedy. Jonas Leatherman. Executors: George Reed and Andrew Wilson. Signed August 5,

44

1846. Witnesses: Boone Wilson and David J. Hobbs.

Page 383 **WILL OF E.E. DISMUKES.** Wife Sarah C. Dismukes. Daughter Sarah E.L. Dismukes. Signed May 23, 1848. Witnesses: James D. Grisard and Hiram Reese. Executors: A.J. Carloss and William Lay, Sr.

Page 383 **WILL OF ARCHER BEASLEY.** Wife Nancy Beasley. Son Liberty Beasley. Ethelbart E. Davis and the heirs of Elizabeth Hobbs. Executor: Son Liberty Beasley. Signed February 2, 1833. Witnesses: Abraham Sumners, William G. Sumners, John Trantham and A.G. Downing. Proven March 26, 1839.

Page 385 **WILL OF STARKEY ROBERSON.** Conveys to his wife Caty Roberson land in District 19, and after the death of Caty, the land is to go to Stephen Sawyers. Signed May 7, 1850. Witnesses: Thomas George and John Spencer.

Page 385 **WILL OF GEORGE GEE (A FREE MAN OF COLOR).** Children: Ruth, Philip, Simeon, Nelson, Wiley, Jenny, Mary, Esther and Cynthia and wife who was not named. Executors: Henry Kelso and John Goodrich. Signed July 22, 1848. Witnesses: Constant P. Beavers, Samuel J. Isaacs and W.D. Blake. George Gee made a will some months ago and is in the possession of one said Elijah M. Ringo and cannot be readily got to or had and since making said will has purchased my son Wiley from James Fulton, Robert Farquharson and R.A. McDonald at the price of $1200.00, etc. Signed November 1, 1848.

Page 388 **WILL OF JAMES TOOLE.** Wife Catharine Toole. Children: William P. Toole, Ruth Ann Toole, grandson Sylvester Dewoody and granddaughter Lucinda Dewoody. Executor: Howell Harris, Jr. Signed June 2, 1849. Witnesses: Joel M. Harris and nathaniel Millard.

Page 391 **WILL OF ANDREW GLEGHORN.** John M. Gleghorn. Children: Betsey Jane, Hugh, Mary Elender, Martha Minerva, Sarah Susan, Rebecca, Urshala and Elgiva. Executors: John Watt and William A. Gault. Signed August 17, 1850. Witnesses: Robert Gleghorn and Joel C. Pigg.

Page 392 **WILL OF JAMES McREE.** Mother Elizabeth McRee. Sister Eliza consort of Jesse McAfee. Sister Cintha Reed consort of George Reed. Brother Carroll McRee. Sister Adaline Paysinger consort of Thomas A. Paysinger. Brother David W. McRee, Gallen McRee. Sister Elizabeth McRee. Sister Delina McRee. Sister Sarah E. McRee. Brother John McRee. Executors: P.W. Harper and John W. Watt. Signed August 21, 1850. Witnesses: P.W. Walton and H.C. Roberts.

Page 394 **WILL OF ROBERT McCLELAN.** Sarah McClelan. Mrs. Sarah McClelan and her three oldest children: Robert J., Margaret B., and Susan J. McClelan. Daughter Jane Davis the former wife of Absolom Davis, Henry Davis, and William Davis. Heirs of Sarah Wilson who was the wife of James Wilson. Heirs of daughter Nancy McNite and her two children: Robert and Samuel McNite. Heir of Eliza McClelan. Mary Gregory's heirs. William and Joseph McClelan. Two youngest daughters of Mrs. Sarah McClelan: Maria Thompson McClelan and Sarah Elizabeth Wilson McClelan. Owned a negro man in Williamson County. Executors: John G. McClelan and John Clark, Jr. Signed July 20, 1850. Witnesses: Robert R. McKinney and Jefferson Kelso.

Page 396 **WILL OF ANDREW W. WALKER.** Wife Elizabeth Walker. Son John F. Walker. Daughters: America Jean Walker, Columbia Walker, Polly Anthony who has five children: Carolina, Andrew, Jacob, George W.A., and Elizabeth W. Anthony. Children: Cincinnatte Edens, Maria, Peggy or Margaret Sullivant, Laureal Walker, James M., Thompson, Nancy Walker, and Harriet Walker. Executors: Elizabeth Walker and James M. Walker. Signed June 18, 1840. Witnesses: B.H. Berry, W.P. Edde and T.H. Shaw.
Codicil: August 3, 1850. Witnesses: J.A. Saintclair, F. Motlow and James H. Shaw.

Page 400  **WILL OF JAMES A. BUCHANAN.** Brother David S. Buchanan. Sister Amanda H.M. Buchanan. Sister Minerva A. Buchanan. Father Moses Buchanan. Aunt Patsey wife of Alfred Smith. Signed August 3, 1850. Witnesses: George Martin and John M. Smith.

Page 401  **WILL OF ALLICE R. SHARP.** Son Benjamin F. Sharp. Daughter Nancy Gray. Granddaughter Allice Ann Reed Sherrell. Granddaughter Bathea Gray. Executor: Benjamin F. Sharp. Signed February 19, 1849. Witnesses: E.M. Ringo and John M. Bright.

Page 404  **WILL OF WILLIAM KENNON.** Two wifes: Amelia and Polly Kennon. Both had children. Samuel D. Buchanan. Two grandchildren: William A. and Francis E. Short. Son Meraweather L. Kennon. Son Ellsworth R. Kennon. Executors: Charles McKinney and John V. McKinney. Signed August 15, 1839. Witnesses: Peter G. McMullen and W.C. Riggins.

Page 405  **WILL OF JAMES WEST.** Heirs of son William West. Son Rhodes West. Son James S. West. Son Alfred West. Daughter Margret Device. Heirs of daughter Elizabeth. Daughter Sarah Luster. Son Josephus West, and Andrew Jackson West. Wife Margaretta West. Executor: Pleasant Halbert. Signed May 6, 1850. Witnesses: Mathew Wilson, John Wood and William McMillen.


## LINCOLN COUNTY, TENNESSEE WILL BOOK 2

Page 1  **WILL OF JOHN W. HORTON.** Letter from John W. Horton to his mother on March 1, 1859, stating that he was leaving the next day for California, if he didn't return, he wanted B.F. Hudson to settle his business. He wanted James to have his cloths. Mentions brothers and sisters but not by name.

Page 2  **WILL OF CHARLES McNATT.** Wife Elizabeth McNatt. Children: John McNatt, James McNatt, Sarah McNatt, Sophia McNatt, Nancy Burns, Mary Wright, and a step-daughter Lucinda Cobb. Executor: Daniel Warren. Signed October 2, 1847. Witnesses: A.G. Harris and J.E. Prosser and James Raby.

Page 3  **WILL OF JOHN DUSENBERRY.** Wife Susan Dusenberry. Green L. McLain. Granddaughter Susan A. Moyers. Granddaughter Martha M. McLain. Granddaughters: Virginia J. McLain, Laury E. McLain. Grandson John D. McLain. Other children: Martha Ann Dusenberry, Henry F. Dusenberry and John Dusenberry. Executors: Paul Ingle and William Tolly. Signed July 18, 1850. Witnesses: N. Whitaker and Joseph Pruitt.

Page 3  **WILL OF DOILEY GRIFFIS.** Wife Nancy Griffis. Mentions children but not by name. Signed March 12, 1857. Witnesses: J.B. Shuffield and Robert Drennan. Proven April Term 1857.

Page 5  **WILL OF CYRENA SMITH.** Son Alfred Smith. Clarissa Smith. Elizabeth Smith. Nancy Smith. Brother-in-law John Smith is the executor. Signed April 23, 1857. Witnesses: William N. Hicks, William Stephens, Emily Street and Martha L. Smith. Recorded March Term 1857.

Page 6  **WILL OF JOEL DOLLINS.** Wife Polly Dollins. Children: David B. Dollins. Sophia E. Stone, Andrew H. Dollins, James D. Dollins, Julia A. Dollins, Nancy I. Dollins, and Joel F. Dollins. Executors: Three sons David B., Andrew A. and James D. Dollins. Signed December 26, 1844. Witnesses: J.M. Dollins, John J. Dollins and Marion P. Dollins.

Page 7  **WILL OF JAMES EDDE.** Mentions his wife but not by name. Children: Hiram, Moses P., Fanny M. Enochs, Patience Reese, and Mitchell Edde. Executors: Son Mitchell and William Edde. Signed September 8, 1850. Witnesses: John Bird and Daniel Brown. Recorded July 1857.

Page 8 **WILL OF ELI MONKS.** Wife Margaret Monks. Son James Monks. Son-in-law John Simmons and wife Sarah. Son-in-law James Henderson and wife Mary. Signed December 18, 1848. Witnesses: James Pinkerton and Joseph Clarke.

Page 9 **WILL OF JEREMIAH HEDGEPETH.** Wife Charlotte Hedgepeth. Thirteen children: Elmira Jane, Charlotte Manerva, Lucinda Lumisa, Matilda Curie, Sarah, Micajah Peacock, Allen Broadway, Jeremiah Walker, David Enochs, Samuel McDaniel, William Robert, Isaac Newton, and Larkin Cleveland. Signed April 16, 1857. Witnesses: Pleasant Halbert, G.W.P. Mooney, A. Cathey and George Oliver.

Page 11 **WILL OF ELIZABETH JENNINGS.** Granddaughter Lucy Ann James. Granddaughter Micha Elizabeth Hindman. Granddaughter Mary Nichols Bledsoe. Grandson Benjamin Pleasant Jennings. Granddaughter Susan Frances Stephenson. Granddaughter Sarah Hamey Jennings. Grandson Pleasant Wilson Weaver. Grandson John William Weaver, and Samuel Madison Weaver. Signed September 16, 1857. Witnesses: Jacob Vance and William E. Hunnicut. Recorded September 16, 1857.

Page 13 **WILL OF FELIX G. GIBSON.** Wife ____. Daughter Nancy A. Carter. Daughter Mary Jane Royester. Son John Gibson and James Gibson. Mentions other daughters but not by name. Executors: S.S. Buchanan and nephew William S. Buchanan. Signed April 17, 1857. Witnesses: Albert G. Gibson and Lee Smith.
NOTE: Wife was Minerva Clayton a daughter of Stephen Clayton, Eds)
Codicil: June 15, 1857. Witnesses: Joel M. Harris and Charles McKinney.
Additional Codicil: April 17, 1857. Signed June 19, 1857. Witnesses: Albert G. Gibson and Robert B. Gibson.

Page 17 **WILL OF JOHN GUTHRIE.** Children: Sarah H. wife of Hugh R. Hodge, James C. Guthrie and his wife Nancy, Susan M. wife of Thomas Baxter, Lucinda A. Guthrie, Mary H. Coleman, Sophia Walker, Reuben F. Guthrie, and Sampson H. Guthrie. His desire is to be buried in the graveyard at Stephen M. Dance's place. Executors: James P. Baxter, Patsey Williams and Elizabeth C. Baxter. Signed June 9, 1848. Witnesses: G.M. Dance and J.W.H(N). Dance.

Page 18 **WILL OF BENJAMIN M. WILLIAMS.** Daughter Emeline K. Coleman. Signed October 28, 1837. Witnesses: John Franklin, Jr. and Robert Smith. Recorded December Term 1837.

Page 19 **WILL OF ELIAS SCOTT.** Wife Margaret Scott. Son John Scott. Daughter Angeline A.(Artififter) Brunts (Brents). Daughter Arena Scott. Daughter Elizabeth Couch. Daughter Mary Jones. Daughter Sarah Wilson, and Nancy Linch. Grandson Eli McGeehee and granddaughter Dorana McGeehee. Executor: Andrew Laws of Marshall County, Tennessee. Signed 1843. Witnesses: John Moorehead and Henry Renegar.

Page 21 **WILL OF JACOB HAMILTON.** Wife Elizabeth Hamilton. Children: Eddey A., Jasper S., Ezekiek Wilson, Alexander, Newton A.G., Sarah, Jane, Lucy Lucinda, Evaline and Nancy. Mentions Jane's grandmother as Jane Brown. Other children named: Mary Enicy, Thomas, James P., and Lucetta B. Son-in-law William Walker. Executors: Son Alexander Hamilton and son-in-law William Walker. Signed October 28, 1851. Witnesses: Gilbert Robertson, James A. Walker and Reuben Stone. Proven and recorded February 14, 1852.

Page 23 **WILL OF TEMPLE TAYLOR.** Wife Jane Taylor. Children: William Y., Henry C., James, A.J., Alexander, Milly, Susan Alexander, Cintha Shelton, Elizabeth Shelton, Emaline Martin Taylor, William and Jane Scott who is living with family. Executor: Young L. Taylor. Signed December 13, 1851. Witnesses: J.B. Griffis and J.T. Landess.

**Page 24** **WILL OF BENJAMIN W. HARDIN.** "We, John S. Fulton, George Gant and Charles C. McKinney, witnessed Benjamin W. Hardin make his last will on September 23, 1851. All estate and negroes be divided between his brothers Wiley and Moses Hardin and his sister who was not named. Made and signed by us October 3, 1851."

**Page 25** **WILL OF SAMUEL BUCHANAN.** Wife Rachael Buchanan. Daughter Martha Jane Buchanan, son William Buchanan, eldest son Greenfield Buchanan and his only child Vesta Buchanan, daughter Millissa P. Buchanan and son Colman C. Buchanan, the heirs of Martha Revis: Mary, John W. and Cyrus A. Revis. Grandchildren: Greenfield and Mary Jane, children of my daughter Elizabeth, granddaughter Martha Revis of my daughter Nancy, and daughter Lucy Adeline Buchanan. Signed January 27, 1852. Witnesses: C.F. Edmiston and John Buchanan.

**Page 27** **WILL OF SUSANAH DOBBINS.** Heirs of my deceased daughter Doshie Hall the consort of Samuel Hall, heirs of my deceased son John Dobbins, the heirs of my deceased daughter Elizabeth Pinson consort of Joel Pinson, and Sally Edmiston former consort of John Dobbins. Executors: T.W. Harper and Samuel Hall. Signed September 4, 1849. Witnesses: John Caldwell and Samuel Caldwell.

**Page 28** **WILL OF STITHE H. MEAD.** Wife Betsy Mead. Four children: Lemuel G. Mead, Mary M. Mead, Marcus L. Mead, and Susan J. Thompson. Executor: Enos Wilson. Signed (no date). Witnesses: Thomas M. Wilson and Andrew Cashion.

**Page 29** **WILL OF NANCY WHITAKER.** Two sons: Madison G. and Newton Whitaker. Executor: Son Newton Whitaker. Signed November 12, 1851. Witnesses: William Moore and Franklin R. Moore. Proven May Term 1852.

**Page 30** **WILL OF B.M.G. RHEA.** Sister Susan McLaughlin and her four daughters: _____, Glenn, Agness and Annah B. McLaughlin. Brother Pleasant V. Rhea. Brother W.B. Rhea. Sister Myra Isham, Polly Smith and Sally Ann Rhea. Signed July 5, 1852. Witnesses: H.F. Robertson and Robert R. McKinney. Proven August Term 1852.

**Page 31** **WILL OF JAMES CREASON.** Wife Rebecca Creason. Children: Sarah Ann, Catharine E., Louisa C., James F., Mary F., Martha R., George, M.D., Margaret E., Susan A., and Permelia E. Creason. Executor: Christian Carriger. Signed April 28, 1852. Witnesses: Samuel Boone and John Cunningham. Proven 1st Monday in August Term 1852.

**Page 32** **WILL OF JOSHUA D. BROWN.** Wife Sarah B. Brown. My wife's child Vesta Carrella and six children: Mary E., Finis H., Martha J., Mariah Ann, Margaret Elizabeth, and Andrew Jackson Brown. Daughter Vesta Carrella willed all the interest my wife Sarah B. Brown may acquire by decent or contribution from her father William Anderson's land estate. Calvin Thomas gets a bound boy. Executors: Robert C. Ewing and W.W. Petty. Signed June 28, 1852. Witnesses: W.M. Byers and John A. Hill. Proven September 6, 1852.

**Page 34** **WILL OF WILLIAM TIMMINS.** Wife Florence Timmins. Daughter Mary Steele and her daughter Margaret Robertson. Owned Lor 78 in Fayetteville. Executrix: Wife Florence Timmins. Trustee: William Timmins, Jr. Signed September 9, 1847. Proven October Term 1852.

**Page 37** **WILL OF WILLIAM McCLELLAN.** Wife Caroline Matilda McClellan. Son William A. McClellan, my eldest child, a daughter Julia wife of James B. Wright and their only son William N. Wright, a son Thomas J., son John G., James C., and grandchildren: Robert Constantine and Matilda Jane Davis all children of my deceased daughter Charlotta who intermarried with Henry Davis, both of whom are dead. Executors: Sons Thomas J. and William A. McClellan.

Signed June 11, 1852. Witnesses: B.W.D. Carty and A.J. Carloss. Proven October Term 1852.

Page 39  **WILL OF JOHN M. EWING.** Wife Mary E.J. Ewing. Children: Mary F. Ewing, William D. Ewing and Robert C. Ewing and they are to windup the estate of Elizabeth Jennings and take in hand the guardianship of four minor heirs of Jacob VanHoozer, deceased. Signed September 18, 1852. Witnesses: Abraham Eddins, M.W. Petty and John A. Sumners. Proven October Term 1852.

Page 41  **WILL OF JAMES WISE.** Children: Louisa, James Wesley, William Riley, Mary Ann, Rhody Malvina, Manuel THomas, Rutha Luhany, Matthew Levi, David, Sarah, Elizabeth, Mahula and Elender Wise. Executor: James M. Bryans. Signed March 3, 1849. Witnesses: Robert M. Cowser and James Kirkland. Proven November Term 1852.

Page 42  **WILL OF COALBY GRAY.** Wife Hannah Gray. Six children: David S., John D., Brice P., Joshua D., Martha Caroline, and Sarah Elizabeth Gray. Executor: Son David S. Gray. Signed August 6, 1849. Witnesses: Young T. Taylor and James Stiles. Proven December Term 1852.

Page 44  **WILL OF DANIEL BROWN.** Wife Elizabeth Brown. Mentioned his children but not by name. Signed November 4, 1852. Witnesses: L.S. Woodard and John E. Gore. Proven January Term 1852.

Page 45  **WILL OF CHRISTOPHER HOWARD.** (Died October 19, 1852) His will was made a few hours before his death on the above date. Wife Jane Howard. Son William Howard. Newton Littrell. Property on west side of the East Fork of Mulberry Creek, also land on Shelton's Creek. Executor: to be James Fulton and if he can't, Charles Bright. Signed October 21, 1852. Witnesses: F.R. Moore, W.A. Wood, George Berry, R.M. Houze and David Roser. Proven December 1853.

Page 46  **WILL OF ANDREW CAUGHRAN.** Wife Sarah Caughran. Three children, which he did not name. Land in Jackson County, Arkansas. Executors: John T. Caughran and Robert Drennan. Signed January 18, 1853. Witnesses: J.A. Stuart and W.P. Caughran. Proven February Term 1853.

Page 47  **WILL OF PRYOR BUCHANAN.** Two daughters: Sarah M. and Mary L. Buchanan. He appointed his friend Pleasant Halbert as guardian for his two daughters. Executors: Samuel S. Buchanan and Joel M. Harris. Signed November 11, 1852. Witnesses: James Fulton and Gideon Lay. Proven February Term 1853.

Page 49  **WILL OF ALFRED H. BERRY.** Wife Rebecca H. Berry. Children: Henry and Joel Alfred Berry. Executor: James H. Cobb. Signed March 15, 1853. Witnesses: W.W. McNeely and N.O. Wallace. Recorded April Term 1853.

Page 51  **WILL OF WILLIAM HAMILTON.** John Hamilton and Newton Hamilton. Executor: Enoch Hamilton. Signed March 20, 1849. Witnesses: William Tally, Alfred Eaton and A.W. Parks. Proven May Term 1853.

Page 52  **WILL OF JOHN LOCK.** Wife Elizabeth Lock. Children: William, Rebecca Crutsinger, Emily Mullins, Eliza Ann, Samuel K., Jacob, Thomas, Erastus, Calvin, Sidney Lock and Mary Lock. Executors: Samuel K. Lock and Calvin Lock. Signed March 29, 1853. Witnesses: William C. Bland and James R. Bland. Proven May Term 1853.

Page 54  **WILL OF JOHN J. WHITAKER.** Son Rufus Whitaker and son Charles Whitaker. $100.00 to Indian Mission Association and $100.00 to China Mission Association. Executors: Son-in-law William Rhea and Harrison Reese. Signed August 16, 1846. Witnesses: W.F. Smith and Robert Martin. Proven June Term 1853.

Page 55    **WILL OF RHODES WEST.** Wife Elizabeth West. Daughter Sarah A. West and the youngest daughters Isabella C. and Eliza C. West. Executor: William Wyatt. Signed June 11, 1853. Witnesses: William Wyatt and John Wyatt. Proven July Term 1853.

Page 56    **WILL OF PHILIP KYSOR.** Sons: Gabrael and James Kysor. Joseph Clark. Dice, a slave woman. Calvin Stone. Executors: Frederick Waggoner and Calvin Stone. Signed June 8, 1853. Witnesses: Alexander Forester and Andrew Waggoner. Proven July Term 1853.

Page 57    **WILL OF EZERIAH McAFEE.** Wife Jane McAfee. Ten children: Mandy, Jane wife of Doak Hoots, Emeline wife of David T.C. Allen, Polly Ann wife of Daniel J. Watson, Benjamin F. McAfee, Martha A., Cintha C., Smith A., George W., Thomas W., and Chloe Lutua McAfee. Executor: Smith Alexander. Signed October 6, 1852. Witnesses: Travis Ashby and Moses W. Yant. Proven August Term 1853.

Page 58    **WILL OF ALEXANDER CAUGHRAN.** Mother not named. Sisters Mary Ann and Sarah Caughran. Brothers Manson and Oliver Caughran. Executors: Brothers Oliver and Manson Caughran. Signed July 8, 1853. Witnesses: Robert Drennan and James Wiley. Proven August Term 1853.

Page 59    **WILL OF WILLIAM PRICE.** Wife Rebecca Price. Daughter Mary J.F. Price. Executor: Thomas Gore. Signed August 16, 1853. Witnesses: L.S. Woodward and T.P. Green. Proven September Term 1853.

Page 60    **WILL OF WILLIAM G. SPENCE.** Fanny Spence. Children: Mary Ann, Martha Elizabeth, Nancy Means, Sarah Jane, Arminta Margaret, Hannah Bryson, Esther Wilson, Samuel Thompson, William Stewart and Alexander Curtis Spence. Executor: A.M. Gallaway. Signed August 6, 1853. Witnesses: James Wiley and Alexander J. Stewart.

Page 61    **WILL OF JAMES McKINNEY.** Wife Sarah McKinney. Eldest son Galen, 2nd son Ira, 3rd son James, and 4th son L.H. McKinney. Executor: Robert S. Woodard. Signed July 22, 1848. Witnesses: William M. McKinney and G.W. Sawyers. Proven September Term 1853.

Page 62    **WILL OF STEPHEN M. DANCE.** Wife S. Dance. Stephen M. Dance died April 25, 1850. Children: S.E.H. Dance and H.S.G. Dance. Witnesses: J.T.S. Dance and D.L. Enochs. August 22, 1853.

Page 63    **WILL OF EDMUND TOWNSEND.** Probate Court of Madison County, May 2, 1853. Petition of Charles H. Patton, John E. Townsend, Samuel Townsend, and Edward G. Townsend witnessed a will of Edmund Townsend, deceased, of Madison County, made and published his will. He left no widow or children but the next of kin a brother Samuel Townsend, a testator, of Madison County, Alabama, John E. Townsend, Montford R. Townsend, Samuel C. Townsend and Park Townsend, children of said testator, deceased, brother Park Townsend, deceased, all of Madison County, Alabama. Elizabeth wife of Archibald Townsend, Jane wife of Upton Craw, Rutha wife of Jones Craw, Celia wife of Thomas Smith, Mary Ann Townsend, Louisa and Joseph Townsend who live in Virginia. Thomas and Daniel Townsend live in Tennessee, all are children of testator's deceased sister. Probated May 14, 1853. (7 pages of will)

Page 70    **WILL OF WILLIS R. MILAM.** Wife Margaret Milam. Children: Betsey, Mary, James Wiley, and Madison Alexander Milam. Brother Wiley G. Milam. Signed September 18, 1853. Witnesses: Jesse Leatherwood and Larkin Smith. Proven October Term 1853.

Page 71    **WILL OF WILLIAM BRIGHT, SR.** Children: William D., James, Catharine Carty, Nancy Crawford and Charles Bright. Grandson Joseph T. Williams. Granddaughter Elizabeth W. Hicks and granddaughter Mary Ann

Bright. Witnesses: D.C. Hall, A.H. Bishop, Robert Drennan, William A. McClellan and William Stephens. Signed September 1, 1853.

Page 74 **WILL OF DANIEL LEE.** Children: Rutha Lee, heirs of my deceased daughter Gincy wife of W.J. Williamson, Elizabeth Neely, Polly Young, Nancy wife of William Whorley. Granddaughter Elizabeth Williams(Williamson). Grandsons Calvin and Coleman Lee. Executors: B.M.G. Allsup and S.M. Emmons. Signed August 6, 1851. Witnesses: Anderson Allsup, Henry Robeson and John Roberson.
Codicil: Graveyard reserved on place and a wall to be built around it, 4 feet high and 18 inches thick. Witness: John T. Wilson. Proven November Term 1853.

Page 76 **WILL OF WILLIAM P. LAND.** Wife Eddy Land who is weak in mind. Children: Vercena Ellen and Eddy M. Land. Father mentioned but not by name. Brother M.B. Land who is to be executor. Signed October 17, 1853. Witnesses: Larkin Smith and William Land. Proven November 7, 1853.

Page 77 **WILL OF RALPH SMITH.** Wife Elizabeth Smith. Children: John, Joseph, Thomas, James, Ralph, Johnathan, Margaret Shorter, or her child Lucinda, Nancy McCown, Elizabeth Hawkins and Suzy Cooper. Signed January 10, 1843. Witnesses: William Stephens and Jesse Hawkins. Proven December 5, 1853.

Page 78 **WILL OF DAVID S. BUCHANAN.** Wife Nancy Buchanan. Sisters: H.M. and Minerva A. Buchanan. Brother James Buchanan. Martha Edmiston. John M. Smith gets his Naval Uniform received from brother James Buchanan also his sword, cap, sash, etc. Nephew James Moffett, William Moffett. A relative Alfred Smith gets his Mexican Saddle, etc. Amanda Dickinson gets large silver mess Spoon which belonged to his brother James BUchanan. Mentions grandfather Robert Buchanan's estate also services of James Buchanan in Naval or Marine Service. Executor: Alfred Smith. Signed October 11, 1853. Witnesses: J.V. McKinney and S.M. McElroy.

Page 79 **WILL OF WILLIAM G. HAMILTON.** Nephew and niece: William Joseph and Mary Elizabeth, heirs of James Hamilton. Elizabeth S. Bledsoe. Executor: Thomas H. Bledsoe. Signed December 17, 1853. Witnesses: L.M. Stephenson and John G. Bledsoe. Proven January Term 1854.

Page 81 **WILL OF ANNA WILLIAMS.** Daughter-in-law Lucinda Williams. Son Morgan M. Williams, son Daniel T. Williams, daughter Sally Childs, and daughter Anna Tooley. Executor: Constant Smith. Signed October 10, 1853. Witnesses: Davis Smith and John Dyer.

Page 82 **WILL OF THOMAS SPENCER.** Wife Mary Spencer. Children mentioned but not by name. Executors: Wife Mary Spencer and William Spencer. Signed September 23, 1848. Witnesses: B.E. Spencer and Alfred M. Spencer.

Page 83 **WILL OF REBECCA HENDERSON.** Son John L. Henderson. Grandson James H. Henderson. Daughter Mary G. Hearlson. Grandson Ephraim L. Hearlson. Granddaughter Elizabeth W. Hearlson. Signed October 21, 1852. Witnesses: Henry Childs, A.W. Stroud and James Dunlap.

Page 84 **WILL OF HENRY CLIFT.** Wife Jane Clift. Three daughters: Susan Moffett, Louisa Clift and Nancy Smith. Two sons: Joseph H. and Alexander P. Clift. Grandson and granddaughter: Charles Henry and Sarah Clift, children of William Clift, deceased. Executor: Aldred (Alfred) W. Smith. Signed January 26, 1854. Witnesses: Joel M. Harris and Howell Harris, Jr.

Page 85 **WILL OF ABNER FREEMAN.** Wife Drucilla Freeman. Six minor heirs, other older children not numbered or named. Signed March 8, 1850. Witnesses: James Wilson, James Barham and John G. Glidewell.

Page 86    **WILL OF GEORGE CUNNINGHAM.**   Wife Permelia A. Cunningham. Daughter Louisa Virginia Cunningham. He owned a house and lot in Fayetteville and owned land on Mulberry Creek. Executor: Peter Cunningham, Sr. Peter Cunningham was appointed guardian of his daughter Louisa Virginia. Signed June 23, 1854. Witnesses: W.B. Rhea and J.L. Dusenberry.

Page 87    **WILL OF HUGH R. HAMILTON.**   Wife Mary Hamilton. Seven children: Susan C., William F., James C., Nancy Ann, Robert B., Samuel W., and also an infant son not yet named. Executors: Peter L. Hamilton and William F. Zimmerman. Signed June 27, 1854. Witnesses: Joseph Askins, Robert H. McMullen and Robert A. Hamilton. Proven September 4, 1854.

Page 88    **WILL OF DAVID W. GEORGE.**   Wife Nancy George. Sons: William P.A. and James N. George. Executors: William P.A. and James N. George. Signed June 27, 1854. Witnesses: C.W. McGuire and Needham George. Proven September 4, 1854.

Page 89    **WILL OF CORNELIUS N. SLATER.**   Friends and kinsman Mr. William T. Ross. He has interest in California Company. Executor: Col. James Fulton. Signed March 2, 1849. Witnesses: John M. Bright and M.W. Robinson. Proven September 4, 1854.

Page 90    **WILL OF ROSINA B. HOWELL.**   Mother Elizabeth Howell. Sister Altabitha C. Howell, and Charles S. Howell. Executor: Charles S. Howell. Signed July 12, 1854. Witnesses: Smith L. Walker and Joshua Smith. Recorded September 4, 1854.

Page 91    **WILL OF MARY SLATER.** (Deceased).   Daughter Mary M. Slater. Appointed her son Peter M. Ross as guardian of daughter Mary M. Slater. Son William T. Ross appointed as guardian of Cornelius N. Slater. Executors: Sons Peter M. Ross and William T. Ross. Signed July 9, 1840. Witnesses: John O. Griffis and S. Gullett. Proven September 4, 1854. Codicil: Proven September 4, 1854.

Page 95    **WILL OF ALLEN PARKS.**   Wife Mary Parks. Four children: Sarah E., Mary E., Martha A., and Susan A. Parks. Executor: John F. Gregory. Signed May 4, 1854. Witnesses: C.B. McDaniel and William M. James. Proven June 5, 1854.

Page 96    **WILL OF MAJOR MITCHELL. (A FREE MAN OF COLOR).**   Wife Milly. Daughter Ann a slave of Dr. William Bonner. Son Milby a slave of William Bonner. His wife Milly a slave, given to Reubin A. McDonald and William F. Kercheval. He lives in the town of Fayetteville. Executors: Friends Reuben A. McDonald and William F. Kercheval. Signed June 8, 1854. Witnesses: Hiram Phillips and B.W.D. Carty. Proven November Term 1854.

Page 99    **WILL OF JUDGE DUNKIN.**   Wife Susan Dunkin. Eldest daughter Rebecca now Rebecca Cothrun, 2nd daughter Mary Ann Elizabeth, and others: Nancy Jane, Susan Caroline, Polly Conger, Sarah P., and Frances Moore. Three sons: John Thomas, William Watson and James Wiley Dunkin. Executors: Christian Carriger and John H. Steelman. Signed October 19, 1854. Witnesses: David Sullivan and Joseph T. Moore. Proven November 6, 1854.

Page 101    **WILL OF CYNTHIA HUNTER.**   Daughter Polly wife of William McElroy, Niece Dicy Taylor widow of James Scott. Grandson P.A. McDonald, grandson William Hunter, daughter Sarah wife of Elijah Davis and their two daughters: Katharine and Polly Davis, grandchildren of Sherrod and Nancy Jane Hunter, Frances Hunter and son-in-law Elijah Davis, son Jackson and Cynthia the wife of John Bronson, Reubin Davis and Frances Davis. Executor: Grandson Reuben A. McDonald, also as guardian of my grandchildren: Nancy Ann, Sherrod and Frances Elizabeth Hunter. Signed August 19, 1840. Witnesses: M.L. Dismukes and A.P. Smith.
Codicil: August 18, 1843. Proven November 6, 1854.

Page 103 **WILL OF DAVID S. GRAY.** Wife Mary G. Gray. Children: John S. Gray, Brice P. Gray, James E. Gray, David N. Gray, George Gray, and W.J. Gray. Executor: John H. Taylor. Signed December 12, 1854. Witnesses: B.H. Berry and H. Whitfield. Proven January 1, 1855.

Page 104 **WILL OF JOHN MOTLOW.** Children: Feliz G., Louisa M., Mary B., James M., John L., Nancy A., and Caroline T. Motlow. He gave one (1) acre of land for the purpose of a Female Academy. Executors: Sons Felix G. and John L. Motlow. Signed December 12, 1854. Witnesses: John A. Motlow and John H. Taylor. Proven January 1, 1855.

Page 105 **WILL OF IREDELL D. BRAY.** Five children, 4 daughters and 1 son William. The other children and his wife are not named. Executor: Wiley M. Newman. Signed January 2, 1855. Witnesses: Wiley M. Newman, William R. Bryan and Hiram Bray. Proven February Term 1855.

Page 107 **WILL OF JAMES PROSSER.** Wife Frances Prosser. Son Mark Prosser. Daughters: Mary Amelia, Elizabeth Frances and Nepsey Prosser. Executors: Lewis Newsom, Esq. and John D. Prosser. Signed May 7, 1854. Witnesses: John Landess, Lewis Newsom and John D. Prosser. Proven March 5, 1855.

Page 108 **WILL OF JOHN J. DOLLINS.** Four brothers: William A., Milton S., Joel M., and Miles M. Dollins. Sister Anna E. Dollins. Three married sisters: Mary A.R. Downing, Jane K. Fuller and Margaret H. Colter. Executors: Brothers William A. and Milton S. Dollins. Signed March 1, 1855. Witnesses: Arthur Washburn and James S. Brown. Proven April 2, 1855.

Page 109 **WILL OF ALVIS FLACK.** Wife Amanda Flack. Executor: James G. Harrison. Signed April 29, 1855. Witnesses: H.H. Rives and William Sorrells. Proven June 4, 1855.

Page 110 **WILL OF WILLIAM WILLIAMS.** Son Thomas S. Williams and Victoria Ray. Executor: Tunstall Gregory. Signed July 13, 1855. Witnesses: Robert T. Searcy and Jacob Stonebraker. Recorded July 7, 1855.

Page 111 **WILL OF ROBERT K. McCONNELL.** Two nephews: Robert F. Holman and Robert F. Hill. Signed August 14, 1855. Witnesses: B.F. Ramsey, H.M. Ramsey, H.M. Edmondson, and R. Farquharson. Proven September 5, 1855.

Page 111 **WILL OF THOMAS A. OWEN.** Only brother Marcus L. Owen. A faithful friend Miss Mary Winn. $500.00 to Cumberland Presbyterian Theological School in Lebanon, Tennessee. Executor: Brother Marcus L. Owen. Signed June 29, 1855. Witnesses: C.A. Diemer and John Goodrich. Proven September 3, 1855.

Page 112 **WILL OF JOHN L. HENDERSON.** Wife Priscilla Henderson. Eight children: Sarah A., James W., William A., Basil L., Maria E., John A., Victoria A., and Spencer J. Henderson. Executor: Norris Leatherwood. Signed August 19, 1855. Witnesses: D.L. Patterson and John Maddox. Proven September 3, 1855.

Page 113 **WILL OF EDWARD MOSS.** Wife ____(Elizabeth) Moss. Children: George W. Moss, Nancy Burton, Drucilla Towry and Robert C. Moss. Grandchildren: James C. Benton and Chambers P. Moss. Executors: James Burton, George W. Moss and J.L. Thompson. Signed June 20, 1854. Witnesses: J.L. Thompson and A.C. Meek. Proven October 1, 1855.

Page 115 **WILL OF SARAH DAVIS.** Daughter Margaret E. Davis. Daughter Sarah Ann Johnson, and granddaughter Sarah Jane McMillen. Executor: Edward Johnson. Witnesses: James L. Thompson and William Rosen. Signed October 7, 1850. Proven October 1, 1855.

Page 116 **WILL OF HENRY TAYLOR.** Wife Katharine Taylor. Children: Mary M., Martha R., Samuel H., Hannah B., Henry B., Katharine H., Sarah A.M., Lucinda Jane and Erastus B. Taylor.

Page 117 **WILL OF WILLIAM A. ROBINSON.** Wife Sophronia Robinson. Son Stephen Lafayette Robinson. Witnesses: Stephen E. Emmons and Henry Robinson. Signed October 1, 1855. Proven October Term 1855.

Page 118 **WILL OF BENJAMIN F. SHARP.** Seven children: Elizabeth Smith, Bethenia Gracy, John H. Gracy, William Gracy, Tranquilla Gracy and Betsena Gracy, all children of my sister Nancy Gracy. Niece Allice Sherrill. Executor: John M. Smith. Signed September 5, 1855. Witnesses: William Weaver and R.M. Weaver. Proven November 5, 1855.

Page 121 **WILL OF JAMES C. ROBINSON.** S.M. Emmons and James Hopper witnesses J.C. Robinson make his will on October 17, 1855. His wife Martha Robinson and her offspring, not named. Executor: Henry Robinson. Witnesses S.M. Emmons and James Hopper. Proven November 5, 1855.

Page 121 **WILL OF DRURY RICHARDSON.** Wife Priscilla Richardson. Son James Richardson, and others not named. Executrix: Wife Priscilla Richardson. Signed May 21, 1853. Witnesses: Thomas Ramsey and Y.R.W. Crane. Proven November 5, 1855.

Page 122 **WILL OF RICHARD CERNELL.** Wife Elizabeth Cernell. Executrix: Wife Elizabeth Cernell. Signed September 17, 1855. Witnesses: Spencer Leatherwood and B.W. Merrell. Proven November 6, 1855.

Page 123 **WILL OF AMANDA H.M. BUCHANAN.** Sister Manerva Ann Buchanan and an Aunt Martha M. Smith. Executor: S.M. McElroy. Signed January 23, 1855. Witnesses: John F. West and Rufus C. McElroy. Proven December 3, 1855.

Page 125 **WILL OF WILLIAM OLD.** Wife Nancy Old. Children: Henry Old, John Old who is deceased, William Old, Elizabeth Stillwell who is deceased, Martha Old, Sarah Smith, Eliza Harris, and Mary C. Curtis who is deceased and leaving one child Nancy Ruth Curtis. Executors: Jacob Gillespie and THomas H. Bledsoe. Signed January 30, 1852. Witnesses James M. Cole and James E. Bell. Proven December 2, 1855.

Page 127 **WILL OF MILES RUFUS SHERRELL.** Eldest daughter Alice Ann Read Sherrell. Son Uty William Sherrell. Daughter Mary Frances Sherrell. Executors: Joseph Lawson and Wormly R. Bruice (Bruce). Signed April 14, 1855. Witnesses: John Maddox and David S. Patterson. Proven February Term 1856.

Page 128 **WILL OF WILLIAM McELROY.** Wife McElroy. Children: Sanford McElroy, Sherod G. McElroy, Micajah L. McElroy, Rufus C. McElroy, Jane Crawford, Cynthia A. Smith, Elizabeth A. Ellis, Jackson McElroy, Thomas H.B. McElroy, and John A. McElroy. Three grandchildren: David, William and Archibald McElroy, all sons of my son Sanford McElroy. Executors: Reuben A. McDonald and Constant Smith. Signed June 7, 1854. Witnesses: E.M. Ringo and John M. Bright. Codicil: Signed April 20, 1855. Proven February Term 1856.

Page 131 **WILL OF RICHARD CARNEL.** Wife Elizabeth Carnel. Signed September 17, 1855. Witnesses: H.M. Bledsoe, S.M. Leatherwood and B.W. Merrell. Proven February Term 1856.

Page 132 **WILL OF HANNAH EDDINS.** Requested that his and his brother's graves near the Crossroads in Madison County, Alabama, be enclosed with a stone wall. Niece Ann H. Drake and her son George K. Moody, her present husband Col. Samuel Drake and their children: Dorinda Ann H. Drake, Marcellus Drake and Adalide Drake. (Ann H. wife of A.S. McRea), Matilda McKinney of Linestone County, Alabama, Abraham Eddins and his wife Clasa Eddins, Parthenia

Elliott, and Thomas Anderson. Signed August 17, 1855. Witnesses: W.W. Petty, Richard Petty and James P. Ewing. Proven March Term 1856.

Page 135 **WILL OF B.W.D. CARTY.** Wife Catharine Carty. Daughter Mrs. Ann Vining. Owns a town lot in Fayetteville, Tennessee and also land in Montgomery County, Virginia, about three miles north of Christiansburg, about 105 acres. Signed March 30, 1848. Witnesses: U.A. Wilson and W.W. Forwalt. Proven March 3, 1856.

Page 136 **WILL OF JOHN REDD.** Wife Susanna C. Redd. Mentions sons and daughters but not by name. Owned land on East Mulberry. Executors: Wife Susanna C. Redd and John F. Redd. Signed June 14, 1855. Witnesses: W.M. Head and Joel Foster. Proven March 3, 1856.

Page 137 **WILL OF WILLIAM MILLARD.** Wife Mary Millard. Children: Mary, Margaret Kimes, Ditie Smith, Sarah Martin, Nathan THomas, Cynthia, Mary Jane, William, and John Millard. Executor: Thomas Hampton. Signed August 16, 1853. Witnesses: Joel Harris and Howell Harris. Proven March 3, 1856.

Page 139 **WILL OF JOHN BUCHANAN.** Wife Hannah Buchanan. Daughter Margery Buchanan wife of Leander Buchanan who now lives in Arkansas. Daughter Jonah Moore wife of Alexander S. Moore. Daughter Arminta Buchanan. Daughter Mary Jane Buchanan. Eleanor Buchanan a sister to my wife Hannah. A deceased son Joseph C. Buchanan. Executors: Son W. Buchanan and Alfred Smith. Signed September 22, 1845. Witnesses: B.W.D. Carty, Henry Kelso and William S. Southworth.
Codicil: Signed November 20, 1849.
Codicil: Signed May 16, 1851.
Codicil: Signed September 20, 1851. Proven March 3, 1856.

Page 143 **WILL OF JAMES FULTON.** Nine children: Alfred, Jane, John, Frank, Martha, James, Laura, Virginia, and youngest not yet named. Wife not named. Signed September 20, 1842. Witnesses: R. Farquharson, W. Bonner and T.M. McElroy.
Codicil: Daughter Margaret Davidson wife of James M. Davidson, deceased. Other children: Robert, Kate, Charles and Victoria. Executors: R.A. McDonald, John S. Fulton and John M. Bright. Signed February 12, 1856. Witnesses: Same as Executors. Proven March 3, 1856.

Page 146 **WILL OF CATHARINE NORMAN.** Son B.S. Norman. Signed January 9, 1856. Witnesses: Wiley M. Newman and W.W. Parker. Proven April Term 1856.

Page 146 **WILL OF SARAH CHILDRESS.** Son Marion Childress. Granddaughter Rebecca Sarah Catharine Smith. Executor: Son Marion Childress. Signed October 23, 1855. Witnesses: John Wood and Joseph Clark. Proven April 7, 1856.

Page 149 **WILL OF JOHN MARLER.** Wife Elizabeth Marler. Children: Charles Dennis, Eliza Ann Deal, William B. Marler and Sintha Jane Marler. Signed October 8, 1854. Witnesses: Chaney Smith and James R. Smith. Proven July 7, 1856.

Page 150 **WILL OF THOMAS R. WYNN.** Mentioned his wife and children but not by name. William F. Blake and Willis G. Rives. Wanted John F. Pack to have $20.00 for damages. Signed June 3, 1856. Witnesses: Robert C. McEwen and J.P. Warren. Proven July 7, 1856 and July 11, 1856.

Page 151 **WILL OF R.L. BROWN.** Wife Martha S. Brown. Owned land in Marshall County, on which Sarah Myers now lives. Adopted daughter Amanda daughter of Sarah Louise, and her son Robert Brown Myers. Mentions brother and sisters but not by name. Executors: J.S. Edmiston and Archibald Wells. Proven July 11, 1856.

Page 152 **WILL OF JOSEPH CLARK.** Wife not named. Son Thomas, daughter Sally Ann. Executor: R.A. McDonald. He had business with Henry Jacob. William F. Richard to settle my business between myself and Thomas W. Sullivan and Newton C. Sullivan and Con Smith. Executor: Brother John Clark, Jr. Signed May 17, 1856. Witnesses: M.H. Bonner and Benjamin March. Proven July 14, 1856.
Codicil: May 18, 1856.

Page 154 **WILL OF GEORGE ALEXANDER.** The State of Mississippi, Panola County, proven by Judge John G.M. Burdudges on 3rd Monday in August 1845.
**WILL:** Wife Rebecca Alexander. Children: Rebecca, George S., Jane B., Eliza D. Diemer, Mary Stratten, and Charles F. Alexander. Owns land in State of Alabama in Benton County. Executors: Son George S. Alexander and son-in-law Charles F. Alexander. Signed January 21, 1845. Witnesses: James M. Rowzier, Robert P. Sorrells and Jonathan Miller. (5 pages of will)

Page 159 **WILL OF STEPHEN COLBERT.** Wife Charlotte Colbert. Executor: Son Richard Colbert. Signed February 26, 1856. Witnesses: A.J. Childress and Isaac Kelso. Proven August 4, 1856.

Page 159 **WILL OF WILLIAM LAY.** Wife Edith Lay. Signed October 18, 1855. Witnesses: A.J. Carloss and Hiram Reese. Proven August 4, 1856.

Page 160 **WILL OF WESLEY LUTTRELL.** Wife and two children but not by name. Witnesses: William Benson and Jackson Luttrell. Signed August 31, 1856. Proven September 17, 1856.

Page 160 **WILL OF HOUSTON McBAY.** Wife Margaret McBay. Daughter Elizabeth Snow. Four other children but did not name. Executor: Chany Smith. Signed August 5, 1856. Witnesses: W.M. Newman and Samuel Irvin. Proven October 6, 1856.

Page 161 **WILL OF JOSIAH B. GIBSON.** Father Thomas Gibson. Mother Mahala Gibson. Brother Thomas W. Gibson. Sister Margaret M. Gibson, and James L. Gibson and Sarah Smith.

Page 161 **WILL OF JACKSON LUTTRELL.** Wife not named. Executor: Newton Luttrell. Signed October 3, 1856. Witnesses: P.R. Whitaker and William Benson. Proven October 11, 1856.

Page 162 **WILL OF WILLIAM T. ROSS.** Wife Martha E. Ross. Two sons William T. Ross and other son not named. Two daughters: Mary M. Ross and Martha G. Ross. Owned land in Alabama and also has about 160 acres in Lincoln County. Executors: William F. Kercheval and Robert Farquharson, and his wife Martha E. Ross. Signed July 7, 1856. Witnesses: Matt M. Marshall and Jonathan Gilliland. Proven September 2, 1856 and October 1, 1856.

Page 164 **WILL OF MARY McELROY.** Daughters: Mary Jane Crawford, Cynthia Smith and Elizabeth Ellis. Sons: Thomas, Alexander, Micajah, Jackson, John and Sanford McElroy. Executors: Sons Sanford and Micajah McElroy. Signed 1856. Witnesses: Pleasant Halbert and David Buchanan. Proven November 3, 1856.

Page 165 **WILL OF JAMES B. DOOLEY.** Son George W. Dooley, son Tindale C. Dooley, son John C. Dooley, daughter Emeline P. Gates, son Alfred W. Dooley. Granddaughter Frances Jemima Smith and also John S. Edmiston is to be guardian, two smaller children: Susan Virginia Boyd and Louisa Jane. Executor: John Washburn. Signed October 8, 1856. Witnesses: A.A. Greer and Jacob Gillespie.

Page 166 **WILL OF SAMUEL H. HOBBS.** Wife Sarah E. Hobbs. Children: Margaret J., William H., Richard C., Joel B., James W., and Mary A. Hobbs. Executor: William Hunter. Signed May 8, 1856. Witnesses: Isaiah Nerren and J.W. Nelson. Proven December 1, 1856.

Page 167 **WILL OF JAMES M. MOORE.** Wife not named. Mother Martha Moore. Executor: John Moore. Signed October 1, 1856. Witnesses: John Caughran and John M. McFerren. Proven December 1, 1856.

Page 168 **WILL OF THOMAS H. McGAUGH.** Wife Catharine McGaugh. Children: Felix G. McGaugh, John M. McGaugh, Martha Waggoner wife of Solomon Waggoner, Elizabeth Hamilton widow of James Hamilton, Caroline T. wife of William Hamilton. Executor: Felix G. McGaugh. Signed February 1, 1847. Witnesses: W.T. Ross and Joseph Clark. (Probated December Term 1856)

Page 170 **WILL OF JAMES HAYS.** Wife Elizabeth Hays. Children: Margarett L. Hays, A.P. Hays, James Alexander Hays son of David Hays, James G. Hays, and Elizabeth who intermarried with John Good. Executors: Alexander P. Hays and Calvin L. Hauge. Signed September 17, 1856. Witnesses: Samuel J. Bland and Jacob W. Rowell. Proven January 9, 1857.

Page 171 **WILL OF JACOB ALLISON.** Wife Eliza Allison. Son Pinkney and daughter Malissa Jane Allison. Executor: Samuel Stiles, who is also guardian of two minors. Signed (no date). Witnesses: W.M. Newman and Samuel Stiles. Proven January Term 1857.

Page 172 **WILL OF STEPHEN WALKER.** Wife Elizabeth C. Walker. Children: Martha A. Hambrick, Mary J. Phillips, William A. Walker, Peter L. Walker, Elizabeth Vance, two youngest daughters Nancy Wilburn and Lucy Walker, and son Stephen Walker. Executors: Stephen L. Walker and Elizabeth C. Walker. Signed December 3, 1853. Witnesses: William A. Smith, Henry Henderson and J.H. Locker. Proven March 2, 1857.

Page 174 **WILL OF BENJAMIN T. PARKS.** Wife Martha Parks. Children: Elisha, Ann Elizabeth, William and Hugh B. Parks. Executor: William Thomison. Signed December 3, 1856. Witnesses: William B. Rhea and Hugh Thomison. Proven March 2, 1857.

Page 175 **WILL OF GEORGE RENEGAR.** Wife Anna Renegar. Children: Andrew Jackson Renegar, William Henry Renegar, George T. Renegar, two son-in-laws Andrew Cashion and William Gattis. Owned land on Tuckers Creek and near Mulberry. Executors: George T. Renegar and William Gattis. Signed February 11, 1857. Witnesses: Thomas H. Freeman, Marcus L. Mead and William H. Reese. Proven March 9, 1857.

Page 178 **WILL OF MARGARET CARMACK.** Deceased husband S.W. Carmack. Children: George Call Carmack, Samuel William Carmack, David Carmack, and Susan McCoy. Owned land in Mississippi and also land in Arkansas. Executors: A.A. Greer and John J. Greer. Signed March 13, 1857. Witnesses: D.R. Smythe and Jacob Gillespie.
Codicil: Gave $100.00 to aid in building of the Presbyterian Church in Petersburg or vicinity. Signed March 13, 1857. Proven April 6, 1857.

Page 179 **WILL OF ALEXANDER McCULLOUGH.** Wife Parthenia McCullough. Her four children: Alfred H. Bell, Eliza V. Bell, Thomas M. Bell and Panis D. Bell. Executor: Alfred H. Bell. Signed November 31, 1853. Witnesses: John P. McGee and Jefferson Kelso. Proven May 4, 1857.

Page 180 **WILL OF DOKE NICKS.** Wife Margaret Nicks. Children: Austin T. Nicks, Elizabeth M. Nicks, Lydia who intermarried with Amos Small, Alvis D. Nicks, Prudence who intermarried with Jesse M. George, Bryan L. Nicks, the children of my deceased son John D. Hicks, Margaret who married Benjamin Cowley, Henrietta who married Samuel Wells, and Edithy who intermarried with Doke Bates, Martha Nicks, John J., and A.T. Nicks. (Six in all) Executor: Friend Moses W. Yant. Signed February 24, 1857. Witnesses: Moses W. Yant and Abraham Washburn. Codicil: Proven May 4, 1857.

Page 183 **WILL OF WILLIAM SMITH.** Wife Sarah Smith. Children: Eldest son Benjamin, James, William B., and Elizabeth Borrow of Texas. He is living in Civil District No. 8. Executors: Benjamin and William B. Smith. Signed April 25, 1856. Witnesses: Samuel J. Bland and Hugh W. Shuffield. Proven May 4, 1857.

Page 187 **WILL OF ALEXANDER McCULLOUGH.** Wife Parthenia. Same as on page 57.

Page 188 **WILL OF JOHN W. BUCHANAN.** Three children: Sina Adaline, Thadeus Sylvester and Cyrus J. Buchanan. Named his deceased father-in-law Henry Kimes and mother Rachel Buchanan. Executor: Brother Thomas W. Buchanan. Campbell F. Edmiston be appointed guardian of his three children. Brother Thomas W. Buchanan be appointed guardian of his three children on that portion of the property from the estate of Henry Kimes, deceased. Signed March 9, 1857. Witnesses: Benjamin F. Clark and William Moffett. Proven May 4, 1857.

Page 190 **WILL OF ANTHONY CRAWFORD.** Wife Elizabeth Crawford. Children: William H. Crawford, the heirs of Thomas Crawford, deceased, Polly Womack, Nancy Douthit, Carter T. Crawford, the heirs of Charles M. Crawford, deceased, Elizabeth Braden, and granddaughter Mary Jane Nelson. Executors: E.H. Womack and William Talley. Signed (no date). Witnesses: Daniel Scivley, Thomas A. Gattis, Abner Brady, George Waggoner and Felix Waggoner. Proven June 1, 1857.

Page 192 **WILL OF WILLIAM COOPER.** Wife Susannah Cooper. Susannah Cowley, son James Cooper, John Cooper, Mathew Cooper, Jacob Cooper, Eli P. Cooper, Phillip Cooper, Noah Cooper, and Asa Cooper. Daughter Phebe Boyd. Executors: Wife Susannah Cooper and John Moore. Signed July 18, 1854. Witnesses: Samuel Merrell and A.M.C. Whitworth. Proven June 1, 1857.

Page 193 **WILL OF POLLY RINGO.** Son Isaac Ringo. Mentions other relatives, John S. Dickson and Robert K. Dickson. Owned lot No. 79 in Fayetteville. Executor: John S. Dickson. Signed December 8, 1856. Witnesses: W.S. Southworth and John S. Fulton. Proven June 1, 1857.

Page 194 **WILL OF SARAH A. McDANIEL.** Children: Sarah J. Parks, Martha and Mary McDaniel. Has land in 7th District. Executor: Woodruff Parks. Signed February 6, 1857. Witnesses: C.B. McDaniel and C.A. McDaniel. Proven July 6, 1857.

Page 195 **WILL OF REBECCA BAGGERLY.** Daughter Ethiel McKee and her son Archibald McKee. Daughters: Rebecca and Emeline Baggerly, the daughters of my son David Baggerly, son Benjamin Baggerly and children, Jerina, Mary, Letum and Buble Baggerly. Daughter Rebecca wife of Lebition Gather. Daughter Lelah Ellis wife of William Ellis. Granddaughters Margaret McDaniel, Mary E. Baggerly, Ruth E. Baggerly. Executors: Archibald McKee and Arthur J. Childress. Signed March 13, 1856. Witnesses: Isaiah Hancock and John Rogers. Proven July 6, 1857.

Page 197 **WILL OF ELENOR KIMES.** Three children: S.H. Kimes, Elizabeth E. Malier and THomas B. Kimes. Three grandchildren: Sina A., Thadeus C. and Cyrus J. Buchanan. Executor: Squire Pickle. Signed September 27, 1856. Witnesses: Benjamin F. Clark, W.B. Beatie and Howell Harris. Proven October 5, 1857.

Page 198 **WILL OF NATHANIEL READ.** Two granddaughters: Elizabeth and Margaret Read the daughters of my eldest son Samuel Read, deceased. Son-in-law Aaron Stiles. Daughter Martha Gilliland and her four children, Benjamin Read, Nancy Patrick and John Read and Amy Smith, deceased, and her children andson James Read, deceased and his heirs. Executors: Chaney Smith and John Read. Signed September 18, 1854. Witnesses: Jeff M. Stone and W.D. Wiseman. Proven October 19, 1857.

**Page 199** **WILL OF WILLIS H. HOLMAN.** Wife Ann R. Holman. Two children: Henry and Caroline Holman. Executor: Mark Whitaker. Signed September 22, 1857. Witnesses: D.W. Holman and James C. Kelso. Proven November 2, 1857.

**Page 201** **WILL OF DANIEL FARRAR.** Wife Nancy Jane Farrar. Children not named. Executors: John Owen, Joseph Farrar and T.A. George. Signed October 18, 1857. Witnesses: George Stewart, Giles Hedgepeth and L.D. Sugg. Proven November 2, 1857.

**Page 202** **WILL OF JAMES BONNER.** Brother William Bonner. Sister-in-law Mahala Bonner. Executor: Joseph H. Greer. Signed September 26, 1853. Witnesses: Joseph G. Moore and Jacob W. Moore. Proven November 2, 1857.

**Page 204** **WILL OF ALLEN STUBBLEFIELD.** Children: Joel, Sarah J., William, Young, Milly Lavina, Hannah C., Mary M., Elizabeth E. Stubblefield and Nancy Solomon. Executor: James H. Taylor. Signed September 28, 1857. Witnesses: Young T. Taylor and W.G. Nix. Proven in Open Court.

**Page 205** **WILL OF WILLIAM GIVENS.** Wife Margat Givens. Step-daughter Sarah Ann Wiley. Executors: Robert Drennan and John T. Caughran. Signed November 26, 1855. Witnesses: Thomas Caughran and John Caughran and S.T. Wilson.

**Page 206** **WILL OF ELIJAH M. RINGO.** Wife Elzira Ringo. Daughter Mary Duval, son Joseph Ringo. Granddaughter Mary Elzira Duval. Executrix: Wife Elzira Ringo. Signed January 28, 1857. Witnesses: James R. Bright and R. Farquharson.

**Page 210** **WILL OF PETER ASHBY.** Wife Mary Jane Ashby. Three children: Rebecca Elzira, Travis David and Sarah Hardin. Executor: S.M. Conger. Signed December 6, 1857. Witnesses: William A. Brown and George S. Carty. Proven January 4, 1858.

**Page 211** **WILL OF JOHN COLE.** Wife Nancy A. Cole. Children not named. Executors: George Stewart and J.J. Finney. Signed September 15, 1857. Witnesses: T.N. Hughes and William F. Zimmerman.

**Page 212** **WILL OF JOHN DUDLEY.** Wife Nancy M. Dudley. Children: Ignatius, Kames L., Wiley Dudley, daughter Polly Mitchell. Other names: Elizabeth Williams, John S. Nicholass, Virgal A. Stewart. Executors: John F. Couser and Nancy M. Dudley. Signed April 9, 1840. Witnesses: John Enochs, Isaac Collins and John F. Couser.

**Page 213** **WILL OF JOHN KING.** Children: Jonathan King who lives in Alabama, George King who lives in Alabama, Mark King lives in Missouri, Mary wife of E.C. Ward, the heirs of Aaron King, and heirs of daughter Martha Newman. Signed March 12, 1857. Executor: W.M. Newman. Witnesses: Isaac H. Eslick and E. Mc Dickey. Proven December 8, 1857.

**Page 214** **WILL OF MARY A. GREER.** Son John Jacob Greer, daughter Eliza McEwen and her daughter Mary Ann McEwen, granddaughter Mary M. Gillespie the daughter of Catharine Gillespie, Julia Evans, Jane Greer, Jefferson Greer and his daughter Kate Greer, and Margaret R. Carmack. A.A. Greer. Signed December 27, 1857. Witnesses: H.M. Blake and A.M. Hall.

**Page 216** **WILL OF JOHN GROCE.** Wife Cincinnatta Groce. Children: Elizabeth, Thomas, William, Martha, Wilsy, Cordely, Nancy, and Ann Groce. Executor: William Ashby. Signed December 12, 1857. Witnesses: Travis Ashby and Morgan H. Conaway.

**Page 217** **WILL OF WILLIAM BRYAN.** Wife Lucinda Bryan. Five sons: William

A., Benjamin B., John, Ephraim B., Newton Bryan. Others: Elizabeth who married John Moddox, Rebecca Bryan, Malinda S. Bryan, Cintha who married Joseph Buchanan and James J. Bryan, deceased, and his heirs: William H., Francis M., John H., Nancy and Henry Bryan. Executors: William A. Bryan and Ephraim Bryan. Signed November 30, 1857. Witnesses: John Smith and John J. Bonner. Has land on Kellys Creek.

Page 219 **WILL OF JAMES B. DOOLEY.** Will contested in Court November 2, 1857, No. 9. Mary E., Susan V.B., Louisa Jane Dooley vs A.W., F.C., John C. Dooley and Emaline Jeter.
Will: Son George W. Dooley, son Findele C. Dooley, son John C. Dooley, daughter Emeline T. Jeters, son Alford W. Dooley, Granddaughter Frances Germima Smith, S. Edmiston should become her guardian. Small children: Susan Virginia Boyd and Louisa Jane. Executor: John Washburn. Signed October 8, 1856. Witnesses: A.A. Greer and Jacob Gillespie. Recorded February 3, 1858.

Page 222 **WILL OF SAMUEL TOWNSEND.** Of Madison County, Alabama. Deceased brother Edmund Townsend, John E. Townsend and Samuel C. Townsend. Executors: S.D. Cabiness and Samuel C. Townsend of Madison County, Alabama. Bond and Security by Joseph C. Bradley and James J. Donegan. Executors: John J. Jackson and nephew Samuel C. Townsend. Witnesses: Joseph Taylor and David Shelby. Signed September 6, 1856. (16 pages)

Page 238 **WILL OF WILLIAM BRYAN.** Wife Lucinda Bryan. Five sons: William A., Benjamin B., John, Ephraim B., and Newton Bryan. Others: Elizabeth who married John Maddox, Anna Bryan, Rebecca Bryan, Malinda S. Bryan and Cintha who married Joseph Buchanan, Anna who married Thomas Maddox, the heirs of Bryan, deceased*, William H., Frances M., John H., Nancy and Henry Bryan. Signed November 30, 1857. Executors: William A. Bryan and Ephraim Bryan. Witnesses: John Smith and John J. Bonner.
* James J. Bryan, deceased.

Page 240 **WILL OF JOSEPH COMMONS.** Nine children: Hiram S. Commons to be Trustee for my daughter Sarah wife of Simpson Buchanan, appointed my son-in-law William Beverly Trustee for my daughter Elizabeth wife of said William Beverly, son John M. Commons, son Henry S. Commons, son Andrew J. Commons, son Carrell J. Commons, son Francis M. Commons. Executor: William W. Farmwalt. Signed February 21, 1858. Witnesses: R.S. Woodard and M.H. Roberts. Proven April 5, 1858.

Page 242 **WILL OF JAMES HIGGINS.** Of Norris Creek. Born in Caroline County, Virginia, in 1772. Daughter Sally Castleman, son Owen W. Higgins, Nurse Eliza Howard, other children: Emily, Nancy Jane, John J. son of my son John A. Higgins, deceased. Appoint Owen W. Higgins as guardian for the children of my daughter Emily. Executor: George W. Higgins. Signed October 6, 1857. Witnesses: L.L. Stone and E.G. Johnson. Proven May 3, 1858.

Page 244 **WILL OF ELISHA BAGLEY.** Wife Elizabeth Bagley. Children: Elizabeth C. Hill who is deceased, Martha wife of my son John R. Bagley, Eliza B. wife of my son Robert H.C. Bagley, daughter Bethenia A. Tally who is deceased, and daughter Eliza W. Norris who is deceased. Executor: E.M. Ringo. Signed November 29, 1855. Witnesses: Lucinda D. Greer and James R. Bright.

Page 246 **WILL OF WILLIAM McCLURE.** Grandson Elisha Moore McClure, son Mark Moore McClure and son William C. McClure. Executor: William C. McClure. Signed April 19, 1858. Witnesses: Young T. Taylor and David A. Franklin. Proven June 7, 1858.

Page 247 **WILL OF MARGARET WATSON.** Children: William, Margaret Jane, Samuel, Sarah Rebekah, Elizabeth Ann who married Rice Williams, and son John Wiley Watson. Executors: Calvin L. Hodge and Edmon D. Hicks. Signed

June 16, 1858. Witnesses: Alfred R. Smith and William W. Vaughn. Proven July 5, 1858.

Page 248 **WILL OF JAMES LOCKER.** Wife Rebekah Locker. Son Robert Locker. Other children not named. Executor: Rufus A. McGee. Signed June 7, 1858. Witnesses: Jefferson Kelso and Needham Koonce. Proven July 5, 1858.

Page 249 **WILL OF WILLIAM WOFFORD.** Wife Judith Wofford. Daughter Lucy, granddaughter Mary Eliza Wofford alias Mary Eliza Wright, five grandchildren: Mary Eliza, William Francis, Isaac Rufus, Robert Harvey, and Luther Wright, all children of my son Isaac Wofford, deceased, and who was begotten out of wedlock upon the body of my present wife Judith whose maiden name was Judith Wright. Said son Isaac Wofford was born in South Carolina and was known in South Carolina as Isaac Wright but was known in the State of Tennessee and in the State of Mississippi by Isaac Wofford. The above children of my son Isaac was known in Tennessee and Mississippi by names: Mary Eliza        William Francis Wofford, Isaac Rufus Wofford, Robert Harvey Wofford and Luther Wright Wofford and daughter Lucy wife of George Mooney and their son Joseph William Mooney. He had interest in gold mine in South Carolina. Executor: Pleasant Halbert. Signed September 24, 1853. Witnesses: W.F. Zimmerman, W.R. Hedgepeth and H.R. Hamilton. Proven July 5, 1858.

Page 252 **WILL OF WILLIAM F. BLAKE.** Daughter Eliza Washington. Other children: Susan Ann, Mary Jane, and Frances Wyatt, all children is to remain at Dr. B.F. Bearden. Executor: Thomas K. Warren. Signed: July 19, 1858. Witnesses: A.A. Greer and Thomas H. Holland. Proven August 2, 1858.

Page 253 **WILL OF JAMES FORRESTER.** Sister Mary Mills, sister Elizabeth Sullivan, brother Isaac Forrester, sister Rebeccah Lane, the heirs of deceased brother Eli Forrester, sister Ellender Mills, nephew James Forrester son of Isaac Forrester. Executor: Nephew James Forrester. Signed April 1, 1858. Witnesses: F.R. Moore and P.R. Whitaker.

Page 254 **WILL OF JULIA GILLESPIE.** Husband Jacob Gillespie. Brothers and sisters: Ellen Moffett, Eliza Ringo, Ella Duval, Louisa Combs, and niece Mary Duval. Executor: Jacob Gillespie. Signed July 24, 1858. Witnesses: John J. Greer and J.H. Ringo.
Codicil: Proven September 6, 1858.

Page 255 **WILL OF SAMUEL BROWN.** Grandson Robert Brown Irvin son of my deceased daughter Nancy H. Irvin, son Robinson Brown, son William A. Brown, daughter Lucy Ann Brown, and son James M. Brown, and son John S. Brown. Executors: Sons James M. Brown and Robinson M. Brown. Signed July 7, 1858. Witnesses: W.B. Robinson and John Brown. Proven September 6, 1858.

Page 256 **WILL OF WILLIAM NEELD.** Wife not named. Children not named, some are single and some are married. Signed November 28, 1854. Proven September 7, 1858.

Page 257 **WILL OF JOHN CLARK.** Robertson Clark, son. Executors: Moses H. Bonner and J.B. Lamb. Signed September 12, 1858. Witnesses: William Bonner and M.D. Hampton.

Page 257 **WILL OF NANCY C. DOLLAR.** Daughter Mary F. Gillam. Executor: Samuel M. Rowell. Signed October 22, 1858. Witnesses: Hiram Reese and Joseph Farrar. Proven December 6, 1858.

Page 258 **WILL OF DAVID SNODDY.** Wife Nancy Snoddy. Youngest son Price M. Snoddy. He mentions both sons and daughters but not by names. Executors: Son David Snoddy, Jr. and David A. George. Signed November 17, 1858. Witnesses: William Benson and F.M. Snoddy. Proven December 6, 1858.

Page 259  **WILL OF HENRY RENEGAR.**  Hon. A.J. March, Judge contest will No.
12.  John M. Renegar, Sanford Renegar and Nicholas Renegar vs Jacob
Hoots and Mary Hoots ... March 30, 1859.
Will: Wife Mary Renegar.  Son Henry Renegar, son David Renegar, and son John
Renegar.  Executors: John Renegar and George Renegar, my sons.
Signed August 18, 1838.  Witnesses: A. Baxter and James Steelman.

Page 261  **WILL OF DAVID BAGGERLY.**  Of North Carolina, Iredel County, City
of Statesville, at Court House on Monday February 15, 1819.  Present
and residing, Collin Campbell, John McLelland and George Robison, Justices of said
county.  Proven by John Forsyth and Libitious Gaither qualified as Executor.
Will: Wife Rebekah Baggerly.  Son Benjamin, daughter Rebekah wife of Lititious
Gaither, daughter Celia wife of William Ellis, son David, and daughter Ethel
Farnale Baggerly.  Signed February 4, 1816.  Witnesses: John Forsyth and
Alexander Reed.  March 2, 1838.

Page 264  **WILL OF HENRIETTA JOHNSON.**  Jackson County, Alabama.  Son
Robert Johnson, son Michael Johnson, daughter Keziah Rye who
intermarried with William Dye, daughter Elizabeth Houston who intermarried with
George V. Houston, and daughter Parthena Stewart wife of James R. Stewart.
Executors: Sons Robert and Michael Johnson.  Signed June 19, 1856.  Witnesses:
G.A. Wyche and William E. Hurt.  Probate Court Jackson County, Alabama.
Robert Johnson, Executor.
        vs
James P. Steely and wife and others
State of Alabama, County of Jackson
Henrietta Johnson, deceased, will was proven and recorded in Will Book "K", page
409 and 410.  Signed August 12, 1858 by John H. Norwood.  Judge of Probate
Court.

Page 267  **WILL OF JOSEPH McMILLEN.**  Wife Rachel McMillen.  Elizabeth A.,
Greer, Willis, John, Emeline, Martha, Lucinda Jane, Rebekah, Niel,
Napoleon and Dick McMillen.  Executors: Sons William and Robert D. McMillen.
Signed January 29, 1859.  Witnesses: Rane McKinney and D.M. Beatie.  Proven
March Term 1859.

Page 269  **WILL OF HENRY SNIDER.**  Harriet M. Hamilton wife of William
Hamilton, Sarah H. Smith and Agnes D. Smith.  Executor: Jacob Vance.
Signed April 1, 1859.  Witnesses: James R. Bright and Thomas Timmins.  Proven
May Term 1859.

Page 271  **WILL OF JOHN W. DOUTHITT.**  Febetta J. Douthitt.  Stacy Minerva,
Isaac Cole and his wife Nancy, Elizabeth Jane McCoy daughter of Ira
E. Douthitt, Nancy Cole mother of Finetta and Stacy.  Signed May 3, 1859.
Executor: L.D. Sugg.  Witnesses: J.E. Yowell and William A. Douthitt.  Proven July
Term 1859.

Page 273  **WILL OF JANE B. MOORE.**  Nephew William H. Moore, niece Mary L.
Beanland wife of E.G.G. Beanland and friend Scion Conger.  Signed
April 15, 1857.  Witnesses: Henry R. Moore and Lucas Groove.
Codicil: Proven January Term 1859.

Page 275  **WILL OF JESSE STOCKSTILL.**  Wife Margaret Stockstill.  Eldest son
William F., James W., daughter Sarah M., and mary M. Stockstill.
Executors: John L. Ashby and John A. Silvertooth.  Signed June 18, 1859.
Witnesses: David P.C. Allen and Peterson Grammer.  Proven July Yerm 1859.

Page 276  **WILL OF WILLIAM R. LOCKER.**  Mother, sisters and brothers are not
named.  Executor: John P. McGee.  Signed December 9, 1858.
Witnesses: Jefferson Kelso and Jesse Ventress.  Proven January Term 1859.

Page 277  **WILL OF JOHN GRAMMER.**  Wife Sarah Grammer.  Son William and son Peterson Grammer. Signed November 16, 1858. Witnesses: William F. Bruce and John L. Ashby. Proven January Term 1859.

Page 278   **WILL OF P.W. HARPER.** Wife Nancy D. Harper. Daughter Martha A.
Jacobs wife of Henry Jacobs, two youngest sons Thomas M. and James
G. Harper, son A.W. and daughter M. Louisa Harper. Executor: James H. Wright.
Signed January 16, 1859. Witnesses: Isiah Nerren and J.R. Nelson. Proven March
1859.

Page 280   **WILL OF ISAAC W. HESTER.** A Lieut. in the Navy of the United
States of America. Mother Mary Hester, sister Ann B. Hester, brother
W.W. Hester, brother Joseph T. Hester, and brother Elijah L. Hester. Executors:
Dr. M.H. Bonner and John M. Bright. Signed March 15, 1857. Witnesses: William
J. Caldwell and M.D. Hampton. Proven June Term 1859.

Page 281   **WILL OF CHARITY PAYNE.** William P. White, Amandory and Charity
Elizabeth and Dianna Frances and Thomas Jefferson, James T. White
and wife Martha V. White. Executors: Paul Ingle and D.B. Cooper. Proven March
Term 1859.

Page 282   **WILL OF ELIZABETH HOLMAN.** Son James W. Holman, daughter
Martha W. Holman wife of James S. Holman, daughter Eliza Cannon
wife of Augustine Cannon, daughter Nancy M. Cannon wife of George M. Cannon,
son Miles H. Holman. Granddaughter Elizabeth Nicks. Executors: James W.
Holman and Willis H. Holman. Signed July 5, 1845. Witnesses: Abner Steed and
Franklin R. Moore.
Codicil: Granddaughter Sophronia A. Holman. Witnesses: Edward Taylor and
William Taylor. Dated: April 12, 1850. Proven June 1859.

Page 284   **WILL OF JOHN BUCHANAN.** Wife Hannah Buchanan. Daughter
Margery wife of Leander Buchanan who resides in Arkansas, daughter
Joannah Moore wife of Alexander S. Moore, daughter Martha M. Smith wife of
Alfred Smith, Frances A. Crawford wife of John Crawford who lives in Arkansas,
son Thomas W. Buchanan, son Joseph C. Buchanan who died in Washington County,
Arkansas in 1843, daughter Emily Buchanan, daughter Arminta Buchanan, daughter
Mary Jane Buchanan and Elanor Buchanan sister to my wife. Executors: Thomas
W. Buchanan and Alfred Smith. Signed September 22, 1845. Witnesses: W.B.D.
Carty, Henry Kelso and William F. Silvertooth.
Codicil:
Additional Codicil:

Page 288   **WILL OF JAMES P. BAXTER.** Wife E.C. Baxter. I.T. Baxter, W.B.
Baxter, M.C. Baxter, S.E.C.B. Dance, and S.M. Dance, M.M. Ferguson,
M.M.D.I. Baxter, and W.A.J. Baxter. Executors: J.T. Baxter and J.F. Baxter.
Signed August 3, 1859. Witnesses: Loderick Robertson and James Martin and J.S.
Bedford. Proven October 3, 1859.

Page 289   **WILL OF THOMAS B. WILSON.** Sister Mary E. Wyatt, brother James
and wife Jane Wilson, sister Elizabeth wife of John M. Wham.
Executor: Morgan D. Hampton. Signed August 20, 1859. Witnesses: John R.
Massey and Isham R. Dismukes. Proven October 3, 1859.

Page 290   **WILL OF WILLIAM CRAWFORD.** Contested will of William Crawford,
deceased. November 7, 1859. Hon. A.J. Marchbanks of 8th Judicial
Circuit. Anderson C. Martin, executor of William Crawford, deceased. vs Thomas
W. Buchanan, B.E. Malier, J.J. Crawford, William T. Malier, John R. Moore, R.A.
Gibson and William A. Crawford. Contested will No. 41, December 2, 1859.
Will: Wife Nancy R. Crawford. Sons: George G. and Joseph W. Crawford, two
daughters Margaret A.E. Crawford and Marietta F. Crawford. First wife Rachel
Crawford. Son William Crawford, son John J. Crawford, daughter Rebecca
Buchanan, heirs of daughter Evaline Sawyers and her three daughters, Elizabeth
Ann Mitchell a daughter, daughter Nancy P., daughter Phebe T. Buchanan, daughter
Rachel S. Hamptonand daughter Sally S. Eastland. Executors: Thomas W.

Buchanan, Anderson M. Martin and John S. Fulton. Signed December 22, 1857. Proven December 23, 1857. Witnesses: S.M. McElroy and J.B. Tigert.

Page 295 **WILL OF ELIZABETH HOWELL.** Daughter Martha, deceased, wife of Gideon Barnett, Jermma R. wife of Lorenzo Harrison deceased, daughterdaughter Susannah C. wife of Lum Benson, daughter Amarilla M. wife of Joseph T. Landers, daughter Tabitha C. wife of David F. Brown, son Charles T. Howell and son Hysen M. Howell. Executor: Hysen M. Howell. Signed January 19, 1856. Witnesses: John Moore and Joshua Smith. Proven November 1859.

Page 296 **WILL OF NANCY ELIZABETH OLD.** Mother Eliza Ann Old. Executor: A.C. Edmiston. Signed August 26, 1858. Witnesses: Rufus Harris and Robert C(H). McEwen. Proven December 5, 1859.

Page 297 **WILL OF JAMES RAMSEY.** Daughter Mary Pigg, daughter Eliza Ramsey, son Thomas W. Ramsey, and daughter Jane Ramsey. Executor: Benjamin F. Clark. Signed August 21, 1856. Witnesses: Squire Pickle and Robert Patterson. Proven December 1859.

Page 298 **WILL OF LUCINDA WHITE.** Daughter Elizabeth wife of Charles McNatt, daughter Christiana wife of Leon Bonner, daughter Mahala wife of Benjamin Fanning, daughter Nancy wife of Major Bedwell, daughter Sarah wife of John Teel, daughter Nancy wife of William McNatt, heirs of son Willis White, and daughter Matilda wife of Thomas White. Executor: Thomas S. Williams. Signed April 14, 1852. Witnesses: Peter C. Webster and Jacob Stonebraker. Proven September 1859.

Page 300 **WILL OF BOON WILSON.** Wife Nancy Wilson. Children: A.M. Wilson, Delina Marshall, Cynthia B. Cathey, Fanny F. Suttle, Martha J. Smith, Sarah E. March, James L. Wilson, and E.S. Wilson. Lived on the east fork of Swan Creek. A portrait of his grandfather Jonas Leatherwood goes to son James L. Wilson. Executors: A.M. Wilson, Jonas L. Wilson and E.S. Wilson. Signed December 15, 1859. Witnesses: John McDaniel and F.M. Wright. Proven January 1860.

Page 303 **WILL OF DAVID COOPER.** Son Samuel M. Cooper, son D.B. Cooper, son H.H. Cooper, son J.J. Cooper, daughter Mary Mitchell, and Sarah White who is deceased. Signed April 27, 1858. Witnesses: Charles Bright and Alex Philpott. Proven April 1860.

Page 304 **WILL OF JAMES L. TATE.** Three brothers: William V., Andrew B., and Robert T. Tate. Sisters not named. Executor: William V. Tate. Signed October 16, 1859. Witnesses: John Carey and S.S. Alexander. Proven November 1859.

Page 305 **WILL OF JAMES H. COBB.** Wife Martha J. Cobb. Brother William Cobb. Martha Ann Woods and James Harvey C. Woods. Executor: James G. Woods. Signed March 5, 1860. Witnesses: James R. Bright and George W. Simms. Proven April Term 1860.

Page 308 **WILL OF JAMES T. JACKSON.** State of Texas, County of Lavaca, February 27, 1860. Sworn to and subscribed before me this 27 of February 1860 by B.B. Walker, Chief Justice, L.E.
Will: Friend Mary M.B. Smith and her children: Jasper R., Tranquilla, James F., and Jackson Smith. Executrix: Mary M.B. Smith. Signed December 15, 1859. Witnesses: William Thomas, William A. East and Frank A. Kelly. Halleettesville, Texas. Proven March 31, 1860.

Page 312 **WILL OF LEMUEL BRANDON.** Wife Mary Brandon. Eldest son B.B. Brandon, 2nd son T.L.D. Brandon, heirs of my 3rd son John M. Brandon deceased, 4th son W.B. Brandon, 2 youngest sons: H.O.G.T(Taylor) Brandon and L(Lemuel).W.B. Brandon. Eldest daughter Rachel Brazier, 2nd daughter Martha L. Davidson deceased and her two daughters. Executors: Mary Brandon and James O.

Norton. Signed July 1, 1857. Witnesses: Daniel Scivally, George W. Brewer, John Scivally and Richard M. Stephens.
Codicil: Granddaughter Susan Bryant daughter of son Burgan and also Lear and Lidia also daughters of Burgan. Executors: Sion M. Conger and Mary Brandon. Signed May 26, 1860. Witnesses: H. Whitfield, R.M. Stephens, Daniel Scivally and G.W. Scivally.
Additional Codicil: Proven July Term 1860.

Page 316    **WILL OF GARLAND B. MILLER.**    Wife Sarah R. Miller.    Children: Sarah Jane Miller, Thomas K. Miller, Garland B. Miller, Ann W. Miller, and William G. Miller. Executor: Wife Sarah R. Miller. Signed February 22, 1860. Witnesses: W.N. Wright, A.J. Carloss and Jacob W. Farmwalt.
Codicil: Proven August 7, 1860.

Page 321    **WILL OF RICHARD WYATT.**    Son Thomas Wyatt, daughter Sarah Morton, daughter Elizabeth West, Rhoda West is deceased, daughter Jane Wyatt, son William Wyatt and Margaret Fullerton. Executors: Thomas Wyatt and John Carey. Signed December 4, 1855. Witnesses: James H. Carey and Robert Carey. Proven September 4, 1860.

Page 323    **WILL OF MARY MOSS.**    Son George W. Moss, son Robert C. Moss, daughter Nancy Burton and daughter Drucilla Towery. Executor: James Burton.    Signed September 22, 1860.    Witnesses: R.L. Templeton and J.H. Hutcheson. Proven November Term 1860.

Page 324    **WILL OF NANCY OLD.**    Daughter Eliza C. Harris, other children but not named. Grandchildren mentioned but not named. Executor: Squire Pickle. Signed February 29, 1860. Witnesses: B.E. Malier and Thomas I. Bryant. Proven December 1860.

Page 325    **WILL OF JOHN SILVERTOOTH.**    Annie P. Davis, Mahaly Laws, Francis Laws, James Blackledge, John H. Blackledge, George Blackledge, John A. Silvertooth, George Silvertooth, Giles Rainey, and Moriah Blackledge. Executors: B.H. Berry, William Tally and John A. Silvertooth. Signed (no date). Witnesses: A.W. Parks, Z. Motlow, David Roughton and E.H. Warnack. Proven December 1860.

Page 326    **WILL OF JOHN HOVIS.**    Wife Betsey Hovis. Daughter Susan, daughter Lavina who married William Gregory deceased, son Ephraim Hovis and W.F. Hovis and a sister Betsey Hovis. Signed September 21, 1860. Witnesses: J.E. Yowell and E. Hovis. Proven December Term 1860.

Page 327    **WILL OF JAMES DUNLAP.**    Wife Elizabeth Dunlap.    Son William Grocy, son David C. Dunlap, son Robert Dunlap, daughter Jane Douthet, daughter Louisa Dunlap, and son Andrew Jackson Dunlap. Executor: William F. Zimmerman. Signed November 4, 1860. Witnesses: D.L. Sugg and D.S. Patterson. Proven December 1860.

Page 328    **WILL OF RUFUS K. FLACK.**    County of Madison, State of Mississippi. August 13, 1860.
Will: James M. Allen, a friend of New Orleans, Louisiana, a brother C.T. Flack, sister Levina Walker, sister Mrs. Matilda Holt, sister Jane Holman, sister Mrs. Susan Chilcoat and heirs of Mrs. Musadora Roundtree. Executors: James M. Walker of Camden, Mississippi and James W. Holman of this county. Signed August 1, 1860.    Witnesses: J.A. Cooper, J.B. Massey and A.V. Montgomery.    Proven November 23, 1860 in State of Mississippi, County of Madison, City of Canton.

Page 332    **WILL OF WILLIS G. RIVES.**    Wife Virginia Rives. Child: N.S.B. Rives. Brother Henry H. Rives and his wife Catharine H. Rives. Executors: H.M. Blake and Jeff M. Stone. Signed December 26, 1860. Witnesses: Hugh McLier and William R. Hanaway. Proven January Term 1861.

Page 333 **WILL OF JOHN DOUTHIT.** Children: James, Absolom, Samuel, Campbell, children of Jane Davis: Nancy, Spencer, Stacy, Brent, Mary and Frost, the children of Margaret Massey now Margaret Davis, and Lucinda Hinkle. Executors: William Tolly and James W. Holman. Signed July 5, 1859. Witnesses: Feliz Waggoner and John L. Ashby. Proven January 1861.

Page 334 **WILL OF JAMES SEATON.** Wife Mary Ann Seaton. Names: William Greer, Andrew Ferrel, Julia Ann Seaton, Dicy Emeline Seaton, Carrol Mims, Drury Morton Mims, Elizabeth Baker, Jane Davis, Ruth Sandland (Sandlin), Mary Cook, Sarah Osteen, Margaret Meaders and Benjamin Erwin McCary Seaton. Executor: Drury Morton Mims. Signed December 28, 1859. Witnesses: Emery Hill and G.W.G. Heath. Proven January 1861.

Page 335 **WILL OF ARCHIBALD KIDD.** Wife Elizabeth Kidd. Five children: Margaret Anderson, Jane B. Anderson, George Kidd and William Kidd, James H. Kidd. Henry T. Anderson son of Jane B. Anderson. Executors: John Anderson, George Kidd and James H. Kidd. Signed June 25, 1860. Witnesses: William Wyatt and Robert Rees. Proven January 1861.

Page 337 **WILL OF BENJAMIN RAMEY.** Children: Phebe wife of William L. Pamplin, Delina wife of Henry H. Pamplin, both of these daughters are now dead, Catharine wife of Jesse Creacey, Abraham Ramey deceased, Milton Ramey deceased, Mary Ann wife of Samuel Hall, Nancy wife of James M. Davis, Jane wife of Constantine A. Hall, Cynthia Ann wife of Armstead Pamplin, and Wesley Ramey, youngest son William D. Ramey, Benjamin F. and Moody S. Ramey, grandson Travis M. Ramey. Owned land and lived on Cane Creek, in Civil District 12. Executor: Benjamin F. Clark. Signed May 5, 1852. Witnesses: A.T. Nicks and B.W.D. Carty.
Codicil: Proven January 1861.

Page 340 **WILL OF ROBERT E. EDMONDSON.** Wife Sophia M. Edmondson. He mentions children but not by name. Signed November 22, 1860. Witnesses: John Wood and William H. Gunter. Proven March 1861.

Page 341 **WILL OF JAMES S. KEITH.** Wife Mary Ann Keith. Two children: Keziah Elzira Elizabeth and Mary Margaret. Father F.W. Keith. Father-in-law Hampton Sims. Signed January 23, 1861. Witnesses: F.W. Keith and Hampton Sims. Proven March Term 1861.

Page 342 **WILL OF JAMES A. WILSON.** Wife Sarah Wilson. Sister Jane Caughran. He did not mention any children. He mentioned his brothers and sisters and his wife's brothers and sisters but not by name. Signed November 23, 1860. Witnesses: A.S. Sloan and W.J. Gallaway. Proven January 1861.

Page 344 **WILL OF MIDDLETON FANNING.** Wife Rachel Fanning. Daughter Rachael, son Benjamin, six oldest children not named. Executor: Young T. Taylor. Signed February 8, 1861. Witnesses: W.H. McLaughlin and N.J. George. Proven April 1861.

Page 345 **WILL OF MOSES C. WOODWARD.** Wife Catharine Woodward. Daughter Eliza C. Harris, mentions other children but not by name. Executors: Wife Catharine Woodward and son James Robert Woodward. Signed September 28, 1860. Witnesses: J.J. Finney and W.C. Sugg. Proven April Term 1861.

Page 346 **WILL OF MICHAEL ROBINSON.** Daughter Amanda wife of Samuel Brown, daughter Helena wife of William B. Robinson, Melissa J. Cassena. Executor: Son-in-law William B. Robinson. Signed 1845. Witnesses: Robert R. McKinney and Hugh P. Penny. Proven April Term 1861.

Page 347 **WILL OF MARGARET GIVENS.** Daughter Mary Caughran wife of John L. Caughran, heirs of James Wiley, John G. Wiley, J. Caughran, Eliza Phagan, Sarah A. Wiley, three children of my daughter Nancy Galloway deceased.

Had property in Camargo. Executor: John L. Caughran. Signed July 13, 1859. Witnesses: Robert Drennan and William Fife. Proven May 1861.

Page 349 **WILL OF JOSEPH P. HARKINS.** T.M. Harkins was his partner in busioness. Susan A. Flack, B.F. Harkins is deceased, sister Jane K. Harrison, sister-in-law Margaret Harkins widow of David A. Harkins who is deceased, three nephews: J.F., James M., and William T. Sorrells. Executor: James G. Harrison. Signed April 15, 1861. Witnesses: D.E. McCants and W.O. Scott. Proven August 1861.

Page 351 **WILL OF RACHAEL HOUSCH.** Granddaughter Amanda Caroline, grandsons William Jacob and John Wesly the children of my son John Hosch, and grandson John Jacob Patterson. Executor: William B. Robinson. Signed April 10, 1859. Witnesses: James and Margaret Jane Coleman. Proven November Term 1861.

Page 352 **WILL OF EZEKIEL SANDERS.** Son James C. Sanders, son Newton C. and his wife Lucretia Sanders, and Neil S.C. Sanders, daughter Elizabeth McAdams and daughter Harriet C. Smith. Executors: Sons L. David and William H. Sanders. William H. Sanders is to be guardian for my sons Newton C. and Neil S.C. Sanders. Signed December 3, 1862. Witnesses: John B. Stephens and W.S. Findley. Proven February 1863.

Page 354 **WILL OF GEORGE HALL.** Children: A.M., Sarah F. Jones, S.S., William C., and Elizabeth Malinda Flynt. Grandchildren: George D., William, Harriet Frances, and John B. Blake children of my daughter Caroline Matilda wife of William C. Blake. Executors: Son Allen M. Hall and David R. Smith. Signed March 8, 1859. Witnesses: Thomas Hampton and A.W. Smith. Codicil: Proven October 1862.

Page 356 **WILL OF JAMES NELSON.** Children: Mary D. Stephenson, Isaac R. Nelson, Permelia Bledsoe, Thomas R. Nelson, Nancy A. McAdams, Lucy Colter, Sarah A. Nelson, John W. Nelson, Emily J. Nelson, and Virginia P. Nelson. Executor: Son Isaac R. Nelson. Signed August 12, 1857. Witnesses: D.A. Gilbert and J.C. Daves. Proven October 1862.

Page 357 **WILL OF JAMES PITTS.** Wife Rachel Pitts. Children: Ephraim B., Riley W., William A., Elizabeth H. Bright, Henry P., Sinthy Dean, Jane M. Blair, Robert K., James L., Thomas B., Isaac R., and Wiley J. Pitts and heirs of my two deceased daughters Edney C. Rowe and Rachel A. Hall. Executors: Robert K. Pitts and Robert Drennan. Signed August 24, 1855. Witnesses: William Stewart and Quinton Marshall. Proven October 1862.

Page 359 **WILL OF MATHEW W. CARTER.** Two children but not named. Proven by M.W. Carter, A.L. Davidson, W.A. Carter and J.H. Sullenger. Proven October 1862.

Page 360 **WILL OF JAMES B. GILL.** Wife Alafair Gill. 2nd wife not named. 1st wife Margaret Gill and three children: William D., Samuel W., and Sally B. Gill. Executrix: Wife Alafair Gill. Signed June 20, 1854. Witnesses: W.W. Wilson and A.L. Myers. Proven November 1861.

Page 362 **WILL OF HENRY LANDESS.** Wife Grace Landess. Children: Susan Eaton, Hannah Ford, Mary Greer, Evaline Tally and Ann Smith, John, Joseph and Herman Landess. Susan Eaton wife of Alfred Eaton. Executor: Son John Landess. Signed October 3, 1854. Witnesses: A.A. Greer, Jacob Gillespie and John W. Blake.
Codicil: Signed January 9, 1862. Jacob Gillespie and A.A. Greer. Proven November 1862.

Page 364 **WILL OF JOSEPH S. HUDSON.** Wife Esther H. Hudson. Child not named. Signed May 13, 1861. Witnesses: James B. Hudson and James G. Harrison. Proven November 1862.

Page 366  **WILL OF V.C. ISOM.** Wife Mary A. Isom. Four children: James, Mary
F., Robert C., and Greenberry F. Isom.   Signed June 27, 1861.
Witnesses: L.G. Mead and J.E. Brown. Proven December 1862.

Page 367  **WILL OF ALFRED W. HARPER.** Mother nancy D. Harper. Executrix:
Nancy D. Harper. Signed August 19, 1861. Witnesses: James H. Wright
and Jacob B. Wright. Proven February 1863.

Page 368  **WILL OF ELIZABETH HAMILTON.** Son James G. Hamilton, daughter
Susan A. Timmins, heirs of John B. Hamilton, heirs of William B.
Hamilton deceased, David R. Hamilton and Samuel P. Hamilton. Executors: H.C.
Cowan and John B. Hamilton. Signed February 7, 1863. Witnesses: H.C. Cowan,
M.A. Carloss and M.G. Stamps. Proven February 1863.

Page 369  **WILL OF JAMES P. CAUGHRAN.** Wife Jane C. Caughran.  Children
not named.  Executor: James E. English.   Signed April 12, 1860.
Witnesses: Hugh P. Penny, Pleasant A. Randolph and Robert Drennan. Proven April
1863.

Page 371  **WILL OF GENERAL S. MARCUM (MARKHAM).** Wife Charlotte M.
Marcum. Children not named. Executrix: Wife Charlotte M. Marcum.
Signed November 29, 1861.  Witnesses: James R. Bright and James W. Bright.
Proven April 1863.

Page 372  **WILL OF JOHN F. COUSER.** Son John F. Couser, Jr., Robert M.
Couser, six daughters: Mary Gore, Elizabeth Floyd, Sarah Long,
Rebecca Neil, Isabella Cates, and Nancy Pearson. Executors: Robert M. Couser
and John F. Couser, Jr. Signed August 25, 1860. Witnesses: A.E.S. Hanes, Hardy
Reavis and S.S. Reavis. Proven May Term 1863.

Page 373  **WILL OF WESLY TURNER.** Wife Frances Turner. Sister Margaret
Duckworth, sister-in-law Elizabeth J. Goode.   Executor: Woodruff
Parks.  Signed March 8, 1863.   Witnesses: William L. Alexander and S. S.
Alexander. Proven May 1863.

Page 374  **WILL OF ELIZABETH KIMES.** Son Campbell E. Kimes. Mentions other
children but not by name.  Mentions grandchildren but not by name.
Executor: Joel M. Harris. Signed January 19, 1861. Witnesses: R.D. McMillen and
W.M. Rosebrough. Proven June 1863.

Page 375  **WILL OF ALFRED C. DICKEY.** Wife Eliza Dickey.   Children not
named.   Executor: Anderson C. Martin.   Signed April 11, 1863.
Witnesses: J.W. Watt and S.S. Buchanan. Proven May 1863.

Page 377  **WILL OF NANCY STEPHENS.** Brother Isom Wells, brother William
Wells, brother Francis Wells, Mary Isom widow of Valentine Isom,
Margaret Crenshaw widow of Pascal Crenshaw, niece Nancy E. Fairbanks. Signed
April 12, 1863. Witnesses: James E. Brown and R.S. Fleming. Proven June 1863.

Page 375  **WILL OF NANCY ANN SMITH.** Mother Martha M. Smith, and deceased
father Alfred Smith. Executor: F.A. Dickinson. Signed July 14, 1857.
Witnesses: John M. Smith and T.G. Smith. Proven May 1868(1863).

Page 379  **WILL OF WILLIAM L. MOORE.** Wife Virginia L. Moore. Son Archie,
son William N., and Lawson Moore. Sister Davidella H. Neil, nephew
William H. Holman.  Co-partnership with Dr. F.R. Moore. Executors: Newton
Whitaker and Cullen Bailey. Signed April 30, 1861. Witnesses: A.B. Carter and
Nathaniel Gattis. Proven May 1863.

Page 381  **WILL OF JOHN REES.** Daughter Charlet T. Rives, son Jacob Rees,
daughter Ann Neece, heirs of Jordan Rees, Sophia Hale and Joel Rees,
John Rees, and heirs of William H. Rees. Executors: Sons W.H. and Jordan Rees.
Signed April 3, 1862. Witnesses: Dempsey Sullivan and Jerome Albright. Proven

May 1863.

Page 383 **WILL OF JOHN McDANIEL.** Wife Mary H. McDaniel. Children: W.F., Martha J., Martha E. Merritt, Mary L. Wilson, L. Ann March, Sarah E. McDaniel, A.W. March and Bethiah J. McDaniel. Executors: W.F. McDaniel and A.W. March. Signed October 16, 1861. Witnesses: R.B. Gibson and I.R. Nelson. Proven November 1861.


## LINCOLN COUNTY, TENNESSEE WILL BOOK 3


PAGE 1 **WILL OF JOHN J. BONNER.** Wife Sarah Ann Bonner. Son John Jefferson Bonner, mentions other children but not by name. Father-in-law John J. Clark. Executor: William R. Martin. Singed February 16, 1864. Witnesses: A. Bonner and John Mullins. Proven February 16, 1864.

Page 2 **WILL OF JOHN MILLIKIN.** Children: M.A., M.J., Sarah Reese, Agnes Millikin, John H. Millikin, and Abra Millikin, also John H. Hughes. Executor: John H. Millikin. Signed March 23, 1864. Witnesses: William Wyatt and Henderson Barnes. Proven July 6, 1865.

Page 3 **WILL OF WILLIAM L. PAMPLIN.** Grandchildren: Elijah Pamplin and Joel Brewer. Mentions children, both sons and daughters but not by name. Executors: Sons James H., Joel K., Benjamin F., and John T. Pamplin. Martha Matilda Mills, Sarah Maddox and Delinda Levetta Pigg. Signed August 14, 1864. Witnesses: C.B. McDaniel and Reuben Woodard. Proven May Term 1865.

Page 5 **WILL OF ENOCH DOUTHET.** Joel E. Yowell in trust for his daughter Lucinda, James K. Moore in trust for daughter Elizabeth Brazier, son Calvin Y., son Felix deceased and his heirs Finetta Jane and Stacy Minerva, son Alfred Douthet the reputed son of my son Alfred who is often called Alfred Swanner, and son Ira E. Douthet. Executor: William Zimmerman. Signed November 19, 1860. Witnesses: George Stewart and S.M. Hampton. Proven May Term 1864.
Codicil: July 6, 1865.

Page 10 **WILL OF JOSEPH SEBASTIAN.** Wife not named. Children: Matilda Randolph, Isaac Sebastian, Nancy wife of Daniel Whitaker, heirs of Benjamin Whitaker deceased, and Jane wife of John Warren. Executors: Son Isaac Sebastian and grandson Henderson Whitaker. Signed June 28, 1859. Witnesses: James W. Holman and Rufus M. Holman.
Codicil: October 9, 1861. Proven July 6, 1865.

Page 12 **WILL OF BENJAMIN W. MERRELL.** Wife Mary E. Merrell. Children not named. Executor: Elijah Smith. Signed April 1, 1862. Witnesses: Willis Smith and Samuel Bond. Proven July 6, 1865.

Page 13 **WILL OF GEORGE K. MOODY.** Mother Ann H. Drake who married Col. Samuel Drake. Executor: Mother Ann H. Drake. Signed December 25, 1860.

Page 14 **WILL OF M.C. (MICAJAH C.) PAMPLIN.** Wife Levina Frances Pamplin. Children: Nancy J.B. Hanks, Mary A.F. Summers, Sarah A.E. Kay, John T. Pamplin. There are eight children but only four are named. Signed May 17, 1863. Witnesses: Sion M. Conger, F.W. Keith, T.B. Pitts and G.W. Beasley. Proven July 6, 1865.

Page 15 **WILL OF WILLIAM C. BRIGHT.** Wife Ann M. Bright. Signed May 26, 1863. Witnesses: Robert Drennan, F.M. Reece and Robert C. Davis. Proven July 6, 1865.

**Page 16**    **WILL OF ARCHIBALD McKEE.**   Wife Ethel McKee.   Son Archibald McKee.   Executors: Archibald McKee and William B. McKee.   Signed November 15, 1859.   Witnesses: W.A. Gill and Isaiah Hancock.   Proven July 6, 1865.

**Page 18**    **WILL OF MARIAH NOLES.**   Son Benjamin W. Noles.   Daughter Henrietta Noles.   Daughter Julia Ann Noles.   Signed (no date). Witnesses: T.C. Loyd and S.D. Loyd.   Proven July 6, 1865.

**Page 19**    **WILL OF JOHN S. FULTON.**   Sister Eliza J. Rodgers.   Mentions other brothers and sisters but not by name.   Executor: James R. Bright. Signed January 11, 1862.
Codicil: January 11, 1862.   Signed February 20, 1864.   Proven July 7, 1865.

**Page 21**    **WILL OF OWEN W. HIGGINS.**   Wife Frances H. Higgins.   Daughter Nancy Y. Tucker, daughter Sally L. Shull, daughter Mary H. Holman, son George W. Higgins, daughter Martha D. Holman, daughter Frances E. Carrigan, Virginia F. Higgins and H. Clay Higgins.   Owned land in Obion County.   Executors: Daniel B. Shull and George W. Higgins.   Signed March 28, 1865.   Witnesses: Hugh Thomison and William Beavers.   Proven July 14, 1865.

**Page 23**    **WILL OF WILLIAM PARKS.**   Son Benjamin T. Parks, daughter Catharine T. Cashion, daughter Elizabeth Thomison, daughter Parthena Isom, daughter Martha D. Roach, heirs of Mary Summerford, son Joel Parks, and brother Woodruff Parks.   Executor: Brother Woodruff Parks.   Signed October 22, 1859. Witnesses: Charles Bright and Benjamin Marshall.   Proven Monday 1st July 1865.

**Page 26**    **WILL OF HUGH SPENCE.**   Daughter Eliza Jones, daughter Nancy Grace, daughter Sarah Ralls (Rawls), son John Spence and wife Mary Spence.   Executor: Robert Drennan.   Signed August 16, 1855.   Witnesses: John H. Drennan and Calvin W. Drennan.   Proven August 7, 1865.

**Page 28**    **WILL OF JAMES COTHEN (COTHREN).**   Wife Frances Cothen. Children not named.   Executor: W.R. Bruce.   Signed June 6, 1861. Witnesses: Joel Bruce and R.J. Nelson.   Proven August 7, 1865.

**Page 29**    **WILL OF ALSEY (ALEX) NOLES.**   Wife Charity Noles.   Children not named.   One son named as Alsey (Alex) Moore Noles.   Signed February 28, 1865.   Witnesses: T.C. Loyd and M.W. Carter.   Proven August 7, 1865.

**Page 30**    **WILL OF EDWARD YORK.**   Wife Martha Eveline York.   Father Edward York.   He mentioned his brothers and sisters but not by name.   Had land on Limestone Creek in Limestone County, Alabama.   Witnesses: J.T. McCauley. Proven July 7, 1863.

**Page 31**    **WILL OF JOHN FULLERTON.**   Wife Margaret Fullerton.   Children not named.   Executor: John Wyatt.   Signed June 3, 1853.   Witnesses: William V. Tate and Adam E. Moore.   Proven August 7, 1865.

**Page 32**    **WILL OF JAMES RANDOLPH.**   Wife Lucretia Randolph.   Son James, son William, daughter Eveline and daughter Martha Randolph. Executor: Arthur S. Randolph.   Signed July 31, 1853.   Witnesses: Robert Drennan and Arthur B. Shuffield.   Proven August 29, 1865.

**Page 35**    **WILL OF GEORGE W. FANON (FANNING).**   Wife Martha Fanon. Executrix: wife Martha Fanon.   Signed Y.T. Taylor and Thomas C. Fanning.   Proven August 31, 1865.

**Page 36**    **WILL OF JOHN MOOREHEAD.**   Wife Elizabeth Moorehead.   Son William D. Moorehead, son John N. Moorehead, son James L. Moorehead, son Rufus A. Moorehead, daughter Mary G. Gray, daughter Nancy A. Waggoner, daughter Elizabeth Gray.   Grandchildren: William and Mandey Taylor.

Daughter Julia McMillen and her children. Granddaughters Elizabeth Harden and Alcy Ann Fox. Executors: William D. Moorehead and John N. Moorehead, sons. Signed March 24, 1862. Witnesses: F.M. Jean, T.M. Ramey and Jacob Neal. Proven September 4, 1865.

Page 39    **WILL OF THOMAS BLAIR.** Mother Jane Blair. Brothers and sisters: James H., Martha E., Mary C., and John F. Blair. Signed March 12, 1863. Witnesses: Jesse Hankins and A.R. Smith. Proven October 7, 1865.

Page 40    **WILL OF WILLIAM ASHBY.** Wife not named. Children: Greenberry, Asbery, James Wiley, William, Minerva Jane, Rebecca, Sally P., and Nancy Davis. Signed March 9, 1862. Witnesses: Travis Ashby and Henry C. Duff. Proven October 7, 1865.

Page 41    **WILL OF FEATHERSTONE REECE.** Wife Martha Reece. Children: James R., Perlina Ann Sullivan, William H., Aramanta D. Brock, and grandson Featherstone Reece. Executors: Littleberry Leftwich and Byas Logan. Signed June 29, 1865. Proven October 7, 1865.

Page 44    **WILL OF HOWELL HARRIS.** Wife Elizabeth Harris. Son Theopulus Harris, children of my deceased son William Harris and children of Any Bledsoe deceased. Names: Rufus, Gustavus, Theodore, Theopulus Bledsoe, Tabithia Bledsoe and Howell Bledsoe. Tabithia wife of Robert Long. executor: Squire Pickle. Signed August 4, 1864. Witnesses: W.R. Bledsoe, Nathaniel Williams and A.C. Martin. Proven October 7, 1865.

Page 46    **WILL OF PAYTON WELLS.** Wife Mary B. Wells. Son-in-law Theophelus Harris. Wife and said Harris to be guardian for my two sons Thomas Jefferson and Rufus Payton Wells, also guardian for my daughter Josephine Cordelia Wells. Theophelus Harris is trustee for my granddaughter Martha M.J. Bearden, son Newton Jasper, son James Marion, son Hildreth Ethen, daughter Eliza E. Harris, daughter Mary J. Routt and son William Henry. Signed September 20, 1860. Witnesses: J.S. Porter and F.M. Ventress. Proven October 6, 1865. (A long will)

Page 53    **WILL OF JAMES TUCKER.** Wife Edith C. Tucker. Children: Malinda Wright, John B. Tucker, William W. Tucker, Nancy B. Pylant, Elizabeth W. Dollar, Thomas J. Tucker, David Tucker, and Sarah W. Pylant. Executors: Sons David Tucker and Thomas J. Tucker. Signed August 19, 1856. Witnesses: John H. Moore and W.W. Moore. Proven November 9, 1865.

Page 55    **WILL OF WILLIAM GEORGE.** Wife Peggy George. Two sons: F.A. George and Joseph George. Five daughters: Mary Williams, Eliza Hobbs, Jane Tucker, Susan Tucker, and Sally Harrison. Signed October 11, 1862. Witnesses: Thomas George and F.A. George. Proven November 14, 1865.

Page 57    **WILL OF WILLIAM C. BUTLER.** Brother Lewis C. Butler, sister Nancy C. Butler, nephew William C. Butler son of E.T. and Frances Butler. A debt to John Clark. Friend William A. Gill and his wife E.F. Gill and their children: Sally G., Mariah M., and William A. Gill, Jr. A namesake William C. B. Lee son of John L. and Tennessee Lee. Owned land in Marshall County, Tennessee. Executors: H.M. Blake and Dr. William R. Smith. Signed February 23, 1864. Witnesses: David McClusky and Joseph McClusky. Proven November 18, 1865. (A long will)

Page 61    **WILL OF REBECCA CARUTHERS (GOOD).** Sarah Lively, Joseph Good and John Good. Executor: John Caughran. Signed July 2, 1864. Witnesses: S.P. McCollough and Robert C. Moore. Proven November 24, 1865.

Page 63    **WILL OF ALEXANDER BRADY.** Children: William Brady, heir of deceased daughter Tempy Marshall, Abner Brady, Mary Steed wife of Augustus Steed, heirs of deceased daughter Martha Steed, Alexander Brady,

Elizabeth Stradford wife of James Stradford, Isaac N. Brady, Jasper Brady, and George Brady heir of my deceased child. Signed November 1, 1865. Witnesses: Ebenezer Hill, Jr. and James Reynolds.
Codicil: November 20, 1865. Witnesses: J.B. Martin and J.C. Reynolds. Proven December 12, 1865.

Page 65     **WILL OF BENJAMIN CATES.** Wife Isabel Cates. Son Timothy Cates and Nancy C. Renfro. Signed March 5, 1865. Witnesses: W.A. Hobbs and William H. Lock. Proven December 15, 1865.

Page 67     **WILL OF THOMAS WISEMAN.** Six children: L.M. Taylor, J.P. Wiseman, Eliza J. Wiseman, Margaret E. Wiseman, Thomas J. Wiseman, and Mary A. Wiseman. Executor: C.H. Bean and J.N. Moorehead.
Codicil: Proven February 9, 1866.

Page 68     **WILL OF JOHN WISEMAN.** Wife Elizabeth Wiseman. Sons: R.C. Wiseman and J.M. Wiseman, and Thomas Wiseman. Executor: Son Thomas Wiseman. Signed October 26, 1864. Witnesses: John N. Moorehead and Mary Moorehead.
Codicil: Proven March 7, 1866.

Page 70     **WILL OF MATHEW T. WILSON.** Wife Jane C. Wilson. Daughter Mary J.D. Wilson and all estate of James M. Paul, late of Galveston, Texas. Brother Robert W. Wilson. William C. West is to be guardian of Mary J.D. Wilson. Owned ½ block No. 566 in the city of Galveston, Texas. Executor: Robert W. Wilson for the Texas estate. Heirs of Andrew Paul are: James M. Paul, Hannah Wilson, Robert W. Wilson and myself Mathew T. Wilson. Executor: John Carey. Signed January 23, 1866. Witnesses: Joseph J. McCown and W.G. Newton.
Codicil: Proven February 6, 1866. Proven March 7, 1866.

Page 74     **WILL OF D.F. ROBERTSON.** Probate Court, December 1865. DeSoto County, State of Mississippi. Hon. J.B. Morgan, Judge of Probate.
Transcript:
Petition of Susan Jeffries, late Susan Robertson widow of David F. Robertson and James Robertson said David F. Robertson died in DeSoto County in 1862, leaving a will.
Will: Wife Susan Robertson. Son James Robertson, namesake David Robertson Bonner son of Dr. M.H. Bonner of Fayetteville, Tennessee. Executors: Susan Robertson and James B. Lamb and a son James Robertson. Signed September 14, 1860. Witnesses: A.J. Carloss, J.D. Scott and T.C. Goodrich.
Codicil: Owned land on Elk River. Proven March 7, 1866. (Long will and probate, 6 pages)

Page 86     **WILL OF MARY A. CUMMINS.** Mother Darcus Cummins and deceased father Harman Cummins. Executor: Mother Darcus Cummins. Signed April 10, 1866. Witnesses: Mary E. Hill and Margaret M. Carter. Proven June 4, 1866.

Page 87     **WILL OF LEWIS SHIPP.** Heirs of daughter Susan Bryant and Louisa J. Franklin, heirs of Nancy Jane Farrar, Sarah Hobbs, Mary Elizabeth Story, Orlinda B. Coats, son-in-law David Hobbs who is also the executor. Signed November 21, 1861. Witnesses: John Wood and Pleasant Hobbs. Proven June 4, 1866.

Page 89     **WILL OF JOEL REES.** Wife Patience Rees. Daughter Eliza Bailey wife of William H. Bailey, Martha Cole wife of William F. Cole, Fanny B. Rees, Nancy A. Rees, Bettie W. Rees, sons Nathan Rees, John Rees, Joel Rees, and James Rees. Executors: William H. Rees and Dempsey Sullivan. Signed December 29, 1861. Witnesses: Andrew B. Conley, B. Franklin, and W.M. Parr. Proven August 15, 1866.

Page 92     **WILL OF WILLIAM MELSON.** Wife Mary A. Melson. Son Peter Melson and son John Melson. Executors: D.A. Gilbert and J.M. Barham. Signed: June 19, 1866. Witnesses: D.A. Gilbert, James M. Barham and W.W. Rees. Proven August 20, 1866.

Page 94   **WILL OF AB. S. BOONE.** Of Bedford County, Tennessee. Mother Cyntha Boone of Lincoln County. Executor: Montgomery Little. Signed October 1, 1861. Witnesses: H.W.L. Little and J.C. Caldwell. Proven July 3, 1866.

Page 96   **WILL OF JOHN W. BLAKE.** Mentions wife and children but not by name. Executors: Sons Hugh M. Blake and G.W. Blake. Witnesses: A.A. Greer and S.D. Blake. Proven September 24, 1866.

Page 97   **WILL OF LUCY HAYNS.** Daughter Lydia Hayns. Sons Samuel W. and William Hayns. Daughters: Rachael, Ruth Inda, Lucy C., Mary and A.E.S. Hayns. Father David Reves. Executors: James M. Byrom and A.E.S. Hayns. Signed February 12, 1858. Witnesses: Stanton J. Green and R.M. Couser, Jeremiah Dean, and A.M. Reves. Proven September 25, 1866.

Page 99   **WILL OF JOHN W. WATT.** Wife Nancy Watt. Children: Mary J., John F., Pleasant W., Martha M., and Joshua C. Watt, five in number. Executrix: Nancy Watt. Signed October 22, 1866. Witnesses: L.F. Arney and W.P. Sawyers. Proven December 3, 1866. In this will, mentions estate of William Owen.

Page 101   **WILL OF SARAH MOORE.** Heirs Martha Ann McCalley and two sons Artimus and James Phagan, Isabella Allen, Caldona Strong, John M. Strong, Susan Strong, Lewis C. Strong, and James M. Strong. Executor: Robert Drennan. Signed August 22, 1866. Witnesses: Moses Fisk and James H. Gray. Proven September 3, 1866.

Page 103   **WILL OF MIDDLETON BEDDINGFIELD.** Wife Christiana Beddingfield. Daughter Sally Bryant, Elizabeth Bolling and Sarah Bolling, children of my son M.M. Beddingfield, James H. Beddingfield, and John T. Curtis. Signed April 22, 1857. Witnesses: F.L. Ezell and C.W. McGuire. Proven November 5, 1866.

Page 105   **WILL OF JAMES PIGG.** Daughter Mary Ann Pigg. Mentions other children but not by name. Grandchildren not named. Executor: W.R. Bledsoe. Signed September 2, 1866. Witnesses: James Massey and E. Pigg. Codicil: Proven November 5, 1866.

Page 107   **WILL OF MRS. MARGRET GUNTER.** Son William A. Wood and his wife Frances Wood. Signed November 15, 1860. Witnesses: Thomas H. Freeman and G.A. Conn, J.P. Sebastian and R.B. Ramsey. Proven.

Page 108   **WILL OF MARGARET ALLEN.** Son D.P.C. Allen (Service of his Country), children in county but not named. Executor: George H. Allen. Signed June 1863. Witnesses: John L. Ashby and W.F. Stocsill (Stockstill). Proven November 5, 1866.

Page 109   **WILL OF JOHN T. HALBERT.** Sister Emily Halbert. Sister Nannie Halbert. Brother William H. Halbert. Father not named. Joel E. Yowell and James C. Halbert. Signed May 27, 1866. Witnesses: Eliza Dickey and W.F. Hamilton. Proven June 3, 1867.

Page 110   **WILL OF MARY EWING.** Youngest son Joshua C. Ewing. Others not named. Owns land on Kellys Creek. September 12, 1864. Witnesses: W.E. Sims and William Fairbanks. Proven April 2, 1867.

Page 111   **WILL OF WILLIAM D. BRIGHT.** Son Charles T. Bright, son John H. Bright, James M. Bright, Martha E. Dunlap, Charles T. Bright, John H. Bright, and grandson Lucius Bright. Mentions Repsey A. Wilkerson and Martha J. Hobbs. He wanted tombstones erected on graves of Mary Ann Hamlin, William C. Bright, Cynthia E. Bright, Catharine L. Bright and Rachel C. Bright, also my own and my wife Elizabeth H. Bright. Executors: James M. Bright and Edmund D. Hicks. Signed March 18, 1867. Witnesses: L.L. Cole and George Kidd. Proven May 6, 1867.

Page 115 **WILL OF LUCY ANN BRIGHT.** Mother Frances D. Bright. Deceased father Charles Bright. Executor: Alexander J. Alexander. Signed December 8, 1866. Witnesses: William W. James and G.W. James. Proven February 4, 1867.

Page 116 **WILL OF WILLIAM H. STEPHENS.** Description: Aged 28 years on the 23 day of September 1866, dark hair, eyes light hazel, weighing about 135 lbs., living in the city of Matamas, land of Cuba. Wanted light metalic coffin and transported home. James M. Bright, William Harris Bright, and Mrs. Sarah E. Brewer in Havanah, Cuba. Executor: D.C. Hall. Matamas, March 22, 1867. Witnesses: Edward A. Saucher and George L. Washington. Proven No. 327, May 6, 1867.

Page 118 **WILL OF WILLIAM HOLT.** Wife Ann Holt. Executor: James C. Kelso. Signed April 22, 1867. Witnesses: Needham Koonce, William Rally (Riley) and J.F. Sandlin. Proven May 6, 1867.

Page 119 **WILL OF MILTON BUCHANAN.** Wife Araminta D. Buchanan. Son Robert M. Buchanan. Three daughters: Elizabeth P., Margaret P., and Marcella R. Buchanan. Executrix: Wife Aramenta D. Buchanan. Signed April 8, 1867. Witnesses: M.H. Caughran and Joel M. Harris. Proven May 6, 1867.

Page 120 **WILL OF JAMES WILEY.** Wife Jane Wiley. Six children: Luther H., Loney J., Martha J., John K., James H., and Alvira C. Wiley. Land in Jackson and Yell Counties in Arkansas. Executors: Robert Drennan and John L. Caughran. Signed August 29, 1861. Witnesses: Robert Drennan, A.S. Sloan and James Stewart. Proven February 9, 1862.

Page 122 **WILL OF RUFUS K. SMITH.** Wife Unice C. Smith. Child Francis C. Smith, Margaret E. Allison wife of Joseph P. Allison. Signed (no date). Witnesses: J.D. Smith, J.P. Allison and M.J. Allison on January 10, 1862.

Page 124 **WILL OF ROBERT K. PITTS.** Wife Elizabeth Ann Pitts. Two younger children: Culpernia and Emma Cordelia. Oldest daughter Eliza Arrena. Eldest son Lyfus L. 2nd son Finton Augustus and others: Rebecca Josephine, Sarah Elizabeth and Theopholus Ira Pitts. Executors: W.A. Rhodes and H.W. Sheffield. Signed May 8, 1867. Witnesses: I.R. Pitts and H.W. Sheffield. Land on road from Fayetteville to Elkton.
Codicil: July 1, 1867. (Will 8 pages long)

Page 131 **WILL OF JOHN C. ANDERSON.** Wife not named. Executor: Samuel S. McCown. Signed July 12, 1867. Witnesses: H.W. Gunter and John B. Clark. Proven September 2, 1867.

Page 132 **WILL OF SAMUEL MURDOCK.** Wife Nancy Murdock. Daughter Amanda C., daughter Sarah E. Finley, daughter Syntha A. Eason, son Alexander, daughter Isabella Finley, daughter Mary Finley, son John, and son Samuel R. Murdock. Executors: Washington Hunter and A. Cathey. Signed April 6, 1867. Witnesses: A.J. Wysong and Isaiah Nerren. Proven September 2, 1867.

Page 135 **WILL OF LUCINDA D. GREER.** Son-in-law Dr. C.A. Diemer. Granddaughter Mollie Garrett daughter of Eliza M. Harris, deceased. Son John T. Greer. Executor: Son-in-law Dr. C.A. Diemer. Signed August 29, 1867. Witnesses: J.M. Bright and E.M. Marshall. Proven September 10, 1867.

Page 136 **WILL OF THOMAS E. SIMPSON.** Wife Selina Simpson. Children: Sarah J. Moore, Rachel M. Browning, Hester R. Brandon, and W.P. Simpson. Granddaughter Selina Jane. Executors: W.P. Simpson, William M. Browning and A.G.H. Brandon. Signed March 2, 1867. Witnesses: G.W. Brewer and John

Chapman. Proven August 5, 1867.

Page 137 **WILL OF M.H. DIEMER.** Mother Eliza D. Diemer. Brother C.A.
Diemer. Executor: C.A. Diemer. Signed April 28, 1861. Witnesses:
S.H. McCord and J.D. Grisard. Proven October 8, 1867.

Page 138 **WILL OF P.T. PHAGAN.** Four children: Cassina Jane, John Thomas,
James Pressley, and May Ella Phagan. Mentions two oldest children by
first wife. Wife Finice Jane and her two children (James Pressley and May Ella).
If no heirs remain, all property is to go to the United Presbyterian Church of
Lincoln County, Tennessee. Executor: Wife Finice Jane Phagan. Signed March 7,
1867. Witnesses: Robert Drennan and C.W. Drennan and R.A. Stewart. Proven
August 5, 1867.

Page 140 **WILL OF JEFFERSON GREER.** Of Crittenton County, Arkansas.
Daughter and only child Catharine Jane Greer. Mother-in-law Mrs.
Catharine Jones. Executor: Robert C. Jones. Signed May 17, 1855. Witnesses:
H.B. Edmundson, J.W. Jones and Dr. William Rives. Proven August 5, 1867.

Page 143 **WILL OF GRIFFITH CUNNINGHAM.** Daughter Elizabeth Gray wife of
Burgess Gray. Son Joseph Cunningham, daughter Maria Moorehead wife
of William D. Moorehead, daughter Malvina Marchbanks of Texas, and daughter Ann
Miller of Iowa, and son George H. Cunningham. Executors: James B. Wright and
Coleman B. McDaniel. Signed March 30, 1867. Witnesses: G.W. Jones, Gideon Lay
and R.A. McDonald. Proven August 5, 1867. Renamed executor: James B. Bright
instead of James B. Wright.

Page 146 **WILL OF JACOB WRIGHT.** Children: William B. Wright deceased,
Jacob L. Wright, Isaac N. Wright, James H. Wright, George W. Wright,
F.M. Wright, Nancy Harper, Polly Bennett, Adaline Benson and grandson William B.
Huff. Executor: F.M. Wright. Signed March 21, 1854. Witnesses: Davis Smith and
Rufus C. Smith.
2 Codicils: Signed January 29, 1867. Witnesses: Davis Smith and Rufus C. Smith.
Proven November 4, 1867. (This will is 7 pages long)

Page 153 **WILL OF T.P. GREEN.** Wife Mary Green. Mentions children but not
by name. Executors: J.T. Dance and Jeff M. Stone. Signed February
11, 1868. Witnesses: Jesse L. Bryant and D.L. Enochs. Proven March 1, 1868.

Page 155 **WILL OF JAMES R. BRIGHT.** Wife Priscilla M. Bright. Two daughters:
Anna and Elizabeth, called Bettie, Bright, son James Henry Bright,
nephew Lewis P. Bright son of William H. Bright. Executor: James H. Gillespie.
Has estate in Texas. Executor: D.C. Hall. Estate in Lincoln County. Signed April
8, 1864. Witnesses: J.M. Bright, H.F. Dusenberry, A.J. Carloss, H.L. Boone and
Ben B, Ingle. Proven April 6, 1868.

Page 157 **WILL OF ANDREW WAGGONER.** Wife Emily Jane Waggoner. Children
not named. Executors: Loderick Robertson, Jr. and Jacob Waggoner.
Signed March 10, 1868. Witnesses: R.B. Parks and Alexander Forrester. Proven
April 6, 1868.

Page 159 **WILL OF CATHARINE CASTLEMAN.** Deceased husband James H.
Castleman of the County Court of Bedford County, Tennessee. Mother
Catharine Carty. Three children: Sallie Kate, Gertrude and Jimmie Castleman.
Brothers: John and George Carty deceased. Joseph Morrison and wife Eliza and
sister Ann Vining. Signed February 21, 1868. Witnesses: J.T. Mitchell and M.R.
Formwalt. Proven April 6 and 14, 1868.

Page 161 **WILL OF ISAAC R. PITTS.** Wife Elvira Pitts. Children: James H.,
Theodosia H., Thomas P., Elizabeth A., Norah L., Minerva E., Isaac R.,
and Robert F. Pitts. Executrix: Wife Elvira Pitts. Signed February 24, 1868.
Witnesses: James M. Bright and R.W. Pitts. Proven June 1, 1868.

Page 163 **WILL OF JOHN McCOWN.** Wife Tabitha McCown. Three sons: James C., Josiah H., and Washington F. McCown. Daughter Pauline Jane wife of Pleasant N. Bryan. Executor: Son-in-law Pleasant N. Bryan. Signed May 7, 1868. Witnesses: W.B. Robinson and Ann Coleman. Proven July 6, 1868.

Page 165 **WILL OF B.M.G. ALLSUP.** Wife Margaret Allsup. Daughter Elizabeth, son Brice Garner Allsup, daughter Emaranda and Lauretta Allsup, and daughter Martha Allsup. Executor: Esq. W.W. Wilson. Signed July 15, 1868. Witnesses: Willis Hardy and A. Allsup. Proven August 8, 1868.

Page 167 **WILL OF JOHN NOWLIN.** Mother Martha Kidd. My guardian Ganoway Nowlin of Tishamingo County, Mississippi. Executor: James Kidd. Signed July 24, 1861. Witnesses: Robert Patterson and John Coleman. Proven September 7, 1868.

Page 168 **WILL OF WILLIAM OWEN.** Wife Nancy Owen. Three daughters: Malissa Hampton, Narcissa Watt and Nancy Jane Hampton. Executor: L.D. Sugg. Signed April 20, 1860. Witnesses: William F. Zimmerman and J.E. Yowell. Proven September 7, 1868.

Page 170 **WILL OF JAMES THORP.** Land on Little Bradshaw Creek. Son C.J., son John, daughter Ruth H. Robinson, son W.F., daughter Susan Scott, son Joseph S., and daughter Elizabeth Cowen, daughter Mary Burks, daughter-in-law Nancy Thorp, and granddaughter Josephine. Executors: Sons C.J. Thorp and John Thorp. Signed September 15, 1866. Witnesses: F.L. Ezell, W.P. Smith and W.S. Curtis.
Codicil: Proven October 5, 1868.

Page 174 **WILL OF CURRAN D. BENSON.** Wife Narcissa Benson. Son Thomas E. Daughters: Elzira Frances and Eleanor Obedience Benson. Executor: Thomas E. Benson. Signed June 17, 1867. Witnesses: F.L. Ezell and J.P. McGuire. Proven November 2, 1868.

Page 176 **WILL OF ALEXANDER BEARD.** Children: Charles M., Margaret Milam, Abslom, Samuel G., William W., George R., Benjamin who is deceased, Elizabeth M. Jones who is deceased, and Alexander Beard. Executor: Theophelius Harris. Signed July 22, 1868. Witnesses: D.B. Downing and J.M. McKinney. Proven November 1, 1868. (Four pages of will)

Page 179 **WILL OF ENOS WILSON.** Wife Mary T. Wilson. Brother Thomas M. Wilson. William D. Roax. Signed October 1866. Witnesses: J.E. Brown and A.G. Gill. Proven December 21, 1868.

Page 181 **WILL OF ANDREW BUCHANAN.** Children: Daughter Elizabeth, son Felix G., son White, daughter Margaret McDaniel, daughter Mary Wright, son Matthew Buchanan in Clay County, Texas. Owned land on Cane Creek. Executors: Son-in-law Coleman W. McDaniel and William N. Wright and son Felix G. Buchanan. Signed June 10, 1867. Witnesses: C.A. French and _____ Farquharson. Proven January 5, 1869.

Page 184 **WILL OF MARIAH H. PERKINS.** The wife of Drewery M. Perkins and married August 3, 1852. Children: A.J.V. Atkinson wife of M.C. Atkinson, William U. Sherrell, Elizabeth Ellinor Perkins, Francis E.B. Perkins, and Drewery V. Perkins. Former husband A.A. Sherrell. Executors: William W. Sherrell and M.C. Atkinson. Appoint brother James H. Patterson as Trustee. Signed August 1, 1868. Witnesses: John Patterson and H.L. Patterson. Proven April 8, 1869.

Page 187 **WILL OF FRANKLIN A. CAMPBELL.** Clira Campbell. Signed October 2, 1868. Witnesses: W.W. James, P.B. Allison and H.F. Dusenberry. proven April 13, 1869.

Page 188 **WILL OF GEORGE STONEBRAKER.** Wife Martha Stonebraker. Signed October 4, 1837. Witnesses: Andrew A. Kincannon and S.E. Gilliland. Proven May 1869.

Page 190 **WILL OF MARY HESTER.** Son E.L. Hester of District No. 22. Grandsons: Isaac William and James Bailey Hester. Granddaughters: Mary Frances and Ann Adlinda Hester. Executor: E.L. Hester. Signed April 12, 1867. Witnesses: M.H. Bonner and B.L. Hester. Proven July 17, 1869.

Page 192 **WILL OF ROBERT CAREY.** Four children: Margaret, John, James H., and Isabella who married James J. Tate. Executor: James H. Carey. Signed September 9, 1861. Witnesses: C.B. McDaniel and Reuben Woodard. Proven August 3, 1869.

Page 195 **WILL OF JOEL K. PAMPLIN.** Wife Cyntha E. Pamplin. Children not named. Signed April 22, 1869. Witnesses: James D. Tillman and M.W. Yant. Proven August 27, 1869.

Page 196 **WILL OF BENJAMIN WHITAKER.** Son N.M. Whitaker, son-in-law M.L. McElroy, daughter Martha V. McElroy, wife's niece Josephine Thornton, son Joseph C. Whitaker, and Benjamin F. Whitaker, daughter M.A. Wilson wife of James B. Wilson, and son Thomas J. Whitaker. Signed April 30, 1868. Witnesses: Benjamin Whitaker and Jacob Vance and S.M. McElroy. Proven October 4, 1869.

Page 199 **WILL OF JAMES B. GILL.** Wife, 2nd and present, Alafair Gill. Three children by 1st wife Margaret Gill: Samuel W., William D., and Sally B. Gill. Executrix: Alafair Gill. Signed June 20, 1854. Witnesses: W.W. Wilson and A.L. Meyers. Proven November 1861.

Page 202 **WILL OF JOHN CUNNINGHAM.** Wife Polly Cunningham. Son Peter Cunningham and a son William Cunningham who is not sound of mind and under the care of Peter Cunningham. Executor: Son Peter Cunningham. Signed December 15, 1868. Witnesses: John E. Frost and Joseph Parker. Proven December 1869.

Page 204 **WILL OF JOHN ADKINS.** Wife Elizabeth Adkins. Only child Nancy Jane Adkins about three years old. Executor: J.E. Gore. Signed October 25, 1869. Witnesses: J.E. Gore and J.M. Runnells. Proven November 15, 1869.

Page 205 **WILL OF THOMAS GIBSON.** Of Hannah's Gap. Wife Elizabeth Gibson. Son THomas W. Gibson, son Nathan F. Gibson, Emily J. Ezell, William H. Gibson, Elizabeth Dollison wife of W.M.W. Dollison, Margarett M. Russell, and James L. Gibson. Executors: James L. Gibson and James M. Dyer. Signed October 25, 1869. Witnesses: James H. Dyer and J.H. Morrison. Proven February 7, 1870.

Page 207 **WILL OF SARAH STORY.** Daughter Celia S., daughter Martha J., son Thomas M., son Moses S., daughter Sarah N. Cunningham wife of Charles H. Cunningham, and daughter E.S. wife of Thomas A. Stewart. Executor: C.H. Cunningham. Signed January 22, 1867. Witnesses: E.L. Bearden and W.F. Zimmerman. Proven February 7, 1870.

Page 209 **WILL OF HENRY P. PITTS.** Wife Harriet S. Pitts. Children: Rachell B. Marshall, James J. Pitts, J.G. Pitts, Cyntha E. Pamplin, Thomas B. Pitts, William P. Pitts, Mary E. Pitts, Tennessee T. Pitts, Henry W. Pitts, and Wiley S. Pitts. Signed May 7, 1869. Witnesses: W.W. James, William C. Sullivan and S.P. Hamilton. Proven March 7, 1870.

Page 211 **WILL OF LEAH JONES.** Daughter Julia F. Jones. Executrix: Julia F. Jones. Signed March 7, 1867. Witnesses: G.W. Jones and J.T. Medearis. Proven March 29, 1870.

Page 212 **WILL OF TUNSTALL GREGORY.** Son Brown Gregory, a deceased
daughter Mary Parkes, daughter Emily Eslick, daughter Elizabeth
McCartney, son John F. Gregory, Ruth A. Hill, Emily Spencer, Moses F. Gregory,
and Tunstall Eslick. Executor: Son-in-law James M. Spencer. Signed March 7,
1870. Witnesses: M.D. Hampton and A.J. Carloss. Proven April 22, 1870.

Page 215 **WILL OF JOHN McADDAMS.** Land in Marshall County, Tennessee goes
to son A.D. McAddams, daughter Mary King gets land in Marshall
County, son Joseph H. McAddams, daughter Susan King, son John J. McAddams and
wife Elizabeth McAddams. Executors: A.D., J.H., and J.J. McAddams. Signed
January 14, 1862. Witnesses: Thomas H. Bledsoe and James S. Gibson. Proven
May 2, 1870.

Page 217 **WILL OF McDONALD TUCKER.** Wife not named. Children: Rufus,
Perry, Georgia Ann, Saweney and Hillery Tucker. Signed February 14,
1870. Witnesses: William C. Stiles and E.C. Loyd. Proven May 2, 1870.

Page 219 **WILL OF MARY CHILDERS.** Nancy and Susannah Childers, Rice and
Marion Hicks sons of T.B. Hicks, nephew E.D. Hicks. Executor: Nephew
E.D. Hicks. Signed January 1, 1862. Witnesses: A.R. Smith and Rufus Smith.

Page 220 **WILL OF WILLIAM CLARK.** Wife Harriett Clark. Four sons: Lilburn
L., James L., William B., and Claiburn S. Clark. Two daughters:
Elizabeth B. and Rebecca M. Clark. Executors: Son Lilburn L. Clark and
son-in-law William L. Thomas who married daughter Elizabeth S. Signed October
22, 1859. Witnesses: G.W. Jones and R.A. McDonald. Proven July 2, 1870.

Page 222 **WILL OF JAMES L. DENHAM.** Wife Esther Denham. Children: Louisa
J., Lucinda J., William J., Robert, Mira, Michael, Nancy, Margaret,
Lavania, Sarah Ann, Martha, George, and Isaac Denham. Executors: Henry Turney
and Pleasant Halbert. Signed July 16, 1859. Witnesses: R.S. Woodard and J.H.
Blair. Proven August 1, 1870.

Page 224 **WILL OF SAMUEL LAUDERDALE.** Wife Elizabeth Lauderdale.
Daughters: Sarah J., Margaret E. and Mary E. Lauderdale. Son William
Lauderdale. Executors: Gideon Lay and William Lauderdale. Signed January 1,
1865. Witnesses: James M. Davis, Austin G. Smith and S.M. Rowell. Proven
November 7, 1870. Recorded in Book D.

Page 226 **WILL OF MARIAH WALKER.** Sister Cincinnatti Edens, sister Nancy M.
Parks, brother James M. Walker, niece Caroline Reeves, niece Mary E.
Anthony, nephew Jacob Anthony, nephew George Anthony, niece Cincinnatta
Cummins, niece Susan T. Taylor, niece Mary E. Parks, niece Emily V. Wamack,
niece Mariah B. Kiser, and niece Elizabeth C. Parks. Executor: Ambrose L. Parks.
Signed August 21, 1870. Witnesses: J.T. Motlow and E.H. Wamack. Proven
December 6, 1870.

Page 228 **WILL OF ANNA A. MADDOX (AMELIA).** Children: Lucinda Josephine,
Armelia Jane, N.G., Ephraim, H.F., James J., Joseph W., and Isaac
Benton Maddox. Executor: Thomas D. Griffis. Signed November 27, 1870.
Witnesses: W.A. Rhodes and M.L. Stedman. Proven December 12, 1870.

Page 230 **WILL OF R.M. STEPHENS.** Wife Lucinda Stephens. Daughter Rutha L.
Grable. Executor: F.H. Brandon. Signed November 2, 1870. Witnesses:
William F. Bruce and W.C. Evans. Proven February 8, 1871.

Page 231 **WILL OF JAMES WILSON.** Wife Dora Wilson. Matilda C. McMillen to
get land in District No. 13. Three kinsman: James R., Thomas A. and
W.C. Wilson all sons of Clinton Wilson. Friend Mrs. Eliza Mullins. Executor: W.W.
Wilson. Signed December 29, 1870. Witnesses: J.E. Yowell and J.H. Milliken.
Proven February 6, 1871.

Page 234 **WILL OF ELIZABETH SMYTH.** Son David R. Smyth and eight grandchildren: Elizabeth Virginia Smyth, Sarah Eglantine Smyth, Johnathan Greer Smyth and David Radford Smyth, others: William Gilliland, Eliza Campbell Smyth and Helen Margaret Rosebrough children of my deceased daughter Sarah M. Rosebrough. Grandson Johnathan Radford Smyth Gilliland. executors: David R. Smyth and Samuel Rosebrough. Signed July 22, 1854. Witnesses: A.A. Greer and A.M. Hall. Proven February 6, 1871.

Page 235 **WILL OF ALEXANDER EDENS.** Wife Cincinnatti Edens. Children: Felix W. Edens, Samuel W. Edens, daughter Susan M.A. Edens, Amanda H. Hobbs who is deceased, Elizabeth A. Parks who is deceased, James Edens, Mary Oliver, Samuel W. Edens, Virginia S.P. Parks, and Emily J. Waggoner. Executors: Felix W. Edens and James Edens. Signed September 24, 1870. Witnesses: R.B. Parks and S.E.H. Dance.
Codicil: January 1, 1871. Proven June 5, 1871.

Page 237 **WILL OF JAMES L. FOSTER.** Wife Mary M. Foster. Children:_____ and Nancy, and Sarah Muse, son R.A. Foster. Executor: W.H. Foster. Signed April 8, 1870. Witnesses: James H. Redd and M.J. Long. Proven May 5, 1871.

Page 240 **WILL OF YOUNG TAYLOR.** Wife Sarah Taylor. Children: Young F., James H., S.(Sanders) W., Sarah C. Nix, Mary Ann Stiles, Sarah Jane Alley and heirs of John A. Taylor deceased, heirs of Mable L. Stubblefield deceased. James Stiles is guardian for Sarah Jane Alley. Executors: Young F. Taylor and James H. Taylor. Signed September 21, 1857. Witnesses: David F. Robertson and Jarred Simmons. Proven June 7, 1871.

Page 244 **WILL OF JEFFERSON KELSO.** Wife Margaret M. Kelso. Children: Henry F. Kelso's two minor children, daughter Louisa Jane wife of John M. Routt, Alfred D. Kelso, Francis M. Kelso, Mary Mandada wife of John McKinney and Newton J. Kelso. Executor: Francis M. Kelso. Signed May 20, 1870. Witnesses: Theo Harris and R.M. Koonce. Proven June 22, 1871.

Page 248 **WILL OF A.J. KING.** Wife Isabella King. Son Sanford being seriously afflicted. Other children: Martha E. Armstrong, E.(Ephraim) J. King, Thomas S. King, Permelia A. King, Eliza J. Delk, M.F. King, J.W. King, William A. King, S.J. King and Allice King. Executors: Wife Isabella King, James W. Barham and E.J. Kimes. Signed June 2, 1871. Witnesses: Joseph M. Dyer and J.A. Stephenson. Proven August 7, 1871.

Page 251 **WILL OF JOSEPH ENGLISH.** Of Madison County, Alabama. Wife Catharine H. English. Joseph C. son of my brother A.M. English. Nephew Joseph Gregg. Mentions other brothers and sisters but not by name. Executor: Brother Andrew M. English. Signed December 18, 1858. Witnesses: James R. Bright and John D. Moore. Proven August 21, 1871.

Page 254 **WILL OF W.A. BRYAN.** Youngest daughter Cynthia Ann, daughter Sarah Ellen, Amanda E. wife of L.M. Steadman, R.M. Bryan, heirs of my son P.N. Bryan deceased, advisors to my two youngest daughters. E.D. Hicks. Signed June 18, 1871. Witnesses: E.D. Hicks and J.J. Summerford. Proven August 26, 1871.

Page 256 **WILL OF ALLEN BROWN.** Wife Sarah Brown. Executrix: Wife Sarah Brown. Signed May 9, 1871. Witnesses: T.J. Shaw and Patterson Grammer. Proven October 30, 1871.

Page 258 **WILL OF ABRAHAM EDDINS.** Wife Clara Eddins. Three sons: Alva Hugh, Thomas Terah and Milton E. Eddins. Lived on Kelleys Creek, Elk River and in District No. 17. Executors: Sons Alva Hugh and THomas Terah Eddins. Signed September 13, 1871. Witnesses: A. McDonald and H.B. Wallace. Proven December 1871.

Page 260   **WILL OF WILLIAM D. GILL.**  Wife Jane Gill.  Mentions children but not by name.  Executors: Wife Jane Gill and George Stuart (Stewart). Signed August 5, 1871.  Witnesses: F.L. Ezell and A.A. Williams.  Proven December 13, 1871.

Page 263   **WILL OF W.J. PITTS.**  Wife Mary Pitts.  Three children: Martha Ann, Miranniah Alice and Wiley Isham Pitts.  Executrix: Wife Mary Pitts. Signed November 25, 1871.  Witnesses: L.L. Cole and R.W. Pitts.  Proven April 1, 1872.

Page 265   **WILL OF JOSEPH ASKINS.**  Children: William and his son Robert H. Askins, John L., Joseph G., Susan H. wife of Joseph F. Montgomery, James W., Peter C., David L., and Amanda J. Askins.  Signed January 19, 1872. Witnesses: J.H. Hamilton and J.W. Griffis.  Proven April 13, 1872.

Page 268   **WILL OF CORNELIUS ALLEN.**  Wife not named.  Children: Elvira who is deceased, son E.L. Allen, son-in-law H.N.P. Ship, son William H. Allen, son John Allen, son Richard Allen and son Clough S. Allen.  Signed April 13, 1872.  Witnesses: G.W. Jones and W.B. Martin.  Proven April 16, 1872.

Page 271   **WILL OF ANDY MULLINS.**  Wife Jane Mullins.  Nephew A.J. Mullins, brothers and sisters: William, George, Vincent, Pleasant, Jefferson, John and heirs of Martin Mullins: Elizabeth Lock, Gery, Betsey Smith and others. Executor: W.A. Rhodes.  Signed April 8, 1872.  Witnesses: Logan Carpenter and W.W. McDaniel.  Proven 1872.

Page 273   **WILL OF DAVID BUCHANAN.**  Children: W.S., H.C., M.T. Buchanan all sons.  Daughters: Emaline deceased, Elizabeth P. Flynt wife of James C. Flynt and their children: David E., Rebecca and James Flynt, Margaret Clark and Rebecca Rutledge.  Executors: Son H.C. Buchanan and L.L. Clark.  Signed September 12, 1871.  Witnesses: U.C. Cowan and M.H. Conaway.  Proven May 4, 1872.

Page 277   **WILL OF SARAH E. WRIGHT.**  Husband Mathew M. Wright.  Father W.A. Bryan who is deceased.  Executor: Husband Mathew M. Wright. Signed and witness by John Y. Gill.  Proven June 3, 1872.

Page 279   **WILL OF SARAH VAUGHN.**  Executor: Friend Edmond D. Hicks. Signed June 1, 1872.  Witnesses: Robert Drennan and A.D. Summerford. Proven July 25, 1872.

Page 281   **WILL OF THOMAS CHILDS.**  Wife Sally Childs.  Son H.T. Childs, grandson Thomas C. Eason, grandson Thomas C. Childs, granddaughter Maggie Lee Childs, and other grandchildren: Troll Childs and Kate Childs.  Owns land on Bradshaw Creek.  Heirs: Nancy M. Childs, Hezekiah Childs, Henry J. Childs and Sally Ann Garrett.  Executors: H.T. Childs and William T. Garrett.  Signed May 6, 1872.  Witnesses: D.W. Clark and A.S. Thomas.  Proven September 2, 1872.

Page 284   **WILL OF STACY McGEE.**  Son A.S. McGee.  executor: Abner S. McGee.  Signed (female) August 21, 1871.  Witnesses: W.B. Jackson and N.S. Forrester.  Proven September 6, 1872.

Page 286   **WILL OF SAMUEL HALL.**  Wife Sarah A. Hall.  Mentions children but not by name.  Executor: D.C. Hall.  Signed October 5, 1872.  Proven October 16, 1872.

Page 288   **WILL OF JAMES BURTON.**  Wife not named.  Three children, all sons: Robert, Edward G. and A.J. Burton.  Executor: Robert M. Burton. Signed August 22, 1872.  Witnesses: George W. Higgins and W.W. Wilson.  Proven November 4, 1872.

Page 290   **WILL OF JAMES B. WRIGHT.**  Wife Julia B. Wright.  Nephew James C.J. McClelland whom he raised and son of John G. McClelland, son

W.N. Wright, grandson James H. Wright son of W.N. Wright. Executor: Son W.N. Wright. Signed January 3, 1867. Witnesses: D.M. Mims and W.A. McClelland. Proven November 28, 1872.

Page 292 **WILL OF EDMOND F. STORY.** Wife Martha Story. Mentions children but not by name. Executors: My last two sons Moses C. and Mathew M. Story. Signed November 10, 1872. Witnesses: George Stewart and Jasper Hames. Proven December 2, 1872.

Page 294 **WILL OF SAMUEL S. BUCHANAN.** Children: John M., Alfred, A.J., a deceased daughter Louisa Martin and her three children: Mary E., W.S. and George Martin, Margaret Moore, Julia Caughran and Mary Ann McCollum. Executors: John M. Buchanan, William P. Moore and Andrew C. Martin. Signed December 28, 1872. Witnesses: J.G. Dickey and J.D. Buchanan. Proven February 3, 1873.

Page 298 **WILL OF E.B. BRYANT.** Wife Margaret L. Bryant. My wife's son Joseph McCoy. Children: Cordelia Jane, William Lewis, Walter E., Elizabeth Ellenora, Henry P., and E.B. Bryant. Executor: Wife Margaret L. Bryant. Signed August 9, 1872. Witnesses: Carroll Cummons and Samuel Gilliland. Proven March 10, 1873.


LINCOLN COUNTY, TENNESSEE WILL BOOK 4


Page 1 **WILL OF CHARLES BRIGHT.** Daughter Catharine H. Bright who is afflicted and her trustee is James B. Lamb. Other children: William B. Bright, Charles L. Bright, John M. Bright, Maria E. Moore, the heirs of my son James R. Bright and my deceased daughters Mary A. Drake and Martha R. Douglas. Mentions Miss Mary A. Wynn. Inventory breakdown as to advancements to each child. Executors: Sons John M. Bright and Charles L. Bright. Signed April 12, 1870. Witnesses: G.W. Jones and J.B. Lamb and George B. Bayless. Proven February 28, 1871.
NOTE: Items of advancements to heirs beginning in 1845. Long will, about 20 pages.

Page 21 **WILL OF ELIZA ARENA MCGEE.** Husband James P. McGee. Executor: James P. McGee. Signed March 14, 1873. Witnesses: W.W. Templeton and A.P. Copeland. Proven March 29, 1873.

Page 22 **WILL OF NANCY RYALS.** Father Noah Ryals who is deceased. Mother Rebecca E. Ryals who is deceased. Brother William E. Ryals and his wife Mrs. Sarah E. Ryals. Sisters Mahala and Eliza E. Ryals. Executor: Brother William E. Ryals. Signed May 19, 1871. Witnesses: T.F. Harris and A.J. Crunk. Proven April 16, 1873.

Page 23 **WILL OF EASON COLTER.** Wife Annie COlter. Children: Son Hardy H. Colter, son Francis Marcus Colter, daughter Elvira Lane, daughter Mary B. Jones, daughter Sarah Ann Pitts, and grandson James E. Hudson. Executor: Son-in-law Eli Lane. Signed May 19, 1873. Witnesses: G.W. Lane and T.H Fuller. Proven July 8, 1873.

Page 25 **WILL OF W.H. GRUBBS.** Wife Martha A. Grubbs. Children: Lucinda M., Ada May, Fountain P., Sterling C., Z.H., Sarah F. Browning, Nancy Ewing, Martha E., Thomas, Missouri A., and grandchild Adelia Byers. Executor: Z.H. Grubbs. Signed May 6, 1873. Witnesses: W.A. Rhodes and Thomas M. Barnett. Proven August 4, 1873.

Page 27 **WILL OF CHARLES MITCHELL.** Wife Mary J. Mitchell. Two daughters: Martha Jane Blackwell and Sarah Elizabeth Neeld, also a daughter by 1st wife Mary Ann Cooper. Executor: William W. James. Signed

81

November 18, 1872. Witnesses: William W. James and W.H. Robertson. Proven August 9, 1873.

Page 28  **WILL OF T.D. JONES.**  Wife S.A. Jones.  Children not named. Executor: J.H. Holman.  Signed August 8, 1873.  Witnesses: William W. James and G.W. Jones.  Proven August 30, 1873.

Page 29  **WILL OF JAMES BRIGHT.**  Niece Mary Crawford.  Bayless F. Marshall who has lived with him for years.  Niece Louisa A. Williams wife of E.D. Hicks.  Sister Catharine Carty.  Deceased brother Charles Bright.  Deceased sister Polly Williamson.  Deceased brother William D. Bright.  Deceased sister Nancy Crawford.  Executor: E.D. Hicks.  Signed August 29, 1873.  Witnesses: C.A. Diemer, J.P. Morrison and John M. Bright.  Proven September 12, 1873.

Page 30  **WILL OF LEVINA ASHBY.**  Deceased husband Alex Ashby.  Deceased son Nathan A. Ashby.  Francis A. Brown, Nancy A. Moore, Marion J. Groce, Mary Ashby.  Granddaughter Lavine Jane Warden daughter of Rachel Warden.  Signed May 12, 1873, Mulberry, Lincoln County, Tennessee.  Witnesses: D.J. Noblitt and G.M. Milstead.  Proven October 7, 1873.

Page 32  **WILL OF S.Y. McCAULA (McCALLA).**  Wife Martha McCaula.  Son Silas and daughter Martha McCaula.  Executors: Robert Moore and Hugh Parkinson.  Signed September 20, 1873.  Witnesses: S.P. McCullough and S.B. Jones.  Proven November 11, 1873.

Page 33  **WILL OF THOMAS BAXTER.**  Wife not named.  2nd son John Franklin Baxter.  Eldest daughter Rosannah Jane Phillips.  Eldest son Alfred William Baxter.  2nd daughter Sarah Stiles.  Youngest daughter Susannah Mary Elizabeth Albright.  Owned land on Hesters Creek.  Executors: Two eldest sons A.W. and John F. Baxter.  Signed January 7, 1871.  Witnesses: Thomas B. Eastland and A.S. Moore.
January 27, 1871.  Present wife not named.  A yellow girl Lucretia wife of Charles Walker, colored.  Proven December 13, 1873.  (Long will, 5 pages)

Page 38  **WILL OF HALIFAX ASHBY.**  Wife Eliza Ashby.  Sons are in Army at Shelbyville: J.B., G.W., and J.R. Ashby.  Daughters: Martha, Josephine and Evaline Ashby.  Signed June 13, 1863.  Witnesses: John McGee and Alexander Waggoner.
Codicil: Proven November 3, 1873.

Page 40  **WILL OF WILLIAM F. ZIMMERMAN.**  Wife Elizabeth R. Zimmerman.  Children: Nancy E., daughter F.C.J., son A.W., son H.L., and son H.W. Zimmerman.  Mentions having seven children.  Executors: Son H.L. Zimmerman and son-in-law M.S. Story.  Signed November 26, 1873.  Witnesses: James K. Moore and R.A. Stewart.  Proven January 31, 1874.

Page 42  **WILL OF CONSTANT SMITH.**  Wife Margaret K. Smith.  Son T.G. Smith, son S.S. Smith, daughter Hala Eliza T. Hunter and her two children: Davis A(H). and Fanny A. Hunter, daughter Amanda A. McElroy wife of R.C. McElroy, daughter Martha Jane Hampton, deceased daughter M. Louisa Moore and her heirs: John, Knox, Cyrus and Ross Moore.  Executors: Thomas Hampton and James K. Moore.  Signed July 26, 1873.  Witnesses: W.R. Bledsoe and W.B. Ellis.
Codicil: Proven January 12, 1874.

Page 45  **WILL OF WILLIAM CONAWAY.**  Four daughters: Judith L. Stephenson, Elizabeth T. Ashby, Emily Ann Woodard, and deceased Julia R. Harris wife of David L. Harris.  Son Morgan S. Conaway who is to be the executor.  Signed February 23, 1874.  Witnesses: H.C. Cowan and L.J. Woodard.  Proven March 14, 1874.

Page 46  **WILL OF JOHN LOYD.**  Wife Catharine Loyd.  Daughters: Lucinda and Malinda and Polly Ann Loyd.  Executors: F.C. Loyd and S.D. Loyd.

Signed August 25, 1873. Witnesses: Charles Bright and Henry Renegar. Proven January 24, 1874.

Page 48 **WILL OF R.G. FULLERTON (ROBERT G.).** Wife Lucy A.J. Fullerton. Two daughters: Willa A. and Lucy G. Fullerton. Father Robert Fullerton who is deceased. Executor: John C. McDaniel. Signed March 8, 1874. Witnesses: H.C. Cowan and C.B. McDaniel. Proven March 23, 1874.

Page 50 **WILL OF NEEDHAM KOONCE.** Wife Burdotta Koonce. Heirs: Eliza Ann wife of John P. McGee, Martha Elizabeth wife of William R. Smith, Mary Fullerton wife of James Ventress, Robert Manley Koonce, Rufus N. Koonce, and Felix P. Koonce who is deceased and his two sons: William and Carrol Koonce. Land in Civil District No. 21. Executrix: Wife Burdotta Koonce and my son Robert M. Koonce. Signed June 4, 1870. Witnesses: Theo Harris and John M. Routt. Proven March 2, 1874.

Page 53 **WILL OF WILLIAM SMITH.** Wife Jane Smith. Son D.M. Smith, M.L. Smith and wife Martha who has filed for divorce, M.L. Smith's son James Douglass Smith, son William F. Smith who resides in the State of Louisiana, son Andrew Smith who is deceased, John F. Smith who died in Mississippi. Executor: Son David M. Smith. Signed November 10, 1867. Witnesses: Davis Smith, Thomas P. Sumners and David M. Smith. Proven February 24, 1873. (4 pages)

Page 57 **WILL OF WILLIAM SMITH.** Wife Julia Smith. Daughter Sarah Whit. Heirs of Elizabeth Austin deceased. Heirs of Willis Smith deceased. Signed December 11, 1873. Executor: Nephew J. Franklin Smith. Had land in Lincoln and Giles County. Witnesses: J.E. Hall of Lincoln County, .L.L. Smith and W.H. Lock. Proven March 5, 1874.

Page 60 **WILL OF THOMAS J. STONE.** Wife Mary E. Stone. Son Benjamin S. Stone, son William H. Stone, and daughter Martha J. Glaze. Land in Civil District No. 9, Giles County on west bank of Elk River near Elkton. Executors: Son Benjamin S. Stone and A.L. Glaze. Signed January 5, 1874. Witnesses: Enoch Hamilton and Jacob M. Simms. Proven May 11, 1874.

Page 62 **WILL OF MARGARET EZELL (MARGARETTA).** Only daughter Araminta Buchanan, son Pinkney H. Ezell, grandson Mat Buchanan, son Madison who is deceased, daughter Maria Cornelia Gardner. Executor: Son Pinkney H. Ezell. Signed (no date). Witnesses: M.H. Caughran and T.W. Stephenson. Proven 1874.

Page 64 **WILL OF JAMES ISOM.** Sons: G.F. Isom and E.A. Isom. Jackson Isom (Col) and Alex Isom (Col). Signed June 20, 1873. Witnesses: H.J. Pamplin and John Warden. Executor: Son G.F. Isom. Proven April 16, 1874.

Page 65 **WILL OF MOSES ARNOLD.** Wife Sarah Arnold. Daughter Sarah Ann Arnold. Executor: Samuel Stiles. Signed May 2, 1874. Witnesses: William T. Baldwin and J.B. Riley. Proven June 1, 1874.

Page 67 **WILL OF FRANK MARKUM (MARKHAM).** Owned a mill known as Elk River Mills. Mentions a child but not by name. Sisters: Mrs. Mary Flannery and Mrs. Bridget Mangrum, brother John Markum. Executor: Brother-in-law Patrick Flannery. Signed September 17, 1872. Witnesses: George B. Boyles and J.H. Burnam. Proven August 3, 1874.

Page 71 **WILL OF ELVIRA CAMPBELL.** Owned land on Gimlet Creek and a lot in Mulberry Village. Names mentioned: Miss Christiana E. Blackwell, Aramantha T. Floyd, Caledonia C. Blackwell, C.C. Blackwell, and Epsa A. Oxford. Executor: William W. James. Signed May 26, 1874. Witnesses: W.R. Robertson and John H. Reese and G.W. Jones. Proven August 10, 1874.

Page 72   **WILL OF BRADLEY KIMBROUGH.**   Wife Martha W. Kimbrough. Son-in-law Cullin Bailey, granddaughter Kate Whitaker and her mother, daughter Lizzie C. Holman, daughter Sarah A. Jones, daughter Mary Kate Bailey and her daughter Delia Thomison. Land east of Wabash Creek. $500.00 to go to the Baptist Educational Society for Union University in Murfreesboro, Tennessee. $100.00 to Foreign Missions at Richmond, Virginia, and $100.00 to Domestic Mission Board at Marion, Alabama. $100.00 to the Baptist Church in Mulberry Village. On tombstone he asked that this be written: "Reverand Bradley Kimbrough died on the __ day of ___, 18__. Aged: __ years." Executor: Son-in-law James H. Holman. Signed May 11, 1874. Witnesses: John H. Rees and G.W. Jones. Proven September 7, 1874.

Page 76   **WILL OF JOSEPH WHITAKER.**   Son John H., son Robert N., son Alexander J., daughter Eliza J. Sebastian, daughter Julia F. Hill, deceased daughter Susan G. Fincher, deceased daughter Vernetta Baxter, Melville Whitaker youngest child of my 1st wife, I.J. Sebastian husband of Eliza J., Julia F. wife of T.D. Hill. Executors: D.W. Holman and son Alexander J. Whitaker. Signed August 20, 1866. Witnesses: N. Whitaker and Cullin Bailey.
Codicil: Daughter-in-law Cornelia S. Whitaker wife of my son Robert N. Whitaker. Land in Fayetteville. Proven October 20, 1874.

Page 79   **WILL OF HENRY BRYSON.**   Wife Hannah Bryson. Executrix: Wife Hannah Bryson and two sons John and Knox Bryson. Signed November 2, 1874. Witnesses: R. Hamilton and S.S. McCown. Proven November 12, 1874.

Page 80   **WILL OF EBENEZER F. COOK.**   Land in DeKalb County, Illinois, being in the south half of the North West Quarter, Section 14, Town 37, Range 4. Cousin Nelly Christopher, daughter of my aunt Emily A. Christopher of Aurora, King County, Illinois. Executor: Mr. Richard Price of DeKalb County, Illinois. Signed July 28, 1874. Witnesses: William A. Gill, Isaiah Hancock and Philip Y. Coleman. Proven February 1, 1875.

Page 82   **WILL OF CORNELIUS W. McGUIRE.**   Wife Sarah McGuire. Two sons: Calvin B. and John P. McGuire. Executors: Two sons, Calvin B. and John P. McGuire. Signed November 28, 1856. Witnesses: William H. Myers and William H. Gibbs. Proven March 9, 1875.

Page 84   **WILL OF CATHARINE CARTEY.**   Joseph P. Morrison and his three children: William Benjamin, Katie Carter and Joseph Diemer Morrison. Brother James Bright deceased. Executor: Edward D. Hicks. Signed November 17, 1873. Witnesses: R.W. Pitts and Joseph G. Carrigan. Proven February 12, 1875.

Page 86   **WILL OF JAMES H. GRAY.**   Wife Emaline Gray. Children: John E., Clemond A., and Elizabeth Nicks. Executor: John E. Gray. Signed January 4, 1875. Witnesses: Arthur Washburn and John D. Wells. Proven February 1, 1875.

Page 87   **WILL OF A.D.V. BENSON.**   Brother D.A. Benson and sister Liddy J. Benson. Executor: D.A. Benson. Signed October 2, 1874. Witnesses: W.A. Pryor and D.A. Benson. Proven March 9, 1875.

Page 88   **WILL OF PETER KENT.**   Wife Lucy Kent. Brother John P. Kent. Nephew John A. Kent. Lived in District No. 9. Executors: William Moffett and William E. Moore. Signed March 19, 1875. Witnesses: Thomas A. Giles and G.W. Wright. Proven March 27, 1875.
Codicil: Wife Lucy Kent. Proven March 27, 1875.

Page 91   **WILL OF D.P. SHACKLEFORD.**   Wife not named. (Cemetery Records has her tombstone: Aletha Young, wife of D.P. Shackleford, Eds.). Two children: Thomas Mitchell and Emma Shackleford. Sister Lida. Wanted to be buried in Rose Hill Cemetery and have the remains of children removed from Old Cemetery near Presbyterian Church and placed at Rose Hill. (No markers for these children in either cemetery mentioned. Eds.). Executor and guardian for the two children, P.T. Murray. Signed May 7, 1875. Witnesses: C.A. Diemer and J.A. Barbee. Proven April 2, 1875.

Page 93    **WILL OF JAMES L. PITTS.** Wife Caroline V. Pitts. John H., Josephus P., Frances O. Pitts, daughter Ophelia E. Moyers, daughter Phelia Ann Lincoln, David F. Moyers, and J.C. Lincoln. Executrix: Caroline V. Pitts. Signed February 16, 1875. Witnesses: L.L. Cole and J.P. McGee. Proven April 5, 1875.

Page 95    **WILL OF JAMES R. GUNTER.** Wife Martha N. Gunter. Lived in District No. 12. Executrix: Wife Martha N. Gunter. Signed February 4, 1875. Witnesses: J.E. Yowell and H.K. Bryson. Proven April 5, 1875.

Page 97    **WILL OF WASHINGTON WILSON.** James F. Cathy and wife Sarah Ann Cathy. Executor: James F. Cathy. Signed July 27, 1869. Witnesses: W.W. Wilson and Eli Barnes. Proven April 5, 1875.

Page 98    **WILL OF JAMES C. DAVES.** Wife Margaret M. Daves. Children not named. Sister Mary Daves. Executrix: Wife Margaret M. Daves and L.L. Stone. Signed April 11, 1875. Witnesses: Thomas Thomison and Hugh Thomison. Proven May 13, 1875.

Page 100    **WILL OF WILLIAM RANEY.** Wife Ruthey Raney. Minor children not named. Executor: J.R. Routt. Signed April 12, 1875. Proven May 14, 1875.

Page 101    **WILL OF VIRGINIA SHUTT DUVALL.** Husband Charles Perry Duvall. Formerly of Wilson County, Tennessee, now residing in Fayetteville. Executor: Charles Perry Duvall. Signed April 10, 1875. Witnesses: J.H. Burnam and William B. Robinson. Proven June 7, 1875.

Page 102    **WILL OF AMOS ANDERSON.** Wife Malinda Anderson. Son William Anderson gets land on west side of Fayetteville and Shelbyville Turnpike about three miles. Daughter Mary Eliza and her children: William A., James M., and Milton C. Gamble. Owned land in District No. 22, about 100 acres. Executor: D.P. Holman. Signed July 8, 1875. Witnesses: L.L. Stone and G.R. Cowan. Proven August 2, 1875.

Page 105    **WILL OF ROBERT J. NELSON.** Wife Mary F. Nelson. Daughter Mattie V. Nelson, and daughter Eveline Stone, and son L.J. Nelson. My attorney Joseph L. Sherrell and also to be executor. Signed November 3, 1873. Witnesses: Joel Bruce and Philip Bruce. Proven August 16, 1875.

Page 107    **WILL OF HENRY RENEGAR.** Children: E. Delinia and Amanda, Stephen Ellis Renegar and deceased daughter Jane Franklin and son Henry J. Renegar. Executor: T.J. Allison. Signed June 25, 1875. Witnesses: W.T. Dickey and W.R. Burnes. Proven August 31, 1875.

Page 109    **WILL OF EDMOND SNOW.** Wife Mary E.D. Snow. Son D.S. Snow and Mrs. Jane Snow. Executor: John Hamilton. Signed February 16, 1875. Witnesses: F.L. Ezell and P.J. Bolin. Proven September 29, 1875.

Page 110    **WILL OF DEMY (DRURY) JEFFRIES.** Granddaughter Melissa Jeffries. Executor: John T. Pamplin. Signed March 2, 1875. Witnesses: J.F. Davis and Joseph T. Moore. Proven October 5, 1875.

Page 111    **WILL OF MARIANNA McEWEN.** Brother Willie McEwen, niece _____ Drake. Executor: Brother Willie McEwen. Signed (no date). Witnesses: M.M. Davidson and M.A. Ross and S.W. Carmack. Proven October 6, 1875.

Page 113    **WILL OF FREDERICK ZIEMER.** Formerly of Germany, City of Berlin. Now a citizen of U.S.A. Two sisters in Germany: Wilhelmina wife of A. Birkholz of No. 18 Thirgarten Street, Berlin, Germany and Emelia Ziemer also of Berlin. Wife Elizabeth Ziemer. Signed December 18, 1875. Witnesses: N.G.

George and Sol Heyman. Proven December 27, 1875.

Page 114 **WILL OF ROBERT STRONG.** S.P. and Eliza McCullough. Executor: Robert Moore. Signed March 1, 1875. Witnesses: J.N. Good and J.L. Stewart. Proven February 4, 1876.

Page 116 **WILL OF DANIEL JONES.** Children: Daughter Dorcas Cummins, two granddaughters, Daniel J. Weigart and Georgeana Moyers wife of John Moyers, the children of John Weigart and his first wife Milberry Ann Weigart who was my daughter, daughter Mary B. Weigart wife of John Weigart and her youngest son Columbus Weigart, grandchildren: Mary F., America B., Berthenia A., and Tabitha P. Weigart, son McMinn Jones, daughter Sarah J. Little wife of Samuel Little and her two sons: Weigart and William Little, a granddaughter the daughter of son McMinn Jones, and son Seaborn Jones. Executor: Coleman A. McDaniel. Signed May 29, 1876. Witnesses: G.W. Jones and H.N.T. Shipp. Proven February 28, 1876.

Page 118 **WILL OF ELIZA ASHBY.** Son George W. Ashby. Mentions daughters and other children but not by name. Executor: Martin V. Groce. Signed February 27, 1876. Witnesses: C.C. Hall and W.G. Commons. Proven March 6, 1876.

Page 119 **WILL OF J.H. ESLICK.** Mentions his wife and children but not by name. Executor: E.F. Tucker. Signed March 10, 1876. Witnesses: John H. Sullenger and Thomas C. Sullenger. Proven April 3, 1876.

Page 120 **WILL OF SARAH JANE NEECE.** Daughter Rebecca Catharine Leftwich, grandchildren: H.H. Neece, Elinetine Pyrdom, Hulda Raney the children of my two sons: J.B. and James K.P. Neece. Executor: D.J. Noblitt. Signed June 23, 1876. Witnesses: T.T. Rives and J.J. Rives. Proven September 4, 1876.

Page 122 **WILL OF ALICE SMITH.** Mother Martha M. Smith. Sister Isanora Smith, sister Mrs. Amanda Dickinson and Elizabeth Davidson. Executor: George J. Stonebraker. Signed September 6, 1876. Witnesses: D.W. Holman and C.B. McGuire.
Codicil: September 9, 1876. Proven September 1876.

Page 123 **WILL OF M.W. WILLIAMS.** Of Blanche, Tennessee. Wife Jane E. Williams. Executrix: Wife Jane E. Williams. Signed September 11, 1876. Witnesses: James F. Byers and J.J. Rawls. Proven November 3, 1876.

Page 124 **WILL OF TRAVIS ASHBY.** Wife Caroline Ashby. Grandchildren: Asberry Ashby, James Ashby, William T. Ashby, Rebecca Ashby, Sallie P. Ashby, Nancy Ashby, Travis D. Ashby, Minerva Waggoner, Sarah Kimes, Eliza Bedwell, Antona Conaway, Minerva Conaway, and Fannie Conaway. Signed: August 29, 1876. Witnesses: Stephen Johnson and James T. Smith. Proven October 17, 1876.

Page 126 **WILL OF WILLIAM KIDD.** Wife Margaret Kidd. Daughter Venicia Jane Phagan, son James F. Kidd, daughter Sarah E. Kidd, son William H. Kidd, and Caroline M.J. Kidd. Executor: James H. Kidd. Signed February 16, 1867. Witnesses: B.E. Melear and John R. Smith. Proven December 2, 1876.

Page 127 **WILL OF ELIZABETH A. REESE.** Daughter Manerva A. Moore, granddaughter Mary A. Millican, granddaughter Elenora Reese, grandson H.S. Reese, granddaughter Olivia H. Newton, daughter Lutitia J. Hubble, son C.A. Reese. C.A. Reese gets the Family Bible. Granddaughter Elizabeth A. Pitts, and other children: Cynthia Surber, Elvira Pitts, Rebecca Marberry, H.S. Reese, Caladonia F. Pitts, and Perlina O. Summerford. Executor: Charles A. Reese. Signed September 13, 1876. Witnesses: L.L. Cole and W.E. Bradford. Proven October 2, 1876.

Page 128 **WILL OF ROBERT S. WOODARD.** Wife Mary Woodard. Four sons: James, Galen, John and William Woodard. Son-in-law T.E. Dryden. Two daughters: Sallie and Ada. Son-in-law Dr. Hatcher. Son Andrew, son Robert Woodard, daughter Mary Hatcher, son M.W. Woodard who is also guardian of Mary Commons and Sina Commons. Land in Madison County, Alabama. Executors: Sons M.W. and A.B. Woodard. Signed May 13, 1877. Witnesses: G.W. Jones, W.N. Wright, James D. Tillman and J.H. Holman. Proven May 26, 1877.

Page 132 **WILL OF JOHN LANDESS.** Children: Mattie A. Terry, Mary R. Goodrich, Eva G. Bobo, John Henry and William J. Landess, Sue K., Ella J., Sallie L., and Fannie L. Holman and Charles S. Landess. Executors: John M. Stone and D.W. Holman. Signed February 4, 1875. Witnesses: R.J. Small, Jr. and Peter Cunningham. Proven March 1877.

Page 134 **WILL OF SANFORD M. McELROY.** Wife Louisa A. McElroy. Children: David S., William, Alfred, Lucy and Charley McElroy. Land in District No. 8. Executor: Son William McElroy. Signed May 18, 1875. Witnesses: John Bateman Smith and J.B. Morgan and George B. Boyles. Proven January 26, 1877.

Page 136 **WILL OF JAMES L. FULLERTON.** Will (J.W.) Lauderdale. Signed October 23, 1876. Witnesses: W.W. McMullen and R.H. Hamilton. Proven February 24, 1877.

Page 137 **WILL OF CATHARINE H. ENGLISH.** A.M. English, sister Amanda Hunter, Nancy E. Wilbanks who is now living with me, daughter Rachel Roach, Catharine Roach now living in South Carolina, niece Sarah Bird, niece Mary Kelly of Tennessee, other nieces: Sarah, Rachel, Mary Jane, Margaret and Amanda Chilits of South Carolina. Land in Tallahatchee County, Mississippi under the control of W.H. Fitzgerald of the town of Charleston of Mississippi. Executor: A.M. English. Signed May 3, 1877. Witnesses: Peter A. Dale and A.S. Randolph. Proven July 7, 1877.

Page 139 **WILL OF GEORGE GANT.** Wife Catharine Gant. Executrix: Wife Catharine Gant. Signed (no date). Witnesses: G.W. Higgins and R.R. McKinney. Proven April 30, 1877.

Page 140 **WILL OF WILLIAM THOMAS.** Three daughters: Harriet Thomas, Emily Bryant and Cynthia Smith. Executors: Hugh D.A. Thomas and William L. Thomas. Signed January 27, 1872. Witnesses: L.L. Clark and J.J. Short. Proven October 6, 1877.

Page 142 **WILL OF JANE S. ROSEBROUGH.** Son John L. Rosebrough and son W.M. Rosebrough. Executor: David M. Beatie. Signed October 12, 1868. Witnesses: W.B. Clark, E.M. Crawford and L.L. Clark. Proven October 22, 1877.

Page 143 **WILL OF MARY ANN SCOTT.** Sons: Andrew J., John W.O. and Joseph M. Scott. Executors: Andrew J. and John W.O. Scott. Grandson Charley R. Scott. Signed February 18, 1874. Witnesses: J.A. Stephenson and R.A. Morrison. Proven April 6, 1874.

Page 144 **WILL OF WILLIAM MOSELEY.** Wife Mary Moseley. Son Robert P., son H.H., son J.B., and son L.H. Moseley. Signed November 11, 1876. Witnesses: Joel Bruce and James Harrison. Proven November 5, 1877.

Page 145 **WILL OF W.H. WARREN.** Wife Lou Warren. Son Thomas H. Warren, son William Henry Clinkscale Warren. To be buried at "Grand Pa Blake's Old Burial Ground." Father Thomas K. Warren. Signed October 4, 1877. Witnesses: George W. Counts, A.A. McAfee and T.R. Rives. Proven November 10, 1877.

Page 146 **WILL OF JOHN S. DICKEY.** Wife Elizabeth B. Dickey. Mentions children but not by name. Executor: Wife Elizabeth B. Dickey. Signed September 29, 1877. Witnesses: H.C. Gaults and Luther H. Dickey. Proven December 10, 1877.

Page 147 **WILL OF DAVID JEAN, SR.** Wive Elizabeth Jean. Signed October 24, 1869. Witnesses: A.D.V. Benson and W.J. Bryant and David L. Harris. Proven January 9, 1878.

Page 147 **WILL OF JOHN HOLLEY.** Wife Elenor M. Holley. Four children: Elenor J., Martha, John S. and Carriah Holley. Executor: N.J. Sorrells. Signed January 23, 1878. Witnesses: T.M. Harkins and W.T Sorrells. Proven February 9, 1878.

Page 148 **WILL OF BERDOTTA CLAUNCH.** Daughter Martha Emaline Claunch. Lived in Civil District No. 21. Executor: James P. McGee. Signed January 21, 1878. Witness: John M. Routt. Proven April 8, 1878.

Page 149 **WILL OF EDWARD SUMMERFORD.** Children: Martha Jane, Catharine, Edward B., Eliza Frances and David A. Summerford. Signed January 10, 1866. Witnesses: Thomas Mallard and Hugh D.A. Thomas. Proven April 13, 1878.

Page 150 **WILL OF HUGH THOMISON.** Wife Elizabeth Thomison. Children: Annie, Susie, Joel P., Julia Ann Cowen, Mary E. McKinney, Ida M. Alexander, Ella C. Cartwright, Franklin Pierce, Hugh, Andrew J. and John H. Thomison. Executors: Wife Elizabeth Thomison and son John H. Thomison. Signed June 13, 1878. Witnesses: T.U. Stephenson, H.B. Bright and R.L. Bright. Proven September 23, 1878. (Long will, 8 pages)

Page 157 **WILL OF SUSAN CARRIGER.** Deceased husband Thomas J. Carriger. John S. Carriger, William Montgomery and wife Louisa Jane, E.M. McClure and wife Susan, Francis Carriger wife of B.F. Carriger, William Norvell and wife Martha, G.W.J. Carriger, son Alonzo Carriger. Executors: Son John S. Carriger and son-in-law E.M. McClure. Signed February 11, 1877. Witnesses: D.J. Noblett and J.M. Noblett.
Codicil: Witnesses: D.J. Noblett and Alonzo Carriger. Proven March 19, 1879. (3 pages)

Page 160 **WILL OF MARY L. BEANLAND.** Five children: J.H., Mattie R. Porter, Jane B. Forbes, Jordan M. and Charlie R.W. Beanland. Aunt Julian Reece, sister F.R. Williams, son James H. Beanland, son Jordan is to get the Family Bible, Charlie gets a Family Bible, son-in-law George Porter, son-in-law Edwin Forbes, brother-in-law O.W. Williams, three grandchildren: _____ Porter, Mary B., and mary Lou Forbes. Mary Curlee. Executors: Son J.H. Beanland. Signed January 21, 1878. Witnesses: D.B. Downing and A.J. Ventress. Proven May 6, 1878.

Page 161 **WILL OF SALLIE B. BEANLAND.** Husband James H. Beanland. Two children: Charlie Eddie and Mary Brown Beanland. Executor: Husband James H. Beanland. Signed September 21, 1877. Witnesses: J.B. Tigert and W.C. Griswell. Proven June 15, 1878.

Page 163 **WILL OF NEWTON WHITAKER.** Wife Frances Ann Whitaker. Lived at Mulberry. Executors: R.A. Rees and Mat N. Whitaker. Signed August 15, 1878. Witnesses: A.J. Whitaker of Mulberry and William W. James. Proven September 26, 1878.

Page 164 **WILL OF SAMUEL TODD.** Of Hanover County, Virginia. Wife Ann G.O. Todd. he was from Spotsylvania. He had land on Duck River in Robertson County, Texas. Youngest son Samuel Dick Todd. Land in Rush County also in Newton and Worton and Jasper Counties in Texas. Daughter Mary Jane Smith to get land in Jasper County, Texas. Daughter Elzira R. Greer, sister Betsey, nephew Samuel Todd son of my brother Levi Todd, son James H. Todd gets land in Rush

County, Texas, son John N. Todd is deceased, and granddaughter Mary Lou Greer gets land in Jasper County, Texas. Executor: Samuel D. Todd. Signed April 29, 1866. Witnesses: C.I. Goodall, Joseph Sitman and George W. Sitman. Proven in Hanover County, Virginia November 22, 1866. Proven May 27, 1878.

Page 166 **WILL OF A.O. BATTLE.** Eugenia Battle. Executrix: Eugenia Battle. Signed January 30, 1878. Witnesses: C.B. McGuire and E.L. Drake. Proven November 5, 1878.

Page 167 **WILL OF WILEY W. ALEXANDER.** Father William L. Alexander. Brother-in-law M.L. Smith who is a partner and also married to my sister Mary C. Mentions two younger sisters but not by name. Executor: M.L. Smith. Signed November 19, 1878. Witnesses: A.C. McClain, Joe Dinwiddie and G.W. Jones. Proven December 11, 1878.

Page 168 **WILL OF THOMAS G. WILLIAMS.** Half sister Victoria Ray, Melia Ray, William A. Williams son of Enoch B. Willilams deceased. Executor: J.H. Southworth. Signed (no date). Witnesses: W.E. Carter and N.M. Jenkins. Proven February 3, 1879.

Page 169 **WILL OF REUBIN WOODARD.** Son Robert S. Woodard, deceased. Daughter Eliza wife of S.H. McKinney, son William M. Woodard, daughter Lucy Ann McElroy wife of Sherrod G. McElroy, daughter Mary M. Commons wife of Hiram Commons, daughter Frances E. wife of James M. Price, daughter Nancy L. wife of James Hamilton, deceased daughter Sinai M. wife of Thomas White, grandson Thomas Price, granddaughters Mary and Sinai Commons. Land in District No. 12. Signed June 30, 1877. Executors: Thomas White and A.B. Woodard. Witnesses: G.W. Jones, E.L. Drake and W.A. Miles. Proven May 24, 1879.

Page 171 **WILL OF A. PETERSON SMITH.** Son Alfred W. Smith is to be the executor. Other children not named. Grandchildren and only one named was Robert J. Blakemore. Signed May 22, 1879. Witnesses: A.H. Bishop, B.F. Hudson and T.W. Clark. Proven June 25, 1879.

Page 172 **WILL OF JAMES McNEAL.** Wife J.C. McNeal. Two sons: James and William McNeal. Signed February 1, 1879. Witnesses: A.S. Moore and W.J. Wiley. Proven July 14, 1879.

Page 173 **WILL OF ELIZABETH C. JEAN.** Son Thomas Jefferson Jean, daughter Eliza, son Wesley Jean. Mentions deceased Daniel Jean, Sr., and his son Wyatt Jean. Brother W.J. Bryant. Executor: Brother W.J. Bryant. Signed August 20, 1879. Witnesses: J.D. Bryant and A. Fitch. Proven August 25, 1879.

Page 175 **WILL OF WILLIAM C. BLAND.** Wife Permelia Bland. Son James R., son J.W., daughter Beatrice J.R. Flynn wife of H.H. Flynn, grandson John S. Bland. Executors: John Smith and son J.R. Bland. Signed June 29, 1875. Witnesses: J.M. Story and L.C. Story and James M. Story. Proven September 4, 1876.

Page 178 **WILL OF MARTHA E. BLAIR.** Brother James H. Blair, sister Mary C. Rowell, sister Rachael J. Blair, and John F. Blair. Executrix: Sister Rachael J. Blair. Signed March 26, 1872. Witnesses: L.L. Cole, R.W. Pitts and A. McDonald. Proven September 23, 1879.

Page 179 **WILL OF ROBERTSON CLARK.** William Clark. Willie Gray son of Ellen Gray, Mrs. H.J. (Mary Ann) Carloss, deceased Lucy Bonner's three children, Ann Bonner wife of Moses Bonner, James Robertson only son of my uncle David Robertson, William H. Robertson, Robertson Clark son of W.H. Robertson, Mary wife of William Clark, Belle R. Robertson. Executor: J.D. Tillman. Signed September 29, 1879. Witnesses: J.G. Woods, C.B. McGuire and F.R. Moorehead. Codicil: Proven October 28, 1879.

Page 181 **WILL OF J.L. (JEFFERSON L.) RAY.** Wife Frances E. (Cox) Ray. Only one son named Jacob S. Ray. Mentioned a family. Signed August 9, 1879. Witnesses: William B. Neeld and Henly Stone. November 5, 1879.

Page 182 **WILL OF JAMES F. BYERS.** Wife Lizzie B. Byers. Children: Adelaid E., Richard H., Ada, Edna E., and Jimmie M. Byers. Mentioned a brother but not by name. Executors: J.A. Holland and T.D. Griffis. Signed December 29, 1879. Witnesses: T.D. Griffis and J.R. Abernathy. Proven January 26, 1880.

Page 184 **WILL OF DAVID JONES.** Wife Ann Jones. Children: Thomas J., James A., L.D., Malissa Stewart, Enoch F., and Isaac M. Jones. Executors: Leroy D. Baggerly and Charles Thompson, Sr. Signed September 30, 1879. Witnesses: J.B. Woodard and D.L. Baggerly. Proven January 27, 1880.

Page 186 **WILL OF M.H (MOSES H.) BONNER.** Of Davidson County, Tennessee. Wife Ann F. Bonner. Land in Fayetteville and also land in Mississippi. Daughter Blanche, J.W. Bonner is trustee and guardian. Mentions other children but not by name. Signed August 6, 1878. Witnesses: G.W. Jones and J.D. Tillman. Proven February 20, 1880.

Page 188 **WILL OF HANNAH WALLACE.** Niece Hepsidans Key wife of C.G. Key (Campbell G.). Willis Satterfield and his daughter Alice Satterfield, nephew William C. Baits. Executor: George W. Higgins. Signed September 11, 1871. Witnesses: Alfred Bearden and James E. Green. Proven January 17, 1880.

Page 189 **WILL OF NANCY D. HARPER.** Deceased father Jacob Wright, deceased son Alfred N. Harper, son Thomas M. Harper, daughter Mary L. Shaw wife of Joseph Shaw. Land on Cane Creek. Executor: Son-in-law Joseph Shaw. Signed January 25, 1869. Witnesses: E.S. Wilson and Jacob R. Wright. Proven March 19, 1880.

Page 191 **WILL OF CHARLES N. THOMPSON.** Wife Mary Ann Thompson. Grandson Robert Lee Thompson. W.W. Thompson. Mentions children but not by name. Executor: Pinkney L. Twitty. Deceased daughter Adie McDonald and her two children, not named. Signed February 26, 1880. Witnesses: W.A. Rhodes and A. McDonald. Proven April 5, 1880.

Page 192 **WILL OF E.H. (ELIZABETH H.) SMITH.** Mary Jane Whitt. Fanny Martin O'Neal. Executor: Nathan Smith. Signed April 26, 1880. Witnesses: J. Franklin Smith and William Hardin. Proven July 5, 1880.

Page 193 **WILL OF DAVID ARMSTRONG.** Children: Deceased son Andrew H. Armstrong, Jane C. Tucker, James B. Armstrong, John F. Armstrong, Mary R. Ford, David M. Armstrong, Martha A. Sorrells, deceased son William T. Armstrong, Margarett E. Armstrong, Albert G. Armstrong, John F. Armstrong has two children: Elnorah H. Armstrong and Leona T. Armstrong, William T. Armstrong has one child Ivey H. Armstrong. Executors: James B. Armstrong and David M. Armstrong. Signed May 2, 1867. Witnesses: James T. Renfrow and Hugh A. Dollins. Proven July 24, 1880.

Page 195 **WILL OF LITTLEBERRY L. STONE.** Daughter Fannie A. Higgins wife of H.C. Higgins, son James D. Stone, grandson Walter J. Higgins and also Eugene J. Higgins. Had land on east and west side of Norris Creek, Civil District No. 7. Deed recorded in Book H, page 172 and 173. Land in Bristers Cove in Etawa County, Alabama. Signed May 5, 1877. Witnesses: M.W. Woodard, J.B. Lamb and J.R. Feeney.
Codicil: Deed Book M, page 299. Executor: James D. Stone. Signed July 26, 1880. Witnesses: G.W. Stone, J.G. Harrison and J.A. Floyd. Proven August 26, 1880. (6 pages).

Page 200 **WILL OF M.L. OWEN.** Wife Susan Owen. Deceased son James M.

Owens and his children: James M.L. Owen son by 2nd wife and two sons: William and Thomas by 1st wife. Mentions his daughters but not by name. Executor: W.W. Wilson. Signed November 11, 1879. Witnesses: J.F. Cathey and A.G. March. Proven August 2, 1880.

Page 205 **WILL OF PARTHENIA GLENN SHORT.** Land in District No. 11, west side of Fishing Ford Road. Bill shoet and his children: John Parthenia, Lemuel and Randall. Joseph Short and his two children: Mollie and Etta. Easter Short and her child Lizetta. William Collier and wife Polly whose maiden name was Garrett. Thomas McGaugh gets land in Marshall County, Tennessee. James Short, Betsey Walls and Betsey Ann Gibson gets land in Marshall County, Tennessee. Theo F. Harris, land in Petersburg. Deceased brother John Short. Executor: Theo F. Harris. Signed January 5, 1880. Witnesses: J.H. Burnam and W.R. Smith.
Codicil: May 31, 1880. Proven November 24, 1880.

Page 210 **WILL OF DAVIS W. CLARK.** Wife Lucy G. Clark. Son John E.T. Clark. Wife's sister Nannie A. Carter. Sister Maria W. Flynt and A.E. Garner. Executrix: Wife Lucy G. Clark. Signed July 17, 1879. Witnesses: A.C. Martin and W.A. Millard. Proven December 16, 1880.

Page 211 **WILL OF WILLIAM WYATT.** At home December 8, 1880. Daughter Margaret J. McCown wife of Samuel McCown, daughter Mollie E. Gordon wife of J.B. Gordon and her heirs. Jane Wyatt, William R. Wyatt, Sam McCown and Roselie McCown. Signed (no date). Witnesses: R.C. Wyatt and P.W. Halbert. Proven January 3, 1881.

Page 213 **WILL OF MARTHA JANE RYALS.** Niece Rebecca Elizabeth Hall. Nephews: A.H. Bruer (Brewer), J.C., Joseph and Denham Bruer (Brewer). Executors: W.F. McDaniel and E.S. Wilson. Signed November 13, 1880. Witnesses: Right (Wright) Luna and M.F. Clark. Proven January 31, 1881.

Page 214 **WILL OF DAVID M. BEATIE.** Brother Andy M. Beatie, son John B. Beatie, daughter Sarah Elizabeth Halbert, daughter Mary A. Millard, and daughter Susan J. Halbert. Land on Cane Creek. Executor: R.D. McMillen. Signed February 15, 1881. Witnesses: H.L. Thomas and R.D. McMillen. Proven February 23, 1881.

Page 216 **WILL OF MARY LETITIA BELL.** Children: William Paris Bell, Jennie Bell, Ora Bell, and Brenda Bright Bell. Paternal Aunt Amanda M. Bright. Sister Ida Vivia Metcalf. Deceased father William H. Metcalf. Executrix: Aunt Amanda M. Bright also guardian of his children. Signed March 1, 1881. Witnesses: Z.P. Gotcher and W.L. Metcalf. Proven March 15, 1881.

Page 217 **WILL OF WILLIAM P. SMITH.** Wife Martha J. Smith. Widow of my deceased brother John W. Smith and their children: John E. Smith, William G. Smith, Samuel Smith, Madora Smith, R.P. Smith, Rufus Smith, Matilda C. Wright, and Martha C. Wright. Sister Parthenia Howell. Sister Nancy Harwell. Nephew William P. Harwell. E.S. Wilson. Executors: F.L. Ezell, E.S. Wilson and W.P. Harwell. Signed February 7, 1877. Witnesses: John Clark and H.G. Swineboard. Proven March 18, 1881.

Page 219 **WILL OF ANDREW McCLAIN.** Sons: George A. McClain and John E. McClain. Three daughters: Eliza H. Warren, Ophelia McClain and Malda McClain. A claim on file at Washington City against United States for 26 or 27 hundred dollars for property taken during the last war, in the hands of J.L. McFaland. Executor: Son-in-law James H. Warren. Signed December 19, 1879. Witnesses: William G. Knowles and W.W. Parkes. Proven April 4, 1881.

Page 221 **WILL OF EMILY G. SPENCER.** November 6, 1880. Husband James M. Spencer. Sister Elizabeth McCartney, sister Ruth A. Hill and her two children, and Charley McCartney. This will was made before she died and not opened until after her burial. Proven May 2, 1881.

Page 222 **WILL OF WILLIS D. COLE.** Wife Martha C. Cole. Son James M. Cole, and younger son Henry Cole. Executor: John B. Cole. Signed April 6, 1881. Witnesses: James E. Randolph and A.J. Childress. Proven May 18, 1881.

Page 223 **WILL OF SAMUEL S. ALEXANDER.** Wife Mary Alexander. CHildren: William L., James I., George J., Harmon H., and Smith M. Alexander and Elizabeth Johnson wife of Angus D. Johnson, Ruthy Tate wife of William V. Tate, Mary Ann Parks wife of Elisha T. Parks, and Amanda Badgett wife of J.R. Badgett. Executors: Sons George J. Alexander and Harmon H. Alexander. Signed February 16, 1880. Witnesses: G.W. Jones and A.C. McClain.
Codicil: Wife Mary Alexander has since died. Signed March 5, 1881.
2nd Codicil: May 30, 1881. Proven June 18, 1881.

Page 227 **WILL OF THOMAS B. EASTLAND.** Wife Florinda Eastland. Daughter Mary Bell Eastland. Signed November 8, 1869. Witnesses: Smith L. Walker and A.S. Moore. Proven August 1, 1881.

Page 227 **WILL OF L.L. CLARK.** Wife Margaret Clark. Son William T. Clark, daughter Mary J. Renfrow wife of L.L. Renfrow, daughter Rebecca B. Clark. Executor: W.L. Thomas. Signed May 6, 1881. Witnesses: Henry C. Harris and W.L. Thomas. Proven October 3, 1881.

Page 229 **WILL OF W.F. HOVIS.** Wife Maranda Elizabeth Hovis. Henry Bryant who is now living with me. Sister Susan Hovis. Deceased brother Ephraim Hovis' heirs, and deceased sister Lavinia Gregory. Mother not named. Executrix: Wife Maranda Elizabeth Hovis. Signed May 17, 1878. Witnesses: N.J. Smith and J.B. Bevels. Proven November 7, 1881.

Page 231 **WILL OF MARY CHAPMAN.** Richard Brown. N.J. Finley's two children by Harriet Ann Finley formerly Brown. Milton Scott. Heirs of Delila Lofton formerly Meadows. Heirs of Mary Ann Kimes: Julia Chitwood, Syntha Kimes, Fannie Ellis, Jose Buchanan, Thomas H. Kimes, Mary A, Kimes, Louisa Kimes, William Kimes, Margaret Kimes, Angeline Taylor. Only living brother Stephen M. Emmons. Executor: Brothers: Brother S.M. Emmons and James M. McAfee. Signed March 20, 1871. Witnesses: Frank B. Terry of near Petersburg and W.B. Gant of near Petersburg, Tennessee. Proven January 28, 1882.

Page 232 **WILL OF JANE NALLY.** Brighton, Lincoln County. Son James Henry Nally. Daughter Printha Elizabeth Nally. Executor: Daughter Printha Elizabeth Nally. Signed March 27, 1882. Witnesses: G.W. Harbin, A.J. Malone, J.A. Malone and J.H.C. Duff. Proven April 3, 1882.

Page 233 **WILL OF SAMUEL M. HAMPTON.** Son H.L. Hampton. Daughters: Martha F. Anderson and Mary E. Woodward. Land north of Elkton and Fayetteville Road. Executor: F.L. Ezell. Signed September 27, 1877. Witnesses: S.A. Hill and J.H. Smith. Proven May 27, 1882.

Page 235 **WILL OF J.W. CUNNINGHAM.** Wife Eliza Cunningham. Son John I. Cunningham, son C.H. Cunningham. Executors: C.H. and John I. Cunningham. Signed December 23, 1879. Witnesses: R.M. Bearden, W.W. Wilson and J.C. Halbert.
Codicil: August 17, 1881. Proven June 5, 1882.

Page 237 **WILL OF WILLIAM BEAVERS.** Daughter Polly Beavers, Asenith Welch, Josie C. Beavers and her children who is the wife of my son William S. Beavers, son Rufus N. Beavers, grandchildren of my deceased children: David Beavers, Rufus N. Beavers, Betsy Parham, Jane Hedgepeth, Asenith Welch, Sallie McClellan and Priscilla Wood. Signed March 21, 1882. Witnesses: F.M. Ventress and James R. Routt. Proven July 3, 1882.

Page 239 **WILL OF JAMES PARKS (COL).** Wife Mecca Parks. Mother Tennessa P Parks (Col). Executor: Elisha T. Parks. Signed July 13, 1882. Witnesses: H.B. Parks and L.R. Steelman. Proven July 29, 1882.

Page 239 **WILL OF MARTHA STONEBRAKER.** Buried at Rose Hill (Cemetery)
Fayetteville. Nephew William C. Yates. Deceased Jacob Stonebraker
and his children: Caroline E. McClelland, George J. Stonebraker, and Mary Ann
McClelland. George W. Jones. Executor: George W. Jones. Signed March 5, 1880.
Witnesses: J.M. Wilson and W.B. Martin. Proven August 1, 1882.

Page 241 **WILL OF JOSHUA P. GAMMILL.** Wife Docia Gammill. Children:
Eddie, Willie, James, Jarrell J., Sanford, Ellenner, Albertia, and
Benedick. Two brothers: James J. and Mitchell Gammill. Signed August 24, 1882.
Witnesses: E.A. Norvell and James M. Barham. Proven September 4, 1882.

Page 242 **WILL OF CHRISTIANNA GREEN.** City of Blanche. Daughter Jane E.
Williams. Signed March 30, 1882. Witnesses: J.J. Rawls and F.R. Rawls. Proven
September 9, 1882.

Page 243 **WILL OF GEORGE A.W. DICKENS.** Wife Lue Dickens. George Vaughn.
Sarah Nancy Scott and daughter G.A. Dickens. Three children: George,
Nancy and Moly. He belonged to the Grand Lodge. Signed April 27, 1880.
Witnesses: B.T. Phelps, G.S. and Wiley Parks and P.P. Renegar. Proven September
25, 1882.

Page 243 **WILL OF JAMES F. McCOWN.** Two brothers: William M. and Lewis C.
McCown. Sister Savilla Stephens. Niece Etta Henderson. Executor:
James E. Green. Signed April 1877. Witnesses: J.W. Dandridge and A.J. Davis.
Proven October 7, 1882.

Page 244 **WILL OF CHARLES B. McDANIEL.** Daughter Martha McDaniel,
daughter Maggie L. McDaniel, son James H. McDaniel, daughter Lucy
A. wife of James M. Wilson, son William T. McDaniel. Executor: William T.
McDaniel. Signed October 8, 1882. Witnesses: John Cary and W.B. Clark. Proven
November 10, 1882.

Page 246 **WILL OF H.H. HARRIS.** Wife Lucinda J. Harris. Grandson Thomas H.
Harris. Granddaughter Mary L. Hill. Granddaughter Leona A. Harris.
Daughter E.C. Harris. Daughter Mary A. Hobbs. Executrix: Wife Lucinda J.
Harris. Signed August 1882. Witnesses: F.L. Ezell and F. A. George. Proven
December 4, 1882.

Page 247 **WILL OF MAHALA RYALS.** Sister Eliza E. Ryals and cousin William
Ellis. Signed February 23, 1880. Witnesses: A.M. Hall and T.F. Harris.
Proven December 4, 1882.

Page 248 **WILL OF E. HELEN BLEDSOE.** Sister Emily V. Blake, nephew Willie
Blackwell, sister-in-law Ella Cummings, sister Martha A. Mitchell, and
brother H.M. Blake. $50.00 is to go to the Cumberland Presbyterian Church in
Petersburg, Tennessee. Executor: H.M. Blake. Signed January 12, 1883.
Witnesses: W.J. Hamilton and J.G. Cummings. Proven April 16, 1883.

Page 249 **WILL OF ANNA W. ROSS.** Husband W.T. Ross. Son Robert C. Ross,
son Garland Ross, daughter Sallie Ross, and daughter Mary Ross.
Codicil: Son William T. Ross. Signed December 20, 1882. Witnesses: E.
Alexander,M.D. and Ida Alexander. Proven May 8, 1883.

Page 250 **WILL OF DELIA A. MOOREHEAD.** Husband F.R. Moorehead. Brother
John S. Moorehead. Mentions other brothers and sisters but not by
name. Executor: Husband F.R. Moorehead. Signed April 30, 1883. Witnesses:
W.C. Morgan and W.S. Morgan. Proven May 14, 1883.

Page 251 **WILL OF THOMAS McDILL.** Wife Elizabeth McDill. Children: Two
youngest, Alis Isabella and Martha Thomas. Five oldest not named.
Executors: James P. McCown and James H. Hamilton. Signed November 14, 1876.
Witnesses: Joseph I. McCown and Robert Drennan. Proven May 15, 1883.

Page 253 **WILL OF MARY E. SISK.** Mrs. Mary E. Sisk died at her residence in Lincoln County. June 28, 1883. Under the witnesses: Mary Gore, M.A. Walker, S.A. Thomas, Martha Derrick, and Ann Michael. She made her will. Proven July 13, 1883.

Page 254 **WILL OF L.F. ARNEY.** Has wife and six children. He has two children by first wife, Daniel and Marshall Arney. Executor: James F. Cathey. Signed July 31, 1883. Witnesses: J.F. Watt and J.O. Watt. Proven September 3, 1883.

Page 255 **WILL OF DANIEL M. SUMNERS.** Wife and children not named. Brother William A. Sumners and brother THomas D. Sumners. Executors: Brothers: William A. and Thomas D. Sumners. Signed 1882. Witnesses: J.V. Alsup and J.T. Harden. Proven September 17, 1883.

Page 257 **WILL OF MRS. SALLIE CHILDS.** Two children: H.T. Childs and Sallie Ann Garrett. Granddaughter Maggie Lee Childs. Executors: H.T. Childs and W.T. Garrett. Signed July 30, 1879. Witnesses: William Ralston and S.H. Taylor. Proven October 24, 1883.

Page 258 **WILL OF JANE TAYLOR.** Daughter Cyntha Taylor, step-granddaughter Milly Taylor, step-son William Y. Taylor, two granddaughters: Mary C. and Willie J. Taylor. Emaline M. Taylor. Executor: David L. Harris. Signed September 21, 1883. Witnesses: William A. Harris and David L. Harris. Proven December 3, 1833.

Page 259 **WILL OF JOHN W. DANDRIDGE.** Wife Mary Jane Dandridge. Children: Ada B., John B., Nannie E. and William S.E. Dandridge. Executrix: Wife Mary Jane Dandridge. Signed (no date). Witnesses: W.A. Rhodes and J.B. Stewart. Proven December 5, 1883.

Page 260 **WILL OF SAMUEL GLEGHORN.** Daughter Nancy P. wife of John H. Job (Jobe), son Samuel W. Gleghorn and his children: Samuel Moses Gleghorn and Mary Rebecca Gleghorn, daughter Mary Ann wife of Henry C. Gant, daughter Elizabeth B. wife of John G. Dickey, and son Andrew C. Gleghorn. Executors: Sons Samuel W. and Andrew C. Gleghorn. Signed August 6, 1878. Witnesses: R.L. Bright and A.B. Bright. Proven December 27, 1883. (3 pages)

Page 263 **WILL OF THOMAS M. BUCK.** The State of Ohio, Preble County, Township of Israel. Journal Vol. No. 9, page 519. Will: Wife Margaret Buck. Children: Samuel A. Buck, William H. Buck, and Charlotte Buck. Executrix: Wife Margaret Buck. Signed May 17, 1879. Witnesses: John P. Buck and James R. McCrearey. Proven in Ohio, December 11, 1883. Certified copy of will. Dated December 24, 1884. (4 pages)

Page 266 **WILL OF SARAH C. DISMUKES.** Daughter Sarah E. Hamilton and her son Samuel E. Hamilton. Samuel P. Hamilton is guardian of Samuel E. Hamilton. Executor: Samuel P. Hamilton. Signed July 24, 1877. Witnesses: J.W. Lauderdale and R.A. Hamilton. Proven February 4, 1884.

Page 267 **WILL OF HENRY SMITH.** Wife Mary B. Smith. Sons and daughters: James D. Smith, John B. Smith, Julyan Jacks, and Martha J. Hunt. Executor: Wife Mary B. Smith. Signed December 14, 1882. Witnesses: E.W. Hamilton and G.M. Bostick. Proven February 4, 1884.

Page 267 **WILL OF JOHN LINDSAY.** Children: Jane Spence, William P. Lindsay, Mary A. Galloway, Jane E. Lindsay, Ebenezer Lindsay, deceased Eliza Stewart, and John Lindsay. Executors: William P. and John Lindsay. Signed January 8, 1884. Witnesses: R.H. Askins and J.T. Kidd. Proven February 4, 1884.

Page 269 **WILL OF SAMUEL RUTLEDGE.** Wife Louisa Rutledge. Isaac C. Rutledge, James H. Rutledge, R.F. Rutledge, and John Rutledge. Three grandchildren: Maggie Lou Motlow, Laura B. Motlow and Fannie E. Motlow the children of deceased daughter Rebecca Motlow. Executors: Isaac C., James H., and R.F. Rutledge and Louisa Rutledge. Signed May 8, 1883. Witnesses: W.G. Commons and Isaac Rutledge. Proven May 7, 1884.

Page 271 **WILL OF MARY M. STONE.** Susan Stone widow of Joel L. Stone, deceased. Nancy Y. Tucker daughter of my sister Frances Higgins, Addaline Shields daughter of my sister Eglantine Old, Mary B. McClusky daughter of Joel L. Stone, the heirs of Sallie Metcalf daughter of my sister Martha D. Rives both are deceased, the heirs of Frances Macon deceased daughter of W.R. Stone. Brother Jeff M. Stone. Executor: Jeff M. Stone. Signed April 22, 1884. Witnesses: D.J. Noblett and John McKenzie.
Codicil: May 7, 1884. Proven May 8, 1884.

Page 273 **WILL OF B.F. HUDSON.** Wife Adeline K. Hudson. Children: James H. Hudson, William J. Hudson, Susan A. Hudson, Edward C. Hudson, Benjamin F. Hudson, Jr., and John M. Hudson. Executors: Newton C. Sullivan and James H. Hudson, and William L. Hudson. Signed April 27, 1884. Witnesses: E.B. Worsham and A.W. Smith. Proven May 28, 1884.

Page 274 **WILL OF MARGARET B. KEITH.** To be buried with mother and father and brother Joseph and sister Josephine on father's home place. Thomas W. Clark, Jane M. Downing and the children of Louisa M. Bishop deceased, to wit: Josie J., Mary E., and Charles T. Bishop. Executor: T.W. Clark. Signed May 21, 1884. Witnesses: John Pigg and W.F. McDaniel. Proven June 12, 1884.

Page 275 **WILL OF JARRED SIMMONS.** Wife Henrietta Simmons. Son Albert and step-son R. Allen Jones. Executor: John P. Cowley. Signed March 3, 1879. Witnesses: J.W. Newman, B.N. Thompson and A.C. Bostick. Proven August 4, 1884.

Page 277 **WILL OF STEPHEN D. BLAKE.** Nephew John E. Crawford who is blind. Sister Margaret E. Carty, sister Jane C. Blake, and niece Annie Bearden. Executors: Henry Henderson and sister Jane C. Blake. Signed June 23, 1884. Witnesses: W.B. Crawford and Isaiah Hancock. Proven August 14, 1884.

Page 278 **WILL OF ROBERT T. GRIFFIS.** Of Limestone County, Alabama. Wife Maggie H. Griffis. Had land known as the Crawford farm. Executrix: Wife Maggie H. Griffis. Signed July 21, 1883. Witnesses: Thomas W. Crowson and John L. Nelson, Jr., both of Limestone County, Alabama. Proven August 8, 1884.

Page --- **WILL OF JOHN F. WHITAKER.** Deceased father John J. Whitaker. Buried at Old Home Place near Mulberry. Wanted his tombstone to read: "Vanity of Vanities, All is Vanity." Sister Martha W. Kimbrough, sister Caroline H. Burdett, brother George Whitaker, brother Alexander Whitaker, niece Mary F. Whitaker daughter of my brother Alexander Whitaker, nephew John H. Rees son of my deceased sister Mary M. Rees, nephew John J. Gill, and niece Mrs. Mary Evans both children of my deceased sister Sallie Ann Gill, niece Mrs. Bettie Sikes daughter of my deceased brother Washington Whitaker, Bettie Sike's children: Jesse Sikes and Stella Sikes. Nephew Charles H. Whitaker son of my deceased brother Charles H. Whitaker. Nieces: Ann R. Bynum, and Mary Bynum. Nephews: William H. Rees, Rufus A. Rees, and Hardy W. Rees children of my deceased sister Elizabeth P. Rees. Niece Mrs. Sarah Ann Jones. Deceased brother Isaac Whitaker. Nephew Ross M. Whitaker son of my brother George Whitaker. Executor: Nephew John J. Gill. Signed Sept 23, 1880. Witnesses: W.B. Martin and D.W. Holman. Proven August 21, 1884. (J.F.: John Franklin)

Page 283 **WILL OF JOHN SMITH.** District No. 1 and District No. 8. Son Rufus Smith. Two grandsons: James S. and Columbus Y. Rhodes. Executors: Son Rufus Smith and H.W. Shefield. Signed January 31, 1884. Witnesses: H.W. Sheffield and L.L. Neece. Proven September 29, 1884.

Page 284 **WILL OF F.R. MOOREHEAD.** Mother-in-law Nancy Alexander. Owned a bar and saloon. His wife and he buried at Rose Hill Cemetery. Brothers and sisters: Martha L. Nix, Elvira C. Freeman, Malvina Dickey, and G.C. Moorehead, D.F. Moorehead, and Rufus A. Moorehead. Executor: William C. Morgan. Signed August 22, 1884. Witnesses: T.P. Fulton and W.J. Morgan. Proven October 6, 1884.

Page 286 **WILL OF JOEL BRUCE.** Wife E.A. (Moore) Bruce. Executors: Sons Phillip and J.K. Bruce. Signed October 20, 1884. Witnesses: F.L. Ezell and D.C. Sherrell. Proven November 3, 1884.

Page 287 **WILL OF GEORGE W. JONES.** Nephew George W. Jones of Texas, nephew George M. Jones of Missouri, nephew George W. Jones of Marshall County, Tennessee, brother William D. Jones, Henry T. Jones, Martin S. Jones who is deceased, Richard M. Jones, and sister Mary J. Small who is deceased. Nieces not named. Agnes K. Little daughter of John Goodrich and the wife of Thomas C. Little. Executors: William N. Wright and John C. Goodrich, of Fayetteville. Signed February 7, 1883. Witnesses: J.G. Woods, P.T. Murray and J.R. Feeney. Proven November 17, 1884.

Page 289 **WILL OF ELI BARNES.** Wife Elen Barnes. Four children: Lucy Orlena, Margaret C. deceased wife of J.A. Millikin, son E.A. Barnes, Martha J. wife of James Halbert, Louisa C. wife of John Swan. Executor: Brother Henderson Barnes. Signed May 14, 1884. Witnesses: W.W. Wilson and James F. Cathey. Codicil: Proven January 5, 1885.

Page 290 **WILL OF ELIZA EDWARD GOODRICH.** Owned a house and lot in Murfreesboro, Rutherford County, Tennessee. Husband T.C. Goodrich. Two daughters: Louella J. and Mary Tommie Goodrich. Proven July 15, 1882, also January 7, 1885.

Page 291 **WILL OF JANE WAGGONER (COL).** Daughter Caroline Waggoner (Col). Mentions other children but not by name. Executor: Dabney Waggoner (Col). Signed December 8, 1884. Witnesses: John G. Waggoner and F.M. Waggoner. Proven January 9, 1885.

Page 292 **WILL OF EADY HONEY.** Husband J.H. Honey. Three children: Virency E. McDougal, Eady M. Tallant and Olle P. Honey. Lived in the Civil District No. 21. Executor: Henry Henderson. Signed October 31, 1881. Witnesses: Smith L. Walker and F.M. Neal. Proven January 31, 1885.

Page 293 **WILL OF ANN GEE.** Grandchildren: Georgina (Anna) Todd and Anderson Todd. Daughter Ellen Gee. Executor: J.D. Tillman. Signed October 10, 1881. Witnesses: J.D. Tillman, J.W. Newman and J.P. Cowley. Proven February 13, 1885.

Page 294 **WILL OF WILLIAM S. BRIGHT.** J.W. Newman drafted the will. Friends Hiram E. Johnson and Ed M. Johnson of Fayetteville. Executor: Ed W. Johnson. My former name was William H. Bright but some years since I changes it to William S. Bright after my grandfather Stephen, whose name was William H. Stephens. Signed December 10, 1884. Witnesses: A.M. Solomon, H.B. Rawls and B.C Newman. Proven February 20, 1885.

Page 295 **WILL OF JAMES STEWART.** Son-in-law A.S. Sloan. Grandchildren: Nora J. Sloan, Mary F. Sloan, James T. Sloan, Oleva C. Sloan, John T.W. Sloan, Ebbie C. Sloan children of Elizabeth J. Sloan, James M. Stewart and Laura M. Stewart heirs of John H. Stewart. Executor: A.S. Sloan. Signed February 14, 1876. Witnesses: George Kidd, W.P. Lindsay and Luther H. Wiley. Proven March 2, 1885.

Page 297 **WILL OF CLINTON WILSON.** Wife Mary M. Wilson. Daughter Elizabeth Lazenberry, son J.R. Wilson, T.A. Wilson, W.C. Wilson and daughter Caldonia A. Perry. Executor: W.W. Wilson. Signed February 8, 1885. Witness: S.S. McCown and W.H. Taylor. Proven April 16, 1885.

**Page 298** **WILL OF WILLIAM M. FRANKLIN.** Wife Amanda Franklin. Daughter Tennessee Ann, nephew Henry M. Renegar. Land on Stevens Creek in District No. 4. Executor: John H. Rees. Signed June 15, 1878. Witnesses: William W. James and G.W. Jones. Proven June 1, 1885.

**Page 299** **WILL OF PHILLIP T. MURRAY.** Wife Mary Ann Murray. Son James A. Murray, youngest daughter Annie Murray, daughter Beulah Murray, and other children not named. Signed February 15, 1882. Witnesses: G.W. Jones and W.N. Wright and W.B. Lamb. Proven June 3, 1885.

**Page 300** **WILL OF MARGARET ANN TIGERT.** Husband J.B. Tigert. Five children: Samuel C., George H., Mary Ann, Annie B. and Jo Ellen Tigert. Executor: J.B. Tigert. Signed April 17, 1885. Witnesses: C.G. Tucker and J.H. Beanland. Proven July 6, 1885.

**Page 301** **WILL OF MARTHA G. MOORE.** Daughter Ellen Moore. Executors: J.S. Sorrells and Susan Ellen Moore. Signed May 15, 1885. Witnesses: John L. Holly and S.T. Stephenson. Proven August 11, 1885.

**Page 302** **WILL OF DANIEL WILSON HOLMAN.** Wife Fannie W. Holman. Father James W. Holman, brother James H. Holman, mentions other children but not by name. Owned land in Fayetteville also land in Lincoln County, holds stock in "New Castle Coal and Iron Company of Alabama," gave lot for Baptist Church to be built. Executor: Brother James H. Holman. Signed September 19, 1885. Witnesses: W.N. Wright, Jr., J. Rufus Hancock and C.H. Holman. Proven September 28, 1885.

**Page 305** **WILL OF JOHN R. TOOL.** Wife Matilda Tool. Children: Mary, Susan, Jane wife of H. H. Sullivan deceased and her two children: Luther and Walter Sullivan, Louis, Frances who went to Arkansas and is deceased. Executor: N.C. Sullivan. Signed September 11, 1885. Witnesses: J.P. Hamilton and J.J. Brandon. Proven October 5, 1885.

**Page 307** **WILL OF REV. D.L. MITCHELL.** Friend Mrs. John W. Orrick. A picture of W.A. Blackwell deceased goes to Walker S. Bearden of Shelbyville, Tennessee. Mrs. M.A. Mitchell is deceased. Executor: Rufus Harris. Signed October 6, 1885. Witnesses: R.C. Rives and A.C. McTier. Proven October 27, 1885.

**Page 308** **WILL OF NANCY MILLIKIN.** NOTED: Her father John Millikin died May 31, 1864. Brother and sisters: Mary A., Margaret Jane and John H. Millikin. Brother John H. Millikin is deceased. Signed May 31, 1881. Witnesses: N.C. Sullivan and Henderson Barnes. Proven December 7, 1885.

**Page 309** **WILL OF JOHN C. GOODRICH.** Wife Ann Goodrich. Oldest son Clarence Goodrich. Daughter wife of J.J. Jones. Mentions other children but not by name. Signed April 25, 1882. Witnesses: G.F. Smith and W.A. Miles. Proven February 5, 1886.

**Page 311** **WILL OF JEPTHA H. SHOFNER.** Wife Nancy Shofner. Son W.L. Shofner is to have the land in District No. 7. Other children may exist but not named. Has land in District No. 5. Executors: Two sons W.L. and James C. Shofner. Signed June 5, 1885. Witnesses: W.G. Commons and D.W. Holman. Codicil: Proven March 25, 1886.

**Page 312** **WILL OF JOHN M. McFARRAN.** Wife Mary Ann McFarran. Daughter Mary J. Clark, daughter Susan, son James P., daughter Minerva, and daughter Margaret R. McFarran. Other children but not named. Executor: John J. Sheffield. Signed May 11, 1872. Witnesses: George W. Higgins and James Parkinson. Proven April 2, 1886.

**Page 314** **WILL OF STEPHEN M. EMMONS.** Mentions wife nut not by name.

Wanted W.F. Gunter and family to live with his wife and three grandchildren. Children: Addie, Thomas, and Winfred McCracken. Heirs: J.I. Emmons, W.F. Gunter and M.M. Emmons, J.W. McAfee, N.J. Smith, Anthony Emmons deceased, and J.A.C. Emmons and William Wilson, son-in-law Thomas Twitty to be guardian for my grandson Sam McCracken. Daughter Sophia Smith. Executor: Son-in-law Thomas Twitty. Signed March 14, 1886. Witnesses: M.L. McDawell and A.J. Compton. Proven April 5, 1886.

Page 315 **WILL OF JOHN CARY.** Wife Nancy C. Cary. Mentions children but not by name. Executors: Wife Nancy C. Cary and J.H. Cary. Signed August 4, 1878. Proven April 9, 1886.

Page 316 **WILL OF B.C. NEWMAN.** Wife L.C. Newman. Brother C.N. Newman, brother John F. Newman, sister Moriah E. Hickman, Julia A. Fayala, sister Mattie J. Wooten and deceased sister Mary A. Cline and her son Benjamin Cline. Land in Jefferson County, Tennessee, also property in Sevier County, Tennessee. Executor: Brother C.N. Newman. Signed April 26, 1886. Witnesses: W.C. Bright and C.A. Diemer. Proven May 3, 1886.

Page 318 **WILL OF ANNIE BEARDEN.** Nephew Eddie Hampton, Aunt Jane C. Blake. Executrix: Jane C. Blake. Signed February 20, 1886. Witnesses: John A. Moore and Henry C. Harris. Proven July 24, 1886.

Page 319 **WILL OF MARGARET COCHRAN.** Niece Jane McGaha and her daughter Carrie McGaha. Executor: C.B. McGuire. Signed September 30, 1885. Witnesses: George B. Boyles and J.L. Woodard. Codicil: Proven August 11, 1886.

Page 320 **WILL OF WILLIAM A. PRYOR.** Sister Anna Pryor. Executrix: Anna Pryor. Signed July 3, 1884. Witnesses: John V. Carter and W.E. Carter. Proven September 7, 1886.

Page 321 **WILL OF MARGARET McC. EDMONDSON.** Sister Jane Edmondson. Executrix: Sister Jane Edmondson. Signed March 18, 1883. Witnesses: A._. Thomas and C.A. Diemer. Proven September 11, 1886.

Page 321 **WILL OF JOHN SULSER.** Nephew John T. Sulser and nephew James D. Sulser. Land in District No. 2. Executor: N.C.E. Sulser. Signed July 28, 1886. Witnesses: Wallace Gee and B.T. Cole. Proven October 13, 1886.

Page 322 **WILL OF T.M. CLAYTON.** Mother Mary Clayton. Youngest sister Miss Donie Clayton. Mother living in McMinn County, Tennessee. Two older sisters not named. Brothers not named. To be buried by the Masons and Odd Fellows and grave to be marked. Signed May 7, 1886. Witnesses: James A. Murray and Hugh D. Smith. Proven November 15, 1886.

Page 323 **WILL OF JAMES P. PHAGAN.** Mother T.J. McCown. Brother John P. Phagan, half brothers and sisters: Rossa J., Archie C., Joseph D., Minnie J., Sallie E., and Knox T. McCown. Executor: James P. McCown. Signed February 7, 1887. Witnesses: S.S. McCown and M.S. Cooke. Proven April 4, 1887.

Page 323 **WILL OF REUBEN F. ROBINSON.** Wife M.C. Robinson. Mother Mildred Robinson. Father Henry Robinson. Brothers and sisters and heirs of two dead sisters not named. Executors: J.H. and J.D. Robinson. Signed April 6, 1887. Witnesses: W.F. Gunter and James B. Davis. Proven May 2, 1887.

Page 325 **WILL OF MAHALA WICKS.** Land in District No. 22, on the Barren Fork of Flint River, bounded in the west by G.W. Crawford, north by land of Florinda Eastland, east by E.C. Walker and heirs of John Wicks deceased, south by A.S. Moore and G.W. Crawford. Mahala J. Pryor, Nancy W. Pryor, Martha G. Pryor and Mildred Pryor. Signed November 4, 1881. Witnesses: N.M. Jenkins and Martha A. Bevel. Proven May 13, 1887.

Page 326 **WILL OF R.A. HAMILTON.** Children: James P., W.A., P.G., O.A., Lou A. Hamilton and B.J. Carter and heirs of Sarah J. Hamilton deceased. Executors: Son O.A. Hamilton and A.F. Carter. Signed February 9, 1887. Witnesses: S.S. McCown and W.F. Hamilton. Proven June 17, 1887.

Page 327 **WILL OF HENRY BECK.** Has five children, all dead. Has no living children. One left no heirs, my son J.C. Beck left heirs, Marsellen Beck left heirs, daughter Rebecca Hughes left heirs, son Boon Beck had not been heard from for many years and supposed to be dead but left heirs. My wife Mary Ann Beck. R.A. Koonce. Executor: R.N. Koonce. Signed (no date). Witnesses: W.A. Rhodes, W.C. Maddox and C.B. Koonce. Proven June 24, 1887.

Page 328 **WILL OF GEORGE STEWART.** Wife Harriet J. Stewart. Children: Sarah A. Lackey, Nancy L. Tucker, Thomas A. Stewart, Milton Green Stewart, Mary C. Sumners, Robert A. Stewart, Martha V. Gill, and Docia A. McMullen, grandson John Oscar Gill. Executor: W.W. Wilson. Signed June 23, 1882. Witnesses: A.M. Downing and R.A. Stewart. Proven June 25, 1887.

Page 329 **WILL OF JAMES E. ENGLISH.** Wife Margaret L. English. Elizabeth, John L., and Harvey E. English. Executrix: Wife Margaret L. English. Signed September 2, 1884. Witnesses: J.P. McCown and J.A. McCown, Jr. Proven August 5, 1887.

Page 330 **WILL OF DAVID SUGG (COL).** John Benson, Jordon Sugg and Emaline Smith. Executor: L.D. Sugg. Signed April 20, 1886. Witnesses: W.L. Moore and Thomas J. Whitaker. Proven September 5, 1887.

Page 330 **WILL OF MARK WHITAKER, SR.** Wife Rosanna Whitaker. Children: V.C. Whitaker, R.M. Eaton, V.J. Terry, Rosanna Holman, Mark Whitaker, Jr., L.F. Whitaker, J.B. Whitaker, J.C. Whitaker, D.G. Whitaker, and my grandchildren: R.B.L. Tolly, W.M. Tolly, J.L. Tolly, M.F. Tolly the children of A.F. Tolly deceased wife of W.P. Tolly, Kate Frost daughter of William Whitaker deceased, and Cornelius W. Taylor son of Ruth Ann wife of F.P. Taylor. Executor: F.P. Taylor. Att. Executor: Mark Whitaker and J.B. Whitaker. Signed April 9, 1881. Witnesses: William W. James and Cullen Bailey. Proven September 5, 1887.

Page 333 **WILL OF JACOB B. BUNTLEY.** Sons: J.V. William and Jack J. Buntley. Mentions his wife and other children but not by name. Executors: J.V. and G.W. Buntley. Signed (no date). Witnesses: George W. Higgins and W.C. Griswell. Proven October 3, 1887.

Page 334 **WILL OF MADALINE STREET.** Nephew George B. Reynolds and sister Julia Reynolds. Land in District No. 7. Signed September 6, 1887. Witnesses: C.A. McDaniel and B.F. Roach. Proven November 4, 1887.

Page 335 **WILL OF MATILDA C. GRAY.** Husband J.H. Gray. Children not named. Signed (no date). Witnesses: W.T. Widener and G.W. Widener. Proven November 7, 1887.

Page 335 **WILL OF L.J. WILEY.** Wife Martha J. Wiley. Five children: Ovid Thomas, John Hamilton, James Thompson, Katie Elvira, and Adolphus Dewite Wiley. Executrix: Wife Martha J. Wiley. Signed October 22, 1887. Witnesses: W.J. Galloway and W.C. Galloway. Proven November 8, 1887.

Page 336 **WILL OF ALLEN TAYLOR.** Wife Mary J. Taylor. Son Lee Knox. 1st children: William H., Julia A. West, heirs of R.M., E.J. and S.C. Childs. Executor: Samuel S. McCown. Signed April 17, 1885. Witnesses: Thomas A. West and T.A. Wilson. Proven January 2, 1888.

Page 337 **WILL OF JANE WILEY.** Neucupative will. October 28, 1887. District No. 20. Her heirs are: L.J. Wiley, Elvira Thompson, and heirs of Martha Lindsay, Ella Sheffield, and Sally Wiley. Executor: W.P. Lindsay. Signed October 28, 1887. Witnesses: John Lindsay and J.T. Kidd. Proven January 5, 1888.

Page 338　**WILL OF J.B. ROCHELL.** Daughter Lissy B. Rochell. Land in District No. 2. Executors: R.W. Stewart and Lissy B. Rochell. Signed December 27, 1887. Witnesses: R.N. Koonce and J.M. Heathcoat. Proven February 6, 1888.

Page 339　**WILL OF GARRETT MANSFIELD.** Daughter and heirs of Patty Ann Montgomery. Four living heirs: Joseph, Garrett, Jr., Nancy Forrester, and Tempy Mills. Executor: D.J. Noblitt. Signed August 12, 1882. Witnesses: C.H. Winford and H.M. Mansfield. Proven February 14, 1888.

Page 340　**WILL OF W.P.A. GEORGE.** Living children: D.W., John, Nancy E. Griffis, W.P., D.J., C.H., and Harriet S. Wisenat widow of H.L. Wisenat, and deceased son Daniel J. George, and deceased daughter Jane Burgess. Executor: Daniel J. George. Signed February 4, 1888. Witnesses: F.L. Ezell and W.L. Moore. Proven February 18, 1888.

Page 341　**WILL OF JOHN PATRICK.** Wife Mary Patrick. Two daughters: Mary J. Patrick and Susan A. Price. Daughter Elizabeth Dennis wife of J.P. Dennis, and Margaret R. Stewart wife of James Stewart, daughter Eliza A. Porter wife of George W. Porter, son William E. Patrick. Executor: Son-in-law George W. Porter. Signed March 7, 1881. Witnesses: John M. Routt and J.C. Kelso. Proven April 7, 1888.

Page 342　**WILL OF SARAH A. GOODRICH.** Son George Goodrich. Mentions other children but not by name. Guardian of his children is John C. Goodrich. Agnes E. Little sister of my deceased husband. Executor: John C. Goodrich. Signed April 27, 1882. Witnesses: G.W. Jones and W.N. Wright.
Codicil: February 24, 1886. Witnesses: W.N. Wright and G.F. Smith. Proven May 19, 1888.

Page 344　**WILL OF JOHN M. BUCHANAN.** Wife Elizabeth A. Buchanan. Son James D., son THomas S., daughter Mary E.C., and Margaret E. Buchanan. Late father S.S. Buchanan. Executors: Two sons James D. and Thomas S. Buchanan. Signed February 7, 1878. Witnesses: J.H. George and W.H. Halbert. Proven June 2, 1888.

Page 346　**WILL OF WILLIAM ROWE.** Five children: Elizabeth M. Gray, Mary C. Downing, Benjamin H. Rowe, Martha J. Moyers, and two grandchildren: Ann Percy and Edna Fisk taking the part of share of their mother Rachel Gilliland. Executor: William T. Moyers. Signed January 30, 1888. Witnesses: George B. Boyles and J.E. Caldwell. Proven July 9, 1888.

Page 347　**WILL OF LOUISA J. GOODNER.** Step-son D.M. Goodner gets my house and lot in Kelso. James D. Buchanan. Executors: D.M. Goodner and James D. Buchanan. Signed July 23, 1888. Witnesses: Frank W. Carter and N.P. Carter. Proven August 6, 1888.

Page 348　**WILL OF W.W. CHRISTIAN.** Wife Vallie S. Christian. Owns Drugs and Drugstore. $1000.00 to Jewell Lodge No. 59. Executor: Charles Waddle. Signed August 11, 1888. Witnesses: T.D. Tillman and W.A. Gill, Jr. Proven August 31, 1888.

Page 349　**WILL OF SUSAN HAGUE.** Of Mulberry. Daughter Anna Hague, daughter-in-law Sarah Hague, daughter Maggie Holt, son Dave Hague, and daughter Maude Bonner, son Buck Hague, deceased mother Paline Cowden, son David Hague, son Lucius Hague, granddaughter Willie Fitzpatrick. Had land near Groveland in Maury County, Tennessee. Executor: J.A.D. Middleton of Mulberry. Signed April 13, 1888. Witnesses: Thomas J. Neeld and James J. Smith, both of Mulberry. Proven November 5, 1888.

Page 350　**WILL OF THOMAS GEORGE.** Wife Polly George. Daughter Mary Patton, Rena George who got the Family Bible. Executor: Relative and friend J.H. George. Signed January 22, 1879. Witnesses: W.A. Patton, J.S. Turner and G.W. Wright. Since will was signed he paid Rena King money. January 2, 1885. On June 6, 1887, appointed Executors: J.B. George and Samuel Haynie. Proven October 1, 1888.

Page 352 **WILL OF MOSES FISK.** Children: Jackson, Virginia Renegar, Susan and Thomey Fisk. Executor: Thomas McFerrin. Signed September 20, 1888. Witnesses: A.L. Morgan and W.C. Morgan. Proven November 27, 1888.

Page 353 **WILL OF ALFRED BEARDEN.** Wife Margaret Bearden. Daughter Mary Delia Josephine and Maggie (these names are not punctuated. Eds.) Thirty five grandchildren. Maybe other children but not named. Executors: John J. Rawls and Matt M. Bearden. Signed November 29, 1888. Witnesses: Theo. Harris and W.H. Burrows. Proven December 24, 1888.

Page 354 **WILL OF R.C. FLETCHER.** Davidson County, Tennessee. To James Fletcher $5.00. Brother Willie Fletcher, Kittie T. Burrows and James Burrows. Signed December 16, 1888. Witnesses: J.L. Davis and Horace G. Wood. Proven January 29, 1889.

Page 355 **WILL OF JESSE P. McGEE.** Son Henry, son Dan, son Jacob McGee. Two grandsons: Joseph A. and Jesse E. Moore. Wife not named. Executors: Two sons Dan and Henry McGee. Signed June 27, 1888. Witnesses: D.J. Noblitt and J.E. Runnells. Proven March 26, 1889.

Page 356 **WILL OF TEMPLE B. LACKEY.** Wife Elizabeth Lackey. Deceased children: William Y. and Rutha F. Lackey. One half of farm to go to Alice Lutitia Sanders. Executor: John M. Dickey. (Mentions he and wife's brothers and sisters but not by name) Signed September 7, 1885. Witnesses: James J. Smith and W.T. Dickey. Proven June 11, 1889.

Page 357 **WILL OF GEORGE ZIMMERMAN.** Son Oskar and son Neil Zimmerman. Ed Hall my illegitimate son. Brother Sam Vaughn to be executor. Signed May 22, 1889. Witnesses: Lewis Smith and H. Ford. Proven June 11, 1889.

Page 358 **WILL OF FLORINDA EASTLAND.** Step-daughter Mary B. Eastland and daughter of my deceased husband Thomas B. Eastland. Land in District No. 22 and known as Lot No. 2 of her father's land, Samuel Hopkins (162 acres). Niece Nancy W. Pryor daughter of my sister Jane C. Pryor. Executrix: Mary B. Eastland. Signed October 23, 1886. Witnesses: C.C. James and J.H. Burnam. Codicil: Nieces: M.J., Martha G. and Mildred Pryor. Signed March 4, 1888. Witnesses: N.M. Jenkins and Mat Bevill. Proven August 10, 1889.

Page 361 **WILL OF ANN F. BONNER.** Children: Blanche, Ella, Lizzie gets her mother's old Bible, Ann's own Bible goes to Ella, Lucy B. Cooper, Ida B. Dallas, J.W. Bonner and M.H. Bonner, son David, grandniece Annie B. Robertson daughter of Dr. James M. Robertson, sister Mary Robertson. Signed December 6, 1882. Witnesses: James D. Tillman and Fannie Neil Lamb.
Codicil: Son-in-law Edmund Cooper and T.B. Dallas. Signed February 14, 1883. Witnesses: J.D. Tillman and M.A. Buchanan.
2nd Codicil: February 9, 1887. Proven September 12, 1890. (5 pages)

Page 366 **WILL OF ANDREW M. BEATIE.** Niece Ann Millard wife of William A. Millard. Executor: William A. Millard. Signed February 13, 1883. Witnesses: Joel M. Harris and Henry C. Harris. Proven September 21, 1889.

Page 366 **WILL OF ANN FRANCES GILLESPIE.** Sister Ellen. Grandmother Greer's estate. Brother George C. Gillespie. Mentions brothers and sisters but not by name. Executor: George C. Gillespie, brother. Signed September 29, 1867. Witnesses: C.A. Diemer and G.C. Carmack. Proven October 9, 1889.

Page 367 **WILL OF ELIZABETH SCROGGINS.** Friend Malinda Brown who also gets the Family Bible. W.W. Poole whom I raised. Executor: Thomas McFerrin.

Signed January 25, 1889. Witnesses: James D. Rives and Thomas B. Tipps. Proven October 9, 1889.

Page 369   **WILL OF JANE E. WILLIAMS.**   Brother Fleming Green, brother Jefferson Green and Safrona C. Cox. Executor: J.A. Holland. Signed May 3, 1887. Witnesses: T.D. Griffis and A.A. Rawls. Proven October 14, 1889.

Page 369   **WILL OF JOHN SIMMONS, SR.**   Daughter Mary Elizabeth Witt, daughter Margaret Jane Simmons and daughter Catharine Monks. Signed July 8, 1889. Witnesses: A.W. Hancock and Isaiah Hancock. Proven October 14, 1889.

Page 370   **WILL OF MARTHA L. CLIFT.**   Three children: W.A. Clift, J.E. Clift and S.A. Bearden. Son J.E. Clift is in Tennessee Insane Asylum. Signed September 2, 1889. Witnesses: H.T. Childs and H.W. Gunter. Proven November 19, 1889.

Page 371   **WILL OF SUSAN G. HARRISON.**   Mattie Bettie Pitts. Clide Pitts. R.H. Pitts. Executor: R.H. Pitts. Signed November 2, 1889. Witnesses: M.R. Luna and Felix G. Buchanan. Proven November 19, 1889.

Page 373   **WILL OF CHARLOTTA MERRILL.**   Daughter Susan Solomon wife of William B. Solomon. Has land in District No. 16, bounded on east by Bradshaw Creek. Willie Hynds. Signed November 3, 1886. Witnesses: W.S. Curtis and Robert S. Hereford. Proven January 23, 1890.

Page 374   **WILL OF ELEANOR COWDEN.**   Husband W.N. Cowden. Deceased father John M. Buchanan. Niece Elizabeth E. Cowden. Cumberland Presbyterian Church at Cane Creek of Howell. Executor: Husband W.N. Cowden. Signed February 19, 1890. Witnesses: Husband W.N. Cowden and George G. Crawford. Proven March 11, 1890.

Page 375   **WILL OF WILLIAM COPELAND.**   Of Flintville. Wife Mary Ann Copeland. Land in District No. 4, also in Moore County, Tennessee. Seven children: William C., Thomas Newton, George Massey, Robert Lee, Mollie Hurt wife of John M. Franklin, Emily Elizabeth wife of H.H. Snow, Ida May Copeland and Thomas Dave son of Jefferson M. Copeland deceased. Executors: William M. Smith, brother-in-law of Moore County, Tennessee and H.H. Snow, son-in-law of Lincoln County. Signed February 22, 1890. Witnesses: C.A. Boyd and W.C. Barry, J.R. Taylor and A.G. Yost. Proven April 16, 1890.

Page 376   **WILL OF J.M. BARHAM.**   Children: James A., John W., Thomas J., Walter A., Rufus C., Samuel D., and Charley E. Barham. Granddaughter Mrs. Sarah Barham, grandson James Ed Bonner son of my daughter Nancy J. Bonner deceased, daughter Gotha E. Barham, son E.L. Barham. Executors: Sons James A. and Thomas J. Barham. Signed August 20, 1889. Witnesses: J.M. Barham, W.B. Freeman and W.H. Foster. Proven August 16, 1890. (3 pages)

Page 379   **WILL OF A.C. McCLAIN.**   Wife Jennie McClain. Son John, Son Joseph, and son Charley McClain. Executor: J.P. Clark. Signed February 20, 1890. Witnesses: E.S. Wilson and A.J. Monday. Codicil: April 23, 1890.

Page 380   **WILL OF H.F. BEATIE.**   Daughter Nannie J. Beatie and brother W.G. Motlow. Land in Register's Office Book "F", page 233. Signed July 26, 1890. Witnesses: John N. Martin and A.A. Woods. Proven August 22, 1890.

Page 382   **WILL OF RICHARD PETTY.**   Wife Margret C. Petty. Children: Gertrude, Annie C., Burton and Mabel Petty. "A Hotel named the Petty House". Executrix: Wife Margret C. Petty. Signed March 12, 1890. Witnesses: C.B. Bagley and R.S. Bradshaw.

Page 384 **WILL OF WILLIAM P. MOORE.** Wife Margaret Moore. Children: William S., Thomas N., Martin Luther, and Mary E. Moore. Executor: Son William S. Moore. Signed April 10, 1878. Witnesses: A.C. Martin and J.M. Buchanan. Proven August 11, 1890.

Page 386 **WILL OF W.J. MARKHAM.** Wife Sarah Markham. Mentions children but not by name. Brother John W. Markham. Signed June 15, 1890. Witnesses: F.N. Jenkins and R.W. Clark. Proven August 28, 1890.

Page 387 **WILL OF T.L. ASHBY.** Wife Ada Ashby. Executors: T.N. Ashby and wife Ada Ashby. Signed September 14, 1890. Witnesses: J.H. Smith and J.C. Pitts. Proven October 4, 1890.

Page 388 **WILL OF H.B. WILLIAMSON.** Deola (Leola) M. Smallman, William E. Smallman and Anna Roberts. Signed November 6, 1890. Witnesses: T.N. Jenkins, J.M. Brady, Epp Harden, and W.B. Brady. Executor: T.N. Jenkins. Proven November 24, 1890.

Page 389 **WILL OF JOSEPH FARRAR.** Wife Elizabeth R. Farrar. Martha Ann daughter of my deceased daughter Mary, daughter Nancy A. West, son J.T. Farrar, son P.E. Farrar, and son M.J. Farrar, and deceased daughter Clemenza Dickey. Signed March 11, 1890. Witnesses: W.L. Moore and G.W. Newton. Proven August 11, 1890.

Page 390 **WILL OF M.E. YOWELL.** Husband J.E. Yowell. Executor: Husband J.E. Yowell. Signed April 29, 1881. Witnesses: R.W. Wilson and E.L. Wilson. Proven September 18, 1890.

Page 391 **WILL OF J.H. FULLER.** Owned property in common with brothers: the heirs of Jackson Fuller deceased, and the heirs of John Fuller deceased, nieces and nephews: Mary, James, John, Nancy and Daisy children of my brother Jackson Fuller, deceased. Executor: Samuel McDill. Signed August 23, 1890. Witnesses: John L. Washburn and Kenneth Stephens. Proven October 2, 1890.

Page 392 **WILL OF JOHN CLARK.** Wife Pricilla Clark. Children: Sins Wand, Rufena G., Richard, Charles, E.G., Margaret wife of Mat Wilson, Prissilla wife of Andrew Cowan, and Molly wife of Will McDaniel. Executor: Son Richard Clark. Signed October 27, 1887. Witnesses: W.W. Wilson and J.W. Templeton. Proven February 2, 1891.

Page 393 **WILL OF G.W. (W.G.) COMMONS.** Of Booneville, Tennessee. Wife Mary C. Commons. Nephew Joel Arthur Commons son of my brother B.L. Commons who now lives in Newton County, Missouri. Nieces: Martha G. Marshall, Lola Commons and Sallie Commons. Sisters to Joel Arthur Commons. Executrix: Wife Mary C. Commons. Signed June 27, 1889. Witnesses: Charles A. Johnson and L.J. Robertson. Proven February 5, 1891.

Page 395 **WILL OF JOHN W. STREET.** Of Mulberry, Tennessee. Wife Ann G. Street. Three children: Oldest Hugh M., Mary L., and Donald M. Street. Executor: John H. Rees. Signed (no date). Witnesses: J.G. Rees, R.A. Rees and R.H. Pitts. Proven July 22, 1890.

Page 396 **WILL OF S.A. McGEE.** Wife Mary Ann McGee. Son Henry McGee living in Texas, daughter Martha A. Faulkner, daughter Stacy McGee, daughter Elizabeth Cates, daughter Louisa Norman, daughter Jane Hamblin living in Texas and her three children: Fanny, Martha Ann and William Hatcher Hamblin, brother John McGee on Gimblet Creek. Signed February 27, 1889. Witnesses: Wesley McGee and T.A. McGee. Proven January 26, 1891.

Page 398 **WILL OF TRAVIS NEWTON.** W.G. Newton, G.W. Newton, Sarah C. Touchstone, and William Travis Newton. Grandchild Eddie Herbert Newton. Signed November 1, 1890. Witnesses: J.H. Deford and J.J. Brandon. Proven January 26, 1891.

Page 399  **WILL OF J.W. CORPIER.**  Wife Mary A. Corpier.  Son Amos S. Corpier.
Mentions other children but not by name.  Executrix: Wife Mary A.
Corpier.  Signed January 29, 1889.  Witnesses: F.L. Ezell and W.L. Stroud.
Codicil: November 18, 1889.  Proven August 11, 1890.

Page 401  **WILL OF T.B. HOBBS.**  Wife Harriet E. Hobbs.  Children: Charlie,
Mary, Minnie, and Clarence Hobbs.  Executrix: Wife Harriet E. Hobbs.
Signed January 3, 1891.  Witnesses: J.W. Wilson and Samuel Cramsil.  Proven
February 10, 1891.

Page 402  **WILL OF W.B. ALSUP.**  J.M. Moore and R.R. McGuire states that on
October 20, 1890, W.B. Alsup being at J.M. Moore's house where he
resided up to ten days before his death made his will.  His sister: Kenedy's wife.
Executor: George Wright.  Signed October 28, 1890.  Witnesses: J.M. Moore and
R.R. McGuire.  Proven March 2, 1891.

Page 403  **WILL OF Z.P. GOCHER.**  Wife and children not named.  Signed
February 7, 1891.  Witnesses: R.C. Kenedy and C.B. Bagley.  Proven
February 11, 1891.

Page 403  **WILL OF ROBERT W. WILSON.**  Died January 1, 1891.  District No. 13.
Son Edward L. Wilson, wife Mary E. Wilson.  Land is east of Swan
Creek and south and west of Fayetteville and on Elkton Turnpike.  Owned land in
District No. 14, also owned a farm known as Sawyers farm on waters of Swan
Creek (East Bank), also Cunningham farm lying north of the Sawyers tract in
District No. 14.  Executrix: Wife Mary E. Wilson.  Signed (no date).  Witnesses:
J.E. Yowell and H.H. Sugg.  Proven March 17, 1891.

Page 404  **WILL OF A.W. SMITH.**  Wife Nancy Smith.  Robert Blackmore
(Blakemore).  Children not named.  Signed October 16, 1890.  Witnesses: T.H. Clark
and R.H. Cunningham.  Proven April 6, 1891.

Page 405  **WILL OF MARTHA W. KIMBROUGH.**  Mentions children and
grandchildren but not by name.  Executor: James H. Holman.  Signed
September 27, 1886.  Witnesses: N.O. Wallace and H.C. Harris.  Proven April 14,
1891.

Page 406  **WILL OF CHARLES S. HOWELL.**  Present wife Celina A. Howell.  Son
Francis M. Howell, daughter Eliza J. Koonce wife of William Koonce.
Lived in District No. 21.  Signed February 22, 1889.  Witnesses: George B. Boyles
and W.B. Martin.  Proven April 21, 1891.

Page 408  **WILL OF MRS. MARY A. MOORE.**  Children: Mattie Fannie Moore,
Cyrus F. Moore deceased, Robert A., Charlie B. and John Henry Moore.
Signed March 12, 1891.  Witnesses: W.C. Goodner and W.H. Wright.  Proven August
8, 1891.

Page 409  **WILL OF JESSE HAWKINS.**  Wife Sabry Hawkins.  Daughter Mary
Hawkins and daughter Milly Wright.  Executrix: Daughter Mary
Hawkins.  Signed September 10, 1881.  Witnesses: J.B. Leatherwood and R.L.
Templeton.  Proven September 7, 1891.

Page 410  **WILL OF SUSAN OWEN.**  To be buried beside her husband.  Grandsons:
William and Thomas Owen.  Granddaughter M.A. Rambo, brother H.O.
Gunter.  Grandson James E. Owen now living with his grandfather Jones.  Mentions
living children but not named.  Executor: W.W. Wilson.  Signed March 4, 1884.
Witnesses: T.J. Lemond and M.M Tuley.  Proven September 7, 1891.

Page 412  **WILL OF HENRY J. BARNES.**  Son John A., son J.H., son H.T., Mary
C. wife of William Wilson, Fannie C. Echols wife of William Echols,
Sarah A. wife of Rufus McAfee, Lucinda A. wife of John Fullerton, Isham G.
Barnes, Lacy Haney son of my daughter Nancy D. Haney.  Executors: H.T. and J.H.

Barnes. Signed March 16, 1891. Witnesses: J.I. Alexander and W.T. McDaniel. Proven July 29, 1891.

Page 414 **WILL OF JAMES W. HOLMAN.** Wife Jane Holman. Children: Son D.W., Thomas P., James H., Sue M. Milhouse, Jennie Tolley, grandson James P. Holman, son Rufus M. Holman. Executors: Sons James H. and D.W. Holman. Signed March 24, 1878. Witnesses: W.W. Petty and O.D. Evans. Codicil: December 8, 1885. Since signing the will, my son Rufus M. Holman has died.
2nd Codicil: February 19, 1892. Proven March 7, 1892.

Page 420 **WILL OF C.C. JAMES.** Wife Tera James. Two children: Clark and Victoria James. Partner in business with W.W. Alexander (Stores). Executors: A.S. Thomas and S.C. Hipsh. Signed August 22, 1890. Witnesses: C.A. Crump and C.B. McGuire. Proven August 7, 1891.

Page 421 **WILL OF L.H. WILEY.** Wife Sallie J. Wiley. Executrix: Wife Sallie J. Wiley. Signed February 24, 1892. Witnesses: N.S.B. Rives and John Lindsay. Proven March 7, 1892.

Page 422 **WILL OF S.W. CARMACK.** Wife Mattie R. Carmack. Son Samuel W. Carmack, Jr., Son Tillman W. Carmack, daughter Margaret G. is to get china belonging to her grandmother Mrs. Martha Ross also china to her Uncle Robert Ross. Margaret G. Carmack gets the Family Bible. Had a contract with Mrs. Nancy A. Woods and is in the hands of Attorney N.P. Carter. Executor: George C. Carmack. Signed February 12, 1892. Witnesses: W.T. Ross and A.A. Wright. Proven March 7, 1892.

Page 423 **WILL OF HARIET CLARK.** Elizabeth B. Thomas gets the Family Bible. W.B. Clark, C.S. Clark, Rebecca M. Daniel, L.L. Clark, E.B. Thomas, and Susan R. Clark. Grandchildren: Hattie Clark, Hariet R. Thomas, Martha Hariet Clark, Elizabeth B. Thomas, Mary Isabel Thomas, Barbara Clark, James Clark, Tony Clark, and George C. Thomas. Executors: L.L. Clark and W.L. Thomas. Signed March 19, 1877. Witnesses: W.M. Rosebrough and J.G. Millard. Proven May 8, 1891.

Page 424 **WILL OF ROBERT WELCH.** Wife nancy V. Welch. Signed February 10, 1882. Witnesses: David Strong and M.E. Welch. Proven April 14, 1892.

Page 425 **WILL OF JAMES W. NEWMAN.** Wife Sallie C. Newman. Son Eugene H. Newman. Mentions children but only named one. Signed January 2, 1892. Witnesses: D.M. Goodner and H.H. Alexander. Proven January 14, 1892.

Page 426 **WILL OF E.R. MORGAN.** Sister Susie J. Carter. Executor: F.W. Carter. Signed April 27, 1888. Witnesses: J.W. Smith, N.E. Petty, Wesley Smith, E.H. Newman, and Pitts Brown. Proven March 28, 1892.

Page 427 **WILL OF MARY M. COMMONS.** Brothers and sisters: David C. Boone, H.L.W. Boone, Sallie Boone, Nathan Boone, S.C. Noblett, and F.A. Childs. Executor: Brother H.L.W. Boone. Signed March 3, 1892. Witnesses: Thomas Bailey and R.T. Shofner. Proven March 14, 1892.

Page 428 **WILL OF MARY M. MEAD.** Brother M.L. Mead and his seven children: Sarah E. Rhea and Marcus W. Thompson the children of my sister Susan Thompson. Brother Lemuel G. Mead and also Maggie Mead. Executor: Brother M.L.D. Signed August 12, 1885. Witnesses: C.A. McDaniel and W.W. Rhea. Proven May 3, 1892.

Page 429 **WILL OF MARGARET CARY.** Brother J.H. Cary, nephew Lex Cary, sister-in-law Letty Cary, sister Abby (Ibby) Tate, brother John Cary, Margaret Sanders. Land in District No. 12. Executor: J.H. Cary. Signed May 20, 1892. Witnesses: W. Hamilton and John T. Hill.

Page 430 **WILL OF ELIZABETH LACKEY.** Alice T. Thompson. Four sisters: Emaline Renegar, Mary Solomon, Viney Smith and Martha J. Renegar. Angeline McGeehee. Niece Mary Ellen Renegar. Brothers: W.B. Taylor and John A. Taylor. Rody Stubblefield. Executor: Brother W.B. Taylor. Sister Sarah Renegar is deceased. Sister Hannah McGeehee is deceased. Signed July 12, 1892. Witnesses: A.H. Hampton and John M. Dickey.

Page 431 **WILL OF B.B. LEATHERWOOD.** Sister Marthy Jane Bills. Brother J.C. Leatherwood. Nephew M.L. Patterson. Brother-in-law J.C. Bills. Signed September 27, 1892. Witnesses: Thomas F. Towery and J.M. Bills. Proven October 25, 1892.

Page 432 **WILL OF NANCY Y. TUCKER.** Children: Owen H., Newton G., Daniel J., Mary, Henry Clay, Robert A. Tucker. Grandson R.A. Rives. Executor: Robert A. Tucker. Signed (no date). Witnesses: W.R. Oldham and J.C. Stephenson. Proven (no date). (NOTE: Died June 28, 1892. eds.)

Page 433 **WILL OF W.B. JENNINGS.** Son R.J. Jennings. Son-in-law Moses Walker are to be executors. Son Burt, daughter Mrs. Alice Dickey. Signed (no date). Witnesses: M.A. Keeling, A.H. Hampton and D.L. Hall.

Page 434 **WILL OF JOHN SEATON.** Present wife Marthy Ann Seaton. Executor: G.D. Wicks. Signed July 26, 1892. Witnesses: G.D. Wicks, T.B. Hopkins, and J.J. Stevenson. Proven September 12, 1892.

Page 435 **WILL OF WILLIAM A. TATE.** Wife Sarah A. Tate. Children not named. Signed November 1, 1887. Witnesses: N.C. Sullivan, Sr. and N.C. Sullivan, Jr.

Page 436 **WILL OF MARY F. RODES.** Husband J.E. Rodes. Land on Elk River about 5 miles from Fayetteville. Sister Lizzie. Father J.B. Lamb. Signed (no date). Witnesses: J.D. Tillman and Mary Frances Tillman. Proven December 22, 1892.

Page 437 **WILL OF JOHN J. MORGAN.** Wife Sarah L. Morgan who is also the executrix. Signed November 30, 1892. Witnesses: James A. Zively and George W. Morgan. Proven December 26, 1892.

Page 438 **WILL OF MARGARET ANN PATRICK.** Son General F. Patrick gets land in District No. 21. Son Pleasant F. Patrick, daughter Fannie B. Walker, granddaughter of my deceased son Henry C. Patrick. Executor: J.B. Patrick. Signed December 31, 1892. Witnesses: H.M. Koonce and J.W. Armstrong.

Page 440 **WILL OF WILLIAM FAULKNER.** Wife Martha Adaline Faulkner. Grandson William Penn, son Frank, son Bud, and son Press Faulkner, daughter Milda Caledona Sullivan, daughter Sarah Jane McGee, daughter Fanny Duncan, and daughter Martha Steel, and daughter Mary M. Faulkner. Signed March 16, 1889. Witnesses: M.V. Groce and J.F. Faulkner. Executors: William C. and James F. Faulkner. Wants them to erect a gravestone to their mother and also over him and his present wife.
Codicil: Two youngest children by ny last wife: Thomas and Vina Faulkner. September 12, 1892.

Page 442 **WILL OF EDWIN L. GILLETTE.** Of Chicago, Cook County, Illinois. Wife Josephine M. Gillette. A friend Henry K. Elkins of Chicago, Illinois. Both to be executors. Son Edwin F. Gillette, daughter Delphine May Gillette. Lived at 306 Michigan Avenue, Chicago, Illinois. Owned stock in Union Stock Yards and also Transit Company. Edwin Gillette son of the late Jeremiah S. Gillette of Ithaca, New York. Richard H. Gillette son of late Samuel Gillette of Pennifon, New York. Mary, Julia and George Kimble are children of Azor and Elizabeth Kimble of Penn Yan, New York. Mrs. Susan Sutherland daughter of William and Sarah Kimble of Penn Yan, New York. To Trustees of Graceland

Cemetery where he is to be buried. Signed February 8, 1882. Witnesses: C.W. Needham and Louis Munson both of Chicago, Illinois. Proven October 31, 1892. (A long will, 13 pages)

Page 454  **WILL OF G.A. SHULTZ.**  Of Louisville, Kentucky, Jefferson County. Wife Helen Shultz. Executrix: Wife Helen Shultz. October 5, 1886, signed. Witnesses: Theo. Cemioti and Louis S. Rosenbaum. Proven February 16, 1893.

Page 457  **WILL OF MARY E. WILSON.**  Husband is deceased. Son E.L. Wilson and his wife Ethel Wilson. Grandson Robbie S. Wilson. Friend T.A. Wyatt, Trustee. Executor: T.A. Wyatt. Signed (no date). Witnesses: J.D. Tillman and W.N. Wright. Proven May 1, 1893.

Page 460  **WILL OF A.S. SLOAN.**  Wife Elizabeth Jane Sloan. Son I.L. Wiley Sloan, Nora Josephine Sloan and her children, Olena C. Parkinson and children, Eben Chalmers Sloan and children. Land in District No. 20 and No. 1 near Molina. Executors: John Lindsay my son-in-law and my son James Thompson Sloan. Signed July 30, 1892. Witnesses: J.W. Rawls, D.C. Waggoner and J.B. Hays. Proven May 16, 1893.

Page 462  **WILL OF JAMES M. STRONG.**  Sister Susan Sanders wife of J.W. Sanders and their child Elma. Brothers: J. Monroe and L.C. Strong. Executor: Brother L.C. Strong. Signed July 19, 1893. Witnesses: N.H. Smith, M.D. and C.C. Carpenter, M.D.

Page 463  **WILL OF MARTIN V. KIMES.**  Seven children. Those named: Son James Samuel Kimes. Five girls and two boys. Executor: N.L. Kimes. Signed April 6, 1893. Witness: John McCollum.

Page 464  **WILL OF W.C. JENNINGS.**  Wife Malessa Jennings. Son W.B. Jennings, daughter Malinda Yeates. Grandsons: George W. Syler and John W. Syler. Granddaughter M.W. Stiles, son James C. Jennings, B.P. Gray and wife Elizabeth. Land on Bean Creek. Deed recorded in Winchester (Tennessee), Book 4, Franklin County, also land on Sheltons Creek. Executors: W.J. Jennings and son-in-law George Syler. Signed April 26, 1873. Witnesses: G.W.L. Heath and Thornton Luttrell.

Page 467  **WILL OF W.S. PATTERSON.**  Wife Belle V. Patterson. Four children: Alma V., Lilla Ethel, Annie Sue, and Mamie Patterson. Lived near Blanche in District No. 18. Mother Priscilla Patterson. Father L.M. Patterson. Had land in District No. 17. Executor: D.H. Patterson. Signed June 17, 1893. Witnesses: D.C. Sherrell and J.H. Patterson. Proven December 23, 1893.

Page 469  **WILL OF THEO. HARRIS.**  Son Theo Harris. Executor: Son Theo Harris. Signed December 31, 1888. Witnesses: Caleb B. Smith and John M. Wells. Proven December 11, 1893.

Page 470  **WILL OF EMILY BRIGHT.**  At Oregon, Tennessee. Charles Warren and children, Fannie Moyers, James P. Warren, and Minnie Ingle and Mrs. Bettie Edwards. Executors: Henry Warren and James P. Warren. Witnesses: W.M. Parker and M.A. Keeling. Proven July 28, 1893.

Page 470  **WILL OF MARTIN V. KIMES (MARTIN VAN BUREN KIMES).**  Seven children. Only named one son James Samuel Kimes. Executor: M.L. Kimes. Signed April 6, 1893. Witness: John McCullum. Proven May 9, 1893.

Page 472  **WILL OF JAMES BRIGHT.**  Wife Rebecca J. Bright. Children: Amanda Orrick, Ede E. Holly, W.D. Wright, H.D. Wright, Anna Stephenson, Margarite Burns and M.J. Wright and J.F. Wright. Executor: William Orrick. Signed February 26, 1892. Witnesses: T.R.W. Crane and W.A. King. Proven November 1893.

Page 473 **WILL OF JAMES M. STRONG.** Suster Susan Sanders and her child
Elma. Elma is the child of Susan and J.W. Sanders. Brither J. Monroe
Strong, brother L.C. Strong. Executor: Brother L.C. Strong. Signed July 19, 1893.
Witnesses: H.W. Smith, M.D. and C.C. Carpenter, M.D.
Codicil: Owned estate with J. Monroe and L.C. Strong. Signed July 19, 1893.
Proven July 25, 1893.

Page 474 **WILL OF LIZZIE BONNER LAMB.** Husband James B. Lamb. Children
not named except the youngest child Lizzie Hester Lamb. Mary J.
Alford shall live with Lizzie Hester Lamb. Signed January 8, 1880. Witnesses:
W.C. Bright and M.J. Alford. Proven January 15, 1892 (1884).

Page 475 **WILL OF JAMES B. LAMB.** Mentions other children but only named
Lizzie Hester Lamb. Charles S. Ivie. Estate from Horton C. Lamb.
executors: C.S. Ivie and W.B. Lamb. Signed January 28, 1892. Witnesses: G.H.
Newman and Kate Gordon. Proven January 15, 1894.

Page 476 **WILL OF CASSINA McCOWN.** Son William Morrison McCown, son
Lewis Carroll McCown. Granddaughters: Emma Stephens, Hattie
Stephens, Ivie Stephens and Etta Pitts. Executors: Sons William M. McCown and
Lewis C. McCown. Signed November 26, 1889. Witnesses: Thomas F. Towry and
T.G. Watson. Proven January 8, 1894.

Page 477 **WILL OF GREENBERRY EVANS.** Wife Julian Ann Evans. Children:
Henry Evans, Alexander C. Evans, Vallenia Evans, and also his eldest
son John C. Evans. Executor: Eldest son John C. Evans. Signed January 20, 1891.
Witnesses: S.W. Fleming, J.P. Keith and W.H. Jones. Proven June 3, 1893.

Page 478 **WILL OF JOHN I(J). McADAMS.** Wife M.M. McAdams. Reserve for a
family graveyard. Daughter Mary Jane, son J. Walter McAdams, and
daughter Lizzie Lake McAdams. Married daughters: M.S. Lovett, Sarah Patton,
Caldonia Morris, Docia A. Dyer and L. Simmons. Son W.B. McAdams. Nephew
George McAdams to be executor. Signed November 18, 1893. Witnesses: W.T.
Porter and J.L. Gibson. Proven December 1, 1893.

Page 481 **WILL OF MATTIE E. WALKER.** Father W.B. Jennings. Husband Moses
Walker. Executor: Moses Walker. Signed February 23, 1893.
Witnesses: W.A. Cashion and R.B. Cashion. Proven October 23, 1893.

Page 481 **WILL OF ROBERT B. GIBSON.** Wife R.J. Gibson. Son W.B., son P.P.,
son S.B. Gibson, daughter _____ Hunter, daughter _____ Warren.
Executors: Sons W.B. and P.P. Gibson. Signed October 26, 1889. Witnesses: W.J.
Markham, M.S. Wilson and J.H. Hudson. Proven November 14, 1893.

Page 483 **WILL OF ISAAC WHITT.** Wife Elmira Elizabeth Whitt. R.D., S.H.B.,
W.F., N.F. Reyer, A.G., I.J., B.F., W.T. Whitt, E.T. Furgerson, J.B.,
L.L. and C.B. Whitt. Executors: R.D. and B.F. Whitt. Signed March 17, 1893.
Witnesses: W.A. Franklin and T.M. Barnett. Proven August 17, 1893.

Page 484 **WILL OF JAMES H. PATTERSON.** Land in District No. 2 to go to
James Campbell son of William Campbell. Recorded in Deed Book T,
page 381, 382 and 383. Mrs. Lizzie Brock. Land in District No. 18. John C.
Patterson and Violet Patterson. Heirs of Martha Sherrell deceased. Heirs of David
Patterson deceased. Heirs of Miriah Perkins deceased. Niece Belle Atkinson.
Nephews: D.C. Sherrell, D.H. Patterson, J.L. Patterson, Mat L. Patterson. Heirs of
W.S. Patterson deceased. Executors: D.C. Sherrell and J.L. Patterson. Signed
February 6, 1894. Witnesses: D.M. Sanders and L.Y. Hays. Proven February 19,
1894.

Page 485 **WILL OF NANCY BUCHANAN.** Husband W.S. Buchanan. Two sons:
John L. and Steele Buchanan. Signed November 29, 1893. Witnesses:
J.B. Hamilton, Sallie A. Mathews and Maggie Woodard. Proven March 17, 1894.

Page 486 **WILL OF GIDEON LAY.** Mary Lay (Col). W.T. Lauderdale, M.E. Turley and May Wilson, Sallie McDaniel, Maggie Wright, and Jennie Wright children of Sarah Jane Wright deceased. Ella Lay (Col). Gertrude Lay, Rosie Lay, Nannie Lay and Olliver Lay children of W.M. Lay deceased. W.L Turley, Samuel Ellis Hamilton, Ella Hamilton, Gideon Fullerton and Mary Ann Lauderdale. Sister Matilda W. Rowell. Executors: W.T. Lauderdale and W.L. Turley. Signed March 10, 1894. Witnesses: D.M. Goodner and W.H. Gray. Proven April 3, 1894.

Page 487 **WILL OF H.C. DUFF.** Wife Rebecca Duff. Son James H.C. Duff. Land in District No. 3. Executors: Wife Rebecca Duff and son James H.C. Duff. Signed November 12, 1889. Witnesses: D.J. Noblitt, U.A. Brazier and R.J. Small. Proven May 28, 1894.

Page 489 **WILL OF PRESLEY V. YATES.** Wife Hattie Yates. Executrix: Wife Hattie Yates. Signed January 28, 1894. Witnesses: J.H. Burnam and Laura Fulton. Proven July 17, 1894.

Page 490 **WILL OF LOUISA A. McELROY.** Daughter Lucy McElroy. Three sons: David, William and Alfred McElroy. Executrix: Daughter Lucy McElroy. Signed September 13, 1887. Witnesses: P.D(O). Boyce and W.B. Martin. Proven July 25, 1894.

Page 491 **WILL OF ELIZABETH W. MOORE.** Son William F. Moore. Executors: W.W. James and R.A. Rees. Signed (no date). Witnesses: James J. Smith and William A. Wood and G.R. Howard. Proven August 14, 1894.

Page 493 **MRS. JANE E. ADAIR.** Deceased husband W.W. Adair. Brother M.M. Rentz, sister Naomi R. Goodner wife of D.M. Goodner. Property in Dallas, Texas to be given to Trinity University of Texarkana, Texas. Desires her body to be buried in Dallas, Texas beside her husband, W.W. Adair, in Trinity Cemetery. Signed Octover 16, 1894. Witnesses: J.E. Poindexter and W.L. Turley. Proven September 5, 1894.

Page 495 **WILL OF JAMES J. FINNEY.** Son William M. Finney of Bryson, Giles County, Tennessee. Daughter Susan Deven deceased. Grandchildren: James H. Finney, _____ Corpier and Mattie Deven. Signed February 19, 1893. Witnesses: W.P. Merrell and John H. Stevenson. Proven September 10, 1894.

Page 496 **WILL OF SAMUEL STEELE McCOLLUM.** Father A.J. McCollum. Mother living but not named. Brother John A. McCollum. Sisters: Emma Blackwell, Lula Clark, Ann and Maggie McCollum. Signed October 5, 1894. Witnesses: George G. Crawford and H.C. Harris. Proven October 13, 1894.

Page 497 **WILL OF TEMPLE C. TAYLOR.** Wife Clemmenza L. Taylor. Daughter Elizabeth Crowder stays and takes care of myself and my wife. Nephew Temple C. Taylor, Jr. is my executor. Martha M. Mims. Signed August 24, 1892. Witnesses: B.F. Isom and John M. Dickey. Proven October 13, 1894.

Page 499 **WILL OF WILEY G. BROWN.** Of Mulberry. Uncle James M. Warden and Aunt Elizabeth Warren. Youngest child Ellander Brown and her guardian is my brother J.F. Brown. Owns a house and lot in Fairmont on Walden's Ridge in Hamilton County, Tennessee. Three children: Ollie Green Brown, Earle Abram Brown and Ellander Brown. Executor: Brother J.F. Brown. Signed November 15, 1893. Witnesses: Felix Forrester, B.M. Brown and J.H.C. Duff. Proven October 25, 1894.

Page 500 **WILL OF ASTOR J. MOORES.** Deceased father not named. Mother D.I. Moores. Executor: S.S. McCown. Signed July 3, 1894. Witnesses: Charlie Hobbs and J.T. West.

Page 501 **WILL OF P.O. GEORGE.** Eight children, not all named: Son M.D.

George, son-in-law U.G. Lane and wife and daughter Mary Fannie, my wife and son is dead. Son Marcus Dister George, son-in-law W.O. Lane and wife, Charley W. Hasty and wife, U.G. Lane and wife. Executors: Son W.D. George and son-in-law U.G. Lane. Signed (no date). Witnesses: John A. Pamplin, H.W. Largen and U.O. Keith. Proven December 12, 1894.

Page 503 **WILL OF MARY STONEBRAKER (COL).** Daughter Eliza Stonebraker now Bonner wife of Major J. Bonner. Executor: Son-in-law Major J. Bonner. Signed December 9, 1890. Witnesses: U.C. Morgan and U.A. Pearson. Proven December 26, 1894.

Page 504 **WILL OF MARY A.E. VANCE.** Niece Laura E. Hamilton, niece Clara F. Smith, niece Lucy A. Eddings, niece Luter Flint, niece Susie V. Eddings, nephew B.T. Eddings, nephew W.H. Eddings, Jennie Richardson, and brother T.T. Eddings. Executor: Brother T.T. Eddings. Signed December 19, 1894. Witnesses: C.A. Crunk and J.B. Hamilton. Proven February 19, 1895.

Page 506 **WILL OF A.J. CARLOSS.** Niece Mary Ann Franklin, sister-in-law Fannie S. Franklin wife of Dr. Robert Franklin. Great niece Jossie Tolliver. Executors: J.P. McGee and J.B. Hamilton. Signed October 27, 1894. Witnesses: Hugh Francis and W.B. Lamb. Proven April 3, 1895.

Page 507 **WILL OF W.S. CURTIS.** Wife N.F. Curtis. Executrix: Wife N.F. Curtis. Signed May 28, 1894. Witnesses: D.C. Sherrell and J.W. Crane. Proven May 6, 1895.

Page 508 **WILL OF I.W. GRIZZARD.** Wife Laura B. Grizzard. Son Irvin Grizzard. Land in Hamilton County, Texas, also land in Fayetteville. Executors: S.C. Hipsh and J.B. Blake. Signed September 3, 1895. Witnesses: C.A. Diener and Tom C. Ragsdale. Proven September 5, 1895.

Page 510 **WILL OF TERA H. JAMES.** Daughter Victoria Roach wife of J.J. Roach gets the house and lot in Fayetteville. Son Clark James. Deceased husband C.C. James. Son-in-law Joseph J. Roach is also executor. Cousin Leroy Smith of Giles County. Guardian of my son Clark is J.J. Roach and Leroy Smith. Signed July 2, 1895. Witnesses: A.S. Thomas and S.C. Hipsh. proven October 1, 1895.

Page 513 **WILL OF SQUIRE PICKLE.** Wife Harriet Pickle. Brother Thomas Pickle. Sister Nancy Stephenson. Two grandsons: William and Rufus Bryant. Executor: E.M. Scott. Signed July 3, 1893. Witnesses: W.B. Moore and N.P. Carter. Proven October 5, 1895.

Page 515 **WILL OF PLEASANT HALBERT.** Wife Martha V. Halbert. Children: Mrs. Martha Yowell, Mrs. Margaret M. Sugg and James Halbert, Mary Jane George, Pleasant W. Halbert, Naomi Clayton, W.H. Halbert, Mrs. Laura Hobbs and Isaac B. Halbert. Executors: Isaac B. Halbert and Pleasant Hobbs. Signed July 28, 1887. Witnesses: A.A. Wright, Joe Denwiddie and George B. Boyles. Proven October 7, 1895.

Page 518 **WILL OF H.H. HUGHEY.** Wife Elizabeth B. Hughey. Land in District No. 13. Daughter Orleany Zimmerman deceased, and her son Robert. Other children not named. Signed August 2, 1895. Witnesses: H.L. Hampton and R.A. Stewart. Proven November 4, 1895.

Page 520 **WILL OF THOMAS W. CLARK.** Mrs. Josie Marshall wife of John R. Marshall who took care of my wife. Sister Martha Goodwin. Sisters: Louisa Bishop, Clarissa Davis and Jane Downing and her daughter Mrs. Mary M. Caldwell. Signed August 20, 1895. Witnesses: E.S. Wilson and John R. Marshall. Codicil: August 23, 1895. Proven October 29, 1895.

Page 522 **WILL OF O.C. TALLENT.** Wife E.T. Tallent. Children not named.

Executrix: Wife E.T. Tallent. Signed October 28, 1895. Witnesses: R.K. Locker and R.W. McMillen. Proven November 8, 1895.

Page 523 **WILL OF J.G. WOODS.** J.H.C. Woods, Joseph G. Woods, Mattie E. Woods. Executor: W.E. Woods. Signed January 1, 1885 at 7:00 P.M. Witnesses: J.R Fenney and P.D. Boyd. Proven November 19, 1895.


## LINCOLN COUNTY, TENNESSEE WILL BOOK 5


Page 1 **WILL OF ABNER BREADY.** Give all my lands to Susan C. Gattis, John W. Hill and George B. Gattis to be equally divided. All personal property, money to go to Susan C. Gattis and George B. Gattis. Executors: J.W. Mitchell and George B. Gattis. Signed September 7, 1894. Witnesses: Martin V. Riddle and F.M. Spencer.

Page 2 **WILL OF J.H. HAMILTON.** Wife M.E. Hamilton gets all personal and real estate. Executors: Sons David S. Hamilton and Herbit H. Hamilton. Signed October 25, 1895. Witnesses: J.L. Wilson and S.H. McDill. Proven January 22, 1896.

Page 3 **WILL OF A.J. PAMPLIN.** Brother John T. Pamplin shall move into, take charge and control of my residence and 40 acres of the tillable land on my farm, to live with and take care of my children until the youngest becomes of age. My afflicted son William O. Pamplin shall have $400.00 more of my estate than my other children. After the death of my mother, I direct that my interest in my father's estate shall be sold and divided amongst my children. Executor: William D. Sims. Signed March 25, 1892. Witnesses: W.C. Morgan and A.A. Parker. Proven December 21, 1895.

Page 5 **WILL OF WILLIAM STEWART.** My executors shall erect a decent monument over my grave as soon as possible. Wife T. Annie Stewart is to hold or donate my farm of 32½ acres in District No. 1 near the village of Molina, together with the lots of land on the oposite side of the creek and known as the Brown Place, also all except my library or books, not be sold but equally dividedbetween my wife and children. The residue goes to my wife and children. Executors: Son J.B. Stewart and H.M. Eakin. Signed July 30, 1892. Witnesses: R.R. Wilson and J.W. Abbott. Probated March 2, 1896.

Page 7 **WILL OF HAMPTON SIMS.** Heirs not named. Appointed oldest son William D. Sims as executor: Signed November 19, 1892. Witnesses: J.H.C. Duff and N.S. Forrester.

Page 9 **WILL OF WILLIAM J. HAMILTON.** Wife Mollie J. Hamilton to receive all property and effects. Three children: William, Herbert and Kate. executrix: Wife Mollie J. Hamilton. Signed September 13, 1895, Shawnee, O.T. Witnesses: James S. Mills and J.G. Street. Territory of Oklahoma, County of Pottawatomie. Died on or about September 16, 1895 in above State. Probated January 16, 1896.

Page 13 **WILL OF A.L. ANDERSON AND E.C. ANDERSON.** Remainder of estate to go to my two sons R.A. and R.R. Anderson and our grandson John Anderson. Our grandson to be made equal with my two sons in the event that he lives in the yard with his grandmother and myself until both of our deaths. Signed April 29, 1894. Witnesses: W. Hamilton and A.L. Matlock. Proven March 20, 1896.

Page 14 **WILL OF MRS. ADA TAYLOR.** Of Fayetteville.Executor is to sell the vacant lot owned by me in Fayetteville, adjoining the residence and lot now owned and occupied by Mrs. Mattie Gill on the south, residence and lot of Mrs. Martha Fulton on the north. Brother Robert Fulton, Trustee in Trust for my daughter Mattie Frank Taylor for and during her life. My residence is on Bridge Street. My late husband, F.P. Taylor. Signed March 6, 1896. Witnesses: C.A. Diemer and Miss Jane Edmondson. Probated 27 March 1896.

Page 16     **WILL OF DELINA A. PIGG.** All property to be sold except the household furniture for use and comfort of my unmarried sister Sarah Elizabeth Pigg. Desires a monument to be put over my grave not to exceed $40.00, and a tombstone to be placed over my deceased sister Ransie Jane Pigg's grave of $20.00. I give my sister Mary C. Patterson $5.00. To my brother James W. Pigg $5.00. Balance to be divided into four equal parts between John Taylor Pigg, William C. Pigg, Fannie E. Prosser, and Virginia E. Ledford. Fannie E. Prosser to be guardian of Sarah E. Pigg and also to be executrix. Signed May 16, 1896. Witnesses: E.T. Hampton and D.A. Hunter. Proven June 16, 1896.

Page 17     **WILL OF S.S. McCOWN.** Wife M.J. McCown to receive everything. Also minor children. Executrix: Wife M.J. McCown. Signed September 8, 1890. Witnesses: W. Hamilton and T.W. McCown. Proven July 6, 1896.

Page 18     **WILL OF W.L. MOORES.** 7 June 1894. Wife Sarah Jane Moores to receive all my property. She is to pay a debt to J.R. Moores for land purchased of him, also settlement of property with William Smith and she become owner of his interests. She is to pay Cyrus Sugg Moores $125.00 if she so desires. Witnesses: E.L. Wilson and C.W. Hobbs. Proven July 21, 1896.

Page 19     **WILL OF W.J. HULSEY.** Wife Sarah A. Hulsey to receive land on which I am now living in District No. 7, on east prong of Norris Creek and bounded on north by Thomas Pitts, east by Joel Parks and C.M. Roach, south by H.J. Pamplin and my wife's Rhea tract, west by W.T. Davis, 136 acres. Children: John W. Hulsey, Mary F. Darnell, W.F. Hulsey, Elizabeth C. Swinney, A.M. Hulsey, G.D. Hulsey, R.L. Hulsey, Morgan Hulsey, Alice Moyers, and James W. Hulsey. Executor: John W. Hulsey. Signed July 2, 1896. Witnesses: H.J. Pamplin, W.T. Davis, Joel Parks, and C.D. Curlie, M.D. Proven July 24, 1896.

Page 20     **WILL OF COLEMAN A. McDANIEL.** Wife Margaret McDaniel receives my 274 acres of land, on which he now lives. Names four children: Mary Lou Whitaker, Andrew C., Fielden C., and Felix W. McDaniel. My executors to divide my lands into two or more tracts, being the tract owned by my wife, given to her by her father Andrew Buchanan by will and then to her children. Mary Lou Whitaker's husband is I.B. Whitaker, to receive my book "Denominations", "History of Methodism", and "Life of John B. McFerrin". My son Fielden C. to have my watch which I have worn so long. To my sons Andrew C. and Felix W., each one of my Derringer Pistols I carried in California.Executors: Son Fielden C. McDaniel, son-in-law Isaac B. Whitaker and my wife Margaret McDaniel. Signed September 13, 1890. Witnesses: Felix G. Buchanan and Jesse W. Parks. Proven July 25, 1896.

Page 23     **WILL OF CHARLES H. QUIMBY.** Of Fayetteville. My sister Sarah Isabelle Quimby to receive my house and lot in Fayetteville, 8th District. My sister Barbary Ann Elliot gets my sewing machine and all my household furniture and one third to S.I. Quimby and one third to W.A. Quimby. Brother W.A. Quimby all my tools, lumber &c. Executors: W.A. Quimby and W.L. Turley. Signed September 17, 1896. Witnesses: C.A. Diemer and W.D. McKenzie. Proven September 26, 1896.

Page 25     **WILL OF J.P. McGEE.** Wife Sallie McGee to have all my household and kitchen furniture. Son Robert McGee gets the tract of land on which he is now residing, 100 acres near Molino. If Robert McGee should die then above goes to his wife and at her death to my brothers and sisters. In Trust: Sallie McGee and R.K. Locker. My cousins: Robert, Jenny and Dora Patterson, under age of 21, to get one third income. Executors: Sallie McGee and R.K. Locker. Signed September 5, 1891. Witnesses: Hugh D. Smith and W.B. Lamb.
Codicil: The interest given to Robert, Dora and Jenny Patterson is hereby revoked

recinded, all of them being now with their uncle J.A. Patterson and no longer under my control. The said interest to be divided between Sallie McGee and son Robert. Signed April 14, 1892. Witnesses: J.D. Tilman and J.W. Davis, M.D. Probated October 6, 1896.

Page 29   **WILL OF RACHEL M. PATTERSON.**   My son James H. Patterson, executor, I making a contract with him in 1866, to take charge of my lands to support me from that date until my death. Daughter Violet M. gets all household and kitchen furniture and a tract of land of 166+ acres, bounded on north by Elk River, east by lands of Violet M. Patterson, south by heirs of David S. and Logan M. Patterson, west by lands of James H. Patterson, being a child's share laid off to me out of the estate of William Patterson. Son John C. Patterson, $1.00. Daughter Moriah H. Perkins $5.00. The heirs of my son David S. Patterson $5.00, to be divided between them. To the heirs of my son Logan M. Patterson $5.00 to be divided. To the heirs of my daughter Martha E. Sherrell $5.00 to be divided. Signed July 31, 1874. Witnesses: F.L. Ezell, John Maddox and J.J. Maddox. Probated September 17, 1896.

Page 31   **WILL OF CHARLES MOORE (COL).**   February 6, 1895. Son W.W. Moore $40.00. Wife Hager to have use of property during her life. Son Wiley $40.00. My four children: Mandy Sprow, Harriet Sebastian, W.W. Moore and George Moore. George Moore $40.00. Executor: R.J. Small. Witnesses: R.J. Small and J.W. Sims. Proven November 2, 1896.

Page 32   **WILL OF H.T. KENNEDY.**   June 23, 1894. Daughter Moly to have the young mare. Wife J.P. Kennedy, land. Six children not named. Witnesses: J.L. Caughran and P.C. Askins. Proven November 19, 1896.

Page 33   **WILL OF S.L. WARDEN (FEMALE).**   Husband Daniel Warden. My land in Marshall County, Tennessee to be sold, being the tract willed to me by my father John Landess, deceased. Daniel and W.J. Landess, Trustees for my brother C.S. Landess $1000.00. My sister Mrs. Eva G. Bobo $500.00. Executors: Husband Daniel Warden, my brother W.J. Landess. Signed October 31, 1896. Witnesses: John Cowden and J.H. Landess. Probated November 25, 1896.

Page 35   **WILL OF JOHN PHAGAN.**   Molino, Tennessee. November 3, 1896. Wife Mary Eliza Phagan to have full control until my oldest boy Carl Thomas Phagan arrives at age of 21 years. After my second boy James O. Phagan arrives at age of 21 years to receive the place known as the middle division joining where son Carl T. Phagan lives, that being his share of real estate. Youngest son William O. Phagan. Witnesses: P.C. Askins and J.L. Caughran. Probated December 10, 1896.

Page 36   **WILL OF NANCY P. JOBE.**   Daughter Elizabeth Jane Jobe and son Pressly Young Jobe, all real estate of 53 acres, deeded to me by my father Samuel Gleghorn. Elizabeth Jane Jobe's children: Leonidas Marion Jobe and James Edmon Jobe. A son Sam Jobe. Executrix: Elizabeth Jane Jobe. Signed November 23, 1896. Witnesses: A.B. Wilson and J.T. Kidd. Proven December 23, 1896.

Page 37   **WILL OF J.M. BROWN.**   Lucindy Brown to have my land and all personal property. Signed June 17, 1899. Witnesses: R.G. Smith and N.E. Keith. Executor: W.J. Cauthran.

Page 38   **WILL OF W.A. PATTON.**   Nephew Charles S. Clark, all personals and interests in a tract of land in District No. 9, 285 acres. Executors: M.L. Thomas. Signed December 1, 1892. Witnesses: C.F. Blakemore and H.D.A. Thomas. Probated December 9, 1896.

Page 39   **WILL OF D.P. HOLMAN (DANIEL P.).**   W.C. Morgan in trust for all my estate. Children: Son W.D. Holman house and lot where he now lives in Fayetteville, daughter Sofronia Jane Gray house and lot she now lives in Fayetteville, daughter Sarah Holman house and lot where I now reside in

Fayetteville. Son James I. Holman gets house and lot in Fayetteville known as "Gracy Lot No. 4". Daughter Mary Frances Perry gets a house and lot in Fayetteville known as "Gracy Lot No. 2". Son R.A. Holman gets a house and lot on north side of Market Street between the Public Square and Dick White College in Fayetteville and known as the "Albright House and Lot", also lot known as "R.A. Holman House and Lot". For Mattie Huggins (Cold) house and lot near the old Cold Baptist Church in Fayetteville and known as "Fletcher Lot". Executor: Friend W.C. Morgan of Fayetteville. Signed November 7, 1893. Witnesses: R.E. Davidson and H.K. Bryson.
Codicil: S.M. Clayton and J.W. Davis. Proven December 22, 1896.

Page 44 **WILL OF JOSEPH H. GREER.** Son Joseph Marion Greer gets all real and personal estate. He cannot sell until he arrives at age of 40 years. 69 acres of land on east of Cane Creek, being part purchased of Joseph Greer. Cousin Margaret Jane Moore, 55 acres of land on Cane Creek and being part of land purchased of my brother Joseph Greer. Brothers and sisters are not named. Signed January 23, 1883. Witnesses: H.C. Moore, W.F. Clark and F.S. McRady. Probated January 4, 1897.

Page 45 **WILL OF JANE C. TUCKER.** Brother Albert G. Armstrong, one half interest in the farm on which I reside. Brother Jas. B. Armstrong to be Trustee for said A.G. Armstrong. To Nancy C. Sherwood, my youngest cow and calf. To James B. Armstrong my other cow. Sisters: Mattie Ann Sorrels and Mary R. Ford. Witnesses: W.C. Goodrich and J.O. Armstrong.

Page 47 **WILL OF JAMES H. PATTERSON.** To James Campbell son of William Campbell, a tract of land in District No. 2 and known as the R.N. Kounce (Koonce) Place, 115 acres. To Mrs. Lizzie Brock a tract of land known as the John J. Clark Place in District No. 18. To John C. Patterson and Violet Patterson each $1.00. To heirs of Martha Sherrell, deceased, $1.00. To heirs of David Patterson, deceased, $1.00. To the heirs of Maria Perkins, deceased, $1.00. One sixth to each to my niece Belle Atkinson, D.C. Sherrell, D.H. Patterson, J.L. Patterson, Mat L. Patterson and one sixth to the heirs of W.S. Patterson, deceased. Signed February 6, 1894. Witnesses: D.M. Sanders and L.Y. Hayes, M.D. Recorded in Minute Book A-4, page 15.

Page 49 **WILL OF URCULER A. CATHRUM.** Sister Martha A. Cathrum all my property both real and personal in the District No. 6, on waters of middle prong of Norris Creek. Executrix: Martha A. Cathrum. Signed November 30, 1888. Witnesses: C.D. Curlee and J.M. Newman. Probated January 19, 1897.

Page 50 **WILL OF ELIZA STONEBRAKER BONNER (COL).** Husband Major J. Bonner all my possessions and also appointed executor. Signed December 9, 1890. Witnesses: W.C. Morgan and N.A. Pearson. Probated March 12, 1897.

Page 52 **WILL OF SEEBIRD PIGG.** Of Petersburg, Tennessee. October 19, 1896. Daughter Emma Pigg to have whole control of my estate provided she stays single. If she should marry, estate is to be sold and divided equally among my children and grandson William F. Crabtree. Son Jackson Pigg. Son Thomas J. Pigg. Son William F. Pigg. Executrix: Emma Pigg. Daughter Sallie who married John Ervin, Josie married William Morrison, Polly married Nathan Ervin, and Fannie married Clara Morrison. Witnesses: W.R. Loving and J.H. Edmiston. Probated March 30, 1897.

Page 54 **WILL OF SUSAN AMANDA FLACK.** May 13, 1897. Nephews: T.E. Harkins and Robert P. Harkins, 23 acres of land in District No. 10. To Mrs. Donie Harkins, Edna Harkins and Ozell Harkins to have my household goods. Executor: J.P. Fox. Witnesses: J.L. Holley and J.P. Fox. Probated June 2, 1897.

Page 55 **WILL OF MARTHA A. FREEMAN.** Mulberry, Tennessee. April 10, 1897. Martha A. Freeman, mother of Thomas H. Freeman, for love and affection bequeath to my son Thomas and wife Florence my building known as the Drugstore and a lot in Mulberry, one fourth an acre. My granddaughter and namesake Martha Ann Freeman household items. To my son Thomas H. and wife Florence my furniture. Executor: My son Thomas H. Freeman. Desires tombstones placed at my grave and also my husband Thomas H. Freeman. Children: Jenny James, Robert N. Freeman, James Frank Freeman, heirs Mamie Day.

Codicil: May 21, 1897. To my son Thomas H. Freeman and wife Florence my entire lot as deeded to my by my father Thomas Whitaker by Deed of Gift on 5 January 1858, recorded in Book W, page 284. Witness: J.W. Adair. Probated May 28, 1897.

Page 57    **WILL OF NANCY ASHBY.** Granddaughter Ida Ashby daughter of Rebecca Ashby, deceased, to be made an equal heir with my other children in the estate of William Ashby, deceased, and my estate of 80 acres I purchased of H.C. Duff in 1868. Appoint M.V. Groce as my executor and guardian of Ida Ashby. Signed May 20, 1893. Witnesses: J.H.C. Duff and T.V. Dusenberry. Probated August 9, 1897.

Page 59    **WILL OF MARTHA V. HALBERT.** To Mrs. Mary Jane Douthatt $25.00 and household items. To Mrs. W.A. Millard my press the same being one that formerly belonged to her father D.M. Beatie. To I.B. Halbert to be paid for taking care of me since my husband's death. To P.W. Halbert to be paid for medical services to me in my sickness. To Mrs. J.H. George and Mrs. I.B. Halbert the remainder of my household goods. To Mrs. J.H. George, J.C. Halbert, Dr. P.W. Halbert, I.B. Halbert and Dr. W.H. Halbert my two horses, farm wagon and other effects and all the money that may be due me. Appointed J.H. George and J.C. Halbert her agents. Signed June 26, 1896. Witnesses: W.A. Millard and S.M. Woodard. Probated August 14, 1897.

Page 60    **WILL OF F.M. CROSS.** Wife P.F. Cross to receive both real and personal to be divided equally between my lawful heirs: L.H. Cross, J.S. Cross, W.M. Cross, Molly Cross, Sue Ella Cross, Sally Cross, Augustus Cross, Caty Cross, Jessee Cross, Franklin Cross, Allis Cross, Robert Cross, and Dick Cross. Three oldest sons: L.H., J.S., and W.M. Cross. Executrix: Wife P.F. Cross. Signed June 5, 1890. Witnesses: T.M. Barnett and F.R. Rawls. Probated October 2, 1897.

Page 61    **WILL OF J.W. INGLE.** Merchant of Booneville, Tennessee. Owns about $4\frac{1}{2}$ acres in Booneville, also a dwelling to go to my wife Lou Ella Ingle, also my personal property and my interest in the business of Ingle & Rees. Executor: H.L.W. Boone of Booneville, Tennessee. Signed April 24, 1897. Witnesses: G.B. Creson and W.C. Faulkner. Probated September 4, 1897.

Page 63    **WILL OF W.W. WILSON.** Wife be allowed $500.00 for burial expenses and erection of a tombstone. To the colored boy known as Shields Wilson, the tract of land on which he now lives and known as the Hamilton Place of about 95 acres. Wife M.A. Wilson gets my entire estate also is my executrix. Signed March 30, 1886.

Codicil: October 1, 1889. To the colored boy Henry, son of Shields Wilson, the sum of $2000.00.

Page 65    **WILL OF GEORGE W. HIGGINS.** To my son Walter J. Higgins, my watch and chain. Wife _____ and girl children living with her. My land to be sold, being located on Coldwater Creek and known as Jas. Bland Place. Son Ralfe H. Higgins. Executors: My three sons Eugene, Owen and Jo. C. Higgins. Signed April 21, 1897. Witnesses: H.L. Moore and J.E. Poindexter. Probated December 6, 1897.

Page 66    **WILL OF J.R. ASHBY.** Appointed J.W. Ashby and G.A. Ashby executors and to sell estate to keep my children or until Willey Green arrives to majority. To Ruthia Steelman $30.00. To J.B. Ashby $230.00. To Eliza Ashby $300.00. And also to Mary Susan Ashby $300.00. All of my heirs. Remainder of estate to be divided equally between Ruthy Steelman, J.W. Ashby, G.A. Ashby, Joseph B. Ashby, Elizia Ashby, Mary Su Ashby, and Willey G. Ashby

Which are my lawful heirs. Signed August 28, 1897. Witnesses: J.F. Faulkner and A.H. Rozar. Probated December 9, 1897.

Page 67   **WILL OF WILLSON ASHBY.** To my sisters $25.00 each. To Ruthy Steelman my old gray colt. The executor is to sell land I own with G.A. Ashby also to sell the Booneville lot. Executors: G.A. Ashby and J.B. Ashby. Remainder of estate to go to my brothers and sisters. Signed October 17, 1897. Witnesses: M.V. Groce and J.F. Faulkner. Probated December 9, 1897.

Page 68   **WILL OF D.C. HALL.** Daughter Emma Hall all my property. Wife Mary A. Hall. Executrix: Emma Hall. Signed April 28, 1897. Witnesses: H.W. Moyers and H.K. Bryson. Probated December 17, 1897.

Page 69   **WILL OF MARY WOODARD.** To James L. Woodard, Sam Woodard a son of my son Galen D. Woodard, M.W. Woodard, Mrs. Ann B. Dryden, Mary E. Hatcher, Andrew B. Woodard, Robert P. Woodard, Willie and Sallie Francis the two children of my deceased daughter Sallie Francis, W.K. Woodard and "Mrs. Addie Higgins", eleven in all. Their deceased mother Sallie Francis or my deceased wife. My son Galen D., the share he is entitled to go to his son Sam who I have kept since he was an infant and still have him yet. Executors: My sons M.W. Woodard and Andrew B. Woodard. Signed April 8, 1894. Witnesses: J.W. Davis and F.F. McGuire. Probated December 16, 1897.

Page 71   **WILL OF G.M. OLMSTED.** Wife Ella Shaver Olmsted all real and personal estate and when she dies to go to my children, Esther Shaver Olmsted and William Harwood Olmsted and any other children to be born to me. Appointed the directors of the Cedar Rapids Savings Bank as Trustee to manage and control the property. Signed March 6, 1891. Witnesses: George M. Howlett and Frederick H. Shaver. Administratrix: Wife Ella S. Olmsted. Probated October 11, 1897. State of Iowa, Linn County confirmed Ella Shaver Olmsted as Admrx.

Page 76   **WILL OF MANSON H. CAUGHRAN.** My two sisters Sarah Wilson and Mary Ann Caughran to get $500.00 each. Wife Julia Caughran, personal property and money. J.D. Buchanan, if living, or if dead, to his heirs $2000.00 and the residue to Mattie Brown wife of Robert Brown, if living and if dead, to her heirs. Executors: J.D. Buchanan and H.K. Bryson. Signed July 12, 1892. Witnesses: W.C. Morgan and A.F. Morgan.

Page 78   **WILL OF GEORGE W. PAYNE.** Of Mulberry, Tennessee. Son Cowden Payne remainder of estate, after expenses and when he arrives at age of 21 years. Son Forney G. Payne, one horse, saddle and bridle. Son Cowden Payne, when he is 17 years, one horse, saddle and bridle. I own two houses and lots in Fayetteville. Children: T.C., F.G., Kalista, Vosie, Edith and Cowden Payne. My four younger children: Kalista, Vocia, Edith and Cowden Payne. Executors: Thomas J. White of Ego, Tennessee and my son T.C. Payne of Lois, Tennessee. Signed February 3, 1898. Mulberry, Tennessee. Witnesses: J.A.D. Middleton and J.C. Jennings. Probated February 21, 1898.

Page 80   **WILL OF MARY ANN CAUGHRAN.** My sister Sarah Wilson my whole estate and at her death to go to my sister-in-law Mary Jane Caughran $200.00 out of estate. To my sister Sarah Wilson and that Elizabeth McCown wife of H---- McCown $50.00 at death of Sarah Wilson. Elizabeth McCown being a granddaughter of Mary Jane Caughran. Signed November 10, 1893. Witnesses: J.W. Rawls and W.D. Rawls. Probated March 16, 1898.

Page 81   **WILL OF W.T. BALDWIN.** To be buried by wife in the Mulberry Cemetery, also to place a tombstone similar to that of my wife. Children not named. Owns 600 acres in District No. 5 in Moore County, Tennessee, remaining about 100 acres in District No. 25 of Lincoln County to be rented out for 14 years or until the youngest child is 21 years of age. Tract of land No. 2, in District No. 5 of Lincoln County on waters of Louce(?) Creek, 450 acres to be sold. Guardians be appointed for minor children out of the family of

Samuel Styles by my executors. My mansion house in which I now live to kept. Executors: James Stiles, John Stiles and Rufus Stiles, brother-in-laws. Signed March 2, 1896. Witnesses: B.K. Bailey and B.A. Spencer. Codicil: March 24, 1896. My heirs, son William E. Baldwin and my daughter O.W. Warren. Signed December 7, 1897. Witnesses: L.M. Shofner and Mathew Waggoner. Probated March 11, 1898.

Page 85 **WILL OF SOLOMON HEYMAN.** Fayetteville, Tennessee. Wife Elizabeth P. Heyman, all real and personal property. Our minor children not named. Signed August 30, 1897. Witnesses: J.H. Burnam and H.A. Weinbaum. Probated May 4, 1898.

Page 86 **WILL OF FANNIE V. LANE.** To husband R.M. Lane, property. Signed Witnesses: J.C. Evans and W.T. Broadway. Probated March 7, 1898.

Page 87 **WILL OF CHARLES B. SLOAN.** May 12, 1898. To my mother Mary E. Sloan, remainder of one $1000.00 of insurance. Two sisters, F.L. Jones and C.Z. Brunson. Executrix: Mary E. Sloan. Signed May 12, 1898. Witnesses: L.Y. Hays and L.L.C. Neece. Probated 1898.

Page 88 **WILL OF JOHN J. SHORT.** Wife Mary A. Short all my household and Kitchen furniture. Two sons, John H. and Oliver N. Short, one bay mare and her increase. Three children, Elizabeth E. Spencer, John H. and Oliver N. Short. Signed January 22, 1898. Witnesses: W.A. Millard and M.L. Kimes. Probated June 21, 1898.

Page 89 **WILL OF H.C. WHITAKER.** Wife Isa R. Whitaker gets money. Son B.A. Whitaker. Daughter Sallie Haines, $600.00. A deceased son Stonewall Whitaker. To Mitcher Whitaker at his majority, a colored boy raised by me, $50.00. Executor: My son Larkin M. Whitaker. Signed March 2, 1898. Witnesses: J.H. Burnam and J.E. Dance. Probated July 28, 1898.

Page 91 **WILL OF WILLIAM A. OLMSTEAD.** Of Chicago, Cook County, Illinois. To my wife Helen M.H. Olmstead, all my property and also my executrix. Signed March 1, 1893. Witnesses: Henry V. Freeman and Arthur E. Kaltenbrum. Recorded April 19, 1898. State of Illinois. Probated in Illinois August 15, 1898.

Page 93 **WILL OF ANN G. STREET.** Three step-children, Hugh McL. Street, Mary Lydia Street and Donald McBryde Street. Executor: Jno. H. Rees. Signed December 14, 1893. Witnesses: W.B. Taylor and R.A. Rees. Probated 1898.

Page 94 **WILL OF S.G. RILEY.** Wife Elisabeth Riley all my lands and at her death to my children and grandchildren, except James Riley my grandson to have $50.00 less, also S.C. Riley, my son, to have $50.00 less and Sarah Gatlin's children, my grandchildren, Martha Lewter, Delia Hozer, Lenna Bevels, Lexaner Spray, Robie Gatlin, Florance Gatlin, Joe Gatlin, and Molly Gatlin, William Simmons, Sam Simmons to have $50.00 less, and also want my son J.H. Riley to have $75.00 less. Executor: G.M. Riley and A.F. Riley. Signed August 25, 1897. Witnesses: Franklin P. Colbert and W.J. Edwards. Probated November 1, 1898.

Page 95 **WILL OF THOMAS BAILEY.** Of Booneville, Tennessee. Two daughters, Candace and Lydia, lands in District No. 5. A daughter Mrs. Bettie Smith. Granddaughter Sallie Smith, my organ and $50.00. Executrix: my daughter Candace Bailey. Signed October 28, 1898. Witnesses: B.E. Noblitt and B.F. Martin. Probated November 21, 1898.

Page 97 **WILL OF WILLIAM THOMAS SORRELLS, SR.** Wife Mary F. Sorrells all household and kitchen furniture. Three minor children, Waldon A., Hoit H. and Glendon Irene Sorrells. Three oldest children, W.T. Sorrells, Jr., Susan P. King and Fannie E. Holley. Susan P. wife of Osker King. Signed February 28, 1898. Witnesses: I.S. Sorrells and B.C. Morton.

Page 100 **WILL OF THOMAS TAYLOR.** Wife M.O. Taylor and our son T.J. Taylor under 21 years, all my lands. If my wife and son should die all goes to Y.A. Taylor and Robert James Taylor, my sons. Executrix: Wife M.O. Taylor. Signed March 26, 1895. Witnesses: W.W. McClelan and Nichless Gray.

Page 101 **WILL OF A.E. McEWEN.** My children to receive all my landed estate. Daughter Mary Ann Ross, deceased, left children: Robert McEwen Ross, Maggie E. and Jennie S. Ross. Brother and sisters of Mary Ann Ross, not named. Robert McEwen Ross is under age of 21 years. Signed February 25, 1886. Witnesses: J.G. Smyth and W.C. Edmiston.
First Codicil: Names a daughter Margarett C. Redman would have inherit land, to go to her two children, Roberta M. and Lou M. Redman. Another daughter of Margarett C. Redman, Mary Bell Swing. Signed November 27, 1890. Witnesses: F.S. McRady and G.A. Jarvis.
Second Codicil: Desires a head and footstone placed over my grave, my husband's grave and my deceased daughter Katharine E. McEwen. Signed June 25, 1896. Witness: J.J. Greer.

Page 104 **WILL OF J.B. RILEY.** To Thomas P. Riley, Sr. and wife and heirs, my home place containing all lands. Executor: W.Z. Jennings. Signed March 30, 1899. Witnesses: G.W. Pickett, R.E. Walker and W.Z. Jennings. To Thomas P. Riley, Jr. his heirs, land known as my (J.B. Riley) school lands of 104 acres. Signed March 30, 1899.

Page 105 **WILL OF LOU (LOUISA) J. ROUTT.** My husband J.M. Routt, my tract of land in District No. 21 on headwaters of Lees Creek and where I now live. Other sons, John E. Routt and R.M. Routt, Trustee of my daughters, not named. Executors: My two sons John E. and R.M. Routt. Witnesses: George J. Moyers and P.R. Powell. Probated: See Minute Book No. 2, pages 47 & 48.

Page 106 **WILL OF H.D.A. THOMAS.** Wife Cynthia Thomas and my children, all my property both real and personal. Two granddaughters Elizabeth Elenora and Cora Eliza Thomas, each a horse and $100.00. Executor: Marcus L. Thomas. Signed May 18, 1889. Witnesses: W.L. Thomas and W.M. Rosebrough.

Page 107 **WILL OF SALLIE A GILES.** Daughter Mary Alta Giles who is under age, all my property. Sister S.L. Giles. Executor: N.C. Harris. Signed April 16, 1894. Witnesses: Jno. A. Moore and T.G. Wade.

Page 108 **WILL OF YOUNG A. TAYLOR.** Wife Martha Taylor and her bodily heirs, Temple C., Young A., W.F., John H., A.W., Zilpha E., Ida B., Cora F., and Ardella Taylor. Youngest son A.W. Taylor under age of 21 years. All my children, to wit, Mary A. Taylor, Sarah J. Little, Susan F. Young, James Taylor, Temple C. Taylor, Young A. Taylor, William F. Taylor, John H. Taylor, Andy W. Taylor, Zilpha E. Taylor, Ida B. Taylor, Cora F. Taylor, and Ardella Taylor. Executor: Son William F. Taylor. Signed July 29, 1895. Witnesses: John M. Dickey and T.J. Winford. Probated February 28, 1899.

Page 109 **WILL OF ALFRED SHARP.** My house and lot in District No. 8 to go to my grandson Willie Wilson. Signed October 12, 1896. Witnesses: D.P. Holman and C.M. Buchanan. Probated April 1, 1899.

Page 110 **WILL OF MARGARETT EAKES.** To S.M. Pitcock all my personal property and land in District No. 19, bordered by John Daniel on north, east by Dan Swinford, south by Arthur Washburn, and west by Peter Dale, 27 acres, it being the land conveyed to me by J.D. Hunter and wife Elizabeth Hunter. Executor: S.M. Pitcock. Signed April 18, 1899. Witnesses: John L. Washburn and J.P. Fife. Probated May 18, 1899.

Page 111 **WILL OF D.C. DOLLAR.** To my grandson W.D. Moore my single barrel shot gun. To my daughter M.R. Moore wife of W.D. Moore all my property. Executrix: Daughter M.R. Moore. Signed October 12, 1897. Witnesses:

R.K. Locker, L.L. Porter and G.W. Porter. Probated May 31, 1899.

Page 112 **WILL OF W.N. WRIGHT.** Of Fayetteville. To my son Andrew B. Wright, my watch, the same I now wear. Wife Mary B. Wright the remainder of estate. To son Andrew B. Wright and James R. Feeney as Trustee, balance of property. To daughter Julia Wright $2000.00. All my children: Eugenia W. Feeney wife of James R. Feeney, Andrew B. Wright, James Holland Wright, W.N. Wright, Jr., Matt R. Wright and Julia Wright. Executors: My son Andrew B. Wright and James R. Feeney. Signed November 9, 1897. Witnesses: J. Rufus Hancock and W.B. Lamb. Probated June 12, 1899.

Page 116 **WILL OF SARAH H. GOODRICH.** Husband George J. Goodrich to get all my real estate. To my nieces Cora Brooks and Gertrude Cumberledge, two diamond rings given to me by my brother M.W. Hatch. The one with 14 diamonds and a ruby goes to Gertrude Cumberledge. If either of the above should die then the rings are to go to the daughter of Ida Canady. To Bessie Canady daughter of Ida Canady, I will my watch and chain. The diamond ring now in the possession of Lucy L. Parks, I will to her. Remainder of jewelry goes to my husband. To sell the two store houses in Columbus, Mississippi, which was given to me and my husband by W.C. Brooks and wife. To the Tennessee Orphan School near Nashville, Tennessee, $500.00. Also $500.00 to Society of the Christian Church for benefit of the aged. Executor: My husband. Signed May 2, 1898.

Page 117 **WILL OF NANCY MARGARET WELSH.** To sister Mary Elizabeth Welsh all the real estate now occupied by me as a homestead and all remaining property. Signed May 25, 1894. Witnesses: Mary E. McCown and Mildred Irwin.

Page 118 **WILL OF JERRY HUDSON (COL).** Fayetteville. Wife Julia Hudson to have all personal and real estate and at her death to be divided among my illegitimate children, Moses or Jerry Cathey a son of Jane Cathey now Jones one fourth of my property. To Caldonia Dobbins wife of John Dobbins (Col) one fourth share, to Mary Willie Bonner wife of Bud Bonner one fourth share, and to Polly Buchanan (Col) a daughter of Jane March (Col) one fourth share in estate, a house and lot in District No. 8. Signed March 17, 1893. Witnesses: A.B. Wilson and Hugh D. Smith. Probated July 25, 1899.

Page 119 **WILL OF A.W. STROUD.** To my wife Rebecca P. Stroud and my son James, all my real and personal property. Executrix: Wife Rebecca P. Stroud. Signed March 28, 1898. Witnesses: J.L. Bishop and D.T. Bowling.

Page 120 **WILL OF ELIZA BELL GREER.** To my two daughters Carrie Bell Greer and Mary Kate Greer, all my possessions. Signed March 11, 1885. Witnesses: John B. Wells and Fannie C. Wells and Will B. Summerford. Kate to get piano, clock, wash stand, parlor carpet and furniture &c. My guitar and square set &c to Carrie. Signed October 29, 1898. Witnesses: John B. Wells and Will B. Summerford.

Page 121 **WILL OF LIZZIE BUCHANAN.** My executor to place a head and footstone to my grave. Son James D. Buchanan to get remainder of estate. Executor: My son James D. Buchanan. Signed June 11, 1890. Witnesses: N.P. Carter and D.M. Goodner. Signed Elizabeth Buchanan.

Page 122 **WILL OF LAURA E. FULTON.** To my sister Virginia Dismukes all my estate also appoint her my executrix. Signed May 18, 1888. Witnesses: A.Y. Stevens and Frank E. Williams.

Page 122 **WILL OF WILLIAM MOFFETT.** January 4, 1888. Wife Susan E. Moffett, if she survives, all my property. Witnesses: D.L. Moore, T.D. Wade and Robert L. Clift.

Page 123 **WILL OF JAMES H. CONANT.** Of District No. 24. Wife Amanda A. Conant, house and lot now occupied by us as our homestead of two

two acres and at her death goes to my daughter Beulah A. Conant. To my daughter Elizabeth P. McCullough $1.00. To my son Leonidas B. Conant $1.00. To my daughter Mollie P. Brown $1.00. To my sons J. Oscar Conant, George E. Conant and Charles H. Conant $1.00 each. Executrix: Wife Amanda A. Conant. Signed September 14, 1899. Witnesses: R.J. Reed, George A. Light, M.D., and E.W. Smith. Probated November 20, 1899.

Page 124 **WILL OF HENRY BONNER.** Property to be divided between my brother and sisters, Wash Bonner, Candes Price and Malvina Bonner. Signed October 14, 1898. Witnesses: R.S. Douthat and J.F. Cannon. Probated November 28, 1899.

Page 125 **WILL OF E.M. BREWER.** To J.C. Brewer, J.S. Brewer, Alice Pettis wife of H.C. Pettis, and Laura Abbott wife of N.B. Abbott, all the real estate which is on the waters of Swan Creek in District No. 15. To granddaughter Annie L. Brewer daughter of J.C. Brewer, one mule and I appoint her father to keep the mule for her. Executor: Son J.C. Brewer. Signed July 31, 1899. Witnesses: A.B. Wilson and James Mills.

Page 126 **WILL OF G.F. SMITH, SR.** Of Fayetteville. Desires to be buried in Rose Hill Cemetery and a monument for himself and wife be erected at their graves. Wife Judith Ann Smith gets all estate. Daughter Ora Lee Carter wife of N.P. Carter gets one fifth, son G.F. Smith, Jr. gets one fifth, daughter Kate L. Robertson gets one fifth, daughter Maggie E. Francis gets one fifth. And to my two granddaughters Lillian Lee Smith and Lena B. Smith children of my deceased son J.B. Smith one tenth each. Executor: My son-in-law N.P. Carter. Signed January 23, 1895. Witnesses: G.W. Morgan and W.A. Miles. Codicil: July 18, 1899. Probated June 14, 1900.

Page 129 **WILL OF JOHN F. HARMONING.** Wife M.E. Harmoning all real estate of 200 acres of land in District No. 3. My son R.E.L. Harmoning and Mattie Lue Harmoning my youngest daughter both under age of 21 years. Executor: John L. Pickett. Signed June 10, 1900. Witnesses: A.M. Hudson and G.W. Pickett. Probated June 13, 1900.

Page 130 **WILL OF W.T. LAUDERDALE.** Wife Josie Lauderdale all my property Children not named. My child Tommie (female) is under age of 21 years. Executrix: Wife Josie Lauderdale. Signed November 2, 1898. Witnesses: Mary F. Tillman and James D. Tillman. Probated July 17, 1900.

Page 131 **WILL OF LUCY RANSOM WARREN.** Desires a monument to mark the grave of my husband and myself. All property to go to my mother and my sisters Mary C. Ransom and Theo C. Ransom to share equally. Brother-in-law Ralph D. Warren to be executor. Signed June 11, 1896.
Memo: To Lucie May Ransom to get my watch to be worn by May H. Ransom and kept in good order for her until she is old enough to wear it. Copy of Brownings Complete Poems and Cooks Guide to Browning to go to Mrs. M.B. Piecher. My Bible and books to go to Lucie Bagley. My copy of Bryant Library of Pasts goes to Lucie May Natier(?) and other books. My husband's Bible to be given to James Wilson Warren. Wish Alford M. Shook to have some books. Probated February 19, 1900.

Page 132 **WILL OF EDMUND C. JONES.** Son James Jones. To Buford Tucker son of my deceased daughter Kate, $5.00. Wants the funeral expenses paid for my mother. Daughter Nannie Myers wife of James Myers, $1.00. Son John to get the place on which I now live in the District No. 8, of 68 acres. One third to children of my daughter Mary E. Dobbins, not named. One third to my daughter Alice Beard's children, not named. One third to be loaned out and interest paid to John Jones and his children, not named. Signed December 30, 1899. Witnesses: B.M. Hopper and C.N. Bates. Probated March 5, 1900.

Page 134 **WILL OF GEORGE WHITAKER.** George Whitaker son of John J.

Whitaker. My grandson William Ross Whitaker son of my deceased son William R. Whitaker, $2000.00, to be held by executor until grandson arrives at age of 21 years. My son J.J. Whitaker, to my daughter Sallie H. Rice, to my son H.R. Whitaker, and to my daughter Mary Sugg, equally $2000.00. Executor: My son H.R. Whitaker. Signed December 9, 1897. Witnesses: B.E. Holman and N.P. Carter. Probated June 25, 1900

Page 135 **WILL OF CORNELIA S. WHITAKER.** Cornelia S. Whitaker wife of R.N. Whitaker of Fayetteville. My house to be held for my family, my four children, to wit, Mrs. Alice Allen, Anna Whitaker, Isabella Whitaker and H. Thurston Whitaker. Other names: Henry Whitaker, Emma March. Executor: My son H. Thurston Whitaker. Signed August 26, 1892. Witnesses: C.S. Colgrove and J.H. Burnam. Probated June 20, 1900.

Page 137 **WILL OF W.G. DUNLAP.** 1st will made 14 June 1898, now revoked. Wife Annie Dunlap, all household and kitchen furniture. To my son James W. Dunlap, a mule &c. To my son James W. and his wife, land. Balance of my land be divided between my two daughters Mrs. Sallie Griffis now of the State of Texas, and Mattie Dunlap. Signed July 5, 1900. Witnesses: R.C. Kennedy, M.W. Woodard and Bert P. Woodard. Probated July 27, 1900.

Page 141 **WILL OF JENNIE PRYOR.** January 9, 1900. Lincoln, Tennessee. To my sister Mattie G. Pryor all my real and personal estate, except my watch and chain which I give to my niece Jolora Love. Witnesses: Mary Love and Ann Harton. Probated August 7, 1900.

Page 142 **WILL OF W.E. PATRICK.** Desires a head and foot stone to be placed at my grave and the graves of my four deceased children. Wife, not named, all my affects. Two sons A.J. Patrick and J.B. Patrick. Executor: A.J. Patrick. Signed July 21, 1899. Witnesses: John A. Formwalt and J.T. Laten.

Page 144 **WILL OF J.K. LEATHERWOOD.** Of Fayetteville. Wife Dillie Leatherwood, household items, house and lot on north side of College Street in Fayetteville and where I now reside, also house and lot on Short Street in Fayetteville. Son R.L. Leatherwood all the property not given to my wife. Executor: My son R.L. Leatherwood. Signed October 10, 1900. Witnesses: H.R. Carter and W.P. Carter. Probated October 22, 1900.

Page 145 **WILL OF S.A.E. WHITWORTH.** Land in District No. 7, 5 acres, being part of the land willed to me by my father M.C. Pamplin. My only heir, a son, G.W.J. Kay, my household and kitchen furniture, which items are to be kept by J.W. Whitworth until my death. My cloths to be divided between Bertha Kay and Ida Kay. One clock I give to Weaver Kay. Signed March 27, 1899. Witnesses: Thomas Daniel, G.W.J. Kay and Josie Daniel. Probated December 3, 1900.

Page 146 **WILL OF W.?. YOUNG.** October 15, 1899. My widow Susan F. Young, home where I now live and other building. Son Madison T. Young. Son Watson Young $50.00. Son G.A. Young $50.00. W.J. Young $50.00. T.H. Young $50.00. D.M. Young $50.00. J.W. Young $50.00. Witnesses: H.C. Young and F.M. Copeland.

Page 148 **WILL OF W.M. BRADY.** Wife Mary P. Brady, all real and personal property. Land in District No. 15. My children: Sarah E. Brady, Emmantta Brady, and Maude M. Brady. Signed June 30, 1892. Witnesses: A.B. Collins and G.W. Collins. Probated March 1, 1901.

Page 149 **WILL OF JOHN LEWIS ALEXANDER.** To my mother Margaret Cordelia Alexander all my property which is one undivided share of my mother's dower tract of land that I bought of my sister Ellen C. Johnson. Executrix: My mother Margaret Cordelia Alexander. Signed January 16, 1901. Witnesses: H.H. Alexander and S.W. Fleming. Probated February 1, 1901.

Page 150 **WILL OF BEATRICE A.P. McMULLEN.** Sister L.M. Alexander all my household goods. She being the wife of J.I. Alexander. Executor: J.I. Alexander. Signed October 16, 1900. Witnesses: F.W. McCown, Alice Waite and J.D. Tillman. Probated February 4, 1901.

Page 151 **WILL OF W.C. SUGG.** Son Thomas F. Sugg and my daughter Victoria Sugg, each $2500.00. Niece Eda Anthony $1500.00. Daughter Wodie Eslick the place known as the Dunlap Place of about 200 acres. My children charges against: J.D. Sugg $3000.00, Jennie L. Billingsley $2600.00, Mary A. Whitaker $2500.00, Victoria Sugg to land mentioned in will $2500.00, T.F. Sugg land mentioned in will $2500.00, Woodie Eslick land mentioned in will $2500.00, and W.C. Sugg $2500.00. Household items to be divided between my daughter Victoria, my son Thomas and my niece Eda Anthony except things I give to my wife. Executors: My sons J.D. Sugg and W.C. Sugg. Signed December 9, 1899. Witnesses: T.A. Dickey and I.W. Kirby. Probated February 4, 1901.

Page 153 **WILL OF M.C. KILPATRICK.** To Willie Bell Patrick $50.00 to be held in trust by my brother W.M. Sned (Sneed) until she is 16 years of age or marries, but should she die before, it goes to my brothers and sisters. Three brothers W.M. Sneed, W.D. Sneed and A.A. Sneed and my sister F.L. Nelson and also the children of John R. Sneed. Executor: Brother W.M. Sneed. Signed January 6, 1901. Witnesses: Sam F. Moss and W.D. Hawkins. Probated July 11, 1901.

Page 154 **WILL OF J.E. RANDOLPH.** Wife Luiza Randolph, all my personal and real estate. After her death, to be sold. Three daughters, Perlina Burton, Ema (Erna ?) Dickey, and Alice Polk to have $50.00 each, remainder to be divided among my children. Signed November 24, 1900. Witnesses: A.L. White and J.F. Clark. Probated January 14, 1901.

Page 155 **WILL OF TOBE PRYOR.** Wife Fannie Pryor. Son Robert Pryor. Mother Lucy Pryor. Three children: James, Albert and Robert Pryor, all estate of 25 acres in District No. 3, to be equally divided between them when the youngest becomes of age. Executor: J.A. McKinney. Signed January 22, 1900. Witnesses: Henry Pryor and H.S. Wells. Probated March 22, 1901.

Page 156 **WILL OF M.D. GEORGE.** Owned about 100 acres in District No. 6 and known as "My Father's Old Home Place". To reserve the old graveyard of about 50 feet square but they will enlarge the same to include not less than three fourths of an acre in the graveyard, which they will not sell but be reserved for a burying place for the George family and connection, that is my father's family and connections. Graveyard to be inclosed with a good stone wall 3½ feet at the base and 4 feet above ground, and an iron gate at entrance. Desires a tombstone erected at my grave. To E.C. Lane and wife Nannie Lane each $75.00 and to be my executor and executrix. My sisters, Estella Hasty, Myrtle Lane, Mary Fannie Lane, May Pamplin, Leola George, Effie Edmondson, and Nannie Lane. Executor and Executrix: N.G. Lane and Myrtle Lane. Signed April 5, 1901. Witnesses: J.A. Lane, J.H. Tillman and M.W. Woodard. Probated April 23, 1901.

Page 158 **WILL OF JAMES H. CAREY.** Nieces, Nannie Carey, Sallie Carey, Maud Carey and Kate Carey, daughters of my deceased brother John Carey, to receive farm upon which I now live in District No. 12, of 190 acres of land. Land bordered by William Hamilton, Dave Hamilton, widow N.C. Carey of the lands of John Carey, deceased, by lands in possession of Marion Clark and owned by Marion or W.R. Wyatt, and lands of John Barnes, and lands of Henry Gault, and lands of widow Elizabeth Dickey or belonging to the estate of John Dickey, deceased. Nephew Alexis Carey a son of my deceased brother John Carey my watch and chair and $2000.00. To Mrs. Nancy A. Carey as trustee to hold for benefit of Gladys Carey daughter of my nephew Alexis Carey $1000.00. Niece Jane Barnes wife of I.G. Barnes $1500.00. Executrix: My nieces Nannie Carey and Sallie Carey. Signed September 5, 1900. Witnesses: W.B. Lamb and Fred C. Gill. Probated April 24, 1901.

Page 160 **WILL OF W.B. FAULKNER.** Three youngest children, Aron, Amy Lee and Maggy Lou Faulkner, to have benefits of my home place until they become of age or marry. Signed July 17, 1900. Witnesses: J.M. Moyers and George W. Syler. Probated June 3, 1901.

Page 161 **WILL OF J.J. RIVES.** Wife Ruth P. Rives gets dwelling house and 100 acres of land in District No. 5. Three children. Son Charley Rives. Names Pearl Davis. Brother J.T. Rives as guardian of my daughter Pearl. Executors: Wife Ruth P. Rives and my son Charley Rives. Signed March 15, 1901. Witnesses: J.W. Gill, J.T. Rives and D.J. Clark. Probated June 29, 1901.

Page 162 **WILL OF T.M. BARNETT.** Wife S.A. Barnett gets all the goods &c that she owned when I married her and $50.00. Daughter M.A. Barnett. Mentions all my children, to wit, John W. Barnett, L.S. Barnett, Martha A. Barnett, Lucy K. Barnett, and Elex Fleming. Executors: L.S. Barnett and Martha A. Barnett. Signed August 24, 1896. Witnesses: B.B. Brock and Frank P. Colbert. Probated July b10, 1901.

Page 163 **WILL OF JAMES B. ARMSTRONG.** Wife Elisabeth J. Armstrong. Son Jas. H. Armstrong. Daughter Ida L. Stone and her children, lena May, Andrew E. and John L. Stone. Executor: Son James H. Armstrong. Signed July 30, 1895. Witnesses: H.C. Sorrells and J.T. Armstrong. Probated July 25, 1901.

Page 164 **WILL OF H.R. WHITAKER.** Wife Pink Whitaker, land where I now reside where the family graveyard is situated on the Shelbyville-Fayetteville Turnpike. Executrix: Wife Pink Whitaker. Signed December 12, 1900. Witnesses: W.B. Lamb and N.P. Carter. Probated July 27, 1902.

Page 165 **WILL OF THOMAS U. STEPHENSON.** Wife Mary R. Stephenson, land where I now live. Sonn John C. Stephenson, 75 acres of land. Daughter Nancy H. Harris, 114 acres of land. Son James R. Stephenson, remaining Buchanan land of 29 acres. Land conveyed to the Duck River Railroad. Executor: Son John C. Stephenson. Signed September 2, 1895. Witnesses: S.T. Walker and C.M. Buchanan. Probated September 28, 1895.

Page 168 **WILL OF JAMES F. RENFROW.** Wife Esther Renfrow. Reserve 3 rods to be reserved for a burying ground for my family. Desires two stones, one for myself and one for my wife. Four children: L.L. Renfrow, Martha J. Daniel, James M. Renfrow, Davis(?) Sorrels and Esther Sorrels to have their mother's (Paralee's) part of my estate and their father to be their guardian. Signed March 7, 1899. Witnesses: G.J. Armstrong and J.H. Armstrong. Probated August 28, 1901.

Page 170 **WILL OF N.J. WOODALL.** Wants father's and mother's graves wired in and twin stones put to their graves with inscriptions on them. Wants grandma Webb to have two quilts and two dresses. Wants Ella Hudson to have all of mother's cloths and wants John J. Stevenson to sell property to pay all expenses also he is appointed executor. Signed August 25, 1901. Witnesses: T.C. Whitworth and R.S. Stevenson. Probated September 10, 1901.

Page 171 **WILL OF MARGARET BUCHANAN.** All my effects to go to my nephews, John Sledge and John Estill. Signed September 1, 1901. Witnesses: R.S. Douthat and Caroline Whitaker. Probated September 16, 1901.

Page 172 **WILL OF SARAH HULSEY.** $250.00 to go toward beautifying the family graveyard with tombstones, monuments, flowers &c. Daughter Bettie Swiney, my organ, one given to me by my husband's estate, and if she should die before I do, then it goes to the oldest child Maud. Son A.M. Hulsey, the dresser in the parlor, and writing desk &c. Son John W. Hulsey, silver watch left me by my husband and if he should die, to go to my other son G.D. Hulsey. Son Morgan Hulsey, other dresser in my room &c. Martha Dunn a daughter of my son John W. Hulsey, household items. Children: John W., G.D., A.M., Morgan, James W., R.L., and to Bettie Swiney whose husband is Mark Swiney. To R.L. Moyers and wife Allice, B.V. Darnell and wife Fannie, and W.T. Hulsey, each $1.00. Executor: Son A.M. Hulsey. Signed February 7, 1900. Witnesses: J.G. Carrigan and M.L. Gregory. Probated October 21, 1901.

Page 174 **WILL OF JESSE LEATHERWOOD.** Wife Malinda G. Leatherwood, all my property. Son James A. Leatherwood, 100 acres of land out of our homeplace which was deeded to me by J.B. Leatherwood and wife N.L. Leatherwood on October 19, 1891. Daughter Beatrice P. McCown and my grandson Albert G. Hayes, residue of my estate. Executor: Son James A. Leatherwood. Signed May 6, 1893. Witnesses: D.C. Rawls and Franklin P. Colbert. Probated October 21, 1901.

Page 175 **WILL OF A.T. PARKS.** Brother W.C. Parks, my one half interest in the farm on which I now reside in District No. 7, of about 516 acres and being the same farm owned by my father Woodruff Parks at the time of his death. Brother Joel D. Parks and my brother W.C. Parks, residue of my property. Executors: Brothers Joel D. and W.C. Parks. Signed May 3, 1901. Witnesses: W.B. Lamb and N.P. Carter. Probated November 15, 1901.

Page 176 **WILL OF ROBERT SUGG (COL).** Fayetteville, District No. 8. Daughter Celista Rodes and daughter Rebecca Meadows, my property. Executor: W.N. Whitaker. Signed January 5, 1900. Witnesses: H.R. Melson and B.T. Roach. Probated December 9, 1901.

Page 177 **WILL OF W.C. HODGE.** Son E.G. Hodge and wife S.E. Hodge and their daughter Ella F. McKnight. To the heirs of Fannie Neece, deceased. Executor: Son E.G. Hodge. Signed October 5, 1899. Witnesses: F.P. Colbert and Robert G. Hayes. Probated December 10, 1901.

Page 178 **WILL OF WILLIAM C. PARKS.** Nephew W.W. Pitts, $500.00. My only living brother Joel D. Parks, all my property. Executor: Brother Joel D. Parks. Signed November 12, 1901. Witnesses: John C. Diemer and N.P. Carter. Probated December 26, 1901.

Page 179 **WILL OF J.S. VAUGHN.** Wife Katie S. Vaughn, all my estate. Executrix: Wife Katie S. Vaughn. Signed July 4, 1901. Witnesses: N.P. Carter and W.B. Lamb. Probated December 3, 1901.

Page 180 **WILL OF D.J. BRADY.** Wife Mary Brady, all my property. Executrix: Wife Mary Brady. Brother G.W. Brady, $25.00. Sam McCullock, $25.00. Mrs. Sarah Toole, $25.00. Ann Bedford, $25.00. Mrs. B.W. Moyers, $25.00. Signed January 9, 1902. Witnesses: G.T. Webb and W.F. Keith. Probated February 13, 1902.

Page 182 **WILL OF HENRY C. GAULT, SR.** Wife Elizabeth Gault, real estate, 50 acres of woodland. Samuel B. Gault, William A. Gault, Henry C. Gault, Davis E. Gault, and Mary Emma Gault now the wife of Telles Jobe, equally division the woodland 3 acres. Martha Gault married John Tate to be made equal with the rest of my children less $100.00 and that John W. Gault be made equal less $200.00. Sallie A. Gault who married Alonzo Tate, deceased, and now wife of a Mr. Smith and her children by Alonzo Tate to have an equal share. Executors: H.C. Garrett and Davis E. Gault. Signed 1901. Witnesses: A.L. Matlock and J.A. Rowel. Probated January 6, 1902.

Page 184 **WILL OF A.J. McCOLLUM.** Howell, Tennessee. Wife Mary Ann McCollum, all my estate. Executrix: Wife Mary Ann McCollum. Signed January 7, 1902. Witnesses: H.F. Taylor and P.T. Rhoads. Probated February 20, 1902.

Page 185 **WILL OF D.A. GILBERT.** Daughter Ruth America $100.00 and use of homeplace, Johnson Organ, and other items. Daughter Francis E. Stephenson one half interest in John Moore farm. Granddaughter Bessie D. Stephenson. Son A.F. Gilbert, son Wash A. Gilbert who is deceased, and his oldest daughter Alice Morton. Executors: A.F. Gilbert and Joe Stephenson. Signed December 19, 1900. Witnesses: R.A. Wagster and David Wagster. Probated March 3, 1902.

Page 187 **WILL OF J.B. DAVIS.** Wife Mary A. Davis and my minor children, not named. Executrix: Wife Mary A. Davis. Signed March 8, 1881. Witnesses: J.M. McAfee and J.V. Alsup.

Page 188 **WILL OF MARY A.F. (MARY ANN FRANCES) HOLLOWAY.** Of Madison County, Alabama. Son Edwin Fletcher Love, $200.00 and other items. Sons William Amelius, Thomas Oscar and Frank Cannon Love, to take charge of Edwin Fletcher Love's portion and interest. Daughter Susan Powers Hatchett and her son Willie Hatchett. Mentions granddaughters but not by name. Son John Bruce Love, $100.00. Son Charles Renfro Love, $100.00. Son Henry Benton Love. Executors: Sons William Amelius Love, Thomas Oscar Love and Frank Cannon Love. Signed August 14, 1879. Witnesses: David C. Crutcher and W.R. Crutcher. Probated May 4, 1881. Lincoln County, Tennessee April 1902.

Page 191 **WILL OF D.B. SHULL.** Wife S.L. Shull and my three children, to wit, Fannie Mary B. who married M.B. March and Rosa with my daughter Ann who married W.B. McKenzie, Susan who married J.D. Stone, $100.00, and my son George O. Shull $100.00. Executors: Son G.O. Shull and J.D. Stone and my wife S.L. Shull. Witnesses: George W. Higgins and W.F. Cole.

Page 192 **WILL OF P.O. NEVILL.** Fayetteville, April 16, 1901. Wife Annie Lee Nevill and my children, not named. Executrix: Wife Annie Lee Nevill. Witness: W.N. Whitaker. Probated May 12, 1902.

Page 193 **WILL OF SUSAN MOFFETT.** February 14, 1900. J.H. Clift to have my land and all personal property except the family Bible, is to be sold and divided among Nancy Smith, Mollie Smith, Fannie Barnes and Robert L. Clift. Mollie Smith to get the family Bible. Executor: John J. Davis. Witnesses: R.M. Buchanan and J.J. Daves. Probated May 31, 1902.

Page 194 **WILL OF J.L. TATE.** Wife Rachel Tate all my property also appointed executrix. Signed May 11, 1902. Witnesses: H.T. Childs and J.T. Pitts. Probated July 19, 1902.

Page 195 **WILL OF R.K. GILLESPIE.** My jewelry "Heart and Hand" goes to Mrs. Nellie Head. Remainder of my property goes to my mother Mrs. Ada P. Gillespie. Executor: William Hall. Signed April 19, 1893.
Sumner County, Tennessee, August Term, 5 August 1895. A paper purporting to be the last will of Robert K. Gillespie, deceased, was this day produced for probate, when William Hall, B.D. Hall and H.A. Gillespie acknowledged the handwriting of said Robert K. Gillespie, saying the paper was found in his bank box in the vault of the First National Bank of Gallatin, Tennessee. Probated August 9, 1895.

Page 196 **WILL OF BRICE P. GRAY.** Wife Mary Ann Elizabeth Gray, all property and 400 acres. Brother J.D. Gray, lands. Nephew John M. Gray son of my brother J.D. Gray, land in District No. 4. Niece Hannah Gattis wife of Charlie Gattis, land in District No. 4. My father-in-law Calvin Jennings, deceased, disinherited and illtreated my wife during his life and failed to recognize her as he did his other children. Executor: Brother J.D. Gray. Signed March 5, 1895. Witnesses: N.P. Carter and A.M. McLaughlin and John A. Formwalt. Probated August 23, 1902.

Page 199 **WILL OF B.A. HARWELL.** Wife Bettie Harwell and minor children not named. Executrix: Wife bettie Harwell. Signed April 23, 1902. Witnesses: J.C. Brewer, B.G. Alsup and James Milton. Probated October 6, 1902.

Page 200 **WILL OF A.J. SUMMERS.** Estate to be divided between the following parties, one third to Mrs. Elizabeth Lane daughter of my brother A.H.

Summers. one third to Roy Summners Noe son of L.R. Noe and Alice C. Noe, one third to Miss Ida Hawkins daughter of W.D. Hawkins. Executor: Col. N.J. George. Signed May 10, 1901.
Codicil: Flintville, Tennessee, May 28, 1902. If I have not disposed of the Flintville place and if Roy Summers Noe is still living, I wish him to take possession. Signed June 7, 1902. Witnesses: George W. Counts and L.R. Noe and N.J. George. Probated September 19, 1902.

Page 202 **WILL OF GEORGE J. GOODRICH.** Fayetteville. To W.C. Brooks and wife Elizabeth P. Brooks of Nevada, Missouri, $3000.00. To Elder David Lipscomb of Nashville, Tennessee, as trustee of the Fanning Orphan School $500.00 also as trustee for the ministers of the Christian Church $500.00. To my sister Mrs. Agnes G. Little, real estate. My sister (above named) is to see that the graves of myself and wife are properly cared for and have inscribed on my monument the date of my birth and death with my full name George Jones Goodrich. Executrix: My sister Mrs. Agnes G. Little. Signed March 25, 1901. Witnesses: J. Rufus Hancock and R. Ed Feeney. Probated October 13, 1902.

Page 203 **WILL OF JAMES E. ASHBY.** Son Thomas Ashby now living in Houston County, Coltharp P.O., Texas $5.00. Son Henry Ashby now living in Rusk County, Henderson P.O., Texas $6.00. Daughter Luanna Payne now living near Winnboro, Wood County, Texas $5.00. Daughter Anna Payne now living near Winnboro, Wood COunty, Texas $5.00. My real estate including the homestead where I now live one and three-fourth miles north east of Fayetteville, the junction of the Mulberry and Norris Creek Turnpike to go to my wife L.E. Ashby. The remaining two-thirds interest goes to my two daughters Ana Lizzie Ashby and Ina May Ashby (under age). Executor: M.V. Groce. Signed August 22, 1896. Witnesses: Jno. W. Boaz and A.J. Monday. Requests that my wife L.E. Ashby be administratrix in place of M.V. Groce. Signed February 23, 1901. Witnesses: B.T. Roach and W.H. Cashion. Probated December 18, 1902.

Page 205 **WILL OF FAUNTLEROY FEENEY.** Executor: Brother R. Ed Feeney. Signed February 28, 1898. Witnesses: George Goodrich and John D. Kelso. Probated January 7, 1903.

Page 206 **WILL OF A.S. THOMAS.** Wife Jane Fulton Thomas All my property. my wife is to pay to my Aunt of Boliver, Tennessee, Mrs. Fannie Neeley $100.00 the amount I owe her. S.C. Hipsh is acquainted with my estate &c. Sisters Kate Thomas and Emma McKinney. My namesake Abednego Thomas Williams son of J.K. and Kate Williams. Another namesake Thomas Bearden son of M.M. Bearden of Fayetteville $500.00. My wife is to get my watch which belonged to my father which is directed to be given to my sister Kate Thomas. Executors: My wife Jane F. Thomas, S.C. Hipsh and J.K. Williams, all of Fayetteville. Signed April 28, 1899. Witnesses: Jos. G. Stritch, W.K. Goodrich and R.A. Culbreath. Probated February 11, 1903.

Page 208 **WILL OF MINERVA S. MILLARD.** Brother John Kimes all my property, also appointed executor. Signed October 2, 1901. Witnesses: W.A. Millard and E.T. Hampton. Probated March 2, 1903.

Page 209 **WILL OF MAHLEY COLLIER.** Children: Ellison Collier, Letty Collier, Alvia Collier, Garrett Collier, John Collier, Lu Collier, Rudder, Clide, and Grover. Desire that our graves shall have a fence around to protect the graves. Signed February 23, 1903. Witnesses: Theo F. Harris and E.J. Brown. Probated March 10, 1903.

Page 210 **WILL OF WILLIE ANN SMITH.** Widow of J.H. Smith, deceased, of Fayetteville. Desires a monument erected at the grave of my late husband, James H. Smith and myself, in Rose Hill Cemetery, a joint monument. To my two youngest children, Carden Henry Smith and Eva Ragsdale Smith $400.00 each. My minor children: Bessie Susie Burr, Carden Henry and Eva Ragsdale Smith to be paid and held by J.M. Smith, Trustee. Executor: J.M. Smith and Trustee of said minor children, Bessie Smith, Susie Burr Smith, Carden Henry Smith, and Eva Ragsdale Smith. Signed March 11, 1903. Witnesses: S.B. Ramsey and N.P. Carter. Codicil: March 13, 1903. To my son James Robert Smith $230.00 and my son Matt Riley Smith $470.00. Probated March 31, 1903.

Page 213 **WILL OF E.T. THOMAS.** Desires a tombstone erected over my grave. Wife Lizzie Thomas, dower &c. Children: Easter McKenzie, Albert G. Th omas, Rebecca Smiley, W.J. Thomas, Josie Smith, Nannie Holland, and Mary Poindexter. Executor: G.C. Thomas. Signed January 19, 1903. Witnesses: O.F. Gill, H.L. Thomas and V.B. Cathey. Probated April 9, 1903.

Page 214 **WILL OF GEORGE W.J. MORGAN.** Fayetteville. I, on 24 December 1866, given by deed to my wife Lizzie Morgan, my dwelling house on High Street and my two story brick store and lot on north side of the public square. Two Children: Frank W.W. Morgan and Lillian H. Morgan, under age of 21 years. Nearest descendants of my sister Susie J. Carter to receive my estate should my wife and children die. I have land in District No. 21 and a store and lot in Fayetteville. Executors: Wife Lizzie B. Morgan and Frank W. Carter, also guardian to my two children. Signed March 7, 1898. Witnesses: H.K. Bryson and H.W. Moyers. Probated June 16, 1903.

Page 216 **WILL OF W.J. STEGALL.** Wife Florence Magnolia Stegall gets all household items, homeplace where we now live, also two houses and lots on west side of Water Street opposite the homeplace, also house and lot known as the "yellow house", and a house and lot known as the Old Fair Ground Tract, also a portion of my place on Harpers Branch about 4 miles south of Fayetteville in the District No. 19 on Fayetteville-Huntsville road. Son E.B. Stegall cash of $500.00 and a house and lot known as the Francis place and where Hugh Francis now lives. Owns many places in Fayetteville. My grandson William J. Stegall son of E.B. Stegall. My Adopted daughter Mrs. Jennie McCown a house and lot in Fayetteville. Desires wife to erect over my grave a gravestone. Executor: M.W. Woodard. Signed December 8, 1899. Witnesses: John C. Diemer, J. Rufus Hancock, E.J. Higgins, R.A. Rees, and W.C. Rodes. Probated June 26, 1903. (A very long will)

Page 220 **WILL OF BRICE P. GRAY,** and Court proceedings of J.D. Gray, Extr. &c. A writing purporting to be the last will and testament of Brice P. Gray, deceased, dated 5th day of March 1895 and which J.D. Gray is nominated Executor and sworn that the writing was the will of Brice P. Gray, deceased. Will was contested. (long Court case)
Will: Desires a monument be erected at my grave. Wife Mary Ann Elizabeth Gray, household items. Brother J.D. Gray gets lands. Nephew John M. Gray son of my brother J.D. Gray gets land in District No. 4. Niece Hannah Gattis wife of Charley Gattis gets land in District No. 4. Father-in-law Calvin Jennings, deceased, illtreated my wife and his children. Executor: Brother J.D. Gray. Signed March 5, 1895. Witnesses: N.P. Carter and A.M. McLaughlin. Probated March 5, 1895.

Page 226 **WILL OF R.A. PORTER.** Wife L.C. Porter all my personal property and real estate of 63 acres in District No. 24. My wife's nephew H.O. Henderson to receive above land and personal property at the death of my wife. Executrix: Wife L.C. Porter. Signed August 8, 1903. Witnesses: R.K. Locker and W.F. Locker. Probated August 22, 1903.

Page 227 **WILL OF A.S. MOORE.** Wife Mary Jane Moore gets all my property both real and estate of 110 acres in District No. 22, also appointed my executrix. Signed March 16, 1903. Witnesses: T.B. Beavers and James Damron. Probated September 7, 1903.

Page 228 **WILL OF A.F. PATTON.** Howell, Tennessee. Mrs. Maggie Winsett and Newman George, all my estate to be equally divided. Executor: My friend W.L. Hatcher. Signed August 18, 1903. Witnesses: Jno. A. Moore and R.L. Clift. Probated November 21, 1903.

Page 228 **WILL OF C.C. PIERCE.** July 23, 1898. My affairs to be settled equally between T.S. Pierce and Lizzie Pierce. $1460.00 to T.S. Pierce ad a house and lot in District No. 10, also a piece of land in same area. My administrators: T.S. and L.L. Pierce. Witnesses: A.B. Winford and G.C. Morrison. Probated January 8, 1904.

Page 229 **WILL OF AMANDA C. RATTIKIN.** Sister Cordelia A. Thompson wife of John D. Thompson, all my property and my land in District No. 4. Signed August 27, 1903. Witnesses: John M. Dickey and W.J. Simmons. Probated December 7, 1903.

Page 230 **WILL OF ELIZABETH MILLER.** Husband W.G. Miller to have a bed, featherbed, pillows and clothing for same, the one he sleeps on, and other items. Oldest daughter Mrs. Mattie Bottom gets her bed and clothing for same. Mrs. Sadie B. Glass gets bed and clothing for same and other items. My farm of 330 acres is in District No. 22. Three children: Mrs. Mattie Bottom, Sadie Glass and E.L. Miller. Signed June 14, 1902. Witnesses: J.E. Ramsey and G.W. Cown. Probated October 17, 1903.

Page 231 **WILL OF WILLIAM T. KENEDY.** Ruth Leah Ringo a child nurtured by my sister Agnes Ringo, gets all the real and personal property except money. To Sophia Buchanan and to Annie McDonald, the former being the wife of Andrew Buchanan and the latter the wife of Allen McDonald, gets remainder of estate. Executor: My friend O.H. Higgins. Signed January 29, 1901. Witnesses: J.J. Jones and George Goodrich. Probated December 29, 1903.

Page 239 **WILL OF ALEXANDER WAGGONER.** Wife Mary Waggoner all my personal property and lands. Son Alexander Waggoner to get the above estate at the death of my wife. Land on Gimlet Creek about 2 acres. Seven children: Cinthia Groce, Orphia Ready, Mary Dunn, Susan Groce, Fannie Bedwell, Alexander Waggoner and Martha E. McGee. Executors: Son Alexander Waggoner and B.E. Noblitt. Signed January 3, 1900. Witnesses: Henry McGee, G.A. Ashby and T.A. Faulkner. Probated November 28, 1903.

Page 241 **WILL OF MRS. N.J.(NARCISSA J.) DYER.** Daughter Dana Dyer gets all her property and after her death to go to my other heirs (not named). Signed January 6, 1899. Witnesses: G.L. Butler and A.G. Butler. Probated February 2, 1904.

Page 242 **WILL OF G.D. WOODARD.** Wife Maggie Woodard gets all personal property and the place I noe live in, an old house near the well to be sold. My land known as "Buchanan Land" willed to me by my father, in all 128 acres to be sold. My three children by her. Remainder of land to be sold and equally divided between my four children by my first wife, except that the executor will give to my daughter Rubie McGee, $50.00 more than the other three. To my son-in-law Will Ashby $75.00. It is agreed by myself and Mr. Alonzo Hughey, who is present at the drafting of this will, that the rental contract for the land from him for this year and not sown down, is to be cancelled and he is to take the land back. Executor: Brother M.W. Woodard. Signed January 31, 1904. Witnesses: C.N. Cowden, A.N. Hughey and A.B. Woodard. Probated February 5, 1904.

Page 244 **WILL OF WALTER S. McWILLIAMS.** Wife Elizabeth Alice McWilliams, all my property. Children: then living, Dana B. McWilliams, Asbury B. McWilliams, Mrs. Elizabeth McWilliams Legg, Jake McWilliams, Bob Lee McWilliams, and Felton McWilliams. Elizabeth McWilliams Legg is wife of Andrew Legg. Executors: My two sons Dana B. McWilliams and Asbury B. McWilliams. Signed October 26, 1903. Witnesses: George Goodrich, J.M. Mansfield and S.C. Hipsh. Probated March 18, 1904.

Page 247 **WILL OF LUCINDA LOYD.** Brother E.C. Loyd gets all landed estate, land where I now live on and hold as tenant in common with E.C. Loyd and my sister Malinda Loyd. Land in District No. 4. Signed January 10, 1901.

Witnesses: John M. Dickey and N.H. Sullenger. Probated March 7, 1904.

Page 248   **WILL OF J.S. LATEN.** June 8, 1900. Wife, not named, gets all my estate. If she marries, land to be sold by W.K. Laten as my administrator and be equally divided between my children which are not named. Witnesses_ W.B. Douthat, Jacob Klein, W.K. Laten and W.J. Malone. Probated March 14, 1904.

Page 249   **WILL OF J.J.(JAMES J.) CRANE.** Wife Sallie P. Crane gets all my real estate of 160 acres in District No. 5, on waters of Gimlet Creek. Executrix: Wife Sallie P. Crane. Two children, Irene and Dixie. Signed August 22, 1903. Witnesses: W.J.H. Campbell and H.W. Pitts. Probated March 24, 1904.

Page 250   **WILL OF J.B.(JOHN B.) THOMISON.** Of Fayetteville. Wife Delia M. Thomison, all my real estate. Sons: James H. Thomison $1200.00 and William C. Thomison $1000.00 and Hubert H. Thomison $200.00 and my other children no advancements (not named). Executrix: Wife Delia M. Thomison. Signed April 9, 1902. Witnesses: W.J. Malone and J.P. Marrs. Probated June 3, 1904.

Page 251   **WILL OF PORTER H. WEBB.** Of Fayetteville. Father James H. Webb, $150.00. Uncle C.M. Webb, $300.00. Uncle W.C. Webb, $100.00. Uncle Frank H. Webb, my gold watch and $100.00. Uncle M.B. Webb, $100.00. Two Aunts, Lillie E. Webb and Mattie Lou Webb, remainder of estate. Executor: Uncle C.M. Webb. Signed July 28, 1904. Witnesses: R. Ed Feeney and N.P. Carter. Probated August 9, 1904.

Page 252   **WILL OF HENRY AUSTIN GILLESPIE.** Wife Eleanor M. Gillespie. She is to take my jewelry and is to be given to my son Henry Austin Gillespie, Jr. when he arrives of age. Executrix: Wife Eleanor M. Gillespie. Signed February 17, 1904. Witnesses: W.B. Douthat, Jno. R. Woodard and H.L. Moore. Probated March 31, 1904.

Page 253   **WILL OF J.B. TIGERT.** Of Howell. Wife Cynthia Tigert, the lot and buildings &c where I now live in District No. 9 in the village of Howell. Two children, Odell and Burney Larkin Tigert, being children of my second wife, all under age. Executors: Wife Cynthia Tigert and son Sam C. Tigert. Signed December 4, 1901. Witnesses: Jno. A. Moore and P.T. Rhodes. Probated June 25, 1904.

Page 254   **WILL OF CASSENA ROBINSON.** Nieces, Anna V. Robinson, Sarah H. Burnam (Pearl), and Mary E. Burnam (Mamie). Anna V. Robinson to take charge of my estate. Signed February 28, 1890. Witnesses: C.C. McKinney and N.E. Petty. Probated July 1, 1904.

Page 255   **WILL OF MELISSA ROBINSON.** Of Fayetteville. Nieces, Anna V. Robinson and Sarah H. Burnam (Pearl) and Mary E. Burnam (Mamie) and Anna V. Robinson. Signed February 28, 1890. Witnesses: C.C. McKinney and N.E. Petty. Probated July 1, 1904.

Page 256   **WILL OF R.W. EDDINS.** Wife Frances J. Eddins, household items, also appointed executrix.Nine children: A.H. Eddins, B.F. Eddins, R.E. Eddins, W.P. Eddins, Mary E. Kidd, Annie Laura Sullivan, B.C. Eddins, W.F. Eddins, and James C. Eddins. Executors: Wife Frances J. Eddins and son A.F. Eddins. Signed April 26, 1904. Witnesses: N.P. Carter and W.B. Lamb, Jr. Probated September 1, 1904.

Page 258   **WILL OF MRS. N.C. HAMILTON.** Near Elora. Step-son Joe A. Hamilton and son I.N. Hamilton, as trustee of all my personal property and estate. Husband N.A. Hamilton. Two single daughters, Arreva Hamilton and Emma Hamilton. My own children, I.N. Hamilton, L.E. Hamilton, Arreva Hamilton, and Emma Hamilton. My step-children and step-grandchildren: The children of my deceased step-daughter Laura E. Murphy, and my step-son Joe A. Hamilton, and the children of my deceased step-son Elisha Hamilton, and deceased daughter Laura E. Murphy. Trustees and Executors: My step-son Joe A. Hamilton and my son I.N. Hamilton. Signed December 12, 1899. Witnesses: W.E. Chick and B.E. Holman. Probated August 13, 1904.

Page 260 **WILL OF LUCINDA S.C. WOODALL.** OfGurley, Madison County, Alabama. My brother L.W. Woodall and wife M.J. Woodall $40.00 and other moneys and real and personal property. My house and lot in the town of Gurley now occupied by Thomas Lancaster and also to Mrs. Adeline Hall $10.00. My niece E.T. Lancaster $40.00. My niece Florence E.R. Young all my landed estate in Tennessee. Remainder of estate to be divided between Florence E.R. Young and Florence J.W. Whitworth. Executor: W.R. Rison of Huntsville, Alabama. Signed January 4, 1892. Witnesses: E.F. Walker and W.T. Roberts. Probated August 2, 1892 and September 4, 1901.

Page 263 **WILL OF MARY J. CLARK.** Two daughters, Fannie L. Clark and Lizzie O. Clark, for life, two parcels of land that C.C. Carpenter and wife conveyed to me on October 22, 1899, in District No. 20. My husband F.S. Clark. Son Robert S. Clark to get $945.00. To Jonathan Sandlin and Smith Towery, in trust. Executrix: Daughter Fannie L. Clark. Signed October 30, 1901. Witnesses: Joseph C. Higgins and Fred C. Gill. Probated August 23, 1904.

Page 266 **WILL OF WILEY COMMONS.** Of Fayetteville. Wife Martha Commons, household furniture and other items. Also a cow devised to my mother Betsey Commons and also the house and lot in Fayetteville where she now lives. Daughter Vinie Commons. Daughter Henrietta Commons. Daughter Lizzie Commons. Son Andrew Commons. Son William Commons. Executrix: Wife Martha Commons. Signed August 6, 1904. Witnesses: W.B. Lamb and John A. Formwalt. Probated August 16, 1904.

Page 269 **WILL OF REBECCA McNIECE.** District No. 5. Mrs. Susie wife of Thomas Solomon, balance of my estate. Husband Henry McNiece. Executor: My cousin James Cunningham, Sr. Signed October 8, 1904. Witnesses: E.F. Holland and Mrs. Fanie Faulkner. Probated October 24, 1904.

Page 271 **WILL OF C.S. WILSON.** Wife Mary E. Wilson who was then living, an insurance policy dated August 20, 1885 and now having died, to go to: my son Charles S. Wilson $1000.00, Daughter Maggie Bulah and husband W.K. Woodard $1000.00, Daughter Cora G. Wallace and husband C.T. Wallace $1000.00. Executors: Son Charles S. Wilson and my son-in-law W.K. Woodard and son-in-law C.T. Wallace. Signed November 22, 1904. Witnesses: J.R. Feeney and R. Ed Feeney. Probated December 2, 1904.

Page 273 **WILL OF JAMES P. McCOWN.** Lincoln, Tennessee. March 6, 1900. Wife Jane A. McCown, all personal and real estate. Children not named. Executors: John C. and Joseph A. McCown. Witnesses: H.T. Kennedy and L.R. Kennedy. Probated December 5, 1904.

Page 274 **WILL OF J.W. JEAN.** Son T.W. Jean $75.00. Son J.D. Jean $117.00. Daughter Mrs. Jennie Boaz $23.50. Daughter Mrs. Mittie Brown $50.00. Son Joel A. Jean, deceased, in his life time $85.00. Granddaughter Viola Hill a daughter of Joel A. Jean $20.24. My son Dr. B.L. Jean to be guardian of said children. Executor: My son J.D. Jean. Signed October 8, 1904. Witnesses: Jas. H. McDaniel, Sam W. Tate and S.W. Neece. Probated January 12, 1905.

Page 275 **WILL OF MAGGIE E. McCOLLUM.** Of Howell, Tennessee. Mother, not named. Wants executor to purchase a bell for Cane Creek C.P. Church. $50.00 to go to the Cumberland University, Lebanon, Tennessee. $100.00 to Missionaries sent from Elk Presbytery. All cloths &c except such as my sisters (not named) want to go to Bervard School, North Carolina. Sister Emma Blacknall and at her death, to Arrie A. Hudson and my butter dish I give to Bessie McCollum wife of J.A. McCollum. Uncle Ike George $100.00. $100.00 to clean off the graves of the A.J. McCollum family twice a year. Remainder of the estate to be divided between my two sisters, Emma E. Blacknall and her heirs and Lula S. Clark and what remains at Lula's death to Annie E. McCollum, J.A. McCollum's daughter. Signed June 19, 1903. Witnesses: W.D. White and Jno. A. Moore. Probated March 10, 1905.

Page 276   **WILL OF MRS. AMANDA R. CHILDRESS.** Of Fayetteville. Son D.L. Childress gets my brick store in Pulaski, Tennessee. Son Marion F. Childress gets my dwelling house in Nashville, Tennessee. Granddaughter Amanda Howell wife of J.T. Howell $300.00. Grandson Mark Lindsay gets $300.00. Grandson John M. Brady gets $300.00. Grandson C.P. Brady gets $300.00. Granddaughter Sadie Kelso wife of James Kelso gets $300.00. Granddaughter Amanda P. Buford gets $300.00. Executors: My two sons Marion F. Childress and D.L. Childress. Signed May 9, 1903. Witnesses: Jno. R. Woodard and N.P. Carter. Probated March 24, 1905.

Page 278   **WILL OF W.B.(WILLIAM B.) MARTIN.** Fayetteville. Step-daughter Ida Goodrich wife of J. Clarnece Goodrich. Son William Barnett Martin. Signed April 2, 1903. Witnesses: John C. Diemer and Robert Fulton. Probated April 7, 1905.

Page 279   **WILL OF A.J. TOON.** Fayetteville, Desires a monument placed on my lot in Rose Hill Cemetery for my deceased wife, deceased daughters and myself, with inscriptions. Great niece Fannie Thomas, now residing in Williamson County, Tennessee, gets my gold watch which belonged to my deceased daughter Susie Toon at the time of her death. Two nieces, Mrs. Mary Oakley and Elizabeth Byers now residing in Nashville, Tennessee. Mrs. Ann Goodrich widow of my deceased kinsman John C. Goodrich. Executor: My friend T.C. Little. Signed October 27, 1904. Witnesses: J.M. Anderson and Charles Waddle. Probated April 12, 1905.

Page 281   **WILL OF F.A. (FENTON A.) PITTS.** Fayetteville. Wife Mary F. Pitts. Daughter Katie Caughran gets land in District No. 20, the farm willed to me by my father, of 35 acres. Two sons, Rufus Knox and Theophilus I. Pitts gets land in District No. 1, being the farm willed to me by my father of 136 acres. Son Ollie P. Pitts and daughter Maud May Pitts gets my house and lot in Fayetteville where I now live. Executors: Wife Mary F. Pitts and my son Ollie P. Pitts. Signed September 10, 1904. Witnesses: H.L. Moore, C.M. Buchanan and W. Towry. Probated March 11, 1905.

Page 283   **WILL OF JOHN STEPHENS.** Near Camargo, Tennessee. I reserve my family graveyard to be blocked out of my lands and never sold. Executor: I.N. McCluskey. Signed November 18, 1903. Witnesses: J.W. Wheeler and John Sanders. Probated February 25, 1905.

Page 284   **WILL OF ALEXANDER M. FREEMAN.** Wife Frances V. Freeman. Children: Nettie Lee, Mattie James, Horace Abner, Maggie Pearl, and Agnes Irmin (Freeman). If Charles Whitman Freeman should die without issue, his share reverts back to his brothers and sisters. Executrix: Wife Frances V. Freeman. Signed January 25, 1899. Witnesses: B.F. Nichols and J.L. Lovett. Probated April 17, 1905.

Page 285   **WILL OF THOMAS HAMPTON.** Wife Elizabeth Hampton and daughter Mary A. Hampton, daughter Sarah Louisa Gleghorn and the heirs of my daughter Margret America Bledsoe, deceased, viz, Nannie Bessie Rives, Alvis Morgan, Bud Walter, and Alexander Bledsoe. Sons, E.T. and W.W. Hampton. Executor: E.T. Hampton. Signed September 10, 1897. Witnesses: T.D. Sims and Andy Moore. Probated May 3, 1905.

Page 286   **WILL OF HENRY M. STEWART.** Wife Josephine Stewart gets all my estate. Daughter Mrs. Martha A. Chick and her children gets $500.00. Four sons, Rev. W.J. Stewart, J. Alonzo Stewart, Joe M. Stewart, and Oscar S. Stewart, gets land including the farm where I now live with my family and known as the "Beavers Farm", located on the Alabama line.  Brother J.L. Stewart. Executors: My four sons.  Signed April 19, 1905.  Witnesses: H.H. Alexander, T.E. Dryden, S.W. Fleming and C.N. Cowden.  Probated May 13, 1905.

Page 288  **WILL OF ROBERT FAULKNER.**  Wife Mary Faulkner, the farm on which we live.  Children of my three daughters, Prudence Emeline Creson, deceased, Regina Kizeat McGee, deceased, and Sarah Bradford Lane, deceased.  Allow $75.00 to be reserved for erection and including grave with iron fence.  Executors: My son-in-law G.M.D. Creson and J.A. Lane.  Signed January 14, 1898.  Witnesses: C.R. Waid and Oliver Waid.  Probated May 24, 1905.

Page 290  **WILL OF GEORGE W. BROWN.**  Wife Catherine Brown, all my property and at her death to go to my daughter Elizabeth Brown, 10 acres and known as the Lum Place, bounded by B. Parkinson on north, east by Sulser heirs, south and west by my lands, the children of my son Lum Brown, deceased.  Lelia, Eugene, Evie and Jim all under age.  Executor: W.M. Smith. Signed April 4, 1903.  Witnesses: F.P. Colbert and W.A. Robertson.  Probated May 6, 1905.

Page 291  **WILL OF SAMUEL STILES.**  Desires a monument erected near graves of myself and my deceased wife.  Own 290 acres of land.  Three daughters, Martha E. Stiles, Julia C. Stiles, and Florence C. Stiles and my two granddaughters, Katie Lee Baldwin and Bessie A. Baldwin.  My children, Margaret A. Jennings wife of W.C. Jennings, James Stiles, William Stiles, Mary J. Koonce wife of R.M. Koonce, Martha E. Stiles, John Stiles, Francis L. Stiles, Julia C. Stiles, R.F. Stiles, and Florence C. Stiles, and the children of a deceased daughter Sarah E. Baldwin, to wit, Samuel Baldwin, Robert B. Baldwin, Rufus Guy Baldwin, John Baldwin, Jesse C. Baldwin, Katie Lee Baldwin and Bessie A. Baldwin. Executors: My sons, John Stiles and R.F. Stiles.  Signed May 14, 1901.  Witnesses: G.W. Pickett and N.P. Carter.  Probated June 3, 1905.

Page 293  **WILL OF DANIEL WARDEN.**  Wife Nancy J. Warden, all my household and kitchen furniture and my one half interest in the farm on which I now reside in District No. 7.  Children, Robert Warden, William Warden, Nathan Warden, John Warden, Ed Warden, and Sallie Fleming wife of S.W. Fleming. Executrix: Wife Nancy J. Warden.  Signed October 27, 1899.  Witnesses: Fred C. Gill and W.B. Lamb.  Probated June 6, 1905.

Page 294  **WILL OF JOHN DALE.**  Son Calvin Dale is executor.  Daughter Frances J. Drennan.  Signed November 29, 1884.  Witnesses: J.P. Fife and William L. Fife.  Probated June 10, 1905.

Page 295  **WILL OF J.W. SOLOMON.**  Desires a headstone placed at my grave. Wife Mary A. Solomon, household furniture &c.  Son J.Y. Solomon, farm in District No. 4 of Franklin County, Tennessee.  Owns land in District No. 4 of Lincoln County.  Five daughters, Hulda Webb wife of George Webb, Rhoda Stubblefield wife of William Stubblefield, Emma Ward wife of Jeff Ward, Anna Franklin wife of Hal Franklin, and Mary Stubblefield wife of Benton Stubblefield. Two sons, now dead, R.A. and G.W. Solomon, both of whom left children surviving them.  Executor: Son J.Y. Solomon.  Signed September 17, 1904.  Witnesses: John A. Formwalt, N.P. Carter, and W.B. Lamb, Jr.  Probated August 5, 1905.

Page 297  **WILL OF FANNIE KATE MILLS.**  Of Fayetteville.  Desires a head and foot stone to my grave.  Sisters and brothers, Minnie Mills, Bessie Mills, Maud Mills, and Sam Mills.  Executor: Dr. D.M. Goodner.  Signed March 14, 1905.  Witnesses: W.N. Whitaker and Willis H. Whitaker.  Probated August 8, 1905.

Page 298  **WILL OF NELSON JOHNSON,(COL).**  Wife Mariah Johnson, about 100 acres of land.  My children (not named).  Executrix: Wife Mariah Johnson.  Signed January 25, 1901.  Witnesses: G.W. Morgan, J.E. McCown, Frank W. Carter, and Bert Buchanan.  Probated September 9, 1905.

Page 299　**WILL OF M.H. CONAWAY.**　Divide my estate between Antonia Conaway, R. Mynerva Ellis, and Fannie Tate, these three children I appoint as my executors. Signed November 15, 1904. Witnesses: J.L. Woodard and S.M. Teel.
Codicil: March 21, 1905. I appoint D.L. Harris to assist as executor. Probated September 7, 1905.

Page 300　**WILL OF L.S. WOOD.**　Fayetteville. October 13, 1896. Executor: J.R. Feeney. To Mary Ed Woods, household items. Others named: Mattie Fleming, Minnie Lou Woods, Pearl Woods and Mattie Bryson. Witnesses: Eugenie W. Feeney and Belle Woods. Probated October 17, 1905.

Page 301　**WILL OF JOHN HAYWOOD SMITH.**　Son Elmer Riggs Smith, my rifle gun. Wife Nancy Maria Smith as executrix. Signed December 4, 1896. Witnesses: E.H. Gregory and J. Harvy Gill. Probated November 9, 1905.

Page 302　**WILL OF JAMES C. KELSO.**　Wife Elizabeth Kelso, all the property. Executors: John D. and Charley Kelso. Signed June 15, 1896. Witnesses: J.W. Feeney and J.E. Routt.
Codicil: June 15, 1896. At Hughey. Appointed my son J.C. Kelso, Jr. as one of the executors in the place of J.D. Kelso who has moved to Chattanooga, Tennessee. Signed March 4, 1905. Witnesses: J.C. Kelso, R.M. Rawls and D.F. Hobbs. Probated December 4, 1905.

Page 304　**WILL OF W.A. MILES.**　Fayetteville. February 24, 1902. To Ellis Woods wife of Jas. M. Blake, the house and lot now occupied by me as a residence and $1000.00 of stock in First National Bank in Fayetteville. To Ella Woods Blake, Susie Woods Bearden, Mary Woods Miller, and my cousin Minnie Walker Woods, each $2000.00 stock in same as above bank. To Master Ellis Miller Bearden, my golf watch and chain. To M.M. Bearden, note for $1000.00 against him. To Mesdames Miller, Bearden and Blake, I leave their deceased sister's piano. Executor: Mat M. Bearden. Witnesses: J.R. Feeney, S.C. Hipsh, R.D. Dryden, M.M. Bearden and N.P. Carter. Probated December 16, 1905.

Page 305　**WILL OF PHILIP DUNAFON.**　Of Fisk P.O., Alabama. Desires a monument be placed at my grave. Wife Jane Dunafon, my estate. Son John Dunafon. Executor: Dr. L.Y. Hayes. Signed June 16, 1905. Witnesses: S.E. Galloway and W.S. Boggs. Probated January 24, 1906.

Page 306　**WILL OF GARRETT D. BUCKNER.**　Of Petersburg, Tennessee. My Cornersville house and lot goes to the three girls and oldest boy, P.M. Buckner, Mrs. L.C. Maxfield, Mrs. Sallie N. Leuter and Mrs. Lollie M. Coker, they are to be made equal with Al. G. Buckner and Charles L. Buckner who is being put through Dental College. Al. G. Buckner gets my practive and books with office fixtures at Fayetteville. Wife Mattie J. Buckner, all my household furniture. Executors: D.M. Dryden and M.J. Buckner. Signed November 17, 1904. Witnesses: D.M. Dryden of Petersburg and Ernest Finch of Petersburg. Probated February 9, 1906.

Page 307　**WILL OF JONATHAN SANDLIN.**　Of Camargo, Tennessee. My oldest daughter July Ann and her six children, $50.00. My nine children (not named). Executors: My sons Morgan and Doc Sandlin. Signed February 23, 1906. Witnesses: J.P. Fife and J.B. Pitts. Probated March 7, 1906.

Page 308　**WILL OF C.B. McGUIRE.**　Of Fayetteville. Daughters, Jimmie McGuire Lamb and Myra McGuire Cowan, all my silver and household and kitchen furniture. Jennie McGuire Lamb wife H.C. Lamb. Myra McGuire Cowan wife of W.G. Cowan. Executors: N.P. Carter and W.B. Lamb. Signed August 18, 1902. Witnesses: J.E. Poindexter and Joseph C. Higgins. Probated March 28, 1906.

Page 310　**WILL OF J.C. (JANE C.) WILLSON.**　Desires a tombstone placed on my grave. One third of my estate to Ettie J. Storment, one third to my son's (W.C. Galloway, deceased) children, Samuel H., Ira C., Jennie C., Clyde

W., Rennie L. and Frank C. Galloway, and one third to my daughter (M.H. Fulton). Executor: James E. McCown. Signed November __, 1899. Witnesses: Jas. E. McCown and S.H. McCown. Probated April 2, 1906.

Page 311 **WILL OF SARAH WILSON.** Friend J.D. Buchanan, $100.00. To Mary Jane Caughran, remainder of estate. Executor: J.D. Buchanan. Signed September 25, 1898. Witnesses: J.E. Poindexter and D.M. Goodner. Probated July 2, 1906.

Page 312 **WILL OF T.L. JOHNSTON.** Wife Susan Adella Johnston, all real and personal property. Children: Beula M., Lenard B., Bunnie L., Edna P., Jessie W., and Eva W. Johnston. My land in District No. 14. Signed September 20, 1906. Witnesses: J.M. Hudson and J.W. Cunningham. Probated October 20, 1906.

Page 313 **WILL OF J.B. DERRICK.** Desires a monument for myself and wife be erected at my grave. Wife Martha J. Derrick, several items and $200.00. Daughter Della McLaughlin wife of J.B. McLaughlin $5000.00. Son Rufus B. Derrick $500.00. My land in District No. 25, 122 acres. To J.B. McLaughlin, as Trustee for my grandchildren, Leon Derrick, Gisell Derrick, and Lewis Derrick, only children of my deceased son W.B. Derrick to get one half of the land in District No. 8. All my grandchildren are under age of 21 years. To W.R. Roach, Trustee for use and benefit of grandchildren, John Thurston Roach, Murrell Jackson Roach, and Helen Roach, only children of my deceased daughter Gertrude Roach, gets the east half of land in District No. 8. Grandchildren all under age of 21 years. Executors: My wife Martha J. Derrick and my son-in-law J.B. McLaughlin. Signed October 28, 1906. Witnesses: A.B. Wright, A.M. McLaughlin, and N.P. Carter. Probated November 10, 1906.

Page 318 **WILL OF M.V. GROCE.** Wife M.J. Groce appointed executrix. Children, not named. Willson named. Signed August 2, 1906. Witnesses: W.M. Groce and C.N. Ashby. Probated August 27, 1906.

Page 319 **WILL OF M.M. BEARDEN.** Of Fayetteville. Wife Susie Woods Bearden, all estate, also appointed executrix. Signed February 27, 1906. Witnesses: N.P. Carter and W.B. Lamb. Probated February 1, 1906.

Page 320 **WILL OF J.L. NEWSOM.** I empower W.R. Newsom and H.O. Newsom to wind up my business and give my wife one half of all the money and personal property. Son J.L. Newsom, Jr., W.R. Newsom, and H.O. Newsom. Probated December 5, 1906.

Page 321 **WILL OF JOSIAH BEATIE.** Desires a head and foot stone erected at my grave. Servant Susan Harris, colored, land where I now reside in District No. 11, 25 acres. Children of my deceased sister Martha McClellan one third of estate. Children of my deceased brother Robert Beatie one third of estate. To my nieces, Sallie E. Halbert wife of P.W. Halbert, and Susan J. Halbert wife of W.H. Halbert 1/12 of estate. To children of my deceased nephew john beatie 1/12 of estate. To children of my deceased niece Mary A. Millard 1/12 less $200.00 estate of which I paid for their father W.A. Millard. Niece Virginia Beatie, only child of my deceased brother John Beatie. Appointed P.W. Halbert as executor. Signed November 23, 1906. Witnesses: George C. Thomas, W.B. Lamb and N.P. Carter. Probated December 10, 1906.

Page 323 **WILL OF MRS. BEULAH BURTON.** My first husband, John Daniel. Brother Hatcher Edgeman to collect $100.00 to pay funeral expenses and place a tombstone over my grave and over the grave of dead husband John Daniel. Three children by my first husband, not named. Oldest daughter Alma Daniel to be given to my sister Mrs. Cora Miller. I want my brother Hatcher Edgeman to have my son Jesse and I want my sister Emma Hosch to have my daughter Bessie Daniel. Signed October 6, 1906. Witnesses: W.J. McAlister, S.V. Beard and Roscoe McAlister. Probated January 7, 1907.

Page 324 **WILL OF D.C. HARRIS.** Wife Sarah E. Harris, all personal property, also appointed executrix. Signed October 9, 1905. Witnesses: D.C. Sherrell and M.F. Story. Probated January 15, 1907.

Page 325 **WILL OF G.R. ALLEN.** Wife Nannie A. Allen, two tracts of land in District No. 20, of about 22 acres. Owns lands in District No. 19 to be equally divided between my named children and grandchildren, William R. Allen, Samuel G. Allen, Thomas M. Allen, Frances M. Allen, Mrs. Mollie Myers, Mrs. Maggie M. Rowell, and granddaughter Nellie Allen. Executor: O. Wiley. Signed December 28, 1906. Witnesses: J.B. Kidd and J.A. Dunman. Probated January 15, 1907.

Page 326 **WILL OF JACK BONNER.** Wife Adlin Bonner, personal property, farm I now live on and after her death to go to my two daughters Fannie Suggs and Elvirie Deberry. Signed March --, 1897. Signed by Jack Bonner and Adline Bonner. Witnesses: A.H. Rull and W.R. Cashion. Probated January 15, 1907.

Page 327 **WILL OF MILTON SMITH.** Two sons, S.B. Smith and A.J. Smith, $1000.00 each. Wife Sarah Smith, one third of my estate. Executors: My two sons, S.B. and A.J. Smith. Signed May 2, 1906. Witnesses: F.R. Mitchell and Nathan Smith. Probated January 21, 1907.

Page 328 **WILL OF F.A. GEORGE.** Wife Betsey Jane George, one third interest in land "Bold Tract". Son J.F. George, two thirds interest in the "Cothren Tract". Daughter M.A. Hallis, one third interest in "Cothren Tract". To heirs of my deceased daughter Martha H. Mitchell, 53 acres on my home place and known as the "McGuire Place". My grandson Luray Harrison, $1000.00. Sons, J.H. George and G.E. George, W.L. George, H.K. George, L.H. George, and E.B. George, balance of my estate. Appointed J.H. George, G.E. George, W.L. George, H.K. George, L.H. George, and E.B. George my agents in the dower of Mrs. M.F. Nelson. I reserve one acre of land where the grave yard is at this time on the Nelson place, also reserve one half acre at the grave yard at the old home place where J.P. Mitchell now lives. Signed March 5, 1898. Witnesses: John D. Simms and T.L. Strain. Probated February 13, 1907.

Page 329 **WILL OF MALINDA LOYD.** Brother E.C. Loyd, all interest I have in landed estate where I now live, also where I am tenant in common with E.C. Loyd and my sister Lucinda Loyd, my interest in said land is one fifth, which I inherited from my father John Loyd, deceased, located in District No. 4. Signed January 10, 1901. Witnesses: John M. Dickey and N.H. Sullinger. Probated February 15, 1907.

Page 330 **WILL OF HUGH PARKINSON.** Wife, not named, to remain on the farm where I now live. Daughter Martha B. Parkinson, son S.M. Parkinson, to remain on said farm. Son Milton B. Parkinson, $100.00. Daughter Mary L. Sloan, $100.00. Daughter Lizzie Phagan, $100.00. Executor: Son S.M. Parkinson. Signed October 16, 1895. Witnesses: W.R. Jones and W.P. Watson. Probated March 1, 1907.

Page 331 **WILL OF E.D. THOMPSON.** Fayetteville. Wife Laura Thompson appointed executrix. Signed January 23, 1907. Witnesses: W.J. Malone and J.R. Hancock. Probated March 4, 1907.

Page 332 **WILL OF R.N. BRADFORD.** Three children, John M., Annie May, and Edith N. Bradford, all under age. Brother W.H. Bradford to be guardian of my children. My land in District No. 1. Executor: January 8, 1907. Witnesses: J.B. Rutledge, J.E. Hereford and J.E. Routt. Probated March 6, 1907.

Page 335 **WILL OF G.W. CAMERON.** Wife Margaret Cameron and my daughter Elizabeth Cameron, $250.00 each. Son J. Lawson Cameron and my two daughters, Minnie Maude Cameron and Letitia Elizabeth Cameron. I own two tracts of land in District No. 15 of about 125 acres. Executor: J.F. Campbell. In case J.F. Campbell should be dead or refuse, I appoint E.E. Eslick as executor. Signed September 20, 1906. Witnesses: Mike D. Sullivan and H.W. Aymett. Probated March 13, 1907.

Page 337 **WILL OF MRS. BETTIE C. BATEMAN.** Of Booneville. Two sons, T.E. Bateman and Benjamin Bateman, personal property. Executor: T.E. Bateman. Signed March 11, 1907. Witnesses: J.C. Shofner and N.F. Boone. Probated April 6, 1907.

Page 338 **WILL OF P.W. HALBERT.** Wife S.E. Halbert, also appointed executrix. She is also to get all my estate. Signed March 8, 1907. Witnesses: J.C. Halbert and E.C. Halbert. Probated April 10, 1907.

Page 339 **WILL OF PENINA CALLAHAN.** September 7, 1899. Isham E. Pylant, household items. Nina Culbreth, household items. Pennina M. Sanders, household items. Ethel Brooks, my press and other items. Mattie A. Crane, sewing machine. Pennina Lancaster, household items. Mary Jane Richardson to have my first husband, Isham Sorrels) bureau and dressing table and his father Neadham Sorrel's trunk. Peggy Morrison, my rocking chair. Gray Jackson Pylant, one horse because he didn't get one from my father. Beatrice Ford, $50.00 to buy her an organ provided she is living at my death. I do this because she is my namesake. Mattie Daniel, my glass pitcher and one goblet. Mary Manafee, my buggy &c. Nancy Pylant, Elizabeth Pylant, Sack Pylant, Mary Pylant, Canthus Pylant, and Josie Loveless, equally divide my clothing. Remainder of my estate to go to Sack (G.M. Pylant's wife) and Josie Loveless to be equally divided. Executor: J.C. Pylant. Signed September 7, 1899. Witnesses: Penina Calahan, H.C. Sorrells and T.B. Daniel. Probated May 11, 1907.

Page 340 **WILL OF RACHEL ANNA KIMES.** Of Bellville. Aunt Exie Jones, $100.00. Brother-in-law Thomas Jones and my brother Mattie D. Kimes, remainder of estate. Executor: Dr. W.F. Cannon. Signed March 24, 1907. Witnesses: G.W. Harris and G.C. Cunningham. Probated May 11, 1907.

Page 341 **WILL OF MRS. L.E. McCOWN.** Daughter Martha J. Galloway, household furniture and other items and land in District No. 20 of 45½ acres. Grandson Willie T. Drenan, one parlor organ and other items and land in District No. 20. Executor: W.P. Galloway. Signed October 8, 1903. Witnesses: J.H. Thompson and T.J. Wiley. Probated June 15, 1907.

Page 342 **WILL OF ELISABETH A. KEELING.** Of Normandy, Bedford County, Tennessee. July 16, 1897. Elizabeth A. Keeling now of Fayetteville, Lincoln County, Tennessee. Youngest daughter Flora Gergie Keeling, all property both real and personal, except my household and wearing apparel &c, I want sold. Two sons, E.B. Keeling and J.G. Keeling. Other heirs, brothers and sisters, not named. Executor: My oldest son, not named. Signed July 16, 1897. Witnesses: J.L. Brandon of Normandy, Tennessee and John A. Troxler of Normandy, Tennessee.
Codicil: "The three named legatees is right where it appears in the above, but they are not the youngest children of mine. I write this to correct this mistake". Signed - Elizabeth A. Keeling. Witnesses: Same as above. Probated May 24, 1907.

Page 343 **WILL OF SUSAN McCLURE.** Of Booneville. Desires to mark the graves of my husband E.M. McClure and myself. Niece Sallie Dawson, $25.00. Husband E.C. McClure, full control of my estate. Desires that the real estate be vested in Earnest A. Carriger for life and the remainder to the heirs of his body. Executor: Earnest A. Carriger. Signed December 17, 1906. Witnesses: N.F. Boone and W.M. Green. Probated July 6, 1907.

Page 344 **WILL OF M.L. WILSON.** Brother Robert A. Wilson to take charge of my property consisting of a dwelling house and lot and a store house and lot in the village of Richmond, Bedford County, Tennessee. Remainder to be divided between brother Robert A. Wilson and my sister Nannie E. Foster. Signed July 8, 1907. Witnesses: J.C. Kelso and J.C. Rucker. Probated July 20, 1907.

Page 345 **WILL OF W.A.E. PITTS.** Wife Parthenia L. Pitts, my estate. Son W.W. Pitts, $625.00. Daughter Jennie May Moore wife of C.L. Moore, $625.00. Executors: Brother-in-law J.D. Parks and son-in-law C.L. Moore. Signed July 17, 1907. Witnesses: N.P. Carter and W.B. Lamb, Jr. Probated July 27, 1907.

Page 347 **WILL OF A.C. McGEHEE.** Wife Sarah T. McGehee, all estate. Children: Etta C. Pitts wife of Clifford Pitts, Elphia M. Howard wife of Clifford Howard, Alda M. Howard wife of Thomas Howard, Harvey M. McGehee, A.C. McGehee, Jr., Mary L. McGehee, Sarah T. McGehee, Farris O. McGehee, Ernest A. McGehee, William R. McGehee, Wilburn R. McGehee, Eldridge M. McGehee, Lily S. McGehee, and such other children as may be born. Executrix: Wife Sarah T. McGehee. Signed September 8, 1906. Witnesses: Jno. H. Rees and W.B. Lamb, Jr. Probated August 3, 1907.

Page 348 **WILL OF M.A. EDMISON.** My land in District No. 12 to be sold. Daughter Susan Adella Johnson, $500.00. Grandson Jno. Irby Cunningham, $300.00. Grandson Jim Bob Cunningham, $200.00. Daughter Mary Hutoca Cunningham, land in District No. 12, land I received from my father's estate and deeded to A.B. Edmison, my husband. I direct my daughter Mary Hutoca Cunningham to take care of my husband and that my household and kitchen furniture be divided between Mary H. Cunningham and Susan Adella Johnson. Executor: A.B. Wilson. Signed June 3, 1907. Witnesses: Mrs. M.A. Edmison. Probated September 11, 1907.

Page 349 **WILL OF R.M. HAGUE.** Desires a monument erected at my grave. Wife Kalista Hague, household and other items, residence and lot in the town of Mulberry, in District No. 5, also R.L. Farrar as Trustee for my two daughters. Daughter Lizzie Hague, my piano, oldest daughter. Daughter Pauline Hague. Executors: Wife Kalista Hague and my friend R.L. Farrar. Signed September 6, 1907. Witnesses: W.B. Lamb, Jr. and N.P. Carter. Probated October 9, 1907.

Page 353 **WILL OF THOMAS H. HARRIS.** Owns land in District No. 9 and 12. Two children, Mary C. and Ernest M. Harris and their Aunt Alice E. Massey, personal property, where I live. Brothers and sisters, not named. Signed March 31, 1883. Witnesses: J.D. Tillman and W.C. Frost. Probated November 2, 1907.

Page 354 **WILL OF C.A. DIEMER.** Wife Rebecca Diemer, all estate. Son John C. Diemer, Trustee for his mother, and my said wife. Owns land in District No. 8, bounded by Franklin Street and Christian Church, known as the "Vineyard Lot" and by Miss Jane Edmondson, Lots No. 68 and 51, respectively. Executor: My son John C. Diemer. Signed February 23, 1903. Witnesses: Jno. R. Woodard and N.P. Carter. Probated December 20, 1907.

Page 357 **WILL OF JAMES H. TAYLOR.** Wife Henrietta C. Taylor, my home farm of 165 acres and where I now reside and other household items. Children, Sarah C. George wife of T.B. George, William Y. Taylor, the heirs of Jarred S. Taylor, deceased, and Franklin P. Taylor, deceased, the heirs of said Jarred and Frank to inherit the part their fathers would have inherited if still living. Executor: My son William Y. Taylor. Signed December 1, 1906. Witnesses: W.A. Copeland and R.W. Gaunt. Probated January 4, 1908.

Page 358 **WILL OF A.B. WOODARD.** Wife Maud L. Woodard, my house and lot which I purchased of Dozier and wife and is situated in front of Richland Park in West Nashville, Tennessee. Daughter Mary Benton Morris, house and lot where she now lives in Fayetteville, District No. 8 and whose husband is

W.W. Morris. Son Bert P. Woodard, $1400.00. Mentions three minor children, not named. Executrix: Wife Maud L. Woodard. Signed June 19, 1906 and June 29, 1906. Witnesses: May 22, 1907 by H.E. Dryden, C.N. Cowden, C.B. Bagley, and P. Mc. Allen and F.C. Guthrie. Probated April 15, 1908.

Page 360 **WILL OF JULIA AMBIRILLA FORRESTER.** Of Bellville. Husband J.W.E. Forrester, all estate. Executor: Dr. W.F. Cannon. Witnesses: R.L. Bolles and T.B. Brown. Probated April 18, 1908.

Page 361 **WILL OF JESSE CARNES.** Of Muncie, Indiana. Wife Mary V. Carnes, all property. Son Lew C. Carnes, son Norwood Carnes, son William W. Carnes and son Edward K. Carnes. Daughters, Dora L. Ingersoll, Emma O. Propst, and Carrie B. Lydick. Executrix: Wife Mary V. Carnes. Signed at Muncie, Indiana January 19, 1899. Witnesses: Cassius M.C. Shanks and James R. Reeves.

Page 362 **WILL OF J.W. SOLOMON.** Will contested by J.Y. Solomon, executor of J.W. Solomon, deceased, VS Mrs. J.C. Solomon next friend &c. Will signed September 17, 1904 and witnessed by John A. Formwalt, N.P. Carter and W.B. Lamb, Jr. The defendants were: Claud Solomon, Hugh Solomon, Thelma Solomon, Thomas Solomon, Adder Solomon, Russell Solomon, Charley Solomon, and Lillie Solomon. Case recorded in Minute Book 7, pages 425, 426, and 427.
Will: Desires a head and foot stone placed at my grave. Wife Mary A. Solomon, all household and kitchen furniture and other items. Son J.Y. Solomon, personal property and land in District No. 4 of Franklin County, Tennessee, where he resides. Wife gets land in District No. 4 of Lincoln County, Tennessee. Five Daughters: Huldah Webb wife of George Webb, Rhoda Stubblefield wife of William Stubblefield, Emma Ward wife of Jeff Ward, Anna Franklin wife of Hal Franklin, and Mary Stubblefield wife of Benton Stubblefield. I have two sons now dead, R.A. Solomon and G.W. Solomon, both of whom left children surviving them, children not named. Executor: Son J.Y. Solomon. Signed September 17, 1906. Witnesses: John A. Formwalt, N.P. Carter and W.B. Lamb, Jr.

Page 366 **WILL OF MINERVA ANNE MOORE, A WIDOW.** Brother H.S. Reese with whom I have been living and since his death with his family, a period of 30 years, and in the fall of year 1899, I made a contract with my brother H.S. Reese, which I delivered all my property. In October 1901, my brother died and I have lived with his widow, Josie Reese and her children, and his daughter by a former marriage, I give to Josie Reese and her children, to wit, Hubert Reese, Alton Reese, Dallas Reese, and Eva Belle Reese, and to Louella Hayes wife of J. Lee Hayes, the only child of my brother by a former marriage. Signed March 18, 1908. Witnesses: W.E. Stewart and W.R. Jones. Probated July 6, 1908.


LINCOLN COUNTY, TENNESSEE WILL BOOK 6

August 1908 - December 1921


Page 1 **WILL OF JNO. W. TRANTHAM.** Red Oak, Tennessee. July 6, 1908. Wife Georgia Trantham, all my estate. Our children that are living, not named. Wife is to deduct $500.00 from Carrie Roden wife of Odie Roden. Witnesses: T.G. Buchanan and W.P. Griffis. Probated August 3, 1908.

Page 2 **WILL OF M.C. STORY.** Wife Mary Elizabeth Story and my five children: T.A. Story, L.E. Story, H.G. Story, D.C. Story, S.E. Cathart and Rosa Dove Mitchell, each one sixth. Executors: L.E. Story and D.C. Sherrell. Signed October 19, 1904. Witnesses: W.S. Robinson and J. Harvey Gill. Probated August 13, 1908.

Page 3 **WILL OF JULIA A. McCRACKEN.** To R.S. and M.E. Hereford, all property of every kind, also they are appointed executors. Signed

January 26, 1900. Witnesses: J.L. Barnes and G.W. Menatree. Probated September 5, 1908. J.L. Barnes of Pulaski, Giles County, Tennessee.

Page 5 **WILL OF JOHN C. STEPHENSON.** Wife Amanda E. Stephenson, land in District No. 8 and 9, of 125 acres. Minor daughter Salome Stephenson. My afflicted son Crawford Stephenson. My six children: Callie M. Clark wife of Charles E. Clark, Mary Myrtle Morgan wife of R.K. Morgan, George T. Stephenson, Crawford Stephenson, Lawrence Stephenson, and Salome Stephenson. Executor: My son George T. Stephenson also guardian of Salome Stephenson. Signed April 8, 1904. Witnesses: A.B. Wright and R. Ed Feeney. Probated November 30, 1908.

Page 7 **WILL OF J.R. BEAVERS.** Wife Eliza Beavers. My eldest son William C. Beavers, all land in District No. 22, bordered by Baxter lands, Myrick lands, Thomas Boles and Patterson lands, 84 acres. The consideration being that the William C. Beavers is to provide a home for his mother, Eliza Beavers, during her life. Signed June 24, 1896. Witnesses: J.E. Ramsey and W.R. Brown. Probated November 30, 1908.

Page 8 **WILL OF M.D.L. WHITAKER.** Of Mulberry, Tennessee. Land in District No. 5. Son Anderson R. Whitaker, $200.00. Two daughters, Agnes Wilson and Johnnie P. Clardy, $100.00 each. My children: W.H. Whitaker, Anderson Whitaker, R. Whitaker, Agnes Wilson wife of C.S. Wilson, Pinkie Hobbs wife of B.H. Hobbs, Johnnie P. Clardy wife of (blank) Clardy and the children and heirs of my deceased daughter Frankie Raby wife of William Raby. Executors: My two sons W.H. and Anderson R. Whitaker. Signed January 15, 1908. Witnesses: W.R. Taylor and Jno. H. Rees. Probated December 7, 1908.

Page 10 **WILL OF MRS. GUSSIE W. WALLACE, WIDOW.** Friend, Miss Ella Dryden, $200.00 for her caring for me during my illness. Sister, Mrs. Beulah Woodard, the dresser made by my father, hand made. Son, Charles Nathaniel Wallace, a minor, to get property to be in trusted by my friend H.C. Harris who is appointed guardian. Executor: H.C. Harris. Brother, C.S. Wilson and my sister-in-law, Mrs. Mary W. Harris, N.O. Wallace, and R.M. Wallace, that is my said sister and brother, to get one half, and my sister-in-law and brother-in-law, take other half. Signed December 9, 1908. Witnesses: M.W. Woodard, Mrs. M.A. Bagley and W.K. Woodard. Probated January 2, 1909.

Page 12 **WILL OF A.C. BLACKWELL.** Of Mulberry. My father and mother, Charles R. and M.J. Blackwell, $300.00 annually. Wife Lucy Blackwell remainder of estate and also appointed executrix. Signed December 16, 1908. Witnesses: J.A.D. Middleton of Mulberry and R.A. Renegar of Mulberry. Probated January 5, 1909.

Page 13 **WILL OF MAYME HUMES INGLE.** Husband, Charles Luther Ingle, one half of all my property. My only heir, Roy Goodner Ingle, remainder of my property. Signed March 4, 1908. Witnesses: S.J. Little and J.M. Stewart. Probated January 9, 1909.

Page 14 **WILL OF M.L. MEAD.** Desires a head and foot stone erected at my grave. To sell all land except the family graveyard which I direct shall be reserved as a burial ground and not sold. Niece, Sallie E. Ray, her land on which she now lives and $25.00. Nieces and nephews: Mrs. Fannie Carrigan wife of Hiram Carrigan, Mary Walker, Mattie Mead, James H. Mead, and Ed Mead, children of my deceased brother L.G. Mead, and Sallie E. Ray and Marcus W. Thompson, children of my deceased sister Susan Thompson. Executor: My grand nephew Felix Ray. Signed July 23, 1908. Witnesses: R.L. Caldwell and N.P. Carter. Probated January 20, 1909.

Page 16 **WILL OF NARCISSIA F. CURTIS.** Son George A. Curtis, land in District No. 16 and known as the Thorp Land, borders John Malone, Albert and Henry Curtis lands, 48 acres. Children: Julia A. Woodward, S.L. Curtis, C.M. Curtis, ?.J. Curtis, A.S. Curtis, and J.H. Curtis. Executors: A.S.

Curtis and J.H. Curtis. Signed September 4, 1908. Witnesses: C.M. Trantham and W.B. Solomon. Probated January 21, 1909.

Page 17 **WILL OF MARIAH WAITE.** December 14, 1908. Wife M.J. Waite. My son Plummer Waite and my daughter Elida Waite, the home farm &c. Remaining children: Roy C. Waite, Henry L. Waite, Alice E. McDaniel, and Coleman B. Waite. Witnesses: David Strang and R.W. McCown. Probated February 1, 1909.

Page 18 **WILL OF MRS. S.S. GLEGHORN.** Daughters Mary Rebecca and Martha Gleghorn, all my money &c. All my children, Chambers, Thompson, Moses, Mary and Martha Gleghorn. Desires a tombstone placed over my grave and their father's grave. Executor: Son Moses Gleghorn. Signed January 15, 1909. Witnesses: A.B. Wilson and F.H. Liles. Probated February 15, 1909.

Page 19 **WILL OF E.J. HIGGINS.** Brothers, not named. Executors: O.H., J.C., and W.W. Higgins. Signed January 18, 1909. Witnesses: Edith G. Higgins and Jos. C. Higgins. Probated February 22, 1909.

Page 20 **WILL OF MARY J. EZELL.** Grandsons, the heirs of my daughter Pattie Ezell, namely, Frank Ezell, Clyde Ezell, Harry Ezell, and Tazwell Ezell, $25.00 each. Son J.L. Ezell, remainder of estate. Executor: J.L. Ezell. Signed September 25, 1908. Witnesses: R.E. Howell and E.G. Bevils. Probated March 1, 1909.

Page 21 **WILL OF ROBERT MOORE.** Wife Margaret Jane Moore, all my real and personal property. Three sons, William G., Thomas G., and Hugh P. Moore. Daughter Mary E. Sloan, $100.00. My invalid daughter Sarah M. Moore. Executor: William G. Moore. Signed March 9, 1899. Witnesses: J.T. Sloan and Albert L. Sloan. Probated March 1, 1909.

Page 22 **WILL OF W.M. ROSBOROUGH.** Of Howell. To W.N. Thomas and William Napier, better known as William N. Rosborough. Executor: H.C. Harris. Signed January 6, 1909. Witnesses: J.W. Clark, A.P. Taylor and Wallace M. Harris. Probated March 10, 1909.

Page 23 **WILL OF LAZARE PILLET.** November 25, 1907. This will is written entirely in French.
Translation: Lazare Pillet, living in Agen, Barsalon Freumentry Street (Villa Mimosa). Wife, Emile, born Calle, living with me. Mistress Pillet to dispose of my property. Josephine Degueuse, Roy's wife, living in Issy, Levergne, Seene and Leire; her sister Cletiles Degueuse living in Paris; their brother Joseph Degueuse living in Geneva, Switzerland; their sister Jeanne Degueuse living in Paris; the four children of my sister Claudine Pillet. And Charles Pillet living in Nevers (Nievre) and his brother Emile Pillet living in Agen, Lot et Gareume; the two childrenof my brother Jean Marie. Written in Agen on November 15, 1907. (A very long will)

Page 29 **WILL OF BENJAMIN M. GLASS.** Of Lincoln. January 18, 1908. Wife Carrie H. Glass and daughter Margaret Anna Glass, under age, all my property both real and personal. Executrix: Wife Carrie H. Glass. Witnesses: S.H. McCown and Tillman Bates. Probated March 31, 1909.

Page 30 **WILL OF DR. W.C. GRISWELL.** March 25, 1909. Wife Mattie Griswell, entire estate. At the death of my wife, to be divided, first, that William Rice Cannon shall have $250.00 and that Martha Virginia Cannon shall have $250.00. W.R. Cannon, Trustee and Executor. Witnesses: W.A. Patterson and J.J. Prosser. Probated May 3, 1909.

Page 31 **WILL OF MARY E. FULLER.** (Died in April) Petersburg. October 28, 1902. At death each of us gives, bequeaths and devises his interests in estate and personal property, should he die single, the following signers of this will. Witnesses: J.S. Edmiston and Lizzie Dwiggins. Probated May 4, 1909.

Page 32   **WILL OF SUSIE J. CARTER, WIDOW.**   Widow of F.W. Carter, deceased, of Fayetteville.   Son Roy R. Carter, $1700.00 in money. Daughter Nena Carter Strong wife of H.R. Strong.   My land in District No. 8. Executor: Son Roy R. Carter. Signed April 9, 1908.   Witnesses: Annie M. Davis, Beulah M. Ralston and N.P. Carter.   Probated May 12, 1909.

Page 33   **WILL OF B.F. FANNING.**   Living near McCalleseter's (McAlister) Store.   Wife Jennie Lula Fanning, my farm.   Four minor children, Thomas Leeton, Ally Ethel, Jabel Andrew Middleton, and John Edward Fanning, land in District No. 19, my homeplace.   Executor: My son William A. Fanning. Signed June 1, 1909.   Witnesses: H.P. Flynt and B.E. Noblitt.   Probated June 12, 1909.

Page 34   **WILL OF T.O. BAGLEY.**   Fayetteville.   June 6, 1893.   Wife Ellen Bagley, all my property.   Children not named.   Witnesses: N. Benedict, H.E. Dryden, William Feeney, and Morgan Eslick.   Probated June 26, 1909.

Page 35   **WILL OF J.J. RAWLS.**   Blanche. September 25, 1905.   Wife Madeleine J. Rawls, all my property.   Witnesses: D.W. Byers and M.P. Woods. Probated July 27, 1909.

Page 36   **WILL OF J.W. MITCHELL.**   District No. 5.   September 22, 1905.   Wife Mollie Mitchell (besides her own property), $100.00 as a year's support and other items.   My land on Farris Creek in Moore County, Tennessee, known as the "Charles Wagoner Tract".   My sons and daughters: J.C. Mitchell and J.L. Mitchell, 100 acres of land, home tract, T.W. Mitchell, Laura Campbell, Martha Copeland, Josie Tipps, Ida Miles and Alice Sullivan.   Grandson Leonard Brown, under age.   Witnesses: Martin V. Riddle and G.B. Gattis.
Codicil: Executors: My sons J.C., T.W., and J.L. Mitchell.   Probated August 2, 1909.

Page 38   **WILL OF H.K. HOLMAN.**   Wife Mattie L. Holman, executrix. Signed June 14, 1909.   Witnesses: W.N. Whitaker and Willis H. Whitaker. Probated August 9, 1909.

Page 39   **WILL OF JAMES R. McELROY.**   Brother Con McElroy, all my real estate in District No. 8, 147 acres.   Brother Clyde McElroy, 105 acres, my father R.C. McElroy estate inherited by myself, Con McElroy, T.T. Elroy, Clyde McElroy and the children of my deceased sister Mrs. Mattie Buchanan, from our mother Amanda McElroy now deceased, subject to the life estate of my father as above stated.   Witnesses: J.E. Poindexter, Hiram Higgins and M.W. Woodard. Probated August 27, 1909.

Page 40   **WILL OF EUGENIA W. FEENEY.**   Fayetteville.   Daughter Mary Battle Rodes wife of H.E. Rodes a note for $2000.00 executed by my husband J.R. Feeney, with J.W. Feeney and R. Ed Feeney as securities all my jewelry to my children, Mary Battle Rodes, Eugene W. Feeney, Ruth Feeney, and Anne Feeney to be divided, also Ruth Feeney.   Executors: Husband J.R. Feeney and son-in-law Henry E. Rodes. Signed June 12, 1905.   Witnesses: W.B. Lamb and N.P. Carter. Codicil: Appointed brother Andrew B. Wright instead of my husband J.R. Feeney. Probated September 15, 1909.

Page 41   **WILL OF HENDERSON BARNES.**   Wife P.A. Barnes, all my estate.   To Eliza Harrison, everything left after my wife's death.   Executor: Henderson T. Barnes. Signed September 5, 1909.   Witnesses: A.B. Wilson and J.B. Hudson.   Probated October 27, 1909.

Page 42   **WILL OF W.F. WRIGHT.**   Wife L.J. Wright, all estate.   Brothers and sister B.L. Wright, P.L. Wright, and H.P. Clift, all property left by my wife. Executrix: Wife L.J. Wright. Signed November 2, 1901. Witnesses: A.B. Wilson and F.M. Liles. Probated October 21, 1909.

Page 43 **WILL OF J.J. CUMMINS.** Wife H.F. Cummins, my farm. Daughter Maud to live with her mother. Two sons, Jack and Clyde Cummins, also live with her and work on farm. Executrix: Wife H.F. Cummins. Signed March 19, 1904. Witnesses: O.F. Gill and J.G. Cummins.
Codicil: We have given all our married children, to date, beds &c. (Children not named). June 27, 1905. Probated October 21, 1909.

Page 44 **WILL OF F.M. COMMONS.** Desires a head and foot stone erected at my grave. Wife Nancy Commons, real estate and personal property. My farm is in District No. 1. Three sons, Alfred, Shields and Otto Commons. Daughters, Clara Randolph wife of Wiley Randolph, Ella Commons, Addie Commons, Fannie Stewart wife of J.G. Stewart, and Minnie Templeton wife of Walter Templeton. Grandchildren, Norah Bradford, Hettie Lewter wife of Ed. Lewter, and Pearl Dunman wife of John Dunman. Executor: My son-in-law J.G. Stewart. Signed October 26, 1908. Witnesses: H.T. Childs and J.B. Gordon, M.D. Probated December 8, 1909.

Page 45 **WILL OF P.B. MARSH.** Petersburg. Desires a monument erected at my grave similar to the one at my deceased wife. Present wife, Mary A. Marsh. Sons, W.H. Marsh, J.D. Marsh and G.C. Marsh. Daughter Mary C. Gant and daughter Minnie P. Hart. Own property with W.H. Marsh, the two brick store house No. 142 Marsh Block in Petersburg, Tennessee, also own 49 acres in old District No. 3 of Marshall County, Tennessee and my son J.D. Marsh owns one half of same. Executors: My son J.D. Marsh, J.D. Hart and Minnie P. Hart. Signed November 24, 1906. Probated December 23, 1909.

Page 47 **WILL OF A.B. SCOTT.** District No. 10. Wife Martha Scott, all property. Children, Sam Scott and Delia Armstrong, personal property. Desires gravestone erected over the graves of myself and my wife, Martha Scott. Executor: G.E. Scott. Signed April 22, 1903. Witnesses: W.R. Ellis and J.T. Land. Probated January 3, 1910.

Page 48 **WILL OF MARY LOU WILSON.** Known as Mollie Lou Wilson. Step-sons, Horace L. Wilson and Robert K. Wilson, $2000.00 divided. Niece Mattie Frank Taylor. Executors: My step-sons Horace L. Wilson and Robert K. Wilson. Signed December 1, 1909. Witnesses: S.C. Hipsh and Virginia Dismukes. Probated (no date).

Page 49 **WILL OF DR. J.L. MADDOX.** To Mrs. Sarah Anderson wife of Lude Anderson, %500.00. To Andrew Maddox, $1000.00. To Susuan (Susan) Lawson Beasley wife of W.H. Beasley, remainder of my estate, both real and personal. Executor: Solon Maddox. Signed July 1, 1909. Witnesses: J.A. Sanders and S.N. Wantland. Probated (no date).

Page 49 **WILL OF HARDY H. COULTER.** June 12, 1908. Wife Manerva Coulter, dower. Three daughters, Mattie Cannon, Josie White and Mollie Bickley. Executor: Jas. T. Bickley. Signed October 15, 1908. Witnesses: H.C. Sorrells and W.H. Wright. Probated (no date).

Page 50 **WILL OF JAMES H. HOLMAN.** Wife Elizabeth Haynes Holman, real estate of 30 acres and land in Fayetteville, all estate along with $30,000.00. Brother Thomas P. Holman, $4000.00. Sister, Mrs. Sue M. Milhouse, $4000.00. Sister, Mrs. Jennie P. Tolley, $4000.00. To Fannie L. Holman widow of my deceased brother D.W. Holman, $4000.00. My nephew James J. Holman son of my deceased brother Robert ?. Holman, $4000.00. To the wife of my nephew J. Hardy Holman son of my deceased brother Rufus M. Holman, $4000.00. To Mrs. Mary Carter wife of George F. Carter, $500.00. To Elizabeth Carter daughter of George F. Carter, $100.00. To Mary Carter, daughter of George F. Carter,

$100.00. To Elizabeth Landess wife of Dr. E.S. Landess, $500.00. Desires a rock wall erected around the graveyard on the place or farm of which Elisha Parks is now the owner and in which my grandfather Hardy Holman and grandmother Elizabeth Holman are buried also a rock wall around the graves of my great grandfather and great grandmother Holman who are buried on the lands now owned by Felix Waggoner, also tombstone to be erected over my grave. Executor: My friend M.W. Woodard. Signed February 6, 1910. Witnesses: A.L. Yearwood and W.F. Cannon. Probated April 4, 1910.

Page 52   **WILL OF VINCIN MULLINS.**   Wife Mary Mullins, all my real and personal estate. Signed December 24, 1891. Witnesses: R.G. Rhodes and D.M. Tafts. Probated March 16, 1910.

Page 53   **WILL OF ANN WRIGHT.** Heirs, Buck, Alfred, and Hosia Wright, sum of $1.00. Children, Eathylenda Murray, W.L. Wright, Jr., J. Hardy Wright, Robert L. Wright, D.U. Wright, Jas. H. Wright, and Cordia Harris. Executor: Jas. H. Wright. Signed March 27, 1907. Witnesses: D.C. Sherrell and J.L. Stone. Probated July 4, 1910.

Page 54   **WILL OF WILLIAM HAMILTON.**   Wife Anna M. Hamilton, also executrix. Daughter Mrs. Cora A. Morton, $850.00. Daughter Nellie Hamilton, $850.00. Grandson W.R. Montgomery, $300.00. Son D. Knox Hamilton. Signed July 12, 1910. Witnesses: J.H. Hudson and D.B. Hamilton. Probated July 26, 1910.

Page 55   **WILL OF N.F. GIBSON.** Sisters, Mahaly C., Emily E., and L.D. Gibson, all the property. Executrix: Mahaly C. Gibson. Signed May 28, 1910. Witnesses: J.R. Nichols, O.W. King and J.M. Young. Probated August 6, 1910.

Page 56   **WILL OF STEPHEN JOHNSON.** Wife Sarah Jane Johnson, entire real and personal estate and appointed executrix. Three children, Walter Johnston, John Alston Johnston, and Maggie Johnston. Sons, C.H. Johnston, E.F. Johnston, sons of my first wife, land. Signed September 17, 1898. Witnesses: B.E. Noblitt, N.F. Boone and H.L. Moore. Probated August 9, 1910.

Page 57   **WILL OF N.J. NICKLES.** Daughter Lizzie who married Sam Jennings and her two children, Ara and Mamy Lee, household items. Husband W.H. Nickles. Daughter Lula Warren, $50.00. Son Moses Nickles. Son-in-law Henry Myers. Son-in-law Benn Price. Son-in-law John Warren. Signed May 30, 1906. Witnesses: Jno. R. Davidson and J.Y. Scott. Probated May 23, 1910.

Page 58   **WILL OF ALONZO BURROUGHS.**   Wife Vinie Burroughs, all my property. Friend Vinie Commons, appointed executrix. Signed July 10, 1910. Witnesses: J.E. Routt and S.B. Ramsey. Probated September 12, 1910.

Page 59   **WILL OF CHARITY JOHNSON.**   Fayetteville.   August 20, 1910. Granddaughter Lenard Dodson, all my personal property, house and lot and also appointed executrix. Witnesses: R.S. Douthat and Vinia B. Commons. Probated December 15, 1910.

Page 60   **WILL OF LEMUEL D. SUGG.** Desires a monument at my grave. Son, William H. Sugg, land in District No. 13 and borders lands formerly owned by William Sugg, deceased, and now owned by T.D. Sugg. Daughter Naomi Sugg. Granddaughters, Bertie Millard wife of D.J. Millard, Margurite Thurston and Elen Thurston. Children, my deceased son Douglas Sugg who has a daughter Ann Sugg. my daughter Siddie Thomison. My daughter Ethel Wilson wife of E.L. Wilson. Executors: Son William H. Sugg and D.J. Millard. Signed April 28, 1910. Witnesses: J.C. Halbert and N.P. Carter. Probated September 30, 1910.

Page 62   **WILL OF WILLIAM CAGER CATHCART.**   Wife Mary J. Cathcart, home where we now reside known as Murf Cathcart Place of 102 acres, also the place known as the Robert Taylor Place of 55 acres. Son J.

Samuel Cathcart gets the above lands at death of my wife. Nieces and nephews, Elbrige Cathcart, Early Cathcart, and Etta Boatright, children of M.C. Cathcart, and Henry Cathcart, Monroe Cathcart and George Cathcart, children of Marion Cathcart whose residence is unknown. Signed August 29, 1910. Witnesses: J.J. Campbell and M.H. Joines. Probated November 9, 1910.

Page 64    **WILL OF J.W. BEDWELL.** Brother J.M. Bedwell, land in District No. 6. Wife and children not named. Executor: Brother J.M. Bedwell. Signed November 2, 1908. Witnesses: W.F. Cannon and E.F. Holland. Probated November 15, 1910.

Page 65    **WILL OF CHARLOTTE PIGG (COL).** Case: John M. Hudson & et al VS Pryor Clark et al: Charlotte Pigg (Col), died ___ day of August 1909 in Lincoln County, Tennessee, made a will, witnessed by Joshua Williams and R.B. Collins. Charlotte Pigg's grandniece Laura Hampton, age about 13 years old, to get all property. Probated October 28, 1910.

Page 67    **WILL OF JAMES L. WOODARD.** Two sons, E.B. and E.M. Woodard, all property. Two daughters, Mrs. Ora H. Waite and Mrs. Ida M. Hamilton, $1500.00 each. Wife Emma Woodard, a confirmed invalid for a number of years. Executors: Sons, E.B. and E.M. Woodard. Signed December 26, 1907. Witnesses: H.F. Dryden, Jno. H. Rees and M.W. Woodard. Probated December 8, 1910.

Page 68    **WILL OF JOHN CAMPBELL.** Wife Mary J. Campbell, all my real and personal property. Son Alexander Campbell and my step-son John Snow. Executor: J.A. McKinney. Signed September 1, 1898. Witnesses: J.D. Corder and J.A. Fitch. Probated December 5, 1910.

Page 69    **WILL OF HELEN HALL.** Fayetteville. Son Green T. Hall, all my lands in District No. 8, three tracts. Executor: Green T. Hall. Signed September 21, 1901. Witnesses: Robert Fulton and E.J. Higgins.

Page 70    **WILL OF JOHN G. TROOP.** Wife Ellen Troop, three houses and lots in Petersburg, Tennessee, District No. 10. Property to be divided equally between James R. Troop, John D. Troop, Clabe C. Troop, Emiline Rambo, Charlie Troop, Nancy Wells, Walter L. Troop, Joe S. Troop and Delphus E. Troop and Caldona Wakefield. Executor: J.C. Morton. Signed March 12, 1909. J.C. Morton is leaving the state and I appoint J.D. Hanaway executor.  March 5, 1909. Witnesses: J.A. Montgomery and J.M. Crick. Probated December 27, 1910.

Page 71    **WILL OF JOSEPH BERRY, (COL).** Wife Lutitia Berry, all my property. At death of my wife, I direct that $30.00 be paid to Ruthy Conger is she is still living. Daughter Lucy now the wife of Alf Bonner. Sons, Joseph Berry and Ed Conger and known as Ed Berry. Executor: Mr. Fayette Spencer. Signed May 20, 1901. Witnesses: R.W. Parks and Jas. W. Byrom. Probated January 31, 1911.

Page 72    **WILL OF JOHN P. STEWART.** Of District No. 20. To the children of my first wife, Joannah K. Kidd, W.E. Stewart, C.L. Stewart, Martha J. Gault, Mary Ella Foster and John L. Stewart, each $300.00. To each child of my last wife (Elizabeth Marsh), Carrol M. Stewart, Annie Lucile Stewart and Sarah Lois Stewart, $300.00 each. Executors: My son John L. Stewart and my wife H.E. Stewart (Henrietta Elizabeth "Lizzie" Marsh).  Signed November 23, 1910. Witness: I.N. Kennedy. Probated February 4, 1911.

Page 73    **WILL OF FRANCIS MARION PAMPLIN.** Wife Cynthia E. Pamplin, all my real and personal estate. Oldest daughter Rebecca A. Elkins, $1.00. Son Rufus S. Pamplin, $1.00. Granddaughter Avis Marrs Stegall, only heir of my daughter Marietta E.C. Marrs who is now dead, $1.00. My farm consists of 110 acres in District No. 7, where I now reside. Executor: R.S. Pamplin. Signed December 17, 1910. Witnesses: J.E. Broadaway, W.T. Broadaway and J.R. Davis. Probated February 17, 1911.

Page 74 **WILL OF THOMAS G. WADE.** Sister Mary Chapman who recently
died, is buried in the Unity Church graveyard near Howell, Tennessee
and I desire to be buried beside her, and direct my executor to erect a monument
for her and myself. Niece Maggie Puryear a daughter of my deceased sister
Permelia Ellington, $100.00. Grandniece Ella Hailey a daughter of my deceased
niece Elizabeth Pool, and a granddaughter of my deceased sister Permelia
Ellington, $100.00. Brother W.D. Wade, and nephew Thomas H. Wade, personal
property in District No. 9. Executor: My nephew Thomas H. Wade. Signed June
6, 1907. Witnesses: J.J. Daves and D.F. Moore. Probated March 6, 1911.

Page 75 **WILL OF JOHN MACK JOHNSON.** Wife Mary Elvirie Johnson, all of
my property also appointed executrix. Signed January 9, 1911.
Witnesses: S.W. Fleming and John Hines. Probated April 10, 1911.

Page 76 **WILL OF MALINDA SUGG.** "I owe no debts and my lodge will bury
me". To my daughter-in-law Della Smith and Ida Sugg wife of my
step-son Lem Sugg, and Mattie Smith daughter of Jack Smith, to be equally
divided, all my personal estate. Son Ben Smith and his children then living, house
and lot where I now reside, in District No. 8, in Fayetteville, known as Lot No.
115. My deceased husband, James Sugg. Executor: My son Ben Smith. Signed
December 19, 1904. Witnesses: H.W. Bonner and R.L. Holman. Probated May 2,
1911.

Page 77 **WILL OF W.C. WEST.** January 9, 1910. Children, J.T. West, Tennie
M. Jean, M.E. Bruce, J.W. West, Marlin West. Wife not named.A
financial distribution listed in will. Probated June 28, 1911.

Page 78 **WILL OF J.F. CLARK.** Wife Lou J. Clark, one fifth interest in my
property and take dower. Son J.K. Clark and my granddaughter Mary
Elizabeth Fife, and my grandson John Wesly Hutchinson, my property to be
equally divided. Executors: My son J.K. Clark and W.A. Hutchinson. Signed
September 26, 1908. Witnesses: J.P. Fife and J.B. Pitts. Probated July 14, 1911.

Page 79 **WILL OF JOHN W. SMITH.** Wife N.M. Smith, all my property. Two
single daughters, Annie Smith and Dollie Smith, all my household and
kitchen furniture. Daughter Minnie Smith wife of Grant Haislip, $125.00.
Daughter Ommer Smith wife of Tom Caldwell, $75.00. Executor: P.B. Smith.
Signed April 3, 1902. Witnesses: J.C. Brewer and F.J. Dever. Probated December
28, 1911.

Page 80 **WILL OF M.A. WILSON, WIDOW.** Widow of W.W. Wilson, deceased.
Desires a neat marble slab placed at my grave. To Charles F. Clark,
Trustee for my faithful servants, Shields Wilson (Col) and Henry Wilson (Col), all
my stock in Elk National Bank of $2000.00. Sister Nancy A. Williams, personal
property. Niece Mrs. Lou Cunningham, my hand organ and personal property.
Sister Nancy A. Williams, $1000.00. Niece Virginia Kirk the only child of my
deceased sister Louisa Bowers, personal property. To the living children of my
brother Nicholas Whitehead, personal property. Nephew Hart Whitehead son of my
deceased brother George H. Whitehead, personal property. To the living children
of my deceased brother John Whitehead, personal property. My lands in District
No. 14. To the living children of my deceased sister Frances Gardner, personal
property. Executor: My friend Charles F. Clark. Signed November 23, 1901.
Witnesses: P.G. Hamilton and N.P. Carter.
Codicil: November 23, 1901. Appointed P.G. Hamilton executor in the room of
Charles F. Clark. Witnesses: P.G. Hamilton, P.W. Halbert and N.P. Carter.
Probated October 24, 1911.

Page 82 **WILL OF JOSEPH M. LOCK.** Wife Jane Lock, all my property. At
death of my wife, to be divided among my children and grandchildren
and step-children, as follows: My grandchild Lila Lock daughter of my son
Marcillus Lock, $1.00. Son James M. Lock. Daughter Leona Balis wife of Arthur
Balis, Cora Jane Lock, my granddaughter and daughter of my son Marcillus Lock.

My step-children, Robert Rodes, Mittie Rodes and Mary Ann Cole wife of Benjamin Cole. My son Marcillus Lock is now in the asylum. Appointed my son James M. Lock, executor and also Trustee of my granddaughter Cora Jane Lock. Signed April 3, 1894. Witnesses: W.A. Robertson and J.L. Robertson. Probated October 17, 1911.

Page 83 **WILL OF W.S. ROBINSON.** Son R.C. Robinson who resides in Colorado, $400.00. Wife Margret Adella Robinson, all personal property and farm in District No. 15. Children, W.H., J.B., O.D. Robinson, Hattie Harrison wife of Wiley Harrison, K.H. Robinson, R.C. Robinson, Minnie Carpenter wife of J.E. Carpenter, and Leon Robinson. I am the administrator of Mrs. E.J. Gill and request that J. Harvey Gill be appointed administrator. Executors: W.H. and K.H. Robinson and J.E. Carpenter. Signed May 13, 1911. Witnesses: Dr. W.S. Harwell and T.A. Story. Probated October 4, 1911.

Page 84 **WILL OF JOHN M. BRIGHT.** Wife Bell Buckner Bright, household and kitchen furniture. Son M.M. Bright, protrait of myself by Halsey and the protrait of his mother Zurilda B. Bright by Carl Brown of Washington City. I have already given to my son S.A. Bright two large photopictures of his grandfather and grandmother Bright. To my son Robert L. Bright, two large protraints of his grandfather and grandmother Bright by Halsey. Daughter Anna M. Jones wife of E.S. Jones, the oil painting by herself of a storm at sea. Grandson, A.B. Bright, Jr., photo of himself in infancy also a group of photos of eminentlawyers of the city of New York, his deceased father A.B. Bright, Sr. being one of the group. Desires a marble monument placed over the graves of my deceased wife Zurilda Buckner Bright and over the grave of my wife Belle Buckner Bright, when deceased, and over my own grave, also over the grave of my deceased son John M. Bright, Jr., and over the grave of my daughter Susan Catherine Bright, one over the grave of Judith Margaret Norwood, and over the grave of my deceased son Anthony Buckner Bright, all of which graves are in the graveyard of the Old Presbyterian Church. Son David M. Bright, $200.00. Executor: H.K. Bryson. Signed July 3, 1911. Witnesses: A.H. Hatcher and C.F. Higgins. Probated November 27, 1911.

Page 86 **WILL OF LEMUEL D. SUGG.** Court Case October 20, 1911. W.H. Sugg and D.J. Millard VS Miss Anne Sugg. Will contest. Will witnessed by J.C. Halbert and N.P. Carter, is a true will.
Will: Desires a plain monument erected at my grave. Son William H. Sugg, two tracts of land in District No. 13. Daughter Naomi Sugg, one half interest. Granddaughters, Bertie Millard wife of D.J. Millard, Margurite Thurston and Ellen Thurston, one sixth interest. My deceased son Douglas Sugg and his daughter Ann Sugg. Daughter Siddie Thomison. Daughter Ethel Wilson wife of E.L. Wilson. Executors: My son William H. Sugg and D.J. Millard. Signed April 28, 1910. Witnesses: J.C. Halbert and N.P. Carter. Probated September 30, 1910.

Page 89 **WILL OF MISS RUTH A TOOLE.** Fayetteville, but for a time residing in Moore County, Tennessee. Desires a tombstone. J.T. Williamson, all my cloths and household goods and $25.00. One third to Mrs. Addie D. Neel. One sixth to J.D. Williamson, one sixth to J.T. Williamson. One fifteenth to Joe S. Hines. One fifteenth to Miss Mary K. Hines. One fifteenth to Mrs. Sallie Gleghorn. One fifteenth to be divided among the children of James T. Hines, deceased. And one fifteenth to be divided among the children of W.G. Hines, deceased. Executor: Rev. C.C. Hines. Signed June 9, 1911. Witnesses: T.J. Fariss and H.H. Holt. Probated November 28, 1911.

Page 90 **WILL OF WILBERN RENEGAR.** Wife Margaret Renegar. Three daughters, Mrs. Mary L. Routt, Mrs. Goodloe C. Martin, and Mrs. Fannie Seaton widow of William Seaton, deceased. Executors: My two sons-in-law James R. Routt and Goodlow C. Martin. Signed April 14, 1910. Witnesses: J.E. Hereford, Eldon Smith and J.E. Routt. Probated November 18, 1911.

Page 91 **WILL OF W.R. CALL.** Wife Fannie Call, our home with everything and $1000.00 for first year and $300.00 each year. Wants $100.00 set aside to pay for covering his house situated in Mulberry. Daughter Janie Call Rutledge, $300.00. Son-in-law J.C. Rutledge to take charge and run the farm. Wants Call Rutledge to have my watch. Executor: My son-in-law J.C. Rutledge. Signed May 22, 1911. Witnesses: J.P. Harrison and E.F. Holland. Probated December 9, 1911.

Page 92    **WILL OF C.S. WEIGART.**  Wife Sarah Elizabeth Weigart, executrix. She is to have all my property. My children, not named. My son George Weigart. Signed August 30, 1911. Witnesses: J.H. McDaniel and J.D. Ralston. Probated December 13, 1911.

Page 92    **WILL OF S.P. HAMILTON.**  Wife Josie Hamilton, residence and lot in Fayetteville and where I now reside. Daughter Bessie Taylor wife of John A. Taylor, and Lillie Hamilton, and to my son Samuel Ellis Hamilton, each one-fourth of personal property. Granddaughters, Mary E. Formwalt and Lillian Farmwalt, children of my deceased daughter Ella Farmwalt, each one-eighth interest. Executrix: My wife Josie Hamilton. Signed December 9, 1911. Witnesses: Thomas A. Patrick and N.P. Carter. Probated December 19, 1911.

Page 94    **WILL OF D.S. DYER.**  Of Fayetteville. My step-mother Susie Barnes, widow of my deceased father Col. William Dyer, my estate, also appointed executrix. Signed July 13, 1908. Witnesses: W.B. Lamb, Jr. and N.P. Carter. Probated January 15, 1912.

Page 95    **WILL OF J.H. HUDSON.**  Sister S.A. Hudson. Brother E.C. Hudson. B.F. Hudson and John M. Hudson, to get the place where I now live, about 440 acres. Sister Sallie Clark. Mary Wright (Col), to have $100.00. I direct that whichever one of my brothers or sister that occupy the home, take care and support Thomas E. Dobbins during his life in the event he is left dependent &c. Executors: E.C. Hudson, B.F. Hudson and J.M. Hudson. Signed March 5, 1911. Witnesses: L.W. Taylor, T.A. Patrick, A.L. Yearwood and A.B. Wilson. Probated February 9, 1912.

Page 96    **WILL OF MARGARET SUSAN BAGLEY, WIDOW.**  Widow of James M. Bagley of near Chestnut Ridge. Sister Ann E. Bolles, personal property. Sister Mrs. Mary Cothrum, personal property. Sister Bettie B. Crane, personal property. Nephews Earnest F. and James L. Bolles, $77.00. Executor: J.E. Bolles. Signed December 11, 1911. Witnesses: Roy Waid and Isaac Morton. Probated December 2, 1911.

Page 97    **WILL OF MARY KATE GREER.**  Sister Carrie Bell Greer. Signed September 25, 1907. Witnesses: Mrs. V.A. Percy and Clara E. Percy. Probated January 26, 1912.

Page 98    **WILL OF D.M. CALDWELL.**  Wife Jane Caldwell, all my property. Grandsons, Haywood Swanner and Hill Swanner. Executor: A.W. Smith. Signed June 23, 1908. Witnesses: H.C. Sanders and S.C. Smith. Probated February 26, 1912.

Page 99    **WILL OF J.C. STEVENSON.**  Wife Ida Cornelia Stevenson, estate of all kinds. My children by my first wife Mary Jane Stevenson and my present wife Ida C. Stevenson. Children not named. Executrix: Wife Ida C. Stevenson. Signed September 9, 1911. Witnesses: I.N. McCluskey and John C. Diemer. Probated February 29, 1912.

Page 100    **WILL OF W.H. ASHBY.**  Wife Ellen E. Ashby, all personal property. Daughter Susan C. Swing, $1134.00. Daughter Willie E. Pamplin, $815.60. Son D.W. Ashby, $1000.00. Son J.M. Ashby, $1000.00. Daughter S.J. Wiley, $500.00. Son B.A. Ashby, $500.00. Son J.H. Ashby, $500.00. Daughter Tinie Caughran, $500.00. Son F.B. Ashby, $185.50. Executors: My sons B.A. and J.H. Ashby. Signed November 10, 1898. Witnesses: R.D. Warren and W.B. Douthat. Probated April 4, 1912.

Page 101  **WILL OF ELIZABETH BOAZ.** Son Thomas Aaron Boaz, land I now live on given to me by my father Jacob Hoots, about one acre. Daughter-in-law Lethiann Boaz wife of my son Thomas Aaron Boaz, personal property. Daughter-in-law Lucy Boaz wife of my son William Benton Boaz, personal property. Executor: My son James Arch Boaz. Signed February 6, 1900. Witnesses: S.M. Fleming, C.D. Curlee and A.A. Parker. Probated March 4, 1912.

Page 102  **WILL OF THOMAS E. DRYDEN.** Children, R.D. Dryden, Mrs. Mamie Naylor, and H.E. Dryden, $1500.00 each. Wife Ann Dryden, remainder of property. Executor: Son H.E. Dryden. Signed September 12, 1910. Witnesses: M.W. Woodard and Ellen Dryden. Probated March 22, 1912.

Page 103  **WILL OF ELIAS WILSON ASHBY.** Step-daughter Elvira Campbell Pitts, $50.00. Wife Rebecka Elzina Ashby, balance of property. Executors: Son Samuel Ashby and my wife's son N.O. Keith. Signed March 9, 1912. Witnesses: J.F. Buntly, S.W. Fleming and Enos Pitts. Probated April 5, 1912.

Page 104  **WILL OF MRS. CLEMENZA L. TAYLOR.** Of Birmingham, Jefferson County, Alabama. Mrs. Lizzie Seaton of Birmingham, Alabama, $1400.00 and other personal property. Lizzie Luttrell, Mary Mimms, J.L. Mimms and Charles Mimms, children of my deceased sister Martha M. Mimms. Husband is dead and is indebted to by William Mimms and Ed Mimms to be cancelled. Executor: J. Howard Perdue of Birmingham, Alabama. Signed September 10, 1910. Witnesses: A.J. Massey, Sr. and M.L. Ward. Probated December 4, 1911.
Those attending the probate of her will: Lizzie Luttrell, Mary Mims, Mrs. Leila Daniel, J.L. Mims, Charlie J. Mimms, and Ed Mimms, heirs of the descendant. Probated April 8, 1912.

Page 106  **WILL OF J.H. LANDESS.** May 23, 1908. Wife H.E. Landess. Son R.T. Landess. I appoint as co-guardian for my son Albert C. Landess, my wife H.E. Landess and son R.T. Landess. Children: Lucy L. Lasater, R.T. Landess, E.S. Landess, J.H. Landess, Jr., and A.C. Landess. Witnesses: G.W. Davidson and J.W. Scott. Probated April 27, 1912.

Page 107  **WILL OF K. HAMILTON.** Granddaughter Eunice Hamilton, $150.00. My seven children: William L., Anna, Milton, Mattie Lou, Tommie, Jacob, and Ed Hamilton. Signed April 7, 1894. Witnesses: George E. Banks and T.A. Embry and Harvey M. Templeton.
Codicil: January 31, 1903. My son M.E. Hamilton be associate executor. Probated May 11, 1912.

Page 108  **WILL OF R.C. McELROY.** Son Con McElroy and son T.T. McElroy, all my property and also executors. Signed November 6, 1909. Witnesses: John C. Diemer and W.N. Whitaker. Probated May 11, 1912.

Page 109  **WILL OF A.K. EDMONDSON.** Sister Jane Edmondson, household and kitchen furniture and personal property. 110 acres in District No. 21, bounded by the Carloss lands, Will Clark (Col), John Taylor, Jane Edmondson. To my niece Anna Lee Edmondson daughter of John F. Edmondson, to have and to hold her entire life and then to the heirs of her body if any. If she died without heirs then it is to go to Charles Edmondson son of John F. Edmondson. John F. Edmondson is to get the Thomerson tract of 104 acres and the barn tract. Signed September 2, 1897. Witnesses: T.M. Roden, C.A. Diemer, Jr. and George L. Diemer.
Codicil: Annie Lee Edmondson is now 21 years old and will not need a trustee. I now will the 104 acre tract to Luella Thompson and also the 62 acres of land south of the 104 tract. Signed May 15, 1907. Witnesses: E.J. Brock, Frank Locker and John C. Diemer. Probated (no date).

Page 110  **WILL OF ELIZABETH McCARTNEY.** Of Madison County, Alabama. Children: Andrew Tunstall McCartney, Ida Izetta McCartney, Beulah

Elizabeth McCartney, and Charlie McCartney, all my land in Lincoln County, it being willed to me by my sister Emily G. Spencer, Charlie McCartney, youngest child, under age of 21 years. Signed June 3, 1881. Witnesses: Eliza Murrell and Glen Gregory. Probated May 24, 1912.

Page 111 **WILL OF WILLIAM E. MOORE.** Wife Mary D. Moore, $1500.00 of my estate or land. Brothers and sisters, David F. Moore (others not named). William Thomas Whitworth, $100.00. Eliza E. Edwards, a breast pin with my likeness, which I now have and was the property of my first wife. Eliza E. Deel have a double hearted finger ring that belonged to my last wife. Executor: Joel Armstrong. Signed March 4, 1909. Witnesses: H.R. Brown and Mrs. W.F. Cannon. Probated June 7, 1912.

Page 112 **WILL OF E.E. SHELTON.** April 8, 1912. To my wife (not named) and son John S. Shelton, all of my household, kitchen goods and land. Witnesses: W.D. Moore, E.O. Stewart and Nora Shelton. Probated June 20, 1912.

Page 113 **WILL OF J.B. HAMILTON.** Of Fayetteville. Wife Sarah Henryetta Hamilton, all my real estate. Children (not named), my daughter Mary wife of E.L. McElroy. Executors: My son-in-law E.L. McElroy and James R. Stephenson. Signed May 1, 1912. Witnesses: H.D. Smith and J.C. Goodrich. Probated June 21, 1912.

Page 114 **WILL OF BENJAMIN A. SHELTON.** Children, Julia A. Dickey wife of John M. Dickey (Jr.), the heirs of Nancy Campbell, deceased, John R. Shelton, Mary L. Howard wife of James P. Howard, and Joel B. Shelton. Maud C. wife of Joel B. Shelton. Executor: James P. Howard. Signed August 23, 1912. Witnesses: M.L. Dickey and John M. Dickey. Probated August 31, 1912.

Page 115 **WILL OF J.J. SHEFFIELD.** Wife Mary Sheffield. My daughter Sallie Stewart. Sons, J.A. and S.M. Sheffield. Granddaughters, Bonnie Hodge and Mirtle Moyers. Executors: My son J.A. Sheffield and son-in-law P.E. Hodge. Signed August 30, 1912. Witnesses: J.P. Fife and A.M. Askins. Probated September 10, 1912.

Page 116 **WILL OF MARIA L. McLAURINE.** To Mary Louise Kilgore, personal property. Niece Rossie Hall Kilgore, personal property and real estate in District No. 8. Executrix: Rossie Hall Kilgore. Signed February 13, 1912. Witnesses: W.E. Jones, J.B. Parks and Mary Roland. Probated October 10, 1912.

Page 117 **WILL OF HENRY THOMPSON.** Wife (not named), 27 acres. Executrix: Betty A. Thompson. Signed April 9, 1894. Witnesses: Coss McDonald and Gilbert Sherron. Probated October 4, 1912.

Page 118 **WILL OF J.T. BRADY.** Wife M.V. Brady, all my estate also appointed executrix. Signed June 17, 1897. Witnesses: J.F. Smith, J.J. Sumners and J.L. Ross. Probated October 15, 1912.

Page 119 **WILL OF W.B. FREEMAN.** The farm on which I now reside, in District No. 8, lying south of the Stone Bridge on Elk River. Wife Kate Freeman and at her death to my daughter Carrie Ena Yearwood wife of Virgil C. Yearwood, to receive the farm and other estate. Signed October 7, 1912. Witnesses: J.M. Fulton and W.C. Dale. Probated October 16, 1912.

Page 120 **WILL OF W.L. McANN.** Desires a monument erected at my grave. Wife Mary Jane McAnn, personal property. Ernest Franklin, a young man who has been reared by myself and wife from infancy, to receive lands and real estate. Brothers and sisters, not named. Signed May 8, 1902. Witnesses: J.R. Feeney and H.K. Bryson. Probated November 18, 1912.

Page 121 **WILL OF MRS. AMANDA ORRICK.** Of District No. 6. Two single daughters, Martha Ellen and Ida Anna Orrick, house and lot in

Bellville, also personal property. My other heirs, not named. Executor: W.H. Wright. Signed March 25, 1909. Witnesses: W.C. Goodrich and W.T. Fergason. Probated December 4, 1912.

Page 122　**WILL OF MARTHA STEPHENSON.** Son S.T. Stephenson, one fourth. To my son W.G. Stephenson one fourth. To my daughter Nancy J. Moore, one fourth. And to my daughter I.D. Young, one fourth of my estate. Executor: Walter M. Morrison. Signed September 15, 1905. Witnesses: I.S. Sorrells and N.J. Wells. Probated December 9, 1912.

Page 123　**WILL OF MRS. E. JANSON.** Of Fayetteville. Children, August Janson, Louis Janson, Josephine Waggoner, and Laura C. DeHaven. Grandchildren, Elizabeth DeHaven and Ellie DeHaven, both under age of 21 years. Appointed my daughter Laura C. DeHaven Executrix and Trustee for the two granddaughters. Signed September 28, 1900. Witnesses: S.B. Ramsey and N.P. Carter. Probated December 13, 1912.

Page 124　**WILL OF R.A. ABLES.** Of Harms. Wife Mary Ables, all property, both real and personal and also appointed executrix. "No real estate be sold until my youngest child becomes 21 years." Signed December 6, 1912. Witnesses: R.W. Hicks, J.R. Wilson and J.W. Hamlin. Probated December 17, 1912.

Page 125　**WILL OF S.D. SMITH.** Wife Lula M. Smith, all property, both real and personal and appointed executrix. Signed January 9, 1907. Witnesses: J.M. Eakin, J.E. Hereford and J.E. Routt. Probated December 31, 1912.

Page 126　**WILL OF MATTIE G. PRYOR.** Of Lincoln. Niece. May L. Quick, all my personal property, tract No. 2. Niece Fannie Wallace, part of my real estate, tract No. 1. Executor: R.H. Quick. Signed January 17, 1910. Witnesses: T.P. Gillham and C.C. Gillham. Probated January 20, 1913.

Page 127　**WILL OF E.M. SCOTT.** Of Petersburg. Desires a monument erected for myself and wife's grave. Grandchildren, Mala Hill, Iva Hill, Lizzie Kate Hill, and Edgar Scott Hill, the only children of my deceased daughter Ophelia Hill. Wife Margarett T. Scott. Sons, J.L. Scott and R.T. Scott, as Trustees in Trust, $3000.00. Son W.L. Scott. Daughters, Clemmie Thomas wife of S.L. Thomas, Ella Lindsay wife of W.E. Lindsay. Executors: My two sons J.L. and R.T. Scott. Signed May 16, 1911. Witnesses: N.P. Carter and W.B. Lamb, Jr. Probated February 10, 1913.

Page 129　**WILL OF J.H. BARNES.** Wife K.J. Barnes. Children or the children of any that may be dead. Daughter Anna May Smith. Youngest son Joseph Lemuel Barnes, under age of 19 years. Executors: H.H. Barnes and W.B. Erwin. Signed October 25, 1912. Witnesses: D.F. Hobbs, W.C. Thomison and M.W. Woodard.
Change of will: Daughter Anna May Smith, $100.00. Signed December 3, 1912. Witnesses: D.L. Nerren, M.W. Woodard and A.O. Barnes. Probated (no date).

Page 130　**WILL OF ALLEN COBLE.** Daughter Martha Joines. Signed April 29, 1911. Witnesses: A.B. Wilson and B.S. Sawyers. Probated January 22, 1913.

Page 131　**WILL OF D.J. FRANKLIN.** George W. Dodd with whom I am now living, all property of all kinds. Signed May 25, 1912. Witnesses: A.B. Wilson and D.L. Childress. Probated November 4, 1912.

Page 132　**WILL OF ELMA SANDERS.** Of Fayetteville. September 18, 1912. My sister Mrs. Lora Gotcher, my insurance. Witnesses: Sam Nerren and Mary Jane Caughran. Probated November 15, 1912.

Page 133　**WILL OF JOHN H. REES.** Of Fayetteville. Daughter Candace Rees,

$1000.00. Son R.W. Rees, $1000.00. Brother J.G. Rees, $2500.00. Son Earnest Rees and my cousin R.A. Rees appointed executors. Signed April 12, 1912. Witnesses: Morgan Eslick and H.E. Dryden. Probated March 10, 1913.

Page 134  **WILL OF L.D. GIBSON.** Desires a stone be erected to mark my grave. Sisters, Mahaly C. and Emily E. Gibson. Brother N.F. Gibson appointed executor. Signed May 28, 1910. Witnesses: J.R. Nichols, O.W. King and J.M. Young. Probated March 18, 1913.

Page 135  **WILL OF SARAH L. MORGAN, WIDOW.** Widow of J.J. Morgan, deceased. Daughter-in-law Beulah Morgan wife of my son George M. Morgan, $1200.00. Three daughters, Allie Adkins wife of Robert Adkins, Emma Adkins wife of Will Adkins, and Kate Jean wife of George Jean, $300.00 each. Son George M. Norgan, $300.00. To Lallie (Sallie, Lottie) Couch, Mabel Harbin and Willie Sue Morgan, children of my deceased daughter Suella who married W.D. Brook, $100.00 each. Annie L. Morgan, minor child and daughter of my deceased son John S. Morgan, deceased, and she is now in Texas. Son George M. Morgan to take charge of Annie L. Morgan. Executor: George M. Morgan. Signed July 9, 1910. Witnesses: J.E. Routt, T.C. Little and J.B. Parks. Probated (no date).

Page 136  **WILL OF M.C. ATKINSON.** Wife A.T.V. Atkinson, all estate and appointed executrix. Signed March 8, 1913. Witnesses: D.C. Sherrell and John M. Wyatt. Probated April 21, 1913.

Page 137  **WILL OF JOSEPH F. MONTGOMERY.** Wife Mary J. Montgomery. Executrix: My daughter Mrs. Mary E. McCown. My heirs are: W.L. Montgomery, Mrs. Mary E. McCown, Mrs. Anna Quick, Mrs. Sarah Pitman, Mrs. Carrie Kidney, and Terry and Worth Saxon sons of daughter Altie Pearl Saxon, deceased, my grandsons. (Five living children and two grandsons). Signed --- --, 1913. Probated April 14, 1913.

Page 138  **WILL OF J.K. SCOTT.** Wife Ruth Arrilla Scott, all my property, real and personal. My children or heirs except two grandchildren, Chales (Charles) Clayton and Mary Ruth Scott, my son Walter deceased children, $200.00. Signed June 14, 1912. Witnesses: Jno. R. Davidson and J.L. Pierce.
Codicil: March 15, 1913. My five sons, Will, John, Rufus, Thomas and Luther to assist my Ruth Arrilla Scott to wind up my business. Probated May 7, 1913.

Page 139  **WILL OF S.W. BRUCE.** Two daughters, Lula B. and Fannie P. Bruce, $400.00 jointly. Changed to $200.00 jointly, January 8, 1913. To W.S. Dickey, $80.00. Executrix: My daughter Lula B. Bruce. Signed December 3, 1912. Witnesses: A.L. Sloan and M.W. Woodard. Probated May 16, 1913.

Page 140  **WILL OF I.G. BARNES.** Desires a head and foot stone erected at my grave. Wife Isabella Jane Barnes, all my estate, real and personal. Son Robert C. Barnes to inherit above at death of my wife. Brothers, H.T. Barnes and John A. Barnes. Sisters, Caroline Wilson wife of William Wilson, F.C. Echols wife of William Echols, Sarah McAfee wife of Rufus McAfee, Anna Fullerton wife of John Fullerton, and the children of my deceased sister Nancy Delila Haynie, and the children of my deceased brother J.H. Barnes. Executors: My wife Isabella Jane Barnes and my son Robert C. Barnes. Signed April 28, 1913. Witnesses: Jesse J. Tucker and A.F. Collins. Probated May 17, 1913.

Page 141  **WILL OF MRS. AGNES RALSTON.** Wife of William Ralston. Children: William Ralston, Jr., J. Huss Ralston, T. Frank Ralston, Mary Ralston, James D. Ralston, Agnes McCown Ralston, Oscar L. Ralston, and Mack N. Ralston. Executrix: My daughter Mary Ralston. Signed November 12, 1909. Witnesses: H.T. Whitaker and Jno. C. Diemer. Probated May 23, 1913.

Page 142  **WILL OF R.S. DOUTHAT.** Fayetteville. May 19, 1913. To Mrs. Ada Belle Taylor wife of W. Adrain Taylor, one half of lot containing the house where I now live and the house and barn occupied by Ad Gustus. I own a store house and lot on College Street, 120 acres of land in Madison County, Alabama, and other possessions to be sold and divided among the following: W.R. Medearis of St. Louis, Mrs. Annie Belle Holman of Nashville, Tennessee, Mrs. S.F. Critz of Cambria, Virginia, Mrs. Lula Taylor of Cambria, Virginia, Mrs. Virginia Driscall of Christianburg, Virginia, Miss Nellie Coper (Copier) of Bristol, Virginia, D.G. Douthat and Houston Douthat of Fayetteville. Desires D.G. Douthat and W.A. Taylor administer on my estate. Household and kitchen furniture with my library and pictures to go to Mrs. W. Adrain Taylor. Witnesses: J.M. Cullum and T.A. Patrick. Probated August 5, 1913.

Page 143 **WILL OF JOHN WEST.** Wife Mary E. West, $1300.00 and household and kitchen furniture. Daughter Mrs. Jennie Brandon, $100.00. Heirs, S.C. West, A.M. West, Mrs. J.M. Johnson, Mrs. Jennie Brandon, and the heirs of Mrs. Anna Johnson, deceased, and the heirs of my daughter Mrs. Lou Brandon, deceased. Executors: S.C. West and J.M. Johnson. Signed April 10, 1913. Witnesses: H.R. Moore, John W. Stovall and B.W. Sutton. Probated September 16, 1913.

Page 144 **WILL OF MILLIE M. TYLER.** Of Fayetteville. Brother Major J. Bonner, all of personal and real estate. Signed September 17, 1900. Witnesses: H.K. Bryson and J.J. Jones. Probated October 4, 1913.

Page 145 **WILL OF B.H. (B. HUGH) STOVALL.** Of Elora. Sister Sarah Stovall, 90 acress including house and barn and when she dies, is to go to my brother G.B. Stovall. Brother G.B. Stovall, 70 acres of land adjoining Sarah Stovall. Sister Leslie Hall, 30 acres adjoining the 70 acres also 60 acres adjoining my land. And 30 acres to her heirs when youngest becomes of age. Executors: A.J. Hardin and G.N. Donaldson. Signed November 27, 1913. Witnesses: J.M. Hardin of Elora and J.E. Hardin of Elora. Signed November 29, 1913. Codicil: 58 acres to sister Leslie Hall. Probated January 24, 1914.

Page 146 **WILL OF R.F. WILLIAMSON.** Wife Nannie C. Williamson, all my land including the place I now live, about 73 acres. Minor children, not named. Executor: My son Eugene Williamson. Signed August 19, 1913. Witnesses: C.B. Sullivan and J.N. Smith. Probated January 24, 1914.

Page 147 **WILL OF J.D. BUCHANAN.** Page blank.

Page 148 **WILL OF WILLIAM WILLIAMS.** Of Fayetteville. Desires a monument erected at my grave. I own a farm in District No. 8 of about 200 acres. Two sons, John R. and G.C. Williams. Wife Ellen C. Williams, residence and lot where I now reside in Fayetteville. Daughter Mary Williams wife of I.M. Williams. Grandchildren, Catherine McElroy and Arthur McElroy with J.E. McElroy their Trustee. Daughter Ethel Bates wife of C.N. Bates and Myrtle Weiss wife of R.G. Weiss. Executors: My two sons, John R. and G.C. Williams. Signed January 17, 1914. Witnesses: C.T. Harms and N.P. Carter.

Page 151 **WILL OF JAMES D. BUCHANAN.** Wife Mary E. Buchanan, household and kitchen furniture and $5000.00. Children and grandchildren, not named. Executors: My four sons, E.C., M.G., Willie B., and John T. Buchanan. Signed November 20, 1911. Witnesses: H.L. Moore and J.E. Routt. Probated January 12, 1914.

Page 152 **WILL OF GEORGE M. MORGAN.** Wife Beulah L. Morgan, house and lot in Fayetteville. Children: Otho George Morgan, John James Morgan, Mildred and Mary Morgan. Own land in District No. 12, 99 acres. Also one half of a tract of land being owned by Mrs. Mary A. Miles wife of A.R. Miles. Executrix: My wife Beulah L. Morgan. Signed March 14, 1914. Witnesses: E.L. Parks and J.F. Smith. Probated May 7, 1914.

Page 154 **WILL OF JAMES F. SMITH.** Nephew L.L. Smith appointed executrix.

Signed April 3, 1914. Witnesses: Frank P. Colbert and Claude B. Brock. Probated June 8, 1914.

Page 155 **WILL OF H.P. CAUGHRAN.** Children, Hugh, Jonney, Alva, and Minnie Caughran. Hugh Caughran is to have the west end of my place, except three acres. Son Alva Caughran to have a place and one acre. Son John Caughran and my daughter Minnie Caughran, one acre. Son John Caughran take my daughter Minnie Caughran and keep her and one acre. Son Alva Caughran to have the home place with three acres cut out of Hugh Caughran's lot. Executors: Sons, John and Alva Caughran. Signed May 21, 1914. Witnesses: J.P. Fife and I.H. Lincoln. Probated June 1, 1914.

Page 156 **WILL OF SALLIE SCALES,** born in slavery but now free in body and mind, though in my 87th year. My only child Joe Scales, my real estate, a house and lot I now live on and which was bought by me of J.M. Metcalf. Five children and one great grandchild, Mollie Scales, Maggie Scales and Joe Scales, Homer Williams, Anna Steel and Robert Scales who is a son of my daughter Sallie Bet, deceased. Signed April 1, 1913. Witnesses: Sam C. Tigert and George N. Harris. Probated July 6, 1914.

Page 157 **WILL OF I.S. SORRELLS.** Desires a monument erected at my grave. Wife Fannie Sorrells, $1000.00. Niece, by marriage, Anita Sorrells a daughter of Theo Sorrells. Brothers, N.J. Sorrells, H.C. Sorrels, and N.A. Sorrels, each one fifth. Nieces, Sue Kate Phillips wife of Jesse Phillips, and Johnnie Curtis wife of Luck Curtis. Niece Alice Morton. Executor: Brother N.J. Sorrells. Signed October 18, 1913. Witnesses: E.S. Raby, J.L. Holly and N.P. Carter. Codicil: May 22, 1914. Witnesses: J.T. Morrison and N.P. Carter. Probated July 7, 1914.

Page 159 **WILL OF F.M. BARNES.** Children, not named. Executors: R.F. Millikin, Bob Williamson and Charlie Barnes. Signed September --, 1909. Witnesses: James A. Barnes and J. Hiram Smith. Probated July 7, 1914.

Page 160 **WILL OF W.L. McANN.** Trial and Judgement: Mary Jane McAnn VS D.B. McAnn. Court said original will was witnessed by J.R. Feeney and H.K. Bryson, to be true. Will: Wife Mary Jane McAnn, all property and appointed executrix. If Ernest Franklin, a young man who has been reared by myself and wife from his infancy, to get all my land. Brothers and sisters, not named. Signed May 8, 1902. Witnesses: J.R. Feeney and H.K. Bryson.

Page 162 **WILL OF A.H. MARSHALL.** Father W.T. Marshall, executor. Owns a farm of 68 acres in District No. 23. To my father W.T. Marshall and his wife Nannie, my real estate. Brothers and sisters, both the full and half blood, not named. Niece Lucy Taylor daughter of Dee Taylor, Oscar Marshall, Beulah Stockstall, Cora Casey, Joe Marshall, Mead Marshall, Thomas Marshall, and Lena Marshall, and Adrain Marshall. Desires improvement of the graves of our family in the Lincoln graveyard by placing monuments at each of our five graves, with inscriptions. Signed May 2, 1914. Witnesses: Sam C. Tigert and W.T. Broadaway. Probated July 17, 1914.

Page 164 **WILL OF C.M.M. TULEY.** Son Jas. S. Tuley, appointed executor. Children: Allie McKnight wife of Clint McKnight, Bettie Finley wife of Ed Finley, Mattie Troop wife of Joe Troop, Clara Butler wife of Earnest Butler, and my son Jim S. Tuley. Also children of Anna May Wakefield. Claburn Wakefield. Ora Foster wife of Sil Foster. Gideon Wakefield. Signed May 1, 1913. Witnesses: A.B. Wilson and G.W. Collins. Probated July 20, 1914.

Page 165 **WILL OF JAMES P. (JIM) BUCHANAN AND AMANDA BUCHANAN.** Son Willie Bedford Buchanan. Son Thomas Ewing Buchanan, appointed executor. Signed September 15, 1909. Witnesses: John A. Moore and J.J. Daves. Probated July 22, 1914.

Page 166  **WILL OF SUSAN E. MALONE.** Of District No. 15.  Son Robert H.
Malone.  Executor: Oscar E. West.  Signed June 13, 1914.  Witnesses:
J.A. Bole, G.W. Evans and W.C. Harwell.  Probated August 1914.

Page 167  **WILL OF ANDREW BROADRICK.** Of Hunt County, Texas.  Sister
Sarah Broadrick, all the property and also appointed executrix.  Signed
November 27, 1912.  Witnesses: E.R. Brown and Ruth Bryant.  Probated August
31, 1914.

Page 168  **WILL OF JENNIE F. THOMAS.** My late husband A.S. Thomas,
deceased.  Sister Corda McDonald, my piano and desk owned by my
late husband.  Sister Mrs. Kate Williams, my silver coffee pot, diamond ring and
all my household and kitchen furniture.  Sister-in-law Mrs. Emma McKinney, my
jet and pearl cross.  Nephew Abednego Thomas Williams.  Sister-in-law Kate
Thomas, $1000.00.  Rev. Thomas F. Gailor, Bishop of the Episcopal Church of
Tennessee, as Trustee, $1000.00, for benefit of St. Mary Magdalene Church in
Fayetteville.  Sister Mrs. Kate Williams wife of J.K. Williams, my residence lot in
Fayetteville.  Executor: J.K. Williams.  Signed June 13, 1908.  Witnesses: W.B.
Lamb and N.P. Carter.  Probated September 21, 1914.

Page 170  **WILL OF NANCY MARIA SMITH.** At present a resident of Leon
County, Florida.  Son Elmer R. Smith.  Daughter Annie Belle Smith
Sherrell.  Grandsons, J. Thomas Smith, Benjamin F. Smith, Samuel C. Smith, and
Elmer R. Smith, Jr., and granddaughter Irene S. Smith, all children of my
deceased son John F. Smith.  Executors: My son Elmer R. Smith and my daughter
Annie Belle Smith Sherrell.  Signed June 10, 1913.  Witnesses: R.C. McDavid of
Tallahassee, Florida, J.A. Wethington of Cross Ties, Florida, and N.E. Bassett of
Tallahassee, Florida.  Probated in Lincoln County, Tennessee October 30, 1914.
Probated in Florida November 6, 1914.

Page 173  **WILL OF W.M. McCOWN.** Desires a monument erected at my grave.
Niece Etta P. Pitts wife of R.A. Pitts.  Executor: Friend R.A. Pitts.
Signed August 9, 1901.  Witnesses: N.P. Carter and Fred C. Gill.  Probated
January 18, 1915.

Page 174  **WILL OF JACKSON BOLANDER.** February 29, 1912.  Wife Elizabeth
Bolander, all property.  Witnesses: W.A. Towry and R.A. Towry.
Probated February 13, 1915.

Page 175  **WILL OF G.J. ALEXANDER.** Of Fayetteville.  Owns house and lot in
Fayetteville.  My single daughter May Alexander.  My single daughter
Edna Alexander.  Daughters, Georgia Roper wife of B.D. Roper, Lizzie McNatt
wife of B. McNatt, and Birdie Baxter, a widow.  Executor: My nephew L.W.
Alexander.  Signed January 12, 1915.  Witnesses: E.K. Blair and N.P. Carter.
Probated February 22, 1915.

Page 176  **WILL OF JACK CARTER.** Of Brighton.  Sister Ida Taylor.  Signed
December 31, 1914.  Witnesses: L.R. Roe and Ralph Noe.  Probated
April 5, 1915.

Page 177  **WILL OF MRS. VIRGINIA DISMUKES.** Of Fayetteville.  Nephew John
Burnam a son of my deceased sister Victoria Burnam.  Niece Virginia
Burnam Bright wife of M.M. Bright.  Niece Veda Rogers Fulton daughter of my
deceased brother Charles Fulton.  Nephew Otho Green son of my deceased sister
Martha Green.  Grand-niece Mary Bright Wilson daughter of my nephew Fulton M.
Wilson.  I own land in District No. 8 of Fayetteville, including two brick two story
business house and lots located on north side of public square in Fayetteville.
Executor: My nephew Fulton M. Wilson.  Signed January 18, 1913.  Witnesses:
William M. Smith and J.L. Heymann.
Codicil: Bequeaths to my nephew Fulton M. Wilson and Otho Green instead of to
my nephew Fulton M. Wilson alone.  April 3, 1915.  Probated May 11, 1915.

**WILL OF T.N. ASHBY.** Of Mulberry. Appointed my daughter Mrs. Mattie Dusenberry executrix. Signed June 5, 1912. Witnesses: L.M. Shofner and T.W. Brown. Probated May 25, 1915.

**WILL OF JAMES R. ROUTT.** Wife Mary L. Routt, land I now own and reside on. Son Willis Routt by my present wife. Son James R. Routt, Jr. who is my son by my first marriage. Executors: B.L. Towry and Lawson Walker. Signed January 9, 1913. Witnesses: Jas. T. Burns and Robert Kelso. Probated July 17, 1915.

**WILL OF CHARLES WEISS.** Wife Maggie E. Weiss. Owns farm in District No. 11. Son Carl Weiss, farm he now lives on in District No. 13, of 77 acres. Daughter Lula M. Weiss Phillips, $100.00. Daughter Mary E. Weiss Sisco, $25.00. Son Goodner Weiss. Executors: Wife Maggie E. Weiss and my two sons Carl and Goodner Weiss. Signed July 8, 1915.

**WILL OF J.C. HARRISON.** Owns land in District No. 16. Son J.W. Harrison, as trustee for my daughter Ida J. Bevels wife of E.G. Bevels. Widowed daughter Mattie B. Bevels and her children. Widowed daughter Lou Jennie Eagin and her children. Daughter Minnie B. West wife of John T. West and her children. Son C.B. Harrison and his children. Daughter Charlotte A. Mansfield. N.L. Mansfield. Executors: My two sons J.W. and C.B. Harrison. Signed April 10, 1915. Witnesses: J.R. Bruce and M.F. Story. Probated August 10, 1915.

**WILL OF MARTIN V. RIDDLE.** Of District No. 5. August 22, 1912. Daughter Emma Riddle. F.E. and J.B. Riddle. James Ed Riddle of Chickasha, Oklahoma sold land to his sister Mrs. Anna Moorehead. Those retaining their original interest in my estate besides Emma are: Martha Jane Spencer, William B. Riddle, Martin Mc. Riddle, Mrs. Ophelia C. Hill, Mrs. Lula McCauley. Executrix: Daughter Emma Riddle. Signed August 28, 1912. Witnesses: Jesse J. Tucker and Ernest S. McGehee and J.T. Allison. Probated August 12, 1915.

**WILL OF PLEASANT HOBBS.** Daughter Sarah H. Sugg wife of J.D. Sugg. Son Beverley H. Hobbs. Son Buchanan M. Hobbs and his children. Daughter Tula H. Stone, a widow. Son David F. Hobbs. Children: Tula H. Stone, Sarah H. Sugg wife of J.D. SUgg, David F. Hobbs, Beverley H. Hobbs, Buchanan M. Hobbs, and Laura H. McLaughlin wife of J.M. McLaughlin. Signed August 26, 1916. Witnesses: H.K. Bryson, W.B. Lamb and W.G. Cowan. Probated December 2, 1915.

**WILL OF H.P. ROWELL.** Desires a plain monument for her and myself. Wife Mary C. Rowell. True friend Sarah Henderson has lived in my family for years in District No. 1. Brothers and sisters, not named. Niece Mary Pearl Williams. Signed November 19, 1910. Witnesses: H.T. McCown and N.P. Carter. Probated December 17, 1915.

**WILL OF P.H. FREEMAN.** Wife Nancy Freeman. My children: Harvey Freeman, Dillie B. Bledsoe, George H. Freeman, Mary Ethel Gilbert, Jessie Redd, Roy Freeman, Fannie Davidson, Nina Ellis, and Johnnie Freeman. Executors: My wife Nannie Freeman and my son Roy Freeman. Signed March 6, 1914. Witnesses: W.S. Joplin and O.F. Gill. Probated August 13, 1915.

**WILL OF MRS. M.V. BRADY.** Brothers and sisters, Elizabeth (Posy) Curtis, Dora Story, Ida Mitchell, Charlie Trantham and W.I. Trantham. Niece Tippie Mitchell. Clyde Mitchell. Signed March 10, 1914. Witnesses: A.B. Wilson, J.O. Milton and Pinkney Owen. Probated January 28, 1916.

**WILL OF MRS. MARY M. CLARK.** Son Roy Conwell and my daughter Susie Belle Conwell, all my property. Present husband W.T. Clark, a house and lot. Executors: My son Roy Conwell and my daughter Susie Belle

Conwell. Signed August 28, 1913. Witnesses: R.T. Hereford and Jas. T. Burns. Probated January 28, 1916.

Page 200 **WILL OF ROBERT S. TAYLOR.** Od Bedford County, Tennessee. Youngest son Erskin G. Taylor. My four children: Myron L. Taylor, Charles W. Taylor, Mrs. Virgie Head wife of Tom Head who is a resident of Oklahoma, and my youngest son Erskin G. Taylor. My lands in District No. 20 of Bedford County, Tennessee, of 103 acres. Signed December 25, 1912. Witnesses: Jack T. Shrim and Fugitt Shrivey. Probated (no date).

Page 200 **WILL OF B.A. CLARK.** Wife Nancy C. Clark, entire estate. At the death of my wife, estate goes to D.M. Wright, A.M. Clark, L.C. Clark, and J. Hester Clark, each my children. Daughter L.C. Clark is still single. Executors: A.M. Clark and Roy A. Clark. Signed April 1, 1911. Witnesses: C. Ernest and C. Eugene. Probated March 15, 1916.

Page 201 **WILL OF M.W. WOODARD.** Wife Ida L. Woodard, all my property and also appointed executrix. Signed February 15, 1909. Witnesses: W.J. Malone, W.K. Woodard, H.B. Haggard and W.G. Cowan. Probated (no date).

Page 201 **WILL OF DUDLEY TIPPS AND JANE TIPPS, HIS WIFE.** Heirs, Davis Tipps, Albert Tipps, Charley Tipps, Nancy Copeland, and Noah Tipps, and our grandson Roy Tipps that we raised. Executors: My two sons Will Tipps and Charley Tipps and my grandson Roy Tipps. Signed May 9, 1911. Witnesses: B.N. Parks and C.S. Massey. Probated (no date).

Page 201 **WILL OF JANE BLAKE CLARK.** Of Howell. Desires my grave be marked. Grandson Joel Harris Clark, an enlarg picture of Dr. Clark. Step-grandson Thomas Blake Clark, my silver waiter. Grandniece Mollie Crawford, my trunk and my wearing cloths. Friend Mrs. Mary W. Harris, silver butter dish. Two nephews William Blake Crawford and John Edward Crawford, remainder of property. Niece Mrs. Alice Blake Cromer and my two step-sons Thomas B. Clark and Edward W. Clark, whatever is left of my estate. Executrix: Mrs. Mary W. Harris. Signed November 30, 1912. Witnesses: A.F. Taylor and R.L. Clift. Probated (no date).

Page 202 **WILL OF BRIDGET L. McKENZIE.** A feme sole. Fayetteville. My two sons Duncan L. McKenzie and John L. McKenzie and my daughter Susie F. McKenzie, all my household and kitchen furniture. My two sons to be Trustees for my daughter. Also my two sons appointed executors. Signed February 19, 1909. Witnesses: Tom Moore and William S. Raby. Probated February 26, 1916.

Page 203 **WILL OF M.M. WOODARD.** Fayetteville. Wife Ida L. Woodard, all my property. Signed February 15, 1909. Witnesses: W.J. Malone, W.K. Woodard, H.B. Haggard and W.G. Cowan. Probated February 26, 1916. (Same as on page 201)

Page 204 **WILL OF DUDLEY TIPPS AND JANE TIPPS, HIS WIFE.** (Same as on page 201)

Page 205 **WILL OF JANE BLAKE CLARK.** (Same as on page 201).

Page 206 **WILL OF MARTHA E. RINGO.** Of Petersburg. February 4, 1916. Desires a stone to mark my grave. Martha Gillespie daughter of George R. Gillespie, $250.00. Presbyterian Church of Petersburg, $200.00. Mrs. Carrie C. Nance and daughter Annie West Nance, remainder. Executor: George R. Gillespie. Witnesses: Carl Hasting, O.F. Gill, and George R. Gillespie. Probated May 1, 1916.

Page 207 **WILL OF N. GARY.** of McBurg. Wife M.E. Gary, all my property. Three children, J.M., C.C., and Gladys Gary. A son Alexander Gary, resident of Texas, $25.00. Executrix: Wife M.E. Gary. Signed February 12, 1916. Witnesses: W.G. Davis and F.F. Mitchell. Probated June 8, 1916.

Page 208 **WILL OF W.H. KENNEDY.** My brother L.R. Kennedy and his wife Minnie Kennedy, land in District No. 22. Brothers and sisters, H.T.Kennedy (sister) of Dwight, Alabama (Citronelle, Alabama, R # 2), L.R. Kennedy of Kelso, J.H. Kennedy of Citronella, Alabama, F.H. Kennedy of R # 3, Kelso, Mrs. Nellie Cora Paxton wife of J.L. Paxton of Grove City, Pennsylvania R # 11, Lizzie Jane Kennedy of R # 3 Kelso, Nina Estelle Kennedy of R # 3 Kelso, and Joe Mack (sister) Kennedy of R # 3 Kelso, and Mrs. Mary Allie Glass wife of William S. Glass of Mercer, Pennsylvania. My father and mother. Own a general merchandise store in Madison County, Alabama, a short distance of what is known as Buck's Mill, Tennessee. My post office being Flintville, Tennessee R # 2. Executors: My brother E.H. Kennedy and my sister Lizzie Jane Kennedy. Signed May 11, 1916. Witnesses: T.P. Gillham and Charles C. Gillham. Probated June 10, 1916.

Page 210 **WILL OF THOMAS L. STRAIN.** Daughter Ella Strain, estate and my interest in the estate of Richard Chapple in the State of Virginia. She is also appointed executrix. Signed October 7, 1896. Witnesses: J.R. Bruce and D.C. Sherrell. Probated June 13, 1916.

Page 211 **WILL OF ENOS PITTS.** Wife Emily Pitts, farm where I now reside in District No, 7, also appointed executrix. Two daughters, Mary Ola Hines and L.C. Hines. Signed December --, 1912. Witnesses: S.W. Fleming and Joel D. Parks. Probated July 3, 1916.

Page 212 **WILL OF THOMAS P. CUNNINGHAM.** Wife Lena Cunningham, entire estate, also appointed executrix. Four children, Maggie Cunningham, Clyde Cunningham, Claude Cunningham and Sarah Cunningham. Signed June 26, 1916. Witnesses: J.E. Sloan and D.L. Childress. Probated July 19, 1916.

Page 214 **WILL OF MRS. ANGELINA McDANIEL.** Desires a head and foot stone placed at my grave. To John Hopkins, all my land on which I now reside. To the children of C.G. and H.B. Key, remainder property except one featherbed which I give to Jack Key. Sister Amanda Key, already given her all of my property. Executor: I.N. McClusky. Signed December 7, 1901. Witnesses: G.W. Simmons and S.M. Hancock. Probated August 5, 1917.

Page 215 **WILL OF MRS. SUE M. MILHOUS.** To Ernest Rees, $1000.00, trustee for my husband Dr. W.A. Milhous. My children, Mrs. R.M. Leslie, Mrs. Mary F. Davis, H.C. Milhous, Mrs. Laura J. Lindsay, Mrs. Beatrice Rees, Ernest Rees, trustee for Mrs. Lucy Garner. Signed May 19, 1912. Witness: Emily H. Milhous. Probated August 7, 1916.

Page 216 **WILL OF OSCAR L. RALSTON.** Desires a tombstone erected at my grave. Brother J.D. Ralston. Wife Susie K. Ralston, executrix. Signed July 10, 1915. Witnesses: R.M. Rawls, R.D. Dryden and Neely D. Crawford. Probated August 7, 1916.

Page 217 **WILL OF ALLEN LAMB, (COL).** Of Fayetteville. Wife Martha Lamb. Granddaughter Josie Johnson, real estate in District No. 8, in Fayetteville. Executor: Mr. A.B. Wright. Signed April 20, 1900. Witnesses: E.H. Smith and W.A. Thompson. Probated August 25, 1916.

Page 218 **WILL OF SAMUEL HAYNIE.** My farm is in District No. 11, on which I now reside, to be sold. To my minor grandson John Haynie one of the children of my deceased son Robert H. Haynie, $100.00. To S.J. Haynie and J.F. Buntley, trustees for my minor grandchildren, Schula Scott, Annie Marie Scott, Robert Scott, and Docia Scott, the only children of my deceased daughter Emma Lee Scott, $500.00. To my living children, S.J. Haynie, H.L. Haynie, T.J. Haynie, and Mary J. Buntley, $500.00. To my grandchildren, Felix N. Haynie, Pearl

Haynie, Willie Haynie, and Annie Bell Thomas and John Haynie. Executors: Son S.J. Haynie and son-in-law J.F. Buntley. Signed August 7, 1915. Witnesses: Giles L. Evans and N.P. Carter. Probated August 25, 1916.

Page 220 **WILL OF J.P. AMOS.** Son D.V. Amos amd my daughter Fannie Smith. Granddaughter Sallie Horton of Albertville, Alabama. Wife Mary Elizabeth Amos appointed executrix. Signed July 25, 1916. Witnesses: R.E. Sawyers and E.H. Gregory. Probated October 3, 1916.

Page 221 **WILL OF THOMAS A. JEAN.** Of Fayetteville. Desires a tombstone similar to the one over the grave of my wife at my grave. Son John A. Jean. Children, John A. Jean, William McHenry Jean, Thomas M. Jean, George Jean, Mrs. Lizzie Campbell, and Mrs. Mary Widener. At the death of Mrs. Lizzie Campbell's two youngest sons, John Westley and Willie Campbell, both under age of 21 years. At death of my daughter Mrs. Mary Widener's oldest boy, Harland Widener. Executors: My two sons John A. Jean and Thomas M. Jean. Signed March 11, 1907.
Codicil: Appointed my son George W. Jean one of the executors. Signed May 8, 1913. Witnesses: F.H. Webb and J.E. Routt. Probated October 12, 1916.

Page 224 **WILL OF MRS. FANNIE CHILDS.** Of Booneville. Grandson Trall McCurdy, all estate. Executors: W.M. Green and Dr. J.T. Graham. Witnesses: D.C. Sullivan and W.N. Reagor. Probated December 4, 1916.

Page 224 **WILL OF MRS. M.A. LINCOLN.** March 19, 1914. Husband J.C. Lincoln to place a tombstone to my grave. He is to have all the personal property and money. Daughter Maude Rawls Woodard, household and kitchen furniture. Son-in-law Robert Woodard be executor. Witnesses: John Henderson and Lula Henderson. Probated December 4, 1916.

Page 226 **WILL OF W.H. GUNTER.** Wife M.S. Gunter, all my property. Three daughters, Willie Eva Gunter, Lucy Minerva Gunter and Mary Amanda Gunter. Son H.O. Gunter, my watch. My four Rambo grandchildren, $1.00 each. Executrix: My wife M.S. Gunter. Signed June 21, 1912. Witnesses: W.G. Collins and Jno. W. Whitaker. Probated November 4, 1916.

Page 227 **WILL OF DON COLLIER.** Desires to buy a plot of ground, known as the Collier graveyard in the County of Bedford, Tennessee, five miles west of Shelbyville, on the farm of Til Gant and shall make a good stone or iron fence around said plot of ground. To Robert Walker, a good horse, bridle, blanket and saddle. Niece Elsie Henly and in no event shall Mahala Collier or any heir of hers, inherit any of my estate. Executrix: Elsie Henly. Signed July 3, 1911. Witnesses: H.T. Childs and Samuel Haynie.
The above will was probated in open court by the oath of H.T. Childs, as to the signature of Don Collier, deceased, and J.E. Poindexter, Morgan Eslick and H.E. Dryden, as the signature of Samuel Haynie as witness to said will, the said Samuel Haynie, being now dead. This November 11, 1916.

Page 227 **WILL OF W.P. LEDFORD.** Desires a monument erected at my grave and also to be used as a monument for my wife Mary Elizabeth Ledford when she shall die. Twelve children, A.S. Ledford, G.Y. Ledford, J.F. Ledford, Sallie Matilda Tate wife of J.F. Tate, P.A. Ledford, J.S. Ledford, T.E. Ledford, Maggie S. Green wife of Joe Green, Clara B. Divens formerly wife of R.L. Divens, Ida M. Little wife of Will Little, C.W. Ledford, and Mary Wilma Ledford, at one time the wife of Carl Phillips. Executors: G.Y. Ledford and J.S. Ledford. Signed May 3, 1913. Witnesses: John C. Diemer and W.B. Lamb, Jr. Probated December 4, 1916.

Page 227 **WILL OF MRS. TABITHA LONG.** Tabitha (Bledsoe) Long. Children, Ava Nora Thomas (his heirs), Fannie, Jennie, Helen and Affa. Executors: J.E. Ellis and Affa C. Long. Signed January 16, 1913. Witnesses: H.C. Sanders and A.M. March. Probated December 14, 1916.

Page 229 **WILL OF A. DERROR.** Desires a monument for myself and wife erected at my grave. Step-daughter J.V. Howard. Wife Huldah Derror and at her death to my son W.H. Derror and three daughters, Docia Logan, Florence Taylor, and Laura Tucker, my farm where I now live in District No. 5. Executor: My son W.H. Derror. Signed September 2, 1909. Witnesses: W.L. Lamb, Jr. and N.P. Carter. Probated December 21, 1916.

Page 230 **WILL OF MRS. ETHEL SUGG WILSON.** Husband Edward L. Wilson, land where we now reside. To Ethel Wilson, my daughter, one bay mare. Son Robert L. Wilson, money to educate Ethel Wilson. Son Clayton Wilson and also mentions daughter Sallie Kate Wilson and daughter Mary Vernie Murphy. Signed July 26, 1916. Witnesses: W.R. Carmack and H.C. Hovis. Probated December 21, 1916.

Page 231 **WILL OF J.N. MARTIN.** Of District No. 23. Wife Allace J. Martin, my entire holdings including the farm on which we now live and she is appointed executrix. Signed June 7, 1915. Witnesses: Oscar Parks and T.G. Yarbrough. Probated February 19, 1917.

Page 232 **WILL OF MRS. ELIZABETH HAYNES HOLMAN.** Of Fayetteville. To Dr. E.S. Landess, Trustee for my two granddaughters, Elizabeth Lee Carter and Mary Anderson Carter, children of my daughter Mary Carter, my store house and lot in Decherd, Franklin County, Tennessee. Son-in-law George F. Carter, the father of my granddaughter. My two daughters, Elizabeth Anderson Landess wife of Dr. E.S. Landess, and Mary Anderson Carter wife of George F. Carter. Own farm in District No. 8, Fayetteville. Executor: N.P. Carter. Son-in-law Dr. E.S. Landess, Trustee for my granddaughters. Signed June 17, 1912. Witnesses: F.M. Bledsoe and R.L. Lasater. Probated February 13, 1917.

Page 235 **WILL OF H.H. BEECH.** Wife, not named, all my estate. Son Thomas Beech and one half to my two grandchildren, Arthur West and Oleda West. Executor: Son Thomas Beech. Signed March 7, 1910. Witnesses: J.D. Carroll and R.R. Haynes. Probated March 7, 1917.

Page 236 **WILL OF MRS. MARGARET TOMLINSON (MAGGIE).** Husband B.W. Tomlinson and Lettie E. Cambron (Cameron) my daughter, my house and lot at McBurg, Tennessee. Mentions Lawson Cameron and Menne M. McDoulde daughter of G.W. Cameron, brother Tom S. Caldwell and brother Tullie M. Caldwell and brother Erskin H. Caldwell. Also mentions Albert Cameron to be guardian of Lettie Cameron and Tullie M. Caldwell, her advisor, this July 22, 1915. Executor: W.H. Robinson. Signed July 22, 1915. Witnesses: Groves Gunter and Robert Porter. Probated March 10, 1917.

Page 237 **WILL OF JAMES I. ALEXANDER.** Friends, A.F. Carter and wife Iva V. Carter, land in District No. 12. Iva V. Carter being the niece of my deceased wife. Myree Bryson youngest daughter of my friend H.K. Bryson, who was a cousin of my deceased wife. Executors: My friends H.K. Bryson and A.F. Carter. Signed October 4, 1911. Witnesses: Jacob Newman and W.B. Lamb, Jr. Probated March 12, 1917.

Page 238 **WILL OF SALLIE H. RICE.** To youngest children, George W. Rice, Holden Rice, and Florence Rice, bed clothing and bed. To George Rice, my trunk, I give to Holden Rice, a gold medal that belonged to and bearing the name of his father Francisco Rice. I give to my daughter Florence Rice all contents of my parlor room and one piano, set of five pieces, table, lamp and one mantel mirrow. To Florence, one fashion clock and other items. Son J.R. Childers, $50.00. Executor: W.F. Cannon. Signed March 23, 1916. Witnesses: A.B. Rhea and Pink Whitaker. Probated April 4, 1917.

Page 239 **WILL OF MARY J. BREADY.** Desires the coffin in which I am to be laid to rest shall cost $50.00, to be enclosed in a cement vault and a monument erected at my grave. To Virgie Hampton (Col), $40.00. To Ida

McCullock wife of Nathan McCullock. To Jeffy McCullock son of Nathan McCullock. Brother James F. McCullock. Sisters, Mrs. Fannie Moyers, Mrs. Sarah Gattis, Mrs. Annie P. Bedford, and my half sister Miss Maggie McCullock. Executors: R.D. Cowley and James F. McCullock. Signed April 3, 1917. Witnesses: G.T. Webb and C.R. McCartney. Probated April 11, 1917.

Page 241 **WILL OF MRS. M.M. BOYLES.** (Mrs. George B. Boyles) December 7, 1909. "If anything should happen to me while away from home for treatment in Nashville, that I may not live"... To my daughter Catharine to have entire control of everything to divide among Margaret, Robert, Charles, Jakie, and Georgie. Witnesses: John C. Diemer and Exie H. Diemer. Probated April 28, 1917.

Page 242 **WILL OF P.E. FARRAR.** Wife Cammilla F. Farrar, residue of my estate. Four daughters, Myrtle Farrar, Nannie Lou Harriston, Annie B. Stewart, and Edna Clark. Executors: Eugene Stewart and Eugene Clark. Signed August 30, 1912. Witnesses: B.W. Markham of Boonshill and J.L. Smith of Booneville. Probated May 4, 1917.

Page 243 **WILL OF J.W. STEELMAN.** Desires a monument erected at my grave similar to the one erected at my first wife's grave. Wife Lula Belle Steelman. Daughter Mrs. Jessie Hunter. Son Fletcher Steelman. Son Rufus Steelman. Son Arthur Steelman. Grandsons, Floyd and Leon Steelman sons of my son Wilson Steelman, deceased, John Willis Warren and Holland Warren sons of my deceased daughter Dollie Ann Warren. Daughter Laura Taylor. Daughter America Cowley and to my daughter Jessie Hunter. Executor: My son Fletcher Steelman. Signed April 5, 1917. Witnesses: A.L. Yearwood, Giles L. Evans and Milus Nisbit. Probated June 1, 1917.

Oage 245 **WILL OF DONIE CLARK.** Daughter Barbara Clark, household and kitchen furniture, she is also Trustee for my minor son Ardell Clark. Land in District No. 8 and 9. Children, Will Clark, Barbara Clark, John Clark, Collie Clark, Ernest Clark, and Charley Clark. Executor: Friend W.S. Clayton. Signed April 24, 1917. Witnesses: S.M. Clayton and N.P. Carter. Probated May 4, 1917.

Page 247 **WILL OF H.T. TRANTHAM.** Wife Sarah Trantham. Children, not named. A son W.R. Trantham. Signed August 16, 1915. Witnesses: A.B. Wilson and Jno. E. Sloan. Probated June 4, 1917.

Page 248 **WILL OF JOSIE HAMILTON, WIDOW.** Of Fayetteville. Granddaughters, Marie Formwalt and Lilliam Formwalt. Land in District No. 8, Fayetteville, borders the Tanyard. Mentions, J.E. Caldwell, J.W. Holman and J.M. Cambron. My late husband S.P. Hamilton died intestate on December 11, 1911 and in his will he bequeathed to the two daughters and son, also two granddaughters and also the said two daughters being named in said will as Bessie Taylor wife of John A. Taylor and Lillie Hamilton and the son named as Samuel Ellis Hamilton, and the two granddaughters named as Mary E. Formwalt or Marie Formwalt and Lillian Formwalt. Executor: Brother-in-law John L. Caughran. Signed March 20, 1917. Witnesses: W.B. Lamb, Jr. and S.D. Lamb. Probated June 21, 1917.

Page 251 **WILL OF E.J. SMITH.** Daughter Lizzie Coble, all the real estate, it being one half interest with J.M. Coble. Daughter Lizzie Coble to pay to Tippie Owen wife of Pinkney Owen $200.00. Signed March 26, 1915. Witnesses: G.E. Wright and E.B. Wright. Probated June 27, 1917.

Page 252 **WILL OF DAVID L. HARRIS.** Desires a tombstone erected at my grave in the family graveyard on my home farm. Wife Sarah Jane Harris, my farm, on which I have resided for years in District No. 23 but now District No. 3. To my sons, W.N. Harris, I.C. Harris, Joel L. Harris, John M. Harris, and S.S. Harris, and to my daughter Sallie L. White wife of Henry L.

White, and to my six grandchildren, the only children of my deceased son D.D. Harris. Daughter Fannie Kate Corder wife of J.F. Corder. The children of my deceased son Thomas H. Harris. Executor: Son W.N. Harris. Signed September 28, 1916. Witnesses: Emma Sebastian and N.P. Carter. Probated July 9, 1917.

Page 254    **WILL OF J.V. PITTS.** Desires a monument erected at my grave. Wife Lula Pitts, all household, kitchen and parlor furniture also appointed executor. Land in District No. 6. Brother H.H. Pitts. Signed July 14, 1917. Witnesses: W.F. Cannon and N.P. Carter. Probated July 23, 1917.

Page 256    **WILL OF A.N. BRYAN.** Desires a monument erected at my grave. Wife F.A. Bryan, real and personal estate. Three daughters, Mary Alice Lincoln wife of John Lincoln, son J.B. Bryan, and my daughter Sallie Green Pitts wife of Thomas Pitts. Executor: My son J.B. Bryan. Witnesses: W.B. Lamb and N.P. Carter. Probated July 26, 1917.

Page 257    **WILL OF MRS. MATTIE E. RUSH, WIDOW.** Widow of A.C. Rush. Desires a double tombstone placed at my husband and myself graves in the Lincoln Cemetery. Son J.M. Rush, daughter Marea Rush, below age. Other four children, A.A. Rush, Myrtle Rush, Robert Eliz Rush and Mattie Elsie Rush, below age. Executor: W.R. Locker. Signed December 10, 1916. Witnesses: J.T. Simms and W.M. Blaylock.
"Births of my children":
A.A. Rush, April 12, 1893
J.M.W. Rush, March 4, 1896
Pearl Maria, March 15, 1898
Myrtle Rush, October 23, 1900
Robert Elic Rush, March 20, 1904
Mattie Elsie Rush, May 3, 1908.    Probated August 1, 1917.

Page 258    **ESTATE OF SUSAN HARRIS, DECEASED.** Marion County, Texas. May 1917. On 8 May 1917, to be heard the application of Mattie A. Blake, for probate for the will of Susan Harris, deceased, H.L. Eldridge, E.C. Webb and C.W. Ray are citizens of Marion County, texas are appointed to appraise the estate both real and personal of Susan Harris, deceased.
**WILL OF SUSAN HARRIS.** Son John Henry Howard Harris who now resides in Lincoln County, Tennessee in Fayetteville. Daughter Mattie A. Blake who now reside at Jefferson, Marion County, Texas. Son of my deceased daughter Mollie McCallin, late of Lincoln County, Tennessee. Children of my deceased daughter Emma Harris, late of Lincoln County, Tennessee. Children of my deceased son George Harris, late of Lincoln County, Tennessee. Executrix: My daughter Mattie A. Blake of Marion County, Texas. Signed March 31, 1916. Witnesses: A.K. Neidermeier and T.H. Stallcup. Probated July 23, 1917.

Page 261    **WILL OF JAS. H. DEFORD.** August 1, 1917. Wife Mrs. M.S. Deford, all my holdings. Mrs. P.C. Breeden and Mrs. T.A. Noah, take charge to act as agent and guardian for her after all debts is paid, but if we go to Texas it will be in charge of Mrs. P.C. Breeden and to sell all household surplus. Witnesses: T.D. Sumners, T.A. Noah and R. Ed Feeney, on August 22, 1917, Fayetteville, Tennessee.

Page 262    **WILL OF MRS. SILENA I. BRIGHT.** (Mrs. John M. Bright, widow) Desires a monument stone placed at my grave. To Anna Bright Jones, $100.00. To Mary Jones Hardin, $50.00. To Margaret Jones, $50.00. To Miss Zue Goodloe $200.00. To Bettie Bright Douglas $100.00. To S.A. Bright $100.00. To the deacons and elders of the First Presbyterian Church of Fayetteville $100.00, to keep John M. Bright lot in the church graveyard adjoining the street between the graveyard and the lot now owned by Robert L. Mason, formerly owned by C.B. McGuire. Also $50.00 for use of church. Executor: B.E. Holman. Signed September 25, 1915. Witnesses: H.E. Dryden, Milus Nesbit and M.W. Woodward. Probated August 12, 1917.

**Page 264**  **WILL OF SARAH BRODERICK.**  Of McBurg.  Brother Hugh Broderick appointed executor. Signed May 24, 1915. Witnesses: W.H. Robinson and C.M. Curtis. Probated September 8, 1917.

**Page 265**  **WILL OF HETTIE GREEN.**  Wife of James Green (Bonner).  Husband James Green, 60 acres in District No. 8.  Daughters, Sarah Patton, Annie Gardner, Maggie Green Lee, Mary Willie Beavers, and Addie Green, all daughters by my husband James Green, alias Kentucky Jim Bonner.  Executor: George W. Sutton. Signed November 15, 1915.  Witnesses: W.B. Hague and Frank Stone.  Probated September 14, 1917.

**Page 267**  **WILL OF G.F. PITTS.**  Wife Martha P. Pitts, farm on which I now reside, located on the Fayetteville-Elkton Turnpike, about one mile west of Fayetteville, bounded by lands of R.A. Rees, Mrs. Cordie McDonald.  At death of my wife Martha P., I give said farm to my children, Daisy Bagley wife of Tom Bagley, Sue E. Young wife of William Young, Jr., Pearl Gwynne wife of Walter Gwynne, Lura Oldham wife of Charles Oldham, Robert E. Pitts, Ephraim Philander Pitts, and Jimmie Ruth Pitts. My wife is to be Trustee for herself and my minor daughter Jimmie Ruth Pitts.  A tract of land in Madison County, Alabama, owned by me and Elgie Hayes, my interest to be sold.  Executors: My son Robert E. Pitts and my son-in-law Tom Bagley. My wife sole executrix of my will.  Signed October 27, 1914.  Witnesses: S.H. Galloway and W.B. Lamb, Jr. Probated October 2, 1917.

**Page 273**  **WILL OF W.M. CATHEY.**  Resident of Lincoln County, Tennessee, temporarily residing in Shelby County, Tennessee. Three children now living on the home place in Lincoln County, Tennessee, Beulah, Sam and J.T. Cathey.  Executor: Jno. O. Flautt of Shelby County, Tennessee. Other children, not named.  Signed June 13, 1916.  Witnesses: R.F. McCaul and Jas. E. McCaul. Probated October 3, 1917.

**Page 274**  **WILL OF W.W. McCLELLEN.**  Wife Marget E. McClellen, all property. Daughter Mrs. Lillian Lee Hamilton wife of W.K. Hamilton and her children.  Signed May 21, 1913.  Witnesses: R.D. Dryden, Jas. T. Burns and J.E. Routt.  Probated (no date).

**Page 275**  **WILL OF LUCY M. RUDD.**  Husband W.H. Rudd.  Children of my husband by a former marriage, Martha N., Robbie L., and Marshal T. Rudd.  Farm in District No. 4, where I now live. Executor: Jno. M. Gray. Signed: October 20, 1917.  Witnesses: C.S. Taylor and John M. Dickey, Sr.  Probated (no date).

**Page 276**  **WILL OF ADA BELL TAYLOR.**  Husband W.A. Taylor, house and lot wherel now live, apart of which was willed to me by R.S. Douthat, deceased, will proven in Will Book # 6, page 142. To Hassie May Taylor daughter of W.A. Taylor.  Executor: W.A Taylor.  Signed July 17, 1917.  Witnesses: T.A. Patrick, M.D. and Neely D. Crawford.  Probated --- --, 1918.

**Page 277**  **WILL OF W.W. TWITTY.**  Of Blanche.  All my lands, residence and other buildings be used by my widow, Mrs. Conley Twitty, and my two daughters, Sadie and Ruth Twitty as a home for them. Executor: Son P.A. Twitty. My widow Mrs. Conley Twitty be left for the use of her and my two daughters. Signed July 27, 1917.  Witnesses: B.C. Wallace and J.E. Watson.  Probated --- --, 1918.

**Page 278**  **WILL OF N.P. CARTER.**  Of Fayetteville.  Wife Orra Lee Carter appointed executrix.  Signed September 24, 1917.  Witnesses: W.B. Lamb and W.B. Lamb, Jr.  Probated --- --, 1918.

**Page 279**  **WILL OF NETTIE CECIL BRYSON.**  Husband H.K. Bryson appointed executor:  Signed August 14, 1915.  Witnesses: J.M. Fulton and S.H. Galloway.  Probated --- --, 1918.

Page 280 **WILL OF MATTIE LULA FLY.** A single woman. Sister Sarah F. Fly appointed executrix. Signed September 15, 1917. Witnesses: T.P. Bryant and S.B. Pigg. Probated March 14, 1918.

Page 281 **WILL OF MRS. KALISTA NEELD HAGUE.** Executor: Anderson Whitaker of Mulberry. Desires a tombstone erected over my grave, also a stone or concrete curbin around our burial lot in the Mulberry Cemetery. To the Stewards of the Methodist Church at Mulberry, $200.00. My property consists of a house and lot in the village of Mulberry. Step-daughter Lizzie Rhea and step-daughter Pauline Johnson. Brother Charles Neeld, house and lot. Nephew Neeld Parks. Niece Alleen Parks. Signed August 28, 1917. Witnesses: E.P. Holt and W.W. Stone. Probated --- --, 1918.

Page 282 **WILL OF JOHN B. HARRIS.** Of Howell. Wife Mary E. Harris appointed executrix. My only child and daughter Mary Bell Conaway wife of William M. Conaway. My now living sister Mrs. F.V. Ward and brother H.C. Harris. Signed October 5, 1915. Witnesses: J.A. McCollum and Jno. A. Moore. Probated --- --, 1918.

Page 284 **WILL OF MATILDA McCLELLAN.** Of Fayetteville. I own the law library and book cases once owned by my brother Judge Thomas N. McClellan, now deceased. Desires a monument erected at the grave of my brother Thomas N. McClellan who at the time of his death was Chief Justice of the Supreme Court of Alabama and who is buried in the cemetery at Athens, Alabama. Sister Mrs. Kate Buchanan $2000.00 to help purchase her home, the house and lot at the corner of Mulberry Avenue and Polk Street, formerly called Fair Ground Street in Fayetteville. Niece Willie McClellan. My deceased brother John B. McClellan had three daughters. Nieces, Netta Davis of Athens, Alabana and Sue Davis. Niece Memory Walker. Deceased brother W.C. McClellan had children. Deceased brother R.A. McClellan had children. Deceased sister Mrs. Sarah M. Davis had children. Executor: My nephew T.C. McClellan. Signed January 30, 1918. Witnesses: A.B. Wright and W.B. Lamb. Probated March 25, 1918.

Page 286 **WILL OF HIRAM SANDLIN.** Wife Mrs. Allie M. Sandlin appointed executrix. Four children, Matie, Jonathan, Lucile and Lorene. To Lawrence Sandlin and Elsie May Sandlin, my farm in District No. 19. Signed March 24, 1913. Witnesses: T.L. Hutchinson and J.G. McAlister. Probated --- --, 1918.

Page 287 **WILL OF JOHN A. McCOLLUM.** Desires a monument erected at my grave. Wife Elizabeth McCollum, all household and kitchen property and other items. To THomas B. Clark, as Trustee, for my minor daughter, Annie Elizabeth McCollum, money &c. Sister Emma Blacknall and her son Arnie Hudson. Executor: Thomas B. Clark. Signed January 1, 1916. Witnesses: H.C. Harris and W.D. White.

Page 290 **WILL OF H.L. MOORE.** Wife Sue E. Moore appointed executrix. Signed October 18, 1917. Witnesses: J.E. Poindexter and D.C. Sherrell. Probated April 2, 1918.

Page 291 **WILL OF FRANK H. WEBB.** Of Fayetteville. Sister Lillie Webb appointed executrix. Signed March 1, 1918. Witnesses: John C. Diemer and T.A. Wyatt. Probated May 7, 1918.

Page 292 **WILL OF THOMAS V. GREER.** Daughter Vadora Ann Percy and her heirs. Heirs of my deceased daughter Elizabeth Vance Moore. Signed August 17, 1904. Witnesses: J.R. Taylor and H.C. Moore. Probated May 9, 1918.

Page 293 **WILL OF SARAH H. THOMPSON.** Grandson Benjamin B. Pitts. Orvel B. Thompson and Mrs. Henrietta Thompson. Desires a marble stone erected at my grave and my deceased husband. Executor: Orvel B. Thompson.

Signed October 16, 1917. Witnesses: J.A. Taylor, Jr., W.F. Simmons and John M. Dickey. Probated June 3, 1918.

Page 294 **WILL OF MARIA (MARIAH) McDONALD, (COL).** Two sons Sam and Adolphus McDonald appointed executors. Signed May 27, 1918. Witnesses: R.P. Smith and W.I. Smith. Probated (no date).

Page 295 **WILL OF J.C. MARCH** Of Molino, Rt 7, Fayetteville. Wide Emma March. Brother Hume March of Dallas, Texas as executor. Signed March 7, 1918. Witnesses: J.P. Farrar and J.B. Hill. Probated (no date).

Page 296 **WILL OF MARY SULLIVAN.** Niece Mary Benson and her husband Claude Benson. Signed November 16, 1908. Witnesses: W.A. Jenkins and B.T. Corder. Probated July 27, 1918.

Page 297 **WILL OF B.S. SOLOMON.** Wife Mary Elizabeth Solomon. Children, Sanford, John, Frank, C.B. Solomon, Anner Mansfield, Katie Bell, and Emma Solomon. Executors: My sons C.B. and B.S. Solomon. Signed August 18, 1913. Witnesses: Hugh D. Smith, R.D. Dryden and M.W. Woodard. Probated July 27, 1918.

Page 298 **WILL OF J.M. CAMBRON.** Son Ebbie J. Cambron, dwelling house and lot in Flintville, where Ebbie J. Cambron and his wife now reside. Son Carl M. Cambron, house and lot near my store house (Dry Goods Store & Grocery). Wife Cora M. Cambron appointed executrix. Also owns lots in Fayetteville known as the Brogan Addition. Signed August 2, 1918. Witnesses: J.B. Goodwin and W.S. Cambron. Probated August 5, 1918.

Page 300 **WILL OF CHARLES M. SUMMERFORD.** Desires a monument erected at my grave. Brother John Small and his wife Anna E. Small. Executor: John Small. Signed May 8, 1918. Witnesses: S.H. Galloway and B.E. Holman. Probated September 28, 1918.

Page 301 **WILL OF R.M. CAMPBELL.** Wife Fannie Campbell, property in District No. 1, where I now live. My minor children by my first wife and my present wife, my nine children, Felix E. Campbell, Lula Agnes Street wife of Eli Street, Mack Campbell, Ben Campbell, Horace Campbell, Eugene Campbell, James Campbell, Clida Lee Campbell, and Rufus Campbell. Executor: O.T. Wiley. Signed October 25, 1916. Witnesses: J.P. Farrar and W.B. Lamb, Jr. Codicil: Appointed my son Felix E. Campbell executor instead of O.T. Wiley. Signed December 23, 1916. Witnesses: C.D. Lamb and W.B. Lamb, Jr. Probated October 1, 1918.

Page 302 **WILL OF HUGH BROADRICK.** Desires a monument erected at my grave. To Miss Ruth Bryant, $5000.00. Brother Charley Broadrick, $4000.00. Nephew Horace Broadrick, land in District No. 2. Executor: T.A. McCracken of McBurg. Signed September 22, 1918. Witnesses: J.T. Rennolds, Rose Sanders and Giles L. Evans. Probated October 7, 1918.

Page 303 **WILL OF J. BONNER GREEN.** Sister Mrs. Ida Green Rogers, all interest in the real estate of my father and mother Mr. J.E. and Mrs. M.F. Green. Executrix: Sister Mrs. Ida Green Rogers. Signed March 19, 1917. Witnesses: John R. Williams and J.W. Danley. Probated November 4, 1918.

Page 304 **WILL OF ELLEN C. WILLIAMS.** Of Fayetteville. Desires a monument erected at my grave and also have a lot at Kelso, where I wish to be buried. Owns a lot in District No. 8, Fayetteville, same deeded to me by John R. Williams and wife. Daughter Mary Williamson. Daughter Esther Bates. Daughter Myrtle Weiss. Son John R. Williams. Son G.C. Williams. Granddaughter Elmer Bates. Executors: My sons John S. Williams and G.C. Williams. Signed August 14, 1918. Witnesses: E.L. Parks and J.M. Waggoner. Probated November 13, 1918.

Page 305 **WILL OF N.J. GEORGE.** Desire to be buried in Rose Hill Cemetery, Fayetteville, in a cedar coffin and a plain monument erected at my grave. Thomas B. George and his wife Sarah and each of their children. Each of the children of Napoleon B. Pearce and his wife Margaret V., both of whom are dead. Mollie P. Adams daughter of D.A. George, Sr., who is dead. Mollie Franklin wife of John M. Franklin. George M. Copeland, my nephew. Nephews, James N. George and William F. George. Signed October 16, 1913. Witnesses (not named). Probated February 25, 1919.

Page 306 **WILL OF P.H. DIETZ.** To Mrs. Alice W. Allen of Fayetteville, all the property, also appointed executrix. Signed January 5, 1918. Witnesses: S.S. Hagie and Mrs. S.S. Hagie. Probated March 14, 1919.

Page 307 **WILL OF JAMES D. STEELMAN.** Fayetteville. August 29, 1917. Sister Jenney Goosby. Witnesses: K.K. Eslick and James Earl Dixon. Probated March 15, 1919.

Page 308 **WILL OF ADDIE N. GILLESPIE.** Son James A. Gillespie. Granddaughter Leila H. Malone. Granddaughters, Mrs. Massey Jones and Mrs. William B. Lamb. Grandsons, Robert Hancock and Henry A. Gillespie. Signed January 16, 1918. Witnesses: Morgan S. Eslick and H.E. Dryden. Probated March 28, 1919.

Page 309 **WILL OF T.S. EDMISTON.** Desires a monument erected at my grave. Wife Daisy Wood Edmiston appointed executrix. Signed August 19, 1916. Witnesses: H.G. Wade and W.A. Ellis. Probated April 18, 1919.

Page 310 **WILL OF CORA M. RIDDLE.** Brother Cruse Brandon to be Trustee for my five children, to wit, Lemuel Riddle, Dixie Riddle, Finis Riddle, J.C. Riddle and Callie Riddle, all under age. Executor: Brother Cruse Brandon. Signed January 16, 1919. Witnesses: H.M. Mansfield and J.M. Cullum. Probated April 25, 1919.

Page 311 **WILL OF COSS McDONALD.** Daughter Martha Smith, ten acres in District No. 8. Son John McDonald, son Charley McDonald. Three children of my deceased son Amos McDonald. Son Alex McDonald. Son J.H. McDonald. The five children of my deceased daughter Katie McDonald Smith. Daughter Mary Ann Finch. Executrix: My daughter Martha Smith. Signed November 20, 1918. Witnesses: S.V (Sam) Beard, T.H.(Tom) Beard and B.E. Holman. Probated May 14, 1919.

Page 313 **WILL OF CELIA ANN TOWRY.** W.A. Towry to have all my property. Executor: H.E. Towry. Signed May 23, 1911. Witnesses: L.O. McClusky and S.M. Hancock. Probated May 17, 1919.

Page 314 **WILL OF SARAH J. ENGLISH.** Son John H. English, $5.00. Two grandchildren, Lillie Woodard, $5.00, and Earl White, $5.00. Son Will English, $125.00. Children of Ada Newton, deceased, $5.00 each. Son Samuel English, $5.00. Sons, Oscar B. English and Ross English, farm I own and live on in District No. 12. Executors: My sons, Oscar B. and Ross English. Signed December 20, 1910. Witnesses: John L. Kidd and W.M. Kidd. Probated May 28, 1919.

Page 315 **WILL OF SUSAN ANN HUDSON.** Mrs. Claudia B. Hudson wife of B.F. Hudson, deceased, $2500.00. Niece Emily A. Hudson daughter of B.F. Hudson, deceased. The heirs of John M. Hudson, that is, one Emily A. Hudson and other John M. Hudson. Executor: John M. Hudson. Signed November 28, 1917. Witnesses: R.W. Gant and D.C. Sherrell and J. Boone Landess. Probated July 28, 1919.

Page 316 **WILL OF THOMAS B. PITTS.** Wife Mary Elizabeth Pitts. Heirs, Delia Hester my oldest daughter, Jennie McGee, Orena Combest, Clifford Pitts, Austin Pitts, Annie Lee Pitts, Oscar B. Pitts, and Ollie Bell Pitts.

Grandson, son of Ed Pitts and my granddaughter, daughter of Clayton Pitts. Executors: My two sons, Oscar B. Pitts and Austin Pitts. Signed February 20, 1915. Witnesses: B.E. Noblitt and T.M. Thornton. Probated August 1, 1919.

Page 317  **WILL OF JOSEPH ALEXANDER EDMISON.** Of Coldwater, RFD 1. Desires my grave be marked. Son R.H. Edmison. Desires that R.H. Edmison and Mrs. M.E. Sowell shall take care of me. My four children: Mrs. M.E. Sowell, Jno. V. Edmison, R.H. Edmison, and Charles Alexander Edmison. Executors: R.H. Edmison and William H. Sowell. Signed July 3, 1919. Witnesses: S.D. Renegar and W.A. Crabtree. Probated August 12, 1919.

Page 318  **WILL OF WILLIAM B. STEVENSON.** Wife Nelia R. Stevenson, 100 acres of land where we reside and also appointed executrix. My children, not named. Signed September 14, 1916. Witnesses: C.E. George and J.R. Bruce. Probated August 21, 1919.

Page 319  **WILL OF GEORGE W. ENOCHS & WIFE MARY FRANCES ENOCHS.** Of Petersburg. Daughters, Mattie G. Hart, Lizzie Naoma Crane, Jessie Lue Sanders, and Pearl Landis Sanders and Mecca An Woosly, and our son Roy L. Enoch. Executor: Our son Roy L. Enoch. Signed July 3, 1915. Witnesses: S.H. Allen and W.A. Muse. Probated September 1, 1919.

Page 320  **WILL OF C.S. MASSEY.** Wife M.J. Massey. Grandson, Raymond Massey. Executor: Wilson Massey. Signed October 24, 1918. Witnesses: Ernest S. McGehee and J.T. Allison. Probated September 1, 1919.

Page 321  **WILL OF TONIE STONE,(COL).** Wife Nancy Stone, farm I now live on. Son Will Stone, 5 acres of land he now lives on including his house. Other four children, not named. Dealia Thomison, the house where she now lives. Appointed Dr. T.E. Ashby and J.Mc. Pamplin as agents for Will Stone and Dealia Thomison. Will written by E.P. Johnson for Tonie Stone on May 3, 1919. Witnesses: J. Mack Pamplin and THomas E. Ashby. Probated September 11, 1919.

Page 322  **WILL OF ELIZABETH McCOLLUM.** Desires my body be sent to State of Tennessee for interment to rest beside my beloved ones who have preceded me. My little niece Sara Bennett Nichols of Franklin, Tennessee, daughter of my deceased brother Sam B. Nichols, her mother, Annie Terrell Nichols be appointed guardian. My nephew, Claude Nichols, son of my deceased brother, George Nichols, deceased. I give to the Board of Trustees of the Howell Presbyterian Church at Howell, Tennessee, $2000.00, in memory of my daughter Annie Elizabeth McCollum, deceased. My son and only living child, Edward K. Jones, who is now a member of the U.S. Army in France. Nieces, Mrs. Ernest Stephenson of Howell, Sarah Bennett Nichols of Franklin, Tennessee, and Mrs. Alfred Barker of Columbia, Tennessee, and my nephews, John Bennett Nichols of Nashville, Tennessee and George Nichols, Claude Nichols and James Nichols of Columbia, Tennessee. Appointed my son Edward K. Jones as executor, if he returns to U.S. Executors: Ernest R. Stephenson of Fayetteville and Bert P. Woodard of Los Angeles, California. Signed February 21, 1919 in Glendale, California. Witnesses: Walter E. Edmonds and M.P. Harrison, both of Glendale, California. Probated September 25, 1919.

Page 323  **WILL OF G.W. CRABTREE.** Of District No. 11. Wife Mary Crabtree, all real estate and at her death to E.L. Crabtree. Executor: E.L. Crabtree. Signed November 17, 1909. Witnesses: Theo. F. Harris and P.M. Harris. Probated September 29, 1919.

Page 324  **WILL OF CARRIE HIRSCH.** Now of Fayetteville. Daughter Mrs. Rachel Kreisman, diamond ear drops and pin. Daughter Mrs. Birdie Brin, diamond ear drops and ring and other personal property. I own a house and lot in Nashville, Tennessee, goes to my husband Carl Hirsch. Daughter Sophie Hirsch. Signed February 24, 1918. Witnesses: B.E. Holman and W.N. Whitaker, Jr. Probated October 7, 1919.

Page 325  **WILL OF C.W. WADE.** Desires a monument erected at my grave. Daughter Pearl Wade, household property. Two sons, W.P. Wade and G.H. Wade, with Pearl Wade Trustee for my two grandchildren Ruth Scott and Clayton Scott, the only children of my deceased daughter Maggie Scott. Son C.K. Wade. Daughter Myrtle Hester wife of W.O. Hester, with Trustee, Pearl Wade. Daughter Mary Eva Ledford wife of Charles W. Ledford, land in District No. 10, on Petersburg-Boonshill Turnpike. My farm and home is in District No. 10 where I now reside. To Ed Rice and wife, 51 acres in District No. 10. Own two lots on east side of the public square in Petersburg. Executrix: My daughter Pearl Wade. Signed April 24, 1916. Witnesses: F.M. Bledsoe and N.P. Carter. Probated October 14, 1919.

Page 327  **WILL OF MRS. MATTIE L. GRISWELL.** Brother Frank and my sister Jane. At my death, articles to Virginia Cannon. Property to W.F. Cannon, also house and lot. Executor: W.F. Cannon. Signed July 12, 1917. Witnesses: Jno. L. Collier and George W. Thomas. Probated October 25, 1919.

Page 328  **WILL OF J.H. CLARK.** Of Boonshill. Desire to be buried in Commerce, texas. Executors: Sons, Jas. M. Clark and Will T. Clark. Signed June 16, 1919. Witnesses: A.W. Wilson and C.A. Couch. Probated December 4, 1919.

Page 329  **WILL OF W.F. COLLINS.** Desires a double monument erected at my grave at the grave of my wife Caledonia Collins, also one at the grave of my deceased daughter Perl---(?) Winsett. My son J.L. Collins. Signed July 12, 1919. Witnesses: W.B. Lamb and W.B. Lamb, Jr. Probated December 6, 1919.

Page 330  **WILL OF J.R. COLE.** Of Flintville. All the children of J.M. Allen, not named. Executor: W.A. Allen. Signed August 30, 1919. Witnesses: W.L. McDonald and L.R. Noe. Probated December 19, 1919.

Page 331  **WILL OF MARY R. ASKINS.** Husband R.H. Askins, all my estate and appointed executor. Signed May 22, 1919. Witnesses: Emma Sebastian and W.B. Lamb, Jr. Probated January 3, 1920.

Page 332  **WILL OF B.B. THOMPSON.** Wife Sarah H. Thompson, all my real estate. Grandson Benjamin Bennet Pitts. O.B. Thompson and his wife Henretta. Sallie Cowley widow of H.D. Cowley. Mattie Catheline Cowley, youngest daughter of John P. Cowley, Sr. Executors: Wife Sarah H. Thompson and added Jno. P. Cowley, Sr. and O.P. Thompson to assist. Signed March 15, 1912. Witnesses: W.A. Jenkins, J.A. Taylor, Jr., and M.W. Woodard. Probated January 13, 1920.

Page 333  **WILL OF JOHN W. FRANKLIN & DELPHIA A. FRANKLIN.** Son Middleton B. Franklin. Son William M. Franklin. To the children of our dead daughter Delia Stiles, Harvey M. Stiles and Etta L. Massey wife of Wilson Massey. W. Mc. Franklin. Executor: Our son Middleton B. Franklin. Signed April 23, 1917. Witnesses: E.F. Dickey and J.M. Nix. Probated January 21, 1920.

Page 334  **WILL OF ROBERT M. KOONCE.** Wife Mary J. Koonce to take charge of my estate and erect a tombstone over my grave also at her grave. Daughter Rosa Koonce. Three other children, not named. Executors: My three sons-in-law, F.B. Kelso, Sam Ashby and Henry Simmons. Signed June --, 1905. Witnesses: C.M. Webb, William M. Smith and Hiram C. Higgins. Probated January 27, 1920.

Page 336  **WILL OF MARY J. TURNEY.** First husband Robert Reese. Daughter Norah Hughey. Last Husband J.B. Turney. Grandson Turney A. Taylor. Executor: D.C. Sherrell. Signed March 28, 1910. Witnesses: W.C. Kidd, E.M. Harris and D.C. Sherrell. Probated January 29, 1920.

Page 337  **WILL OF DAVID STRANG.** Springfield. Mass. September 19, 1913. David Strang of Lincoln, Lincoln County, Tennessee. Daughter Isabella, Mrs. I.S. Lansing. My unhappy wife Mrs. Mary F. Strang, nee Lawrence, also appointed executrix, assisted by Mr. Thomas P. Gillham of Lincoln. Witnesses: Matilda Strang Hyde and L.S. Hyde. Probated February 4, 1920.

Page 338  **WILL OF ELLA C. STRANE.** Petition filed in probate in Linestone County, Alabama. Petitioner, O.W. Strane, a resident of Limestone County, Alabama, who is over age of 21 years. On March 14, 1917, Ella C. Strane departed this life in Limestone County, Alabama. Witnesses: Era Strane and Monroe Strane, both reside in Limestone County, Alabama. Ella C. Strane was unmarried at the time of her death and her next of kin as follows: O.W. Strane, C.W. Strane, R.R. Strane, J.E. Strane, each are brothers living in Limestone County, Alabama, Oce Strane a brother who lives at Dellrose and Mrs. Lula R. Harrison a sister who resides at Altus, Oklahoma, all are over age of 21 years. Will on file: Wills everything to my brother O.W. Strane, the place known as the T.L. Strane place, my home in Dellrose, Tennessee. Witnesses: Era Strane and Monroe Strane.
Proof of will. Era Strane of Limestone County, Alabama and Monroe Strane in Pulaski, Giles County, Tennessee, age 19, each knew Ella C. Strane for many years, saying she did sign her will. Probated in Lincoln County, Tennessee February 6, 1920. (Long will)

Page 342  **WILL OF ELMORE BONNER, (COL).** Late of Coldwater. February 4, 1920. Witnesses: Pete Smith and A.D. White, both of Lincoln County. Will made in the home of his mother near Coldwater, where he had previously resided with his mother for some time. My mother, Fannie Bonner, everything. "I don't want my mother to have to plow anymore and she won't have to, for I have enough to keep her to". "I know I am going to die right away", and he did die shortly afterwards. Done in sick chamber of Elmore Bonner. Probated February 13, 1920.

Page 343  **WILL OF F.M. WAID.** Desires a foot stone to be placed at my grave, similar to the one at the head of my first wife's grave. Desires Elder T.C. Little of Fayetteville to conduct services. To the elders of the Christian Church at Fayetteville, $600.00. Desires to keep up my burial lot in Rose Hill Cemetery, to paint once every three years, the iron fence aroung my lots in the cemetery. My present wife Mary Waid, full share of my estate of $500.00. My sons, William Oscar Waid, Joel B. Waid, Charles R. Waid, James A. Waid, and Oliver Waid, and my granddaughter Willie May Waid the only child of my deceased son E. Marion Waid. Executors: My two sons, Charles R. Waid and James A. Waid. Signed May 9, 1919. Witnesses: H.E. Dryden and B.E. Holman. Probated March 8, 1920.

Page 345  **WILL OF HENDERSON FANNING.** Of Fayetteville. Son John E. Fanning, gold watch and fob. Daughter Mamie Fanning, $1000.00. I own barber chairs, hat-rack, pool tables and other items in a Barber & Pool Table business. Wife Sarah E. Fanning. Four children, Mamie Fanning, Annie Fanning Cunningham, John R. Fanning, and Nora Fanning Brock. Executor: My son John E. Fanning. Signed July 12, 1916. Witnesses: K.K. Eslick and H.B. Webb. Probated March 8, 1920.

Page 346  **WILL OF OVID T. WILEY.** Wife Jennie A. Wiley, two farms and appointed executrix. Children, not named. Signed March 6, 1920. Witnesses: Frank C. Galloway and Thompson J. Wiley. Probated March 26, 1920.

Page 347  **WILL OF HENRY W. BONNER.** Of Fayetteville. Wife Lexie Bonner, all estate and appointed executrix. Signed July 12, 1905. Witnesses: W.B. Lamb, N.P. Carter and W.B. Lamb, Jr. Probated April 14, 1920.

Page 348  **WILL OF MARY ANN COPELAND, WIDOW.** Widow of William Copeland, deceased. Directed to erect a tombstone placed at my grave. My five living children, Mollie H. Franklin wife of John M. Franklin, Emma E. Snow Wife of H.H. Snow, Ida May Jennings wife of B.L. Jennings, George M. Copeland, and Robert L. Copeland. Seven living grandchildren whose fathers are dead, children of my deceased son William C. Copeland, namely Sarah Ann Tucker wife of James Tucker, Fannie Copeland, Newton Copeland, Ross Copeland, and Mollie H. Syler wife of William Syler. Grandson Tom Dove Copeland son of my deceased son Jeff M. Copeland. Johnsey Copeland daughter of my deceased son Newton Copeland. Executors: Charley Copeland and M.L. Spencer, Sr. Signed November 2, 1901. Witnesses: W.P. Gilliam, George W. Counts and W.Y. Taylor. Probated June 19, 1920.

Page 349 **WILL OF MISS MARY E. WELSH.** Nephew Howard M. Welsh, all the property. Signed March 31, 1902. Witnesses: J.E. Poindexter, Mildred Irwin, B.M. Welsh, R.A. Welsh and R.Ed Feeney. Probated August 2, 1920.

Page 350 **WILL OF MRS. S.B. WINFORD.** Of Fayetteville. Nephew Carlos Pamplin, one half of my government bonds and stamps. Niece Sadie Pamplin, one half of my government bonds and stamps. Sister Ruhamah Pamplin, remainder of my estate. Executor: My brother-in-law J. Mack Pamplin. Signed June 29, 1920. Witnesses: Mrs. J.W. Sullivan, Mrs. S.B. Ramsey, J. Mack Pamplin and wife Ruhamah Pamplin. Probated July 5, 1920.

Page 351 **WILL OF J.F. CRESON.** Merchant of Booneville. Wife Mary Creson. Daughter Mattie Lou Creson. Each following to have equal share, J. McDonald Creson, George B. Creson, Mattie Lou Creson, William Creson, Benjamin Creson, Carroll Creson, Edward Creson, Roscoe Creson, and Pearl Waggoner and Mary Creson. Executor: My son J. McDonald Creson. Signed June 26, 1920. Witnesses: W.J. Russell and J.A. Waggoner. Probated August 12, 1920.

Page 352 **WILL OF P.A. CRAMSIE.** Wife Affie Cramsie, estate and appointed executrix. My mother, not named. Four children, Edward, Arthur, Russell, and Richard Cramsie. Signed August 5, 1920. Witnesses: R.W. McCown and W.V. Lindsay. Probated August 23, 1920.

Page 353 **WILL OF M.H. JOINS.** Wife Martha J. Joins, all my personal estate in District No. 15, 94 acres. Daughter Eudora Sawyers, a widow and her two children, Conroy and Lois, under 18 years. Daughters Irene and Dalia or Docia Joins who are living with me as part of my family. Executors: C.B. Davis and my son J.A. Joins. Signed August 18, 1920. Witnesses: J.L. Sawyers and W.C. Harwell. Probated September 3, 1920.

Page 354 **WILL OF WILLIAM W. CHICK.** Wife Lizzie Chick and my four children, Walter Chich, Mamie Chick, Clarence Chick, and Mary Willie Chick or any unborn. Executor: S.W. Fleming. Signed January 3, 1905. Witnesses: Jno. A. Moore and J.A. Boaz. Probated September --, 1920.

Page 355 **WILL OF J.D. SUGG, SR.** Daughter Malcom Patterson Sugg, all my land near Coldwater road, with W.C. Sugg her guardian. Wife Sallie Sugg, my Perkins farm. Heirs, J.D., Jr., and Malcom Patterson Sugg. Eda Anthony Blair. T.D. Sugg and Dave Hobbs is my wife's advisors. Executors: J.D. Sugg, T.D. Sugg, W.C. Sugg and D.F. Sugg. Witnesses: T.D. Sugg, W.C. Sugg, A.L. Sloan, W.G. Cowan, and R. Ed Feeney. Probated September 8, 1920.

Page 356 **WILL OF L.C. STRONG.** Of Harms. Son Charles Waddle Strong. Daughter Cleo Strong. My five children, Retha May Ashby wife of Samuel Ashby, Wennie Cole Fleming wife of Aaron Fleming, Tom G. Strong, Charles Waddle Strong, and Cleo Strong. Executors: My sons Tom G. Strong and Charles Waddle Strong. Signed August 21, 1920. Witnesses: S.C. McCown and J.E. Rawls. Probated September 10, 1920.

Page 357 **WILL OF C.W. WADE.** Contesting will. Court decided the will is a true will.

Will: Desires a monument erected at my grave. Daughter Pearl Wade, all my household furniture &c. Two sons, W.P. Wade and G.H. Wade, with Pearl Wade their Trustee for my two grandchildren, Ruth Scott and Clayton Scott, only children of my deceased daughter Maggie Scott. Daughter Myrtle Hester wife of W.O. Hester. Daughter Mary Eva Ledford wife of Charles W. Ledford, land in District No. 10. My land is in District No. 10 where I now reside. Executrix: Pearl Wade. Signed April 24, 1916. Witnesses: F.M. Bledsoe and N.P. Carter. Probated (no date).

Page 360    **WILL OF MARY C. ROWELL.** Great niece Frances Templeton. Niece Mary Pearl Blair daughter of my deceased brother J.F. Blair. The seven children of my deceased brother J.F. Blair, to wit, William J. Blair, Mary Pearl Blair, Allie Permelia Good wife of R.A. Good, Edna Rachel Blair, Sidney H. Blair, Annie Viola Good wife of D.C. Good, and Addie Thelma Blair. Mary Pearl Templeton niece of my deceased husband, who was reared by me. My deceased husband H.P. Rowell. Executor: R.A. Good, the husband of my niece Allie Permelia Good. Signed August 8, 1919. Witnesses: H.T. Cown and S.H. Galloway. Probated September 24, 1920.

Page 361    **WILL OF MRS. JOHNYE LEE REAVIS.** Desires a monument erected at my grave. Five sisters, Mrs. Dillie B. Bledsoe, Mrs. Ethel M. Gilbert, Mrs. Jessie E. Redd, Mrs. Fannie D. Davidson, and Mrs. Carl B. Ellis. Brother Roy N. Freeman appointed executor. Signed August 18, 1920. Witnesses: R.C. Barham and T.J. Barham. Probated November 22, 1920.

Page 362    **WILL OF H.T. CHILDS.** Land in District No. 11, also to set apart and survey the graveyard lot as it stands, making the north boundary line of my land the north boundary line of said graveyard to contain about two rods square or four square rods and it is to remain a family burying ground. Son Thomas Allen Childs. Daughters, Mattie O. Smith and Annie N. Cunningham, and to my two grandsons, Thomas Swanner and Earl Swanner the children of my deceased daughter Mollie L. Swanner. Executor: My son Thomas Allen Childs. Signed June 1, 1916. Witnesses: W.C. Kidd and E.M. Harris. Probated December 21, 1920.

Page 363    **WILL OF JOE S. HINES.** Of Fayetteville. Children, Walter J. Hines, Smith Hines, Miss Emma Hines, Charles C. Hines, Mrs. Sallie Pylant, Mrs. Exie Hines Diemer, John J. Hines, Newell Hines, and Mrs. Edith Pack. Executors: My five sons. Signed September 18, 1920. Witnesses: F.M. Bledsoe and R. Ed. Feeney. Probated January 3, 1921.

Page 364    **WILL OF JOHN M. DICKEY, SR.** Children, William Mc. Dickey, Dr. E.W. Dickey, Fannie L. Burns wife of John L. Burns, Fred C. Dickey, John M. Dickey, Jr., Hugh D. Dickey, Laura E. Crawford, Joe T. Dickey, and Rose E. Freeman, and my grandchildren, Mattie L. Spencer, Fannie, and William Spencer, Joe Spencer and James Spencer, and only children of my deceased daughter Julia M. Spencer. Executors: My three sons, Dr. E.W. Dickey, Fred C. Dickey, and Hugh D. Dickey. Signed May 9, 1914. Witnesses: J.A. Taylor, Jr., C. Wilson Taylor and Jno. B. Thompson. Probated January 10, 1921.

Page 366    **WILL OF JENNIE HUTTON.** Desires a monument placed over my grave. Niece Mrs. Sallie Brown, all my jewelry, clothes and household furniture. Executor and Trustee: Jo. L. Hutton and if he fails, then John D. Hutton shall act as Trustee. Signed August 15, 1916. Witnesses: J.J. Moyers and C.F. Bagley. Probated January 19, 1921.

Page 367    **WILL OF W.R. NOAH.** Wife S.E. Noah. Son E.L. Noah. Daughter Nancy Jane Gunter. Daughter Mollie Collins. Grandchildren, the children of my deceased daughter Sallie Campbell, namely, Robert, Albert, Maggie, Nora, Talmadge, Eunice, Lelia, and Ross Campbell. Desires a tombstone at my grave also one at the grave of my wife at her death. Granddaughter Mary Frances Noah, daughter of my son F.A. Noah. Executor: Henry Arney. Signed March 8, 1920. Witnesses: A.B. Wilson and F.E. Bearden and H.M. Hopper. Probated February 10, 1921.

Page 369 **WILL OF YOUNG A. TAYLOR.** Wife Lucy M. Taylor, all estate. Signed October 4, 1920. Witnesses: W.E. Barnes and Charles C. Gillham. Probated February 15, 1921.

Page 370 **WILL OF MARY L. WISEMAN.** Nephew Ross Felps, one large Bible and other personal estate. Edna Felps daughter of Ross Felps, my Story & Clark organ. Nephew Albert Felps, personal property. Hasty Felps and sister Annie Felps, son and daughter of Albert Felps. Niece Miss HUghey Parks, personal property. Children of my deceased brother George Felps, viz, David Felps, Birdie Felps and Pearl Felps, Lucy Felps, Edgar Felps, Mrs. Era Felps Jones. Children of my sister Callie Terry, deceased, viz, Mrs. Lucy Carroll, Mrs. Mary Johnston, Mrs. Clair Renegar, Claud Terry and Robert Terry. The two sons of my sister Bettie Parks, deceased, viz, Ben Parks and Charly Parks. Brothers and sisters, Andrew J. Felps, Jack Felps, Brit Felps and Mrs. Mattie Martin. To Hugh Rees, Col., who has lived on place many years, have one horse. Mrs. Hughey Parks. Executor: Dr. J.T. Graham of Booneville. Signed July 2, 1920. Witnesses: Mary L. Wiseman, Trall T. McCurdy and William Creson. Probated February 21, 1921.

Page 371 **WILL OF FRANCES B. TILLMAN.** Of Fayetteville. Children of my brother-in-law Edwin H. Tillman. Frances Bonner Tillman Smith daughter of my brother-in-law Lewis Tillman. Sister-in-law Almeda Tillman Brannan, personal property and a picture of my deceased husband and myself and portraits of her father and mother. My sister-in-law Mrs. G.N. Tillman and also my sister-in-law Mrs. Abram M. Tillman. Great niece Mamie Lamb Smith and her mother Eva Stone Lamb. Great niece Fannie Neil Lamb Carter. Great Niece Lizzie Lamb Jean. Great niece Elise Lamb Dozier and her little daughter Natalia Dozier. Great grand niece Madeline Jean. Nieces, Fannie Bonner Morgan, Elizabeth Lamb and Lucy Bonner Diemer. Nephews, W.B. Lamb, Sr. and Henry Bonner. Niece Jimmie M. Lamb. Martha H. Lamb wife of my grand nephew W.B. Lamb, Jr. Bettie Moore wife of my cousin William H. Moore. Matilda Phagan wife of Jas. O. Phagan. Cora Leatherwood Gault. Cousins, Lizzie Bonner Flint, Annie B. Robertson and James Tillman Robertson. Lexie M. Bonner. Miss Minnie Coleman and Miss Emma Sebastian. Great grand nephews, "Billy" and "Bobby" Lamb. Josie D. Lamb. Cousin Noreen Evans of Florida. Executor: My nephew W.B. Lamb also to assist my grand nephew W.B. Lamb, Jr. Signed January 29, 1919. Witnesses: C.F. Bagley and R. Ed. Feeney.
Codicil: My nephew Henry Bonner, having died. Jennings Bryan Thompson to be educated at Bryson College in Fayetteville. Probated March 25, 1921.

Page 374 **WILL OF WILLIAM BRIGGS DANCE.** Village of Mulberry. Mother Mrs. Olivia A. Dance. Signed October 18, 1920. Witnesses: Olivia A. Dance and J.E. Dance. Probated May 13, 1921.

Page 375 **WILL OF LOUISA C. REED.** Daughter Hattie C. Caldwell wife of Will Caldwell. Executor: A.B. Wilson. Signed May 29, 1901. Witnesses: A.B. Wilson and A.M. March. Probated June 17, 1921.

Page 376 **WILL OF CHARLEY S. BROADRICK.** Nephew Dick Broadrick, all estate and appointed executor. Signed June 6, 1921. Witnesses: W.T. Ables and W.F. McCown. Probated June 18, 1921.

Page 377 **WILL OF BENTON L. TOWRY.** Son Middleton Towry, my home in District No. 19. Wife Louisa C. Towry appointed executrix. Signed February 7, 1920. Witnesses: W.B. Goodrich, Z.M. Wilson and J.E. Routt. Probated June 25, 1921.

Page 378 **WILL OF MARY W. MILLER.** Brother Paul Woods. Susie Bearden and Ellis Be-k. Lash Miller gets my part of his father's estate. Witness: D.M. Goodner. Signed January 1, 1920. Probated June 28, 1921.

Page 379 **WILL OF J.M. MULLINS.** Delrose. Desires a monument erected at my grave. Six children, Mary Mitchell, Ella Mitchell, Maudie Solomon, Ollie Mitchell and Jennie Mullins wife of Willie Mullins, and my son Ben Mullins. Land in District No. 16 and 17. Executors: My son Ben Mullins and my son-in-law Oscar Mitchell. Signed April 8, 1921. Witnesses: R.E. Harwell and Giles Evans and Gladys Davidson. Probated July 2, 1921.

Page 380 **WILL OF C.M. PEARSON.** Desires a monument placed over my grave and wife. Daughters, Mrs. Jennie Billions, Mrs. Hollie Hill, Mrs. Fannie Woodard. Sons, J.R. Pearson and John W. Pearson. Daughter Lizzie Pearson, land in District No. 8. Executor: My son John W. Pearson. Signed March 27, 1920. Witnesses: B.E. Holman and Tennie May Easley. Probated July 22, 1921.

Page 381 **WILL OF JAMES R. YOUNG.** June 12, 1918. Co. C 144th Inf. Camp Bowie, Texas. James R. Young is writing to Bertha. Bertha is to get a picture and Bible to take care of for him. Probated July 22, 1921.

Page 382 **WILL OF MRS. FRANCES V. WARD, WIDOW.** Widow of John F. Ward, deceased, of Howell. My farm in District No. 9, near Howell, on which I now live and on which my deceased father Joel M. Harris resided for many years before his death. Son John H. Ward. Daughters, Laura S. Halbert wife of I.B. Halbert and Elizabeth March wife of A.H. March. Four grandchildren, Mrs. Erma Barnett wife of Dr. W.L. Barnett, Ward K. Halbert and Marion F. Halbert, children of my daughter Laura S. Halbert, and Benjamin S. March only child of my daughter Elizabeth March. Desires a monument erected at my grave and also fenced and kept the family graveyard where my grandfather, father, mother, my deceased brothers, and both of my deceased husbands are buried. Executor: My son-in-law I.B. Halbert. Signed October 6, 1915. Witnesses: W.B. Buchanan and L.L. Stephenson. Probated July 23, 1921.

Page 383 **WILL OF MARY JANE McANN.** Ernest R. Franklin, entire estate also appointed executor. Signed November 18, 1912. Witnesses: W.B. Jobe, R. Ed. Feeney and W.B. Lamb, Jr. Probated August 1, 1921.

Page 384 **WILL OF JANE R. TIPPS.** Owns 23 acres in District No. 4. Desires a monument erected at my grave and at my husband's grave and also to the graves by Emma, Nora, Henry and Davis Tipps. My heirs are, Albert Tipps, Nannie Copeland, Will Tipps, Charlie Tipps, and the children of Davis Tipps, deceased, namely, Roy Tipps, Beuna V. Tipps, Clifford Tipps, Fannie May Tipps, Mary Lee Tipps, Terrace Tipps, and Jennie Pearl Tipps. I direct to reserve enough ground from my estate for a family graveyard where there is always a graveyard started in my garden. Executors: W.G. Tipps and Charlie Tipps. Signed September 25, 1916. Witnesses: J.M. Eslick and B.W. Tipps. Probated August 2, 1921.

Page 385 **WILL OF H.H. WAGGONER.** Of Mulberry. Wife Bolen Waggoner, the dwelling house, lands and all estate, also appointed executrix. Sons, Riley McNeece Waggoner and Eugene Rowland Waggoner. Signed August 18, 1921. Witnesses: J.T. Allison and Thomas W. Swanner, both of Mulberry. Probated September 5, 1921.

Page 386 **WILL OF W.M. ABLES.** April 22, 1921. Age 56 years. Wife Mrs. Sallie Ables, entire estate. Desires to be buried in the Lebanon Church Graveyard and a monument placed at my grave also to my wife's should she die before me. Mrs. Josie E. Cheek, lands on Cyruston-Pearl City Road, known as the Bud Ables place, my brother's place. My homeplace where I now live, on west side of Swan Creek, I give to my two sons, Robert and Louis. The Columbus Farra(r) lands and the Walter Mills lands is to be sold and proceeds be divided between the following children or their heirs, viz, Bud Ables, Mrs. Sarah Barnes wife of J.M. Barnes, Louella Askins, Mrs. Melia Newton, Gus Ables, Tennie Ables, and Della Ables. Witnesses: H.G. Hunter and Willie E. Webb. Probated October 19, 1921.

Page 287  **WILL OF JAMES H. DALE.** Of McBurg. February 14, 1921. Wife Mary E. Dale, sole executrix. Children, W.C. Dale, D.W. Dale, T.G. Dale, R.B. Dale, and the children of J.A. Dale, deceased, consisting of Claud Dale, Clyde Dale, Frank Dale, and Lillian Dale. Witnesses: J.A. Harris and J.M. Prosser. Probated November 28, 1921.

Page 388  **WILL OF GEORGE W. LOYD.** Sister Mary Jane Loyd, all estate and appointed executrix. Signed June 21, 1913. Witnesses: W.F. Fanning and W.E. Tucker. Probated December 3, 1921.

Page 389  **WILL OF H.H. ALEXANDER.** Wife Lucinda A. Alexander, land in District No. 7. Son I.G. Alexander. Children, H.B. Alexander, H.L. Alexander, W.S. Alexander, L.W. Alexander, I.G. Alexander, Mrs. Mary Lou Stewart wife of J.A. Stewart, H.K. Alexander. Executor: I.G. Alexander. Signed May 30, 1918. Witnesses: Morgan Eslick and J.W. Holman. Probated December 5, 1921.

Page 391  **WILL OF J.H. "HAM" SULLINGER.** My land is in District No. 4. Wife Josie Bell Sullinger, lands, also appointed executrix. Children, Howace D. Sullinger and Loney Sullinger Tucker. Brother W.H. "Sul" Sullinger. Signed October 8, 1921. Witnesses: J.P. Cowley and Cruse Brandon. Probated December 9, 1921.

Page 392  **WILL OF CHARLES M. GRIGSBY.** Brother R.S. Grigsby appointed executor. Signed December 8, 1921. Witnesses: W.B. Lamb, Jr. and George L. Diemer. Probated December 12, 1921.

Page 393  **WILL OF F.M. BLEDSOE.** Executor: Charles F. Bagley. My land is in District No. 5. Signed December 6, 1921. Witnesses: R. Ed. Feeney and J.J. Moyers.
Codicil: Bequeath to the following parties, Allen Cummings, W.J. Hamilton, Kate Hamilton, Herbert Hamilton, J.M. Blake, Floyd E. Taylor, J.A. Montgomery, Miss Emma and Joe Hanaway, Landess and Bob Sanders, Luther Rives, Ella Talley, C.F. Bagley, J.J. Moyers and R. Ed. Feeney, Jno. C. Hampton and John Newman, Judith Andrews, Jno. C. Hooper, Jr., B.D. Wilson, Tom Woods and C. Diemer Lamb, Mrs. Sue B. Owens, Miss Lena Brazzelle, Miss Esther Wiggs, Lincoln Carter (Col), and Zora Massey (Col). Signed December 7, 1921. Witnesses: J.A. Moores and Nelson P. Carter. Probated December 12, 1921.

# INDEX